THE GLOBAL EMPLOYMENT CHALLENGE

"I could liken myself to an explorer making a rapid survey of the horizon before plunging into thickets from which the wider view is no longer possible. The gaps in my account are naturally enormous. I have done my best not to conceal any deficiencies, whether in the state of our knowledge or in my own documentation … When the time comes for my own work to be superseded by studies of deeper penetration, I shall feel well rewarded if confrontation with my false conjectures has made history learn the truth about herself."

Marc Bloch, Preface to *French rural history: An essay on its essential characteristics* (1931; reprint London, Routledge and Kegan Paul, 1978)

THE GLOBAL EMPLOYMENT CHALLENGE

Ajit K. Ghose
Nomaan Majid
Christoph Ernst

INTERNATIONAL LABOUR OFFICE • GENEVA

Copyright © International Labour Organization 2008
First published 2008

Publications of the International Labour Office enjoy copyright under Protocol 2 of the Universal Copyright Convention. Nevertheless, short excerpts from them may be reproduced without authorization, on condition that the source is indicated. For rights of reproduction or translation, application should be made to ILO Publications (Rights and Permissions), International Labour Office, CH-1211 Geneva 22, Switzerland, or by email: pubdroit@ilo.org. The International Labour Office welcomes such applications.

Libraries, institutions and other users registered with a reproduction rights organization may make copies in accordance with the licences issued to them for this purpose. Visit www.ifrro.org to find the reproduction rights organization in your country.

Ghose, A. K.; Majid, N.; Ernst, C.
The global employment challenge
Geneva, International Labour Office, 2008

Employment, promotion of employment, employment policy, trend, developed countries, developing countries.
13.01.3

ISBN 978-92-2-120305-6

ILO Cataloguing in Publication Data

The designations employed in ILO publications, which are in conformity with United Nations practice, and the presentation of material therein do not imply the expression of any opinion whatsoever on the part of the International Labour Office concerning the legal status of any country, area or territory or of its authorities, or concerning the delimitation of its frontiers.

The responsibility for opinions expressed in signed articles, studies and other contributions rests solely with their authors, and publication does not constitute an endorsement by the International Labour Office of the opinions expressed in them.

Reference to names of firms and commercial products and processes does not imply their endorsement by the International Labour Office, and any failure to mention a particular firm, commercial product or process is not a sign of disapproval.

ILO publications can be obtained through major booksellers or ILO local offices in many countries, or direct from ILO Publications, International Labour Office, CH-1211 Geneva 22, Switzerland. Catalogues or lists of new publications are available free of charge from the above address, or by email: pubvente@ilo.org

Visit our website: www.ilo.org/publns

Typeset by Magheross Graphics, France & Ireland *www.magheross.com*
Printed in Switzerland

CONTENTS

Acknowledgements xiii

1 INTRODUCTION 1
   Appendix 5

2 WORLD LABOUR FORCE STRUCTURE AND ITS EVOLUTION   9
2.1 Structure and characteristics 10
2.2 The main trends 24
2.3 Future outlook 35

3 GLOBALIZATION IN AN UNEQUAL WORLD 37
3.1 Asymmetric distribution of productive resources 38
3.2 Capital flows and investment in developing countries 41
3.3 Labour flows and supply of labour and skills in developing countries 45

4 PRODUCTIVE EMPLOYMENT IN DEVELOPING COUNTRIES . 57
4.1 The nature of employment and unemployment in developing countries .. 57
4.2 Assessing the employment situation in a developing country 61
4.3 The current state of employment 83
4.4 Recent trends 89
4.5 Economic growth and employment 99
4.6 Employment effects of capital inflow and trade growth 102
4.7 Policy challenges 107

5	THE EMPLOYMENT–POVERTY INTERFACE IN DEVELOPING COUNTRIES	123
5.1	Reducing global poverty	123
5.2	Did poverty decline in the 1990s?	127
5.3	Economic growth and poverty reduction	130
5.4	The employment–poverty interface	134
5.5	Trade growth and the poor	139
5.6	Policies for poverty reduction	144
6	PERSISTENT EMPLOYMENT PROBLEMS IN DEVELOPED COUNTRIES	155
6.1	Employment and unemployment in developed countries	156
6.2	Persisting trends	173
6.3	Finding explanations	184
6.4	The labour market reforms of the 1990s and their effects	190
6.5	Policies for the future	195
7	SYSTEMIC TRANSITION AND JOB CRISIS IN CENTRAL AND EASTERN EUROPEAN COUNTRIES	213
7.1	The current state of employment	213
7.2	Recent trends	221
7.3	Explaining the trends	229
7.4	Policy challenges	234
8	EMPLOYMENT DRIFT IN COUNTRIES OF THE COMMONWEALTH OF INDEPENDENT STATES	247
8.1	Overall employment situation and its evolution	247
8.2	Identifying the drivers	255
8.3	Policy perspective	258
9	A SUMMING-UP	265
References		271
Index		279

Boxes

2.1	Women's labour force participation: India, 2000	15
2.2	Religion, culture and women's labour force participation	16
2.3	Skill, education and employment: India, 2000	20
2.4	Demographic transition	26
2.5	Population and labour force ageing	33
3.1	Does foreign aid help poor countries?	44
3.2	Data on international migration	45
3.3	High-skilled migrants and remittances	52
4.1	Formal and non-formal segments	58
4.2	Surplus labour	59
4.3	How does the labour market work in a dual economy?	60
4.4	Identifying formal and non-formal segments	64
4.5	Dualism within sectors: Brazil and India	65
4.6	The skill gap between formal and non-formal segments	69
4.7	Unemployment rate: Nature of the data	78
4.8	Unemployment in South Africa	80
4.9	Chronic unemployment rate as a measure of queuing: India and Brazil	81
4.10	Job queuing and gender: India and Brazil	90
4.11	Formal employment in China in the 1990s	98
5.1	Strategies for poverty reduction: The shift in focus	125
5.2	Counting the poor	128
5.3	Economic growth and poverty: Some other evidence	132
5.4	Poverty and output per worker in non-formal segment	138
5.5	Trade orientation, economic growth and poverty	139
5.6	Trade growth and output per worker in non-formal segment	142
5.7	Trade growth and poverty reduction: China's experience	143
6.1	Level of education and non-standard employment	169
6.2	Earnings inequality	172
6.3	Explaining unemployment: Macroeconomic shocks and labour market institutions	184
6.4	OECD recommendations for labour market reforms	185
6.5	Offshoring and employment	190
7.1	Labour market institutions in CEE countries	229
8.1	Emigration from CIS countries	253
8.2	The output fall in CIS countries	256

Tables

2.1	Global labour force, 1980–2007	9
2.2	Labour force by country group, 2003	10
2.3	Female labour force by country group, 2003	13
2.4	Distribution of labour force by age group and gender, 2003	18
2.5	Distribution of young workers, older workers and total labour force by country group, 2003	19
2.6	Educational attainment by gender and country group, 2000	21
2.7	Distribution of unskilled, skilled and total labour force by country group, 2000	24
2.8	Growth of world labour force, 1990–2003	25
2.9	Labour force participation rate by country group, 1990–2003	28
2.10	Population growth, labour force participation and incidence of HIV/AIDS, selected countries, 1980–2003	30
2.11	Share of females in labour force, 1990–2003	31
2.12	Labour force participation rate, male and female, 1990–2003	31
2.13	Age structure of labour force, 1990–2003	32
2.14	Educational attainment of the labour force, 1990–2000	34
2.15	Gender disparity in education, 1990 and 2000	35
3.1	Distribution of productive resources by country group, 1990–2000	39
3.2	Investment per worker and skill per worker: Developed versus developing countries, 1990–2000	40
3.3	Net foreign capital inflow as share of GDP, selected countries, 1990–2003	42
3.4	Saving and investment as share of GDP, selected countries, 1990–2003	43
3.5	Migrants as share of total population, 1960–2005	46
3.6	Adult migrants from developing to developed countries as share of adult population of developing countries, 2000	47
3.7	Distribution of countries by incidence of migration to developed countries, 2000	48
3.8	Distribution of countries by incidence of brain drain, 2000	50
4.1	Dual economy indicators, ca. 2003	66
4.2	Distribution of total employment by employment status, ca. 2003	70
4.3	Value added per worker in non-formal segment, ca. 2003	74
4.4	Unemployment rate, 2003	76
4.5	Ranking by employment situation, selected countries, 2003	84
4.6	Gender disparity in employment	86
4.7	Trends in employment situation, selected countries	92
4.8	Trends in two employment indicators, selected countries	94
4.9	Trends in gender disparity, 1990s	96
4.10	Growth of output and employment in formal segment, 1990s	97
4.11	Trade performance, selected economies, 1990s	105

5.1	Poverty in the developing world, 1990s	127
6.1	Employment and unemployment, 2003	157
6.2	Labour force participation rate in developed countries, 2003	158
6.3	Composite Employment Indicator (CEI) estimates, 2003	162
6.4	Key employment indicators by gender, 2003	164
6.5	Gender disparity in employment, 2003	166
6.6	Employment, unemployment and level of education, 2003	168
6.7	Labour force participation by gender and level of education, 2003	171
6.8	Labour force participation rate by gender, 1991–93 and 2001–03	180
6.9	Rate of unemployment by level of education, 1997 and 2003	182
6.10	Growth of labour force by level of education, 1997–2003	183
6.11	Economic growth and the labour market, 1991–2003	187
6.12	Growth of output and employment by sector, 1991–2003	188
6.13	Changes in the unemployment benefit system, 1994–2001	194
7.1	Employment and unemployment in Central and Eastern European countries, 2004	214
7.2	Overall employment situation, 2004	215
7.3	Employment profile by gender, 2004	217
7.4	Gender disparity in employment, 2004	218
7.5	Unemployment and labour force participation by level of education, 2004	220
7.6	Growth and recovery, 1990–2004	222
7.7	Change in employment profile, 1994–2004	223
7.8	Change in overall employment situation, ca. 1997–2004	224
7.9	Change in gender disparity in employment, ca. 1997–2004	225
7.10	Unemployment by level of education, ca. 1997–2004	227
7.11	Growth of labour force by level of education, ca. 1997–2004	228
7.12	Economic growth and employment, ca. 1994–2004	230
7.13	Employment growth by sector, ca. 1994–2004	232
7.14	Growth of working-age population by level of education, ca. 1996–2004	233
7.15	Emigration to developed countries by level of education, period up to 2001	234
7.16	Growth of output and labour productivity by sector, ca. 1994–2004	235
8.1	Employment and unemployment in countries of the Commonwealth of Independent States (CIS), 2004	248
8.2	Employment levels, 1990–2004	250
8.3	Growth in employment by sector, 1992–2000	251
8.4	Growth in labour productivity by sector, 1992–2000	252
8.5	Key indicators of employment situation in CIS countries, selected years, 1992–2004	254
8.6	Real GDP, selected years, 1990–2004	256
8.7	Growth in GDP and employment by sector, 2000–04	257

The global employment challenge

Figures

2.1 Labour force participation rates by country group, 2003 11
2.2 Labour force participation rate and level of economic development, 2003   12
2.3 Labour force participation rates by gender, 2003 13
2.4 Labour force participation rate (male and female) by level of economic development, 2003 14
2.5 Average age of labour force, 2003 19
2.6 Average years of education and level of economic development, 2000 ... 22
2.7 Gender disparity in education and level of economic development, 2000   23
2.8 Average annual growth rates of total and working-age population by country group, 1990–2003 28
2.9 Population growth and level of economic development, 1990–2003 29

4.1 Unemployment rate and incidence of self-employment, ca. 2003 79
4.2 Unemployment rate and level of economic development, ca. 2003 81
4.3 Gender disparity in unemployment and in irregular wage employment, ca. 2003 88
4.4 Gender disparity in unemployment and in self-employment, ca. 2003 ... 89
4.5 Employment situation and level of economic development, ca. 2003 ... 100
4.6 Economic growth and employment situation, 1990s 101
4.7 Trade growth and formal employment, 1990s 104
4.8 Trade growth and formal segment's share of total employment, 1990s .. 104
4.9 Trade growth and output per worker in non-formal segment, 1990s 107

5.1 Trends in incidence of poverty in developing countries, 1990s 130
5.2 Poverty and GDP, 43 countries, 1990s 132
5.3 Poverty and growth of mean expenditure/income, 43 countries, 1990s .. 133
5.4 Poverty and output per worker in non-formal segment, 20 countries, 1990s 135
5.5 Output per worker in non-formal segment and per capita GDP, 20 countries, 1990s 136
5.6 Poverty and GDP, 20 countries, 1990s 137
5.7 Trade growth and output per worker in non-formal segment, 1990s 141

6.1 Short-term unemployment and temporary employment, 2003 159
6.2 Long-term unemployment and part-time employment, 2003 160
6.3 Labour force participation and part-time employment, 2003 161
6.4 Unemployment rate and overall employment situation, 2003 163
6.5 Gender disparity and overall employment situation, 2003 167
6.6 Average rate of unemployment, 1991–93 versus 2001–03 173
6.7 Average share of short-term unemployed in all unemployed, 1991–93 versus 2001–03 174
6.8 Incidence of part-time employment, 1991–93 versus 2001–03 175

6.9	Incidence of temporary employment, 1995–97 versus 2001–03	175
6.10	Labour force participation, 1991–93 versus 2001–03	176
6.11	Composite Employment Indicator (CEI), 1991–93 versus 2001–03	177
6.12	Adjusted Composite Employment Indicator (CEI*), 1991–93 versus 2001–03	177
6.13	Gender disparity (in terms of Composite Employment Indicator), 1991–93 versus 2001–03	178
6.14	Gender disparity (in terms of adjusted Composite Employment Indicator), 1991–93 versus 2001–03	179
6.15	Change in gender disparity and in overall employment situation, 1991–2003	181
6.16	Employment protection index (EPI) for regular employment, late 1980s and 2003	191
6.17	Employment protection index (EPI) for temporary workers, late 1980s and 2003	192
6.18	Unemployment benefit index (UBI), 1994 and 2001	193
7.1	Unemployment and overall employment situation, 2004	216
7.2a	Gender disparity and employment situation, 2004	219
7.2b	Gender disparity and employment situation (excluding Poland), 2004	219
7.3	Change in gender disparity and in overall employment situation, ca. 1997–2004	226

Appendix tables

A3.1	Migration from developing to developed countries, 2000	54
A4.1	Employment in formal segment, 1990–2003	111
A4.2	Value added per worker in non-formal segment, 1990–2003	117
A4.3	Employment Situation Index (ESI), 1990–2003	119
A4.4	Employment and unemployment by gender	120
A5.1	Proportion of population living on less than PPP$1.08 (1993 prices) per person per day, 1990–2004	146
A5.2	Proportion of population living on less than PPP$1.08 (1993 prices) per person per day, selected sample	149
A5.3	Average annual rate of change in some key variables, selected countries, 1990s	151
A5.4	Average annual rate of change in growth indicators, selected countries, 1990s	153
A6.1	Average annual rate of unemployment in developed countries, 1960–2004	197
A6.2	Part-time and temporary employment, 1960–2004	198
A6.3	Unemployment rate, 2003–05	199
A6.4	Modified Composite Employment Indicator (MCEI), 2003	200

A6.5 Voluntary part-time employment as percentage of
total part-time employment, 2003 202
A6.6 Modified Composite Employment Indicator, female to male ratio, 2003 204
A6.7 Growth of employment and labour force, 1991–93 and 2001–03 205
A6.8 Composite Employment Indicator, 1991–2003 206
A6.9 Adjusted Composite Employment Indicator, 1991–2003 209

A7.1 Key employment indicators by gender and level of education, 2004 238
A7.2 Change in employment situation by gender, ca. 1996–2004 239
A7.3 Change in employment by sector, selected countries, 1996–2004 240
A7.4 Change in employment by level of education,
selected countries, 1998–2004 241
A7.5 Participation rate by level of education, ca. 1998–2004 242
A7.6 Employment elasticity in services, selected CEE countries
and European developed countries 243
A7.7 Composite Employment Indicator (CEI), 1997–2004 244

A8.1 Registered and actual unemployment rates in CIS countries,
selected years, 1992–2004 260
A8.2 Population, working-age population and labour force, 1992–2004 261
A8.3 Distribution of output and employment by sector, 1990, 2000 and 2004 262

Appendix figures

A5.1 Poverty (log difference) and mean expenditure/income (log difference) 154

A6.1 Unemployment rate and overall employment situation, 2003 201
A6.2 Gender disparity and overall employment situation, 2003 203

ACKNOWLEDGEMENTS

Our greatest debts are to Tito Boeri, Paul Collier, Pietro Garibaldi, Michael Landesmann, Luca Nunziata and Hermine Vidovic who wrote background papers for this book; to Martina Lubyova, Monica Castillo, Bolivar Pino, Vandeli dos Santos Guerra and Marcia Quintslr who made valuable statistical data available to us; to Radhicka Kapoor, Smita Barbatini, Cinzia Alcidi and Juan Manuel Blanco who provided invaluable assistance in data processing at different stages of the work; to Kaushik Basu and Michael Landesmann who read an early draft of the book and provided very helpful comments and suggestions; to Duncan Campbell, Riswanul Islam and José Manuel Salazar-Xirinachs who gave valuable advice, suggestions and criticisms; to Eddy Lee with whom one of the authors endlessly debated a variety of issues; to Ksenija Bovet whose careful scrutiny saved us from stylistic clumsiness and errors; to Christine Alfthan who provided invaluable secretarial support throughout; and to Anne Drougard who helped produce a clean manuscript. We have benefited from comments and suggestions generously given to us by our colleagues: Claude Akpokavie, Rashid Amjad, Peter Auer, Ibrahim Awad, Azita Berar Awad, Janine Berg, Sandrine Cazes, Philippe Egger, Christine Evans-Klock, Michael Henriques, Rolph van der Hoeven, Ralph Hussmanns, Steve Kapsos, Karin Klotzbuecher, David Kucera, Alena Nesporova, Stephen Pursey, Gerry Rodgers, Dorothea Schmidt, Hamid Tabatabai, Jyoti Tuladhar and Sylvester Young. To all of them, our sincere thanks.

INTRODUCTION   1

The world faces a huge challenge of creating productive jobs for its expanding labour force. Unlike the challenge of sustaining global economic growth or that of correcting global trade imbalances, this global employment challenge is barely recognized and its nature and magnitude are certainly not well understood. Indeed, there is a widespread (though rarely stated) belief that even in an era of globalization employment remains a national concern, so that there can be no such thing as a global employment challenge. Yet the employment challenge today is global in several important respects. Inadequate availability of productive jobs is now a worldwide phenomenon. Global forces – cross-border flows of trade, capital and labour – have significant consequences for employment in individual countries. Also, international policies are now as important as national policies for expanding opportunities for productive employment in less developed countries, which is where most of the world's workers live and where almost all of the world's new workers will live.

This study is about the nature and magnitude of the global employment challenge and about ways of meeting that challenge. It seeks to provide (i) an assessment of the current state of employment in the world, (ii) a review of the developments since 1990, (iii) an analysis of the interactions among structural factors, global forces and national policies that explain those developments, and (iv) a perspective on the policy responses required from the international community and national governments.

The study begins with an analysis of the structure, characteristics and evolution of the world's labour force. It then focuses on a key factor underlying the global employment problem – the asymmetry in the distribution of productive resources across countries. The context thus set, the study goes on to provide detailed analysis of the nature of the problem, of its evolution since 1990 and of the challenges that must now be confronted in different categories of countries. It concludes with a summary of the findings.

The focus on different categories of countries in the analysis of the employment situation warrants an explanation. The countries of the world are extremely diverse in terms of economic structure and level of development. This fact can be ignored in studying the world's labour force, which is more a demographic than an economic variable; no serious conceptual difficulties arise in comparisons of the labour force or of its characteristics across countries. But the fact of diversity cannot be ignored in analysing the employment problem, i.e., the problem of inadequacy of productive jobs in relation to the labour force. Indeed, the nature and manifestations of this inadequacy very much depend on the structural characteristics and the level of development of an economy. Thus a single investigative framework is simply not appropriate for all countries of the world. For purposes of analysis, therefore, we have classified countries into a manageable number of typological categories, keeping structural characteristics and level of development in view.

The typological categories that we develop are: *developed* countries, *Central and Eastern European (CEE)* countries, *Commonwealth of Independent States (CIS)* countries, *other high-income* countries, *petroleum exporter developing* countries, *medium-income developing* countries and *least developed* countries (a detailed list of countries is given in the annex to this chapter). For reasons of data availability, however, much of the analysis focuses on four groups: developed, CEE, CIS and developing, the last group being composed of *medium-income developing* and *least developed* countries together with a few of the *petroleum exporter developing* countries.

Inadequacy of information actually poses a more general problem. Statistical data required for a meaningful analysis of the employment situation are lacking for many countries. For basic statistics relating to the labour force (which moves steadily and has a fairly stable relation with population) it is possible to fill in the gaps by using indirect methods of estimation, but an analysis of the employment situation must obviously be based on actual data available from sample surveys. The availability of such data, unfortunately, is quite limited.

Apart from the problem of inadequate availability of data, there are also conceptual problems involved in using the data that are available. While there is a standardized method of collection of statistics on employment and unemployment, which is used worldwide, the statistics thus collected do not actually give us the same kind of information for all countries. This is well illustrated by the fact that the standard estimates of employment and unemployment, when compared across countries, give us a highly misleading picture of the employment situation around the world. On a straightforward comparison, for example, India would appear to have a much better employment situation than Germany, and the United Republic of Tanzania would appear to have achieved much more impressive growth of employment over the last decade than China.

The standard measures of employment and unemployment are not good indicators of employment or labour market situation in developing countries, where unemployment is not a real option for most workers and where employment hides underemployment as well as engagement in extremely low-productivity work (discussed in Chapter 4). The standard measures are appropriate in the context of developed countries, though even here, arguably, they no longer constitute adequate indicators as non-standard forms of employment (e.g., part-time employment) have now become quite widespread (see Chapter 6).

In preparing this study, considerable efforts were made to add to the database already available at the ILO by collecting additional data from international and country-level sources. Nevertheless, several important limitations remain. First, even the basic statistics on employment and unemployment are simply not available for a fairly large number of developing countries as well as for some CEE and CIS countries; for many others, they are available only for very few years. Second, even for the countries for which the basic statistics on employment and unemployment are available, the data are often not up to date. In many countries, labour force surveys are conducted only at irregular intervals. Moreover, there is often a long lag between the time when surveys are carried out and the time when processed data become available. Third, certain types of information (on formal employment and casual wage employment, for example), which are of critical importance in analysing the employment situation in developing countries, are not always collected and, even when they are collected, are not made readily available. Our efforts to obtain such information from country-level sources yielded results only in a limited number of cases.

These limitations of data imposed two limitations on the empirical analysis in the book. First, the period covered could not be extended beyond 2003–04 because that would have reduced the coverage of countries quite sharply. Second, it has not been possible to avoid using different samples of countries for investigating different issues. These limitations pose some real difficulties, which we have tried to overcome by combining theory with empirics. Although the study is based on empirical evidence, it relies on matching empirical findings with theoretical expectations for drawing conclusions.

In an effort to deal with the conceptual difficulties that arise in the use of data, we have introduced some methodological innovations. As already stated, the categorization of countries has been done in such a way as to ensure that the countries in any particular category are sufficiently similar in terms of economic structure for a single analytical framework to be applicable; this makes comparisons across countries within a category meaningful. More importantly, we have developed some new indices that, we believe, are more appropriate as indicators of the employment situation than the standard measures of employment and unemployment. We hope readers will agree.

CATEGORIZATION OF COUNTRIES AND TERRITORIES

APPENDIX

A total of 193 countries and territories, for which at least some data are available, are classified into seven categories as follows:

Developed: Australia, Austria, Belgium, Canada, Denmark, Finland, France, Germany, Greece, Iceland, Ireland, Italy, Japan, Luxembourg, Netherlands, New Zealand, Norway, Portugal, Spain, Sweden, Switzerland, United Kingdom, United States.

Central and Eastern Europe (CEE): Albania, Bosnia-Herzegovina, Bulgaria, Croatia, Czech Republic, Estonia, Hungary, Latvia, Lithuania, the former Yugoslav Republic of Macedonia, Montenegro, Poland, Romania, Serbia, Slovakia, Slovenia.

Commonwealth of Independent States (CIS): Armenia, Azerbaijan, Belarus, Georgia, Kazakhstan, Kyrgyzstan, Moldova, Russian Federation, Tajikistan, Turkmenistan, Ukraine, Uzbekistan.

Other high-income: Bahamas, Barbados, Channel Islands, Cyprus, French Guiana, French Polynesia, Guadeloupe, Guam, Hong Kong (China), Israel, Republic of Korea, Macau (China), Malta, Martinique, Netherlands Antilles, New Caledonia, Puerto Rico, Réunion, Singapore, Taiwan (China), Virgin Islands.

Petroleum exporter developing: Algeria, Bahrain, Brunei, Congo, Gabon, Islamic Republic of Iran, Iraq, Kuwait, Libyan Arab Jamahiriya, Nigeria, Oman, Qatar, Saudi Arabia, Syrian Arab Republic, Trinidad and Tobago, United Arab Emirates, Venezuela (Bolivarian Republic).

Medium-income developing: Argentina, Bolivia, Botswana, Brazil, Cameroon, Chile, China, Colombia, Costa Rica, Côte d'Ivoire, Cuba, Dominican Republic, Ecuador, Egypt, El Salvador, Fiji, Ghana, Guatemala, Guyana, Honduras, India, Indonesia, Jamaica, Jordan, Kenya, Democratic People's Republic of Korea, Lebanon, Malaysia, Mauritius, Mexico, Mongolia, Morocco, Namibia, Nicaragua, Pakistan, Panama, Papua New Guinea, Paraguay, Peru, Philippines, Saint Lucia, Saint Vincent and the Grenadines, South Africa, Sri Lanka, Suriname, Swaziland, Thailand, Tonga, Tunisia, Turkey, Uruguay, Viet Nam, West Bank and Gaza Strip, Western Sahara, Zimbabwe.

Least developed: Afghanistan, Angola, Bangladesh, Belize, Benin, Bhutan, Burkina Faso, Burundi, Cambodia, Cape Verde, Central African Republic, Chad, Comoros, Democratic Republic of the Congo, Djibouti, Equatorial Guinea, Eritrea, Ethiopia, Gambia, Guinea, Guinea-Bissau, Haiti, Lao People's Democratic Republic, Lesotho, Liberia, Madagascar, Malawi, Maldives, Mali, Mauritania, Mozambique, Myanmar, Nepal, Niger, Rwanda, Samoa, Sao Tome and Principe, Senegal, Sierra Leone, Solomon Islands, Somalia, Sudan, United Republic of Tanzania, Timor-Leste, Togo, Uganda, Vanuatu, Yemen, Zambia.

The category "developed" includes the most advanced economies of the world. The CEE countries are the erstwhile centrally planned economies of Central and Eastern Europe. The CIS countries are those that constituted the former Soviet Union. The "other high-income" countries are defined as those that had a per capita GDP of US$10,000 or more in 2003, that are not usually considered as "developed" and that are not major exporters of petroleum. A country is defined as a "petroleum exporter developing" country if more than 50 per cent of its exports is accounted for by petroleum and related products. The category "least developed" is as defined by the United Nations. The remaining countries are categorized as "medium-income developing" countries.

The criteria used for the above categorization of countries are economic structure and level of development. Thus the CEE category includes countries that are members of the European Union (Bulgaria, Czech Republic, Estonia, Hungary, Lithuania, Latvia, Poland, Romania, Slovakia and Slovenia) as well as countries that are members of the OECD (Czech Republic, Hungary, Poland and Slovakia). Cyprus, Malta and the Republic of Korea are OECD members but are classified as "other high-income" countries. Mexico and Turkey are classified as "medium-income developing" countries even though they are members of the OECD.

Any categorization embodies some distortions and ours is no exception. There are a few countries whose status is ambiguous. Singapore, for example, could have been classified as a "developed" country but we chose to classify it as a "high-income" country. Azerbaijan could have been categorized as a "petroleum exporter developing" country but we chose to classify it as a CIS country. And so on. Arbitrariness is hard to avoid in certain cases. On the whole, however, the countries in each of these categories are sufficiently similar in terms of economic structure and level of development for a common investigative framework to be applicable.

WORLD LABOUR FORCE STRUCTURE AND ITS EVOLUTION 2

The most recent ILO estimates show that the world today has a labour force[1] of 3.1 billion, nearly 1.2 billion more than in 1980 (table 2.1). The growth of the world's labour force, however, has been decelerating since 1980: while the average annual growth rate was 2.1 per cent in the period 1980–90, it dropped to 1.6 per cent during 1990–2000 and then to 1.5 per cent during 2000–07. This notwithstanding, about 46 million workers are currently being added to the global labour force every year.

This chapter looks at the structure, characteristics and evolution of the world's labour force and then briefly considers the outlook for the future. Data availability limits precise analysis to the period 1990–2003, in this chapter

Table 2.1 Global labour force, 1980–2007

Year	Labour force (millions)	Annual increment (millions)
1980	1 930	
1990	2 406	47.6
2000	2 823	41.7
2007	3 144[a]	45.9[a]

Note: Based on data for 193 countries and territories (for detailed list, see annex to Chapter 1).

[a] ILO estimate.

Source: ILO (LABORSTA/LABPROJ/KILM) database (http://laborsta.ilo.org/).

[1] "Labour force" refers to working-age persons who are either engaged in economically gainful activities, or are seeking or available for engagement in economically gainful activities. Unless specified otherwise, "working-age persons" and "labour force" refer to persons aged 15 years or more.

and throughout the book. This is unfortunate but unavoidable. As already noted in Chapter 1, survey-based estimates of employment and unemployment for the years following 2003 are simply not available for many countries. Whenever reliable post-2003 data are available, however, they are taken into account at relevant points in the analysis.

2.1 Structure and characteristics

Labour force concentration in low-income countries

The most striking fact about the world's labour force is its concentration in poorer countries (table 2.2): 73 per cent is in developing countries (medium-income developing countries and least developed countries taken together) while less than 15 per cent is in developed countries; China and India alone are home to 40 per cent of the world's workers.

This pattern of cross-country distribution is, of course, primarily a reflection of the fact that developing countries account for a large majority of the world's population: in 2003, the proportion equalled 73 per cent. However, these countries' share in the world's working-age population (i.e., persons aged 15 years or more) was lower, at 71 per cent. This highlights the important fact that the labour force participation rate tends to be higher at lower levels of economic development.

Table 2.2   Labour force by country group, 2003

Country group	Labour force (millions)	Distribution (%)
Developed	435.4	14.7
CEE	58.9	2.0
CIS	135.1	4.6
Other high-income	45.2	1.5
Petroleum exporter developing	128.0	4.3
Medium-income developing	1 845.8	62.4
(China)	(760.8)	(25.7)
(India)	(423.6)	(14.3)
Least developed	309.2	10.5
World	2 957.6	100.0

Note: Based on data for 193 countries and territories (for detailed list, see annex to Chapter 1).

Source: ILO (LABORSTA/KILM) database (http://laborsta.ilo.org/).

World labour force structure and its evolution

Figure 2.1 Labour force participation rates by country group, 2003

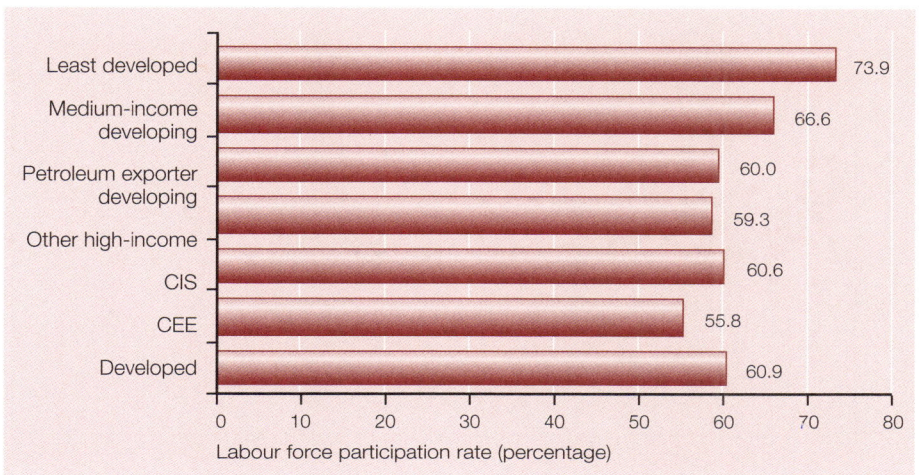

Note: Based on data for 193 countries and territories (for detailed list, see annex to Chapter 1).

Source: Derived from ILO (LABORSTA/KILM) database (http://laborsta.ilo.org/).

As figure 2.1 shows, participation rates in developing countries are significantly higher than those in developed and other high-income countries. More generally, across countries the labour force participation rate varies with level of economic development (as indicated by per capita GDP in Purchasing Power Parity (PPP) dollars) along a flattened U-shaped curve (figure 2.2). Most developing countries are clustered around the downward sloping segment of the curve, while most of the developed and other high-income countries are clustered around the upward rising segment. This indicates that, as growth occurs, the participation rate tends to decline in developing countries and increase in developed and other high-income countries. Since the share of developing countries in the world's working-age population is far higher than that of developed and other high-income countries, the global participation rate can be expected to show a mild tendency to decline over time.

Gender composition of the world's labour force

Women workers constitute 40 per cent of the world's labour force (table 2.3). The cross-country distribution of the world's female labour force is slightly less skewed than the distribution of the total labour force in favour of poorer countries. Developed countries account for 16 per cent of the world's female labour force (compared to less than 15 per cent of the world's labour force),

The global employment challenge

Figure 2.2 Labour force participation rate and level of economic development, 2003

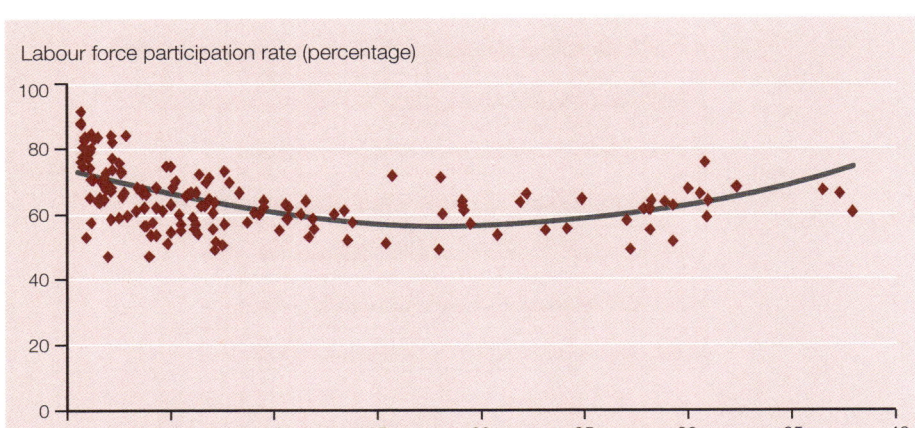

Notes: The regression equation is: $Y = 72.992 - 1.808 X + 0.047 X^2$, $R^2 = 0.301$. Both coefficients are significant at less than 1 per cent.
Based on data for 156 (of the 193) countries and territories for which data on per capita GDP in PPP$ are available. The following 37 countries and territories are excluded as the relevant data for 2003 are not available: Afghanistan, Bahamas, Bhutan, Brunei, Channel Islands, Cuba, Equatorial Guinea, French Guiana, French Polynesia, Guadeloupe, Guam, Iraq, Korea (Democratic People's Rep.), Liberia, Libya, Luxembourg, Macau (China), Maldives, Martinique, Montenegro, Myanmar, Netherlands Antilles, New Caledonia, Puerto Rico, Qatar, Réunion, Sao Tome and Principe, Serbia, Somalia, Suriname, Taiwan (China), Timor-Leste, United Arab Emirates, Virgin Islands, West Bank and Gaza Strip, Western Sahara, Zimbabwe.

Sources: Derived from ILO (LABORSTA/KILM) database (http://laborsta.ilo.org/) and World Bank, World Development Indicators database (CD-ROM, 2005).

while developing countries account for 71 per cent of the female labour force (compared to 73 per cent of the total labour force). The labour force in developed countries is thus more "feminized" than that in developing countries.

The explanation lies in the pattern of variation of female labour force participation with level of development (figures 2.3 and 2.4). While the male participation rate tends to decline mildly but steadily as we move from less to more developed countries, the female rate moves along a fairly pronounced U-shaped curve. With rising level of development, women's participation in the labour force first declines and then increases. The flattened U-shaped curve along which the overall participation rate moves as level of development rises is generated essentially by the behaviour of women's labour force participation.

World labour force structure and its evolution

Table 2.3 Female labour force by country group, 2003

Country group	Female labour force (millions)	Share in total labour force (%)	Distribution (%)
Developed	192.6	44.2	16.3
CEE	26.5	45.0	2.2
CIS	65.4	48.4	5.5
Other high-income	18.7	41.4	1.6
Petroleum exporter developing	39.7	31.0	3.3
Medium-income developing	710.0	38.5	60.0
(China)	(339.7)	(44.7)	(28.7)
(India)	(121.1)	(28.6)	(10.2)
Least developed	131.0	42.4	11.1
World	1 183.9	40.0	100.0

Note: Based on data for 193 countries and territories (for detailed list, see annex to Chapter 1).

Source: Derived from ILO (LABORSTA/KILM) database (http://laborsta.ilo.org/).

Figure 2.3 Labour force participation rates by gender, 2003

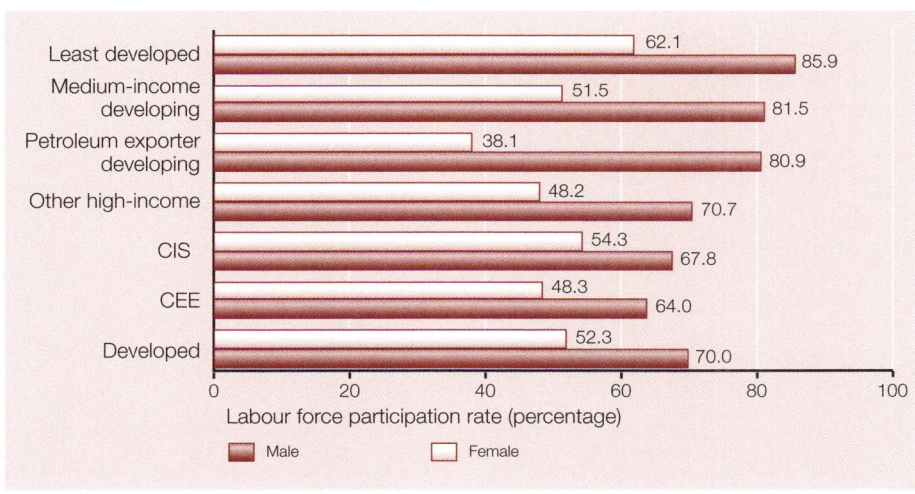

Note: Based on data for 193 countries and territories (for detailed list, see annex to Chapter 1).

Source: Derived from ILO (LABORSTA/KILM) database (http://laborsta.ilo.org/).

Figure 2.4 Labour force participation rate (male and female) by level of economic development, 2003

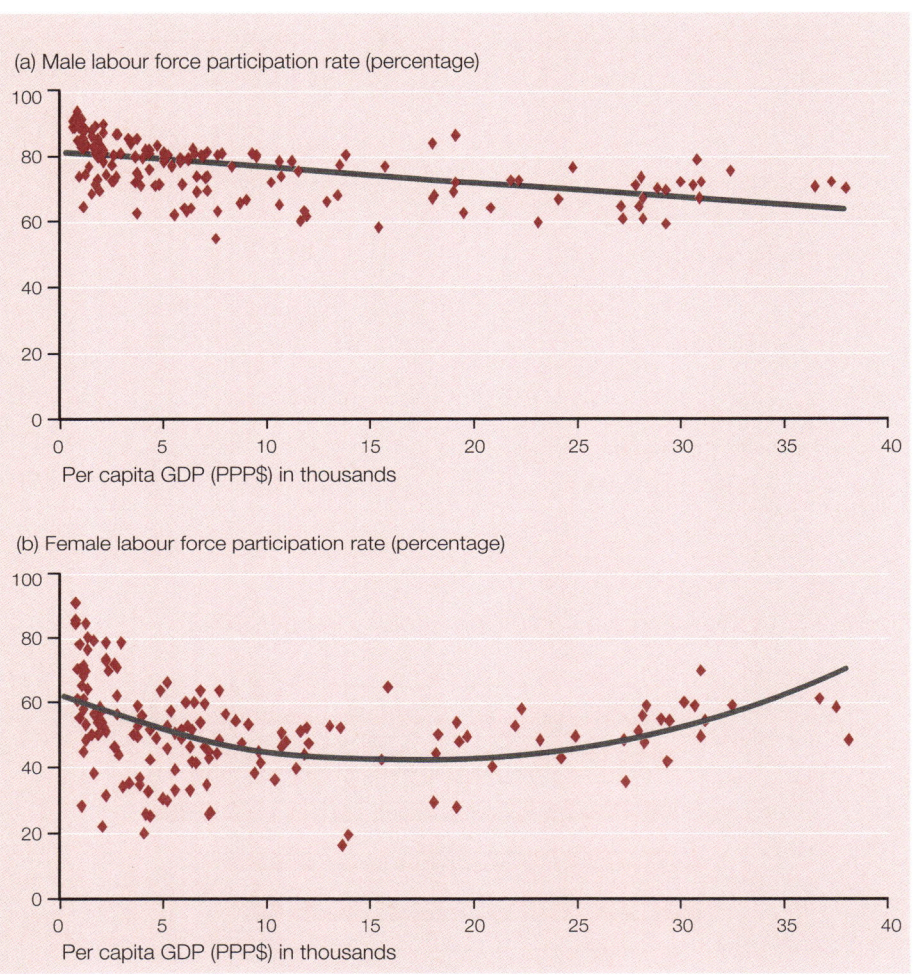

Notes: The regression equations are:
(a) $Y = 81.702 - 0.465\ X$, $R^2 = 0.274$. The coefficient is significant at less than 1 per cent.
(b) $Y = 61.270 - 2.228\ X + 0.065\ X^2$, $R^2 = 0.176$. Both coefficients are significant at less than 1 per cent.
Based on data for 156 (of the 193) countries and territories for which data on per capita GDP in PPP$ are available. The following 37 countries and territories are excluded as the relevant data for 2003 are not available: Afghanistan, Bahamas, Bhutan, Brunei, Channel Islands, Cuba, Equatorial Guinea, French Guiana, French Polynesia, Guadeloupe, Guam, Iraq, Korea (Democratic People's Rep.), Liberia, Libya, Luxembourg, Macau (China), Maldives, Martinique, Montenegro, Myanmar, Netherlands Antilles, New Caledonia, Puerto Rico, Qatar, Réunion, Sao Tome and Principe, Serbia, Somalia, Suriname, Taiwan (China), Timor-Leste, United Arab Emirates, Virgin Islands, West Bank and Gaza Strip, Western Sahara, Zimbabwe.

Sources: Derived from ILO (LABORSTA/KILM) database (http://laborsta.ilo.org/) and World Bank, World Development Indicators database (CD-ROM, 2005).

> **Box 2.1   Women's labour force participation: India, 2000**
>
> Within countries, women's labour force participation tends to move along a U-shaped curve with rising income level. The table below shows the pattern of variation of women's labour force participation with level of education in India where, as in most developing countries, a worker's level of education is a good indicator of the income status of the household to which she belongs.
>
> | Years of education | Labour force participation rate (%) |
> |---|---|
> | 0 | 37.9 |
> | 1–5 | 26.1 |
> | 6–8 | 17.6 |
> | 9–10 | 16.2 |
> | 11–12 | 14.9 |
> | 12+ | 32.7 |
>
> **Source:** National Sample Survey Organisation (Government of India), *Employment and unemployment situation, 1999–2000* (New Delhi, 2001).

The pattern of cross-country variation in the female labour force participation rate is in fact remarkably similar to the pattern of its variation within countries (see box 2.1). For women there exists a trade-off between housework, for which they have the major responsibility in most countries, and economically gainful activities. At very low levels of income, housework has little welfare value (food must be there for cooking to be useful); most of the adults – male and female – in a poor population need to engage in some kind of gainful activity in order to ensure even basic survival. But as household incomes rise, the welfare value of housework increases and exceeds the welfare value of income from gainful activities. And as household incomes rise above a certain threshold, the welfare value of housework begins to decline (as purchase of goods and services in the market begins to substitute for housework), while earning opportunities from work outside home increase.

The way in which work opportunities evolve with economic development is also relevant in this context. At low levels of development, family enterprises predominate and this facilitates women's participation in the labour force. As development occurs, the growing importance of wage employment sharpens the trade-off between housework and gainful activities outside the home. At high levels of development, growth of service jobs again facilitates women's employment. While socio-cultural norms also influence female labour force participation, level of economic development remains more influential (see box 2.2).

Box 2.2 Religion, culture and women's labour force participation

It is widely believed that women's labour force participation is greatly influenced by religious/cultural norms. In particular, women's participation is thought to be more restricted in countries where Muslims constitute a large majority of the population. However, the evidence suggests that, apart from level of economic development, social rather than religious norms are relevant in explaining the behaviour of women's labour force participation (see table below). While religious norms do have a role in setting social norms, there are also other, more powerful forces. For example, other things being equal, women's labour force participation is consistently higher in Socialist or ex-Socialist countries than in others.

Country	Per capita GDP* (PPP$)	Women's labour force participation rate* (%)
Egypt[a]	3 950	20.9
Syrian Arab Republic[a]	3 721	37.0
Azerbaijan[a,b]	3 617	59.6
Turkey[a]	7 068	26.6
Iran (Islamic Republic)[a]	6 995	35.2
Turkmenistan[a,b]	5 943	60.4
Philippines	4 278	52.3
Indonesia[a]	3 401	50.7
Viet Nam[b]	2 490	72.4
China[b]	5 003	66.9
India	2 893	34.6

* 2003 figures.
[a] Mainly Muslim population.
[b] Socialist or ex-Socialist.

Sources: Col. 1: World Bank, World Development Indicators database (CD-ROM, 2005); Col. 2: ILO (LABORSTA/KILM) database (http://laborsta.ilo.org/).

Overall, the observed patterns suggest that there is some degree of what might be called distress participation of women in the labour force in low-income countries, i.e., participation forced by poverty. Rising incomes (declining poverty) naturally lead to withdrawals by the distress participants. Declining female labour force participation in developing countries, therefore, indicates welfare gains rather than welfare losses.

Given the variation in patterns of male and female labour force participation rates with level of economic development, the degree of feminization of the labour force across countries also tends to vary with level of economic development along a U-shaped curve. Since most developing countries (which account for an overwhelmingly large share of the world's labour force) are clustered around the downward segment of the curve, we can expect the degree of feminization of the world's labour force to decline as economic growth occurs in all countries. And it would be incorrect to interpret this as something regressive.

Age structure

Developing countries have a much younger labour force than other countries, and this holds for both male and female labour force (table 2.4). Indeed, there is a fairly neat positive relation between average age of the labour force and level of development (figure 2.5), principally a reflection of the fact that the less developed a country, the younger is its population (because its population growth is higher and average life expectancy lower). Moreover, the age of entry into the labour force tends to be lower in poorer countries since fewer young persons are able to pursue education and most people have to work in order to survive.

At the same time, the problem of an "ageing labour force" has become a matter of serious concern in more developed parts of the world. Ageing emerges as a problem when the percentage of labour force in the age group "55 or older" exceeds that in the age group "15–24". By this criterion, ageing has clearly emerged as a problem in two groups of countries: developed and other high-income (table 2.4). This is a source of concern because, apart from signalling an imminent decline in labour supply and increased need for social security provisions, it can potentially alter the skill structure of the labour force.

The pattern of cross-country variation in the age structure of the labour force implies that the world's young workers are even more concentrated in poorer countries than the world's labour force as a whole. Table 2.5 explicitly shows this to be the case. Medium-income developing countries and least developed countries together account for nearly 80 per cent of the world's young workers (compared to 73 per cent of the world's labour force). Correspondingly, the cross-country distribution of the world's older workers is less skewed in favour of poorer countries than the distribution of the world's labour force; medium-income developing countries and least developed countries together account for 68 per cent of the world's older workers.

The global employment challenge

Table 2.4 Distribution of labour force by age group and gender, 2003 (percentages)

Country group	All				Male				Female			
	15–24	25–54	55–59	60+	15–24	25–54	55–59	60+	15–24	25–54	55–59	60+
Developed	13.5	71.4	8.1	7.0	12.9	71.2	8.3	7.5	14.2	71.7	7.9	6.2
CEE	12.1	76.3	5.7	5.8	12.7	75.3	6.2	5.8	11.5	77.6	5.0	5.9
CIS	14.4	75.8	4.4	5.4	15.4	74.5	4.9	5.2	13.4	77.1	3.9	5.6
Other high-income	12.4	73.5	6.2	7.9	11.5	74.1	6.5	7.9	13.6	72.7	5.8	7.9
Petroleum exporter developing	27.3	63.4	3.7	5.6	26.9	63.5	3.7	6.0	28.2	63.4	3.7	4.7
Medium-income developing	21.3	68.4	4.5	5.8	20.8	67.5	4.9	6.8	22.0	69.8	3.8	4.4
Least developed	31.4	58.2	4.1	6.3	30.5	58.6	4.2	6.8	32.6	57.7	4.0	5.7
World	20.8	68.2	5.0	6.1	20.5	67.5	5.3	6.8	21.2	69.2	4.5	5.0

Note: Based on data for 193 countries and territories (for detailed list, see annex to Chapter 1).

Source: Derived from ILO (LABORSTA/KILM) database (http://laborsta.ilo.org/).

World labour force structure and its evolution

Figure 2.5 Average age of labour force, 2003

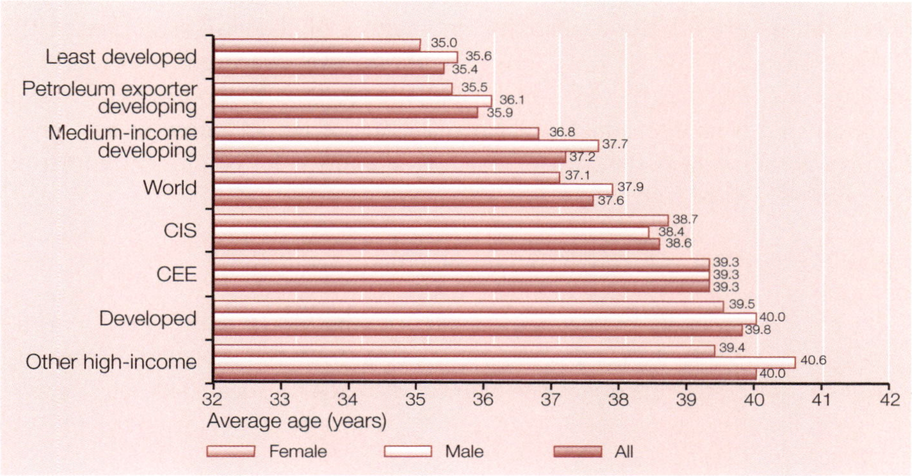

Country group	Female	Male	All
Least developed	35.0	35.6	35.4
Petroleum exporter developing	35.5	36.1	35.9
Medium-income developing	36.8	37.7	37.2
World	37.1	37.9	37.6
CIS	38.7	38.4	38.6
CEE	39.3	39.3	39.3
Developed	39.5	40.0	39.8
Other high-income	39.4	40.6	40.0

Note: Based on data for 193 countries and territories (for detailed list, see annex to Chapter 1).

Source: Derived from ILO (LABORSTA/KILM) database (http://laborsta.ilo.org/).

Table 2.5 Distribution of young workers, older workers and total labour force by country group, 2003 (percentages)

Country group	Young workers (age 15–24)	Older workers (age 55+)	Total labour force
Developed	9.5	20.1	14.7
CEE	1.2	2.1	2.0
CIS	3.2	4.1	4.6
Other high-income	0.8	2.0	1.5
Petroleum exporter developing	5.7	3.6	4.3
Medium-income developing	63.9	58.2	62.4
Least developed	15.8	9.9	10.5
World	100.0 (615.4)	100.0 (326.1)	100.0 (2 957.6)

Notes: Based on data for 193 countries and territories (for detailed list, see annex to Chapter 1).
Figures in parentheses show world totals in millions.

Source: Derived from ILO (LABORSTA/KILM) database (http://laborsta.ilo.org/).

Skill structure

Given the nature of data availability, an analysis of the skill structure of the world's labour force is only possible if we are prepared to make two assumptions: (1) that the level of formal education is a good proxy for skill level, and (2) that the educational profile of the labour force in any given country is the same as that of the working-age (15 years or older) population (see, however, box 2.3).

> **Box 2.3 Skill, education and employment: India, 2000**
>
> The empirical analysis of the skill structure of the labour force rests on two assumptions: (1) that the number of years of formal education is a good indicator of skill level, and (2) that the distribution of the labour force by years of education is the same as the distribution of the working-age (15 years or older) population by years of education in any given country.
>
> The first assumption is quite plausible, although more precise information (e.g., general education, vocational/technical training, tertiary education in science and technology, etc.), which we currently do not have for many countries, would obviously be desirable. The plausibility of the second assumption, however, is open to question. Evidence from India, cited below, seems to suggest that the assumption leads to an underestimation of the skill level of the male workforce and overestimation of the skill level of the female workforce. These patterns are likely to hold for all developing countries as this is consistent with the fact that, as noted earlier, there is distress participation of poor women (without education) in low-income countries.
>
> **Educational attainment: India, 2000**
>
> | Category | Share of population with no education (%) | Share of population with tertiary education (%) | Average years of education |
> |---|---|---|---|
> | Population | 38.2 | 3.9 | 3.4 |
> | Males | 28.3 | 5.0 | 4.2 |
> | Females | 48.9 | 2.6 | 2.7 |
> | Labour force | 42.4 | 6.3 | 3.9 |
> | Males | 33.0 | 7.3 | 4.6 |
> | Females | 68.5 | 3.7 | 1.9 |
>
> Note: Age group 5 years or older.
> **Source:** Ghose (2004a).

Table 2.6   Educational attainment by gender and country group, 2000 (percentages)

Country group	All			Male			Female		
	Share of labour force with no education	Share of labour force with tertiary education	Average years of education	Share of labour force with no education	Share of labour force with tertiary education	Average years of education	Share of labour force with no education	Share of labour force with tertiary education	Average years of education
Developed	2.3	30.6	10.2	2.2	32.0	10.4	2.4	29.4	10.1
CEE	3.3	10.2	9.4	1.8	10.2	9.8	4.8	10.3	9.1
Other high-income	8.0	23.8	10.3	4.5	29.7	11.1	11.5	18.0	9.6
Petroleum exporter developing	27.0	8.8	5.7	20.7	10.5	6.3	32.5	7.2	5.2
Medium-income developing	25.9	4.8	5.8	17.7	6.0	6.7	33.8	3.6	4.9
Least developed	50.8	1.7	2.6	41.8	2.9	3.3	59.6	0.6	2.0
World (excluding CIS countries)	22.8	9.7	6.5	16.3	10.6	7.2	28.5	8.9	5.8

Note: Based on data for the following 99 countries and territories: **Developed:** Australia, Austria, Belgium, Canada, Denmark, Finland, France, Germany, Greece, Iceland, Ireland, Italy, Japan, Netherlands, New Zealand, Norway, Portugal, Spain, Sweden, Switzerland, United Kingdom, United States. CEE: Bulgaria, Croatia, Hungary, Poland, Romania, Slovakia. **Other high-income:** Barbados, Hong Kong (China), Israel, Korea (Rep.), Singapore. **Petroleum exporter developing:** Algeria, Bahrain, Congo, Iran, Syria, Trinidad and Tobago, Venezuela. **Medium-income developing:** Bolivia, Botswana, Brazil, Cameroon, Chile, China, Colombia, Costa Rica, Dominican Republic, Ecuador, Egypt, El Salvador, Fiji, Ghana, Guatemala, Guyana, Honduras, India, Indonesia, Jamaica, Jordan, Kenya, Malaysia, Mauritius, Mexico, Nicaragua, Pakistan, Panama, Paraguay, Peru, Philippines, South Africa, Sri Lanka, Swaziland, Thailand, Tunisia, Turkey, Uruguay, Zimbabwe. **Least developed:** Bangladesh, Benin, Central African Republic, Congo (Dem. Rep.), Gambia, Guinea-Bissau, Haiti, Lesotho, Malawi, Mali, Mozambique, Nepal, Niger, Rwanda, Senegal, Sierra Leone, Tanzania, Togo, Uganda, Zambia.

Sources: Derived from ILO (LABORSTA/KILM) database (http://laborsta.ilo.org/) and Barro and Lee (2000).

Assuming the above, it can be said that the world's labour force is only moderately skilled: 23 per cent have no formal education while only 10 per cent have tertiary education. As would be expected, the lower the level of development, the less skilled is the country's labour force (table 2.6). The contrast between developed and least developed countries is stark. Only 2 per cent of workers in developed countries lack formal education, while the corresponding figure for least developed countries is 51 per cent. On the other hand, 31 per cent of workers in developed countries have attained tertiary

Figure 2.6 Average years of education and level of economic development, 2000

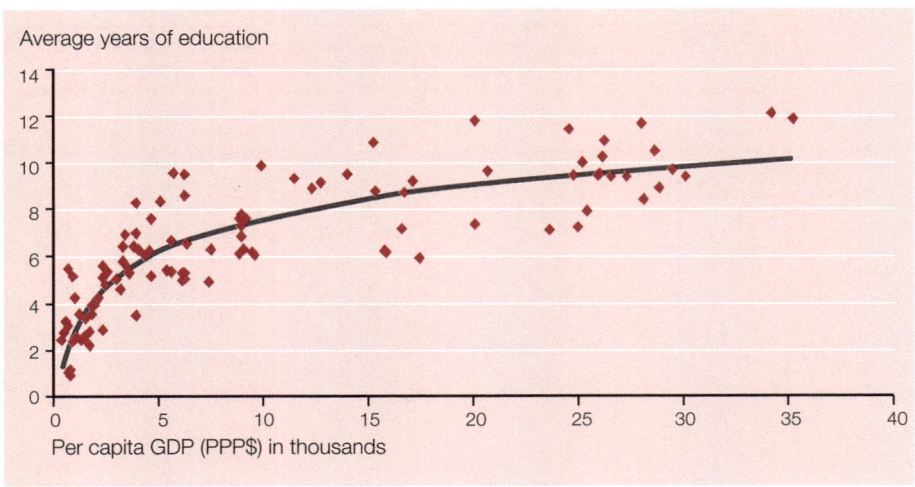

Notes: The regression equation is: Y = – 11.324 + 2.050 Ln (X), R² = 0.756. The coefficient is significant at less than 1 per cent.
Based on data for the following 99 countries and territories: **Developed:** Australia, Austria, Belgium, Canada, Denmark, Finland, France, Germany, Greece, Iceland, Ireland, Italy, Japan, Netherlands, New Zealand, Norway, Portugal, Spain, Sweden, Switzerland, United Kingdom, United States. CEE: Bulgaria, Croatia, Czech Republic, Hungary, Poland, Romania, Slovakia, Slovenia. **Other high-income:** Barbados, Cyprus, Hong Kong (China), Israel, Korea (Rep.), Singapore. **Petroleum exporter developing:** Algeria, Bahrain, Congo, Iran, Kuwait, Syria, Trinidad and Tobago, Venezuela. **Medium-income developing:** Argentina, Bolivia, Botswana, Brazil, Cameroon, Chile, China, Colombia, Costa Rica, Dominican Republic, Ecuador, Egypt, El Salvador, Fiji, Ghana, Guatemala, Guyana, Honduras, India, Indonesia, Jamaica, Jordan, Kenya, Malaysia, Mauritius, Mexico, Nicaragua, Pakistan, Panama, Papua New Guinea, Paraguay, Peru, Philippines, South Africa, Sri Lanka, Swaziland, Thailand, Tunisia, Turkey, Uruguay, Zimbabwe. **Least developed:** Bangladesh, Benin, Central African Republic, Congo (Dem. Rep.), Gambia, Guinea-Bissau, Haiti, Lesotho, Malawi, Mali, Mozambique, Nepal, Niger, Rwanda, Senegal, Sierra Leone, Sudan, Tanzania, Togo, Uganda, Zambia.

Sources: Derived from ILO (LABORSTA/KILM) database (http://laborsta.ilo.org/), Barro and Lee (2000) and World Bank, World Development Indicators database (CD-ROM, 2005).

education, while this is the case only for less than 2 per cent of workers in least developed countries.

Interestingly, the cross-country relationship between level of education and level of economic development is non-linear (figure 2.6): "average years of education" increases more than proportionately with level of economic development in countries below a threshold level of development, but less than proportionately in countries above the threshold. This pattern reflects the fact that there is a *de facto* upper limit (this appears to be 12 years) to which "average years of education" can potentially increase in any given country. But it also suggests that low skill levels of workers in low-income countries reflect the resource constraints that their governments face in

World labour force structure and its evolution

Figure 2.7   Gender disparity in education and level of economic development, 2000

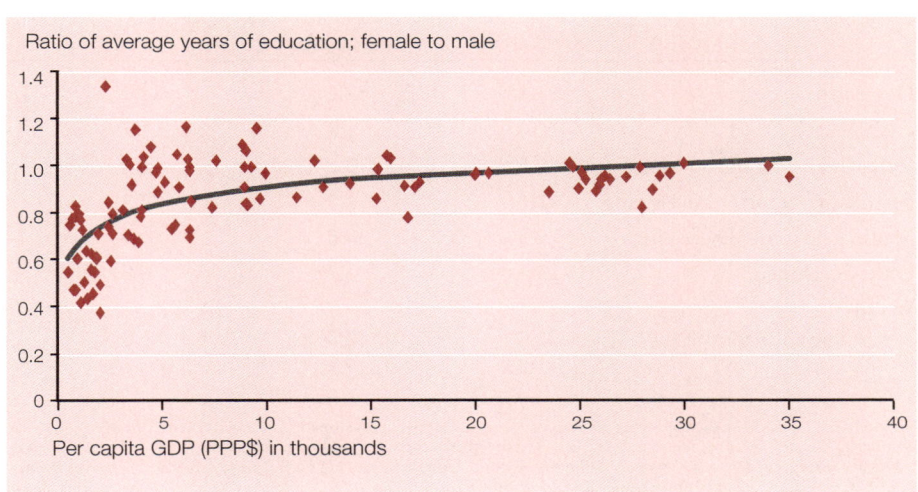

Notes: The regression equation is: $Y = -0.008 + 0.989 \ln(X)$, $R^2 = 0.393$. The coefficient is significant at less than 1 per cent.
Based on data for the following 106 countries and territories: **Developed:** Australia, Austria, Belgium, Canada, Denmark, Finland, France, Germany, Greece, Iceland, Ireland, Italy, Japan, Netherlands, New Zealand, Norway, Portugal, Spain, Sweden, Switzerland, United Kingdom, United States. CEE: Bulgaria, Croatia, Czech Republic, Hungary, Poland, Romania, Slovakia, Slovenia. **Other high-income:** Barbados, Cyprus, Hong Kong (China), Israel, Korea (Rep.), Singapore. **Petroleum exporter developing:** Algeria, Bahrain, Congo, Iran, Kuwait, Syria, Trinidad and Tobago, Venezuela. **Medium-income developing:** Argentina, Bolivia, Botswana, Brazil, Cameroon, Chile, China, Colombia, Costa Rica, Dominican Republic, Ecuador, Egypt, El Salvador, Fiji, Ghana, Guatemala, Guyana, Honduras, India, Indonesia, Jamaica, Jordan, Kenya, Malaysia, Mauritius, Mexico, Nicaragua, Pakistan, Panama, Papua New Guinea, Paraguay, Peru, Philippines, South Africa, Sri Lanka, Swaziland, Thailand, Tunisia, Turkey, Uruguay, Zimbabwe. **Least developed:** Bangladesh, Benin, Central African Republic, Congo (Dem. Rep.), Gambia, Guinea-Bissau, Haiti, Lesotho, Malawi, Mali, Mozambique, Nepal, Niger, Rwanda, Senegal, Sierra Leone, Sudan, Tanzania, Togo, Uganda, Zambia.

Sources: Derived from ILO (LABORSTA/KILM) database (http://laborsta.ilo.org/), Barro and Lee (2000) and World Bank, World Development Indicators database (CD-ROM, 2005).

expanding education, rather than policy bias.

The average skill level of female workers is generally, though not universally, lower than that of male workers. Indeed, there are a number of countries where female workers have a higher level of education than their male counterparts.[2] The skill gap between men and women shows a tendency to narrow at higher levels of development (figure 2.7). But this narrowing, once again, tends to be faster at lower levels of development.

---

[2] These countries are: Argentina, Bahrain, Botswana, Colombia, Dominican Republic, Guyana, Ireland, Jamaica, Kuwait, Lesotho, Nicaragua, South Africa, Swaziland, Sweden, Trinidad and Tobago, Uruguay and Venezuela (Bolivarian Republic). However, it is highly probable that the ratio of "average years of education" of female workers to that for male workers is being overestimated (see box 2.3).

Table 2.7 Distribution of unskilled, skilled and total labour force by country group, 2000 (percentages)

Country group	Labour force with no education (%)	Labour force with tertiary education (%)	Total labour force (%)
Developed	1.8	57.0	18.0
CEE	0.3	1.8	1.7
Other high-income	0.5	3.1	1.3
Petroleum exporter developing	2.6	2.0	2.2
Medium-income developing	79.5	34.8	69.9
Least developed	15.3	1.2	6.9
World (excluding CIS countries)	100.0 (541.9)	100.0 (229.8)	100.0 (2 378.6)

Notes: Based on data for the following 99 countries and territories: **Developed:** Australia, Austria, Belgium, Canada, Denmark, Finland, France, Germany, Greece, Iceland, Ireland, Italy, Japan, Netherlands, New Zealand, Norway, Portugal, Spain, Sweden, Switzerland, United Kingdom, United States. CEE: Bulgaria, Croatia, Hungary, Poland, Romania, Slovakia. **Other high-income:** Barbados, Hong Kong (China), Israel, Korea (Rep.), Singapore. **Petroleum exporter developing:** Algeria, Bahrain, Congo, Iran, Syria, Trinidad and Tobago, Venezuela. **Medium-income developing:** Bolivia, Botswana, Brazil, Cameroon, Chile, China, Colombia, Costa Rica, Dominican Republic, Ecuador, Egypt, El Salvador, Fiji, Ghana, Guatemala, Guyana, Honduras, India, Indonesia, Jamaica, Jordan, Kenya, Malaysia, Mauritius, Mexico, Nicaragua, Pakistan, Panama, Paraguay, Peru, Philippines, South Africa, Sri Lanka, Swaziland, Thailand, Tunisia, Turkey, Uruguay, Zimbabwe. **Least developed:** Bangladesh, Benin, Central African Republic, Congo (Dem. Rep.), Gambia, Guinea-Bissau, Haiti, Lesotho, Malawi, Mali, Mozambique, Nepal, Niger, Rwanda, Senegal, Sierra Leone, Tanzania, Togo, Uganda, Zambia.

Figures in parentheses show world totals in millions.

Sources: Derived from ILO (LABORSTA/KILM) database (http://laborsta.ilo.org/) and Barro and Lee (2000).

The cross-country distribution of skilled workers is highly skewed in favour of developed countries (table 2.7). In a sample of 99 countries, developed countries account for only 18 per cent of the world's labour force but 57 per cent of its high-skilled workers. In sharp contrast, developing countries account for 77 per cent of the world's labour force but only 36 per cent of its high-skilled workers.

2.2 The main trends

The growing concentration of the world's labour force in developing countries

Between 1990 and 2003, the world's labour force grew by about 552 million (table 2.8). The developing countries accounted for nearly 467 million (or close to 85 per cent) of this incremental labour force, while developed countries

World labour force structure and its evolution

Table 2.8 Growth of world labour force, 1990–2003 (millions)

Country group	Labour force		
	1990 (millions)	Change: 1990–2003 (millions)	Average annual growth rate (%)
Developed	394.5	40.9	0.8
CEE	63.2	–4.3	–0.5
CIS	140.3	–5.2	–0.3
Other high-income	36.5	8.7	1.6
Petroleum exporter developing	83.0	45.0	3.4
Medium-income developing	1 466.6	379.2	1.8
Least developed	221.8	87.4	2.6
World	2 405.9	551.7	1.6

Note: Based on data for 193 countries and territories (for detailed list, see annex to Chapter 1).

Source: Derived from ILO (LABORSTA/KILM) database (http://laborsta.ilo.org/).

accounted for only 41 million (or just over 7 per cent). Remarkably, labour force in CEE and CIS countries actually declined in absolute terms over the same period. The overall result was a rapidly growing concentration of the world's labour force in low-income countries.

These trends are primarily explained by the growth of population and working-age population, which has been much faster in developing economies (figure 2.8 on page 28). As a matter of fact, at a cross-country level the rate of population growth is found to vary inversely with the initial level of economic development (figure 2.9 on page 29). This relationship itself calls for an explanation, and the key to the explanation lies in what is called the process of demographic transition (see box 2.4). This refers to the behaviour of population growth in the course of economic development. As a country embarks on development, population growth, starting from an initial low level, first accelerates, then reaches a plateau, then decelerates and finally reaches stability at a low level once again. In most of today's developed countries, the process of demographic transition had started in the early part of the nineteenth century and ended in the early part of the twentieth century. In today's developing countries, however, the process started only in the recent past, in the 1920s in some and around 1950 or even later in others. The observed cross-country inverse relation between population growth and initial level of economic development reflects these different starting points of the process of demographic transition.

> **Box 2.4 Demographic transition**
>
> Over a long period of human history, population growth was insignificant and unstable. Periods of some growth in some parts of the world were followed by periods of decline. Steady and accelerated population growth began in Western and Northern Europe around 1800 as industrial revolutions ushered in modern economic growth. Technological change in food production and discovery of drugs and vaccines led to reduced mortality. Other parts of Europe and the New World (Australia, Canada, New Zealand and the United States), as well as Japan, soon caught up with these trends. Since fertility remained unchanged, the result was accelerated population growth. With a time lag, fertility responded to the decline in mortality and began to decline. As the decline in fertility gathered pace, the decline in mortality slowed down (because of naturally diminishing marginal effects of improved nutrition and medical care). The rate of population growth reached a peak and then decelerated. By the early part of the twentieth century, it had stabilized at a level much lower than the peak.
>
> This pattern of change has come to be known as demographic transition. From around 1920, a succession of developing countries embarked upon modern economic growth, thereby setting off processes of demographic transition. These facts are well reflected in the changing cross-country distribution of the world's population. As shown in the graphs below, the share of Europe (including Russia), the New World and Japan in world population steadily increased between 1820 and 1913 while the share of the developing world declined. The trends were reversed around 1930.
>
> However, there is one noteworthy difference between past demographic transitions in today's developed countries and present transitions in today's developing countries. Even at its peak, population growth in the former group never even approached 2 per cent per annum, whereas in some of today's developing countries it exceeds 4 per cent per annum. This difference is attributable to an "advantage" of late development. Mortality decline in today's developing countries tends to be quicker and sharper because advanced drugs and vaccines from developed countries are available. For the same reason, however, fertility decline also tends to be sharper and more rapid so that there is a shortening of the period required for completing the transition. Many developing countries are already well into the phase of decelerating population growth.

World labour force structure and its evolution

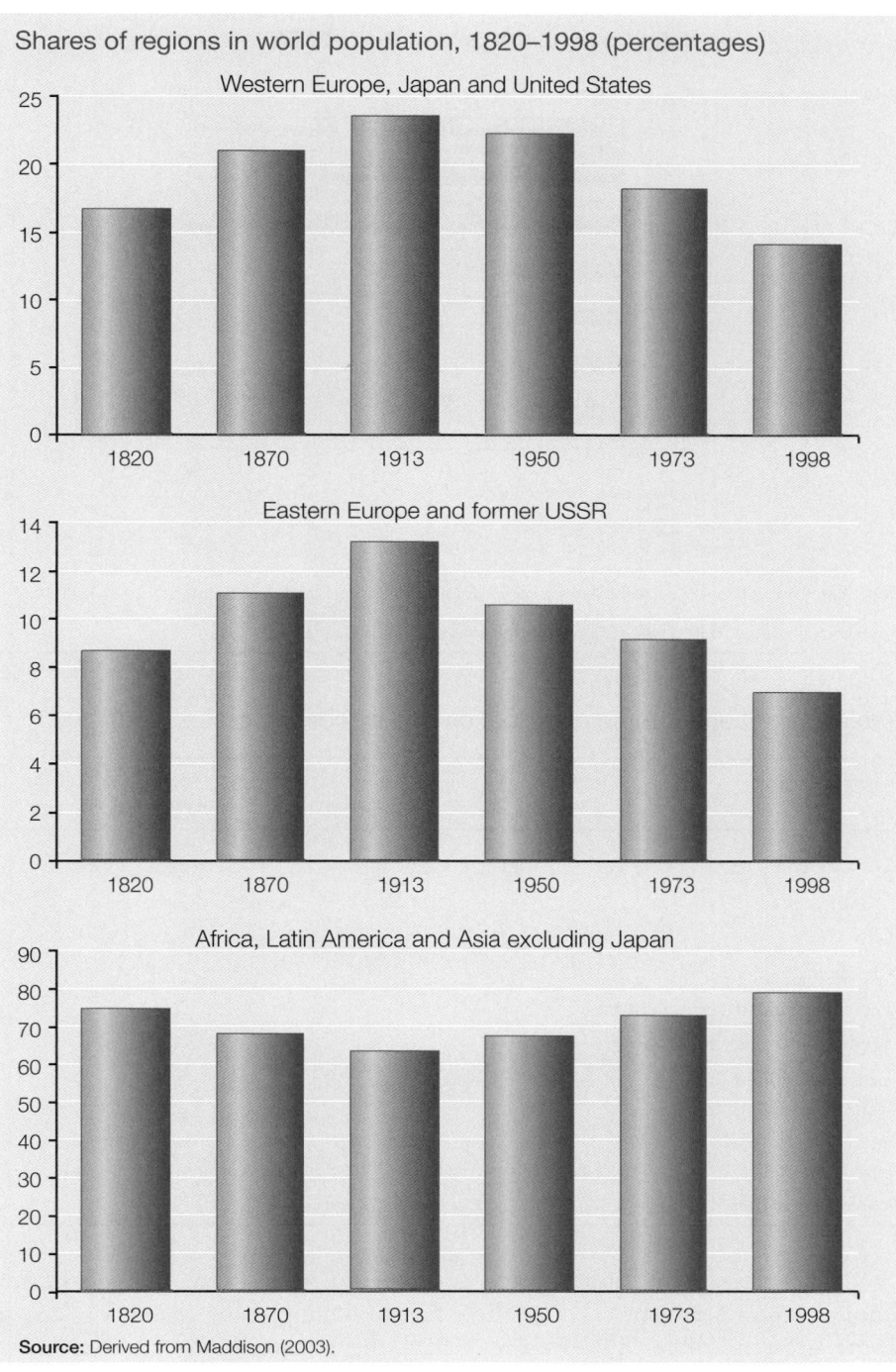

Shares of regions in world population, 1820–1998 (percentages)

Source: Derived from Maddison (2003).

The global employment challenge

Figure 2.8   Average annual growth rates of total and working-age population by country group, 1990–2003

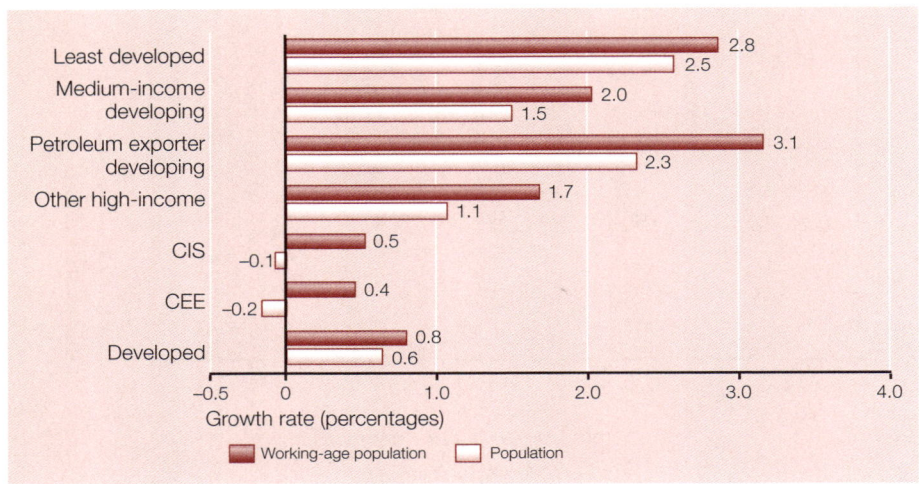

Note: Based on data for 193 countries and territories (for detailed list, see annex to Chapter 1).

Source: Derived from ILO (LABORSTA/KILM) database (http://laborsta.ilo.org/).

Table 2.9   Labour force participation rate by country group, 1990–2003

Country group	1990 (percentages)	Change: 1990–2003 (percentage points)
Developed	61.0	–0.1
CEE	63.5	–7.7
CIS	67.2	–6.6
Other high-income	59.3	–0.1
Petroleum exporter developing	58.0	2.0
Medium-income developing	66.5	–0.1
Least developed	76.3	–2.3
World	65.8	–0.5

Note: Based on data for 193 countries and territories (for detailed list, see annex to Chapter 1).

Source: Derived from ILO (LABORSTA/KILM) database (http://laborsta.ilo.org/).

The changes in labour force participation rates were not significant enough to moderate or enhance the effect of demographic change on labour force growth (table 2.9). In the 1990s, the participation rate showed a

World labour force structure and its evolution

Figure 2.9 Population growth and level of economic development, 1990–2003

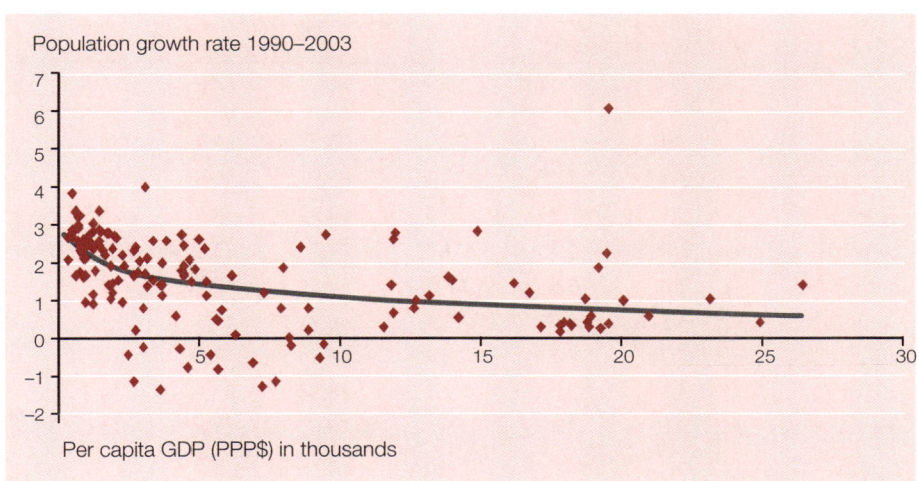

Notes: The regression equation is: $Y = 5.895 - 0.526 \ln(X)$, $R^2 = 0.238$. The coefficient is significant at less than 1 per cent.
Based on data for 152 (of the 193) countries and territories for which the relevant data on per capita GDP in PPP$ are available. The following 41 countries are excluded as the relevant data for 1990 are not available: Afghanistan, Azerbaijan, Barbados, Bhutan, Bosnia and Herzegovina, Brunei, Cambodia, Channel Islands, Cuba, Czech Republic, Djibouti, Eritrea, Fiji, French Guiana, Guadeloupe, Guam, Iraq, Korea (Democratic People's Rep.), Kuwait, Liberia, Libya, Maldives, Martinique, Moldova, Montenegro, Myanmar, Netherlands Antilles, Qatar, Réunion, Saint Vincent and the Grenadines, Sao Tome and Principe, Serbia, Slovenia, Somalia, Suriname, Taiwan (China), Timor-Leste, Uzbekistan, Virgin Islands, West Bank and Gaza Strip, Western Sahara.

Sources: Population growth rate: ILO (LABORSTA/KILM) database (http://laborsta.ilo.org/); per capita GDP: World Bank, World Development Indicators database (CD-ROM, 2005).

declining trend in CEE, CIS and least developed countries, a rising trend in petroleum exporter developing countries and stability elsewhere in the world. The sharp decline in participation rates in CEE and CIS countries is known to have resulted from the economic decline that accompanied the transition from centrally planned to market economies (see Chapter 7 and Chapter 8). The decline in participation rates in least developed countries is in all probability a result of economic growth: at low levels of development, we may recall, participation rates tend to fall as incomes rise. Overall, the labour force participation rate in the world as a whole showed only a slight decline.

During the period under review, in a number of developing countries HIV/AIDS reduced the natural increase in population and/or in the labour force participation rate; countries with a high incidence of HIV/AIDS saw an increase in mortality. Moreover, since the disease mainly affects prime-age persons, its high incidence also had the effect of reducing the participation rate. The available evidence certainly suggests such outcomes for some

The global employment challenge

Table 2.10 Population growth, labour force participation and incidence of HIV/AIDS, selected countries,[a] 1980–2003 (percentages)

Country	Average annual rate of population growth		Labour force participation rate[b]			Incidence of HIV/AIDS[c]
	1980–90	1990–2003	1980	1990	2003	2003
Swaziland	3.4	1.4	58.9	55.6	50.4	38.8
Botswana	3.1	1.7	73.4	65.9	56.8	37.3
Lesotho	2.1	0.9	70.0	69.2	58.6	28.9
Zimbabwe	3.7	1.5	74.7	74.7	73.1	24.6
South Africa	2.3	1.9	66.8	66.5	62.7	21.5
Namibia	3.5	2.7	53.3	56.9	55.3	21.3
Zambia	3.3	2.3	77.6	77.5	77.8	16.5
Malawi	4.3	2.1	87.8	88.3	87.4	14.2
Central African Rep.	2.6	2.1	78.3	79.6	79.8	13.5

[a] Only countries with incidence of HIV/AIDS greater than 10 per cent are included in the table. Other countries identified as having a significant incidence are, in descending order: Mozambique, Cameroon, Côte d'Ivoire, Rwanda, Burundi, Tanzania, Congo, Djibouti, Sierra Leone, Liberia, Ethiopia, Burkina Faso, Haiti, Togo, Nigeria, Angola, Congo (Democratic Rep.), Uganda, Benin, Chad, Gabon, Bahamas, Equatorial Guinea, Eritrea, Ghana, Guinea-Bissau, Cambodia, Guyana, Sudan, Dominican Republic, Trinidad and Tobago, Belize, Myanmar, Guinea, Thailand, Honduras, Gambia and Mali.

[b] Refers to age group "15 years or older".

[c] Incidence of HIV/AIDS is the percentage of persons in age group 15–45 carrying the virus.

Sources: Derived from ILO (LABORSTA/KILM) database (http://laborsta.ilo.org/) and ILO (2004).

individual countries (table 2.10). However, given the low weights of these countries (in terms of population) within the category, the overall effects of HIV/AIDS on population growth and labour force participation rates in developing countries as a group have not turned out to be significant.

Changes in gender composition

The share of females in the labour force remained stable in the 1990s (table 2.11). Contrary to a widely held impression, there is no clear trend towards feminization of the world's labour force. Indeed, in view of the cross-country pattern of feminization discussed above, the surprise is that the degree of feminization of the world's labour force did not decline.

Of course, the global picture hides diverse trends observed in different types of countries. There is a clear trend towards feminization of the labour force in three categories of countries: developed, other high-income and petroleum exporter developing. On the other hand, the share of females in the labour force declined in least developed countries and remained stable in CEE, CIS and medium-income developing countries.

World labour force structure and its evolution

Table 2.11 Share of females in labour force, 1990–2003

Country group	1990 (percentages)	Change: 1990–2003 (percentage points)
Developed	42.1	2.1
CEE	45.3	−0.3
CIS	48.2	0.2
Other high-income	38.7	2.7
Petroleum exporter developing	27.5	3.5
Medium-income developing	38.4	0.1
Least developed	43.0	−0.6
World	39.8	0.2

Note: Based on data for 193 countries and territories (for detailed list, see annex to Chapter 1).

Sources: Derived from ILO (LABORSTA/KILM) database (http://laborsta.ilo.org/).

The observed movements in male and female labour force participation rates confirm these conclusions (table 2.12). In three country groups – developed, other high-income and petroleum exporter developing – the female participation rate was rising while the male participation rate was declining; these are the countries where feminization can be seen as a substantive trend. In CEE and CIS countries, participation rates of both males and females

Table 2.12 Labour force participation rate, male and female, 1990–2003

Country group	Male		Female	
	1990 (%)	Change: 1990–2003 (percentage points)	1990 (%)	Change: 1990–2003 (percentage points)
Developed	73.2	−3.2	49.7	2.6
CEE	72.2	−8.2	55.5	−7.2
CIS	75.7	−7.2	60.0	−5.7
Other high-income	73.1	−2.5	45.6	2.7
Petroleum exporter developing	82.1	−1.2	32.7	5.4
Medium-income developing	81.2	0.0	51.5	−0.1
Least developed	87.8	−1.9	65.0	−2.9
World	79.7	−1.0	52.1	−0.1

Notes: Based on data for 193 countries and territories (for detailed list, see annex to Chapter 1).

Source: Derived from ILO (LABORSTA/KILM) database (http://laborsta.ilo.org/).

decreased in rather unusual circumstances (see Chapter 7 and Chapter 8). In the least developed countries, economic growth expectedly reduced the female participation rate more sharply than the male participation rate. In medium-income developing countries, participation rates of both males and females remained basically stable. This very probably reflects the fact that medium-income developing countries are clustered around the bottom segment of the U-shaped curve representing the relationship between female labour force participation and the level of economic development.

Changes in age structure

The world's labour force is ageing (table 2.13): between 1990 and 2003, the average age of workers worldwide increased from 36.5 years to 37.6 years. In general, the share of young workers (aged 15–24) in the total labour force has been declining while the shares of prime-age (aged 25–54) and older (aged 55 or more) workers have been rising.

The process of ageing has obviously gone much further in some countries than in others. Indeed, in two groups – petroleum exporter developing and least developed countries – it has not even properly started. In developed and other high-income countries, on the other hand, it has been rather rapid; it was

Table 2.13   Age structure of labour force, 1990–2003 (percentages)

Country group	Age group 15–24		25–54		55+	
	1990 (%)	Change: 1990–2003 (percentage points)	1990 (%)	Change: 1990–2003 (percentage points)	1990 (%)	Change: 1990–2003 (percentage points)
Developed	17.5	–4.0	69.7	1.7	12.8	2.3
CEE	16.2	–4.1	72.3	4.0	11.5	0.0
CIS	15.3	–0.9	75.3	0.5	9.4	0.4
Other high-income	17.6	–6.1	73.8	0.5	8.6	5.6
Petroleum exporter developing	27.2	0.1	62.3	1.1	10.6	–1.3
Medium-income developing	28.4	–7.1	61.7	6.7	9.8	0.5
Least developed	31.9	–0.5	57.1	1.1	11.0	–0.6
World	25.7	–4.9	63.9	4.3	10.4	0.6

Note: Based on data for 193 countries and territories (for detailed list, see annex to Chapter 1).

Source: Derived from ILO (LABORSTA/KILM) database (http://laborsta.ilo.org/).

during the period under review that in these groups of countries labour force ageing emerged as a serious problem. The labour force has also been ageing in medium-income developing countries but still remains relatively young.

Labour force ageing is evidently related to population ageing, which in turn is linked to the process of demographic transition. Population ageing begins as countries enter the phase of demographic transition characterized by decelerating population growth. In developed, CEE, CIS and other high-income countries, all phases of demographic transition were completed by the middle of the twentieth century. Most of the medium-income developing countries are in the phase of decelerating population growth. As for petroleum exporter developing and least developed countries, some have entered the phase of high but stable population growth while a few are still in the phase of accelerating population growth.

There are two other factors, however, that influence labour force ageing (box 2.5). On the one hand, the existence of universal social security systems in advanced countries allows people to withdraw from the labour force at a specified age (between 60 and 65). In developing countries, many elderly people do not enjoy the benefit of social security support and are therefore forced to remain in the labour force. On the other hand, the average number of years for which younger people pursue education is stable in advanced countries but is growing in less

---

Box 2.5   Population and labour force ageing

In 2000, the share of population aged 65 years or more in total population equalled about 16.5 per cent in countries of Western Europe and Japan, about 13.5 per cent in Eastern Europe (including the Russian Federation, Georgia and Ukraine) and the developed countries of North America and Oceania, about 9 per cent in other high-income countries and the countries of Central Asia, about 5 per cent in medium-income developing countries and, finally, about 3 per cent in least developed countries as well as in many petroleum exporter developing countries.

The ageing of the labour force, however, does not simply depend on population but also on the extent to which older people participate in the labour force. Across countries, the labour force participation rate of older people is found to vary inversely with the share of older people in total population. In 2000, the participation rate for people aged 65 years or more varied between 1 and 10 per cent in developed, CEE and CIS countries, between 10 and 25 per cent in other high-income and petroleum exporter developing countries, between 25 and 40 per cent in medium-income developing countries, and between 40 and 60 per cent in least developed countries.

Source: United Nations (2002).

developed countries. Consequently, in advanced countries labour force ageing is slower than population ageing, while in less developed countries the reverse is true.

It is not surprising, therefore, that we are seeing overall effects in terms of a growing concentration of both younger and older workers in developing countries. The share of developing countries (medium-income developing and least developed countries combined) in the world's youth labour force (persons aged 15–24) increased from 78.9 per cent in 1990 to 79.7 per cent in 2003, while their share in the world's elderly labour force (persons aged 55 or more) increased from 66.9 per cent in 1990 to 68.1 per cent in 2003.

Changes in skill structure

The average level of education of the labour force has been rising in all parts of the world (table 2.14). In 1990, 27 per cent of the world's workers had no

Table 2.14   Educational attainment of the labour force, 1990–2000

Country group	Share of labour force with no education		Share of labour force with tertiary education		Average years of education	
	1990 (%)	Change: 1990–2000 (percentage points)	1990 (%)	Change: 1990–2000 (percentage points)	1990 (%)	Change: 1990–2000 (percentage points)
Developed	2.5	−0.2	24.4	6.2	9.7	0.5
CEE	2.7	0.6	7.2	3.0	9.2	0.2
Other high-income	9.6	−1.6	13.6	10.2	9.6	0.7
Petroleum exporter developing	37.7	−10.0	5.6	3.2	4.4	1.3
Medium-income developing	32.2	−6.3	3.3	1.5	5.1	0.7
Least developed	57.1	−6.3	1.2	0.5	2.3	0.3
World (excluding CIS countries)	27.2	−4.4	7.6	2.1	6.0	0.5

Note: Based on data for the following 99 countries and territories: **Developed:** Australia, Austria, Belgium, Canada, Denmark, Finland, France, Germany, Greece, Iceland, Ireland, Italy, Japan, Netherlands, New Zealand, Norway, Portugal, Spain, Sweden, Switzerland, United Kingdom, United States. **CEE:** Bulgaria, Croatia, Hungary, Poland, Romania, Slovakia. **Other high-income:** Barbados, Hong Kong (China), Israel, Korea (Rep.), Singapore. **Petroleum exporter developing:** Algeria, Bahrain, Congo, Iran, Syria, Trinidad and Tobago, Venezuela. **Medium-income developing:** Bolivia, Botswana, Brazil, Cameroon, Chile, China, Colombia, Costa Rica, Dominican Republic, Ecuador, Egypt, El Salvador, Fiji, Ghana, Guatemala, Guyana, Honduras, India, Indonesia, Jamaica, Jordan, Kenya, Malaysia, Mauritius, Mexico, Nicaragua, Pakistan, Panama, Paraguay, Peru, Philippines, South Africa, Sri Lanka, Swaziland, Thailand, Tunisia, Turkey, Uruguay, Zimbabwe. **Least developed:** Bangladesh, Benin, Central African Republic, Congo (Democratic Rep.), Gambia, Guinea-Bissau, Haiti, Lesotho, Malawi, Mali, Mozambique, Nepal, Niger, Rwanda, Senegal, Sierra Leone, Tanzania, Togo, Uganda, Zambia.

Sources: Derived from ILO (LABORSTA/KILM) database (http://laborsta.ilo.org/) and Barro and Lee (2000).

World labour force structure and its evolution

Table 2.15 Gender disparity in education, 1990 and 2000

Country group	Average years of education: female to male ratio	
	1990	2000
Developed	0.976	0.974
CEE	0.929	0.933
Other high-income	0.849	0.870
Petroleum exporter developing	0.764	0.822
Medium-income developing	0.667	0.722
Least developed	0.515	0.587
World	0.777	0.811

Note: Based on data for the following 96 countries and territories: **Developed:** Australia, Austria, Belgium, Canada, Denmark, Finland, France, Germany, Greece, Iceland, Ireland, Italy, Japan, Netherlands, New Zealand, Norway, Portugal, Spain, Sweden, Switzerland, United Kingdom, United States. **CEE:** Bulgaria, Croatia, Hungary, Poland, Romania, Slovakia. **Other high-income:** Hong Kong (China), Israel, Korea (Rep.), Singapore. **Petroleum exporter developing:** Algeria, Bahrain, Congo, Iran, Syria, Trinidad and Tobago, Venezuela. **Medium-income developing:** Bolivia, Botswana, Brazil, Cameroon, Chile, China, Colombia, Costa Rica, Dominican Republic, Ecuador, Egypt, El Salvador, Ghana, Guatemala, Honduras, India, Indonesia, Jamaica, Jordan, Kenya, Malaysia, Mauritius, Mexico, Nicaragua, Pakistan, Panama, Paraguay, Peru, Philippines, South Africa, Sri Lanka, Swaziland, Thailand, Tunisia, Turkey, Uruguay, Zimbabwe. **Least developed:** Bangladesh, Benin, Central African Republic, Congo (Democratic Rep.), Gambia, Guinea-Bissau, Haiti, Lesotho, Malawi, Mali, Mozambique, Nepal, Niger, Rwanda, Senegal, Sierra Leone, Tanzania, Togo, Uganda, Zambia.

Sources: Derived from ILO (LABORSTA/KILM) database (http://laborsta.ilo.org/) and Barro and Lee (2000).

education at all; by 2000, the proportion had fallen to 23 per cent. In 1990, less than 8 per cent of the world's workers attained tertiary education; by 2000, this proportion had risen to nearly 10 per cent. Overall, there was a rise in the mean years of education from 6.0 to 6.5 in the course of the decade. The gap between developed and developing countries in terms of educational attainment of the labour force has also been narrowing. Mean years of education, expressed as a ratio of that in developed countries, rose from 0.454 to 0.559 in petroleum exporter developing countries, from 0.526 to 0.569 in medium-income developing countries and from 0.237 to 0.255 in least developed countries. The gender gap in education has been narrowing in all parts of the world (table 2.15) and this narrowing has been faster in developing than in developed countries. Overall, education is one area where a process of convergence, albeit slow, is visible.

2.3 Future outlook

Since 1980, the growth of the world's population, working-age population and labour force has been decelerating, and this trend can be expected to continue in the foreseeable future. Most developing countries have now reached the phase of demographic transition where there is stable or decelerating population growth, and many CEE and CIS countries have reached a stage in which population growth has turned negative. All this means decelerating growth of the world's working-age population. The labour force participation rate should also be declining as economic growth in poorer countries lowers the participation rates there. The growth of the world's labour force will thus continue to decelerate. ILO estimates suggest that between now and 2015 the world's labour force will grow at an annual rate of 1.3 per cent.

Going by past trends, we should also expect the world's labour force to be older and better educated. The problem of ageing will become increasingly serious in developed and other high-income countries, and will emerge as a serious problem in CEE and CIS countries. Gender disparity in education is expected to decline. Change in the degree of feminization of the world's labour force is hard to predict. In many developing countries, economic growth will tend to lower labour force participation for women more than for men; in developed and other high-income countries, economic growth will increase women's labour force participation while reducing that of men. The overall result is not easy to forecast. ILO projections suggest that the degree of feminization will remain stable.

The labour force will continue to grow at a faster rate in developing countries than in developed and other high-income countries. As a result, the level of concentration of the global labour force in developing countries will continue to rise. According to ILO estimates, the share of developing countries (medium-income developing and least developed countries combined) in the world labour force will rise to 75 per cent by 2015, while the share of developed countries will fall to 13 per cent.

These facts already give a preview of the difficulties that lie ahead: the less developed a country, the greater will be the challenge of expanding the opportunities for productive employment and the lower, naturally, will be its capacity to meet that challenge. The international community will have a major role to play in meeting the employment challenge in the developing world.

GLOBALIZATION IN AN UNEQUAL WORLD

3

Productive employment generally results when productive resources – labour, capital and skills – are brought together for purposes of production of goods and services. The current cross-country distribution of these productive resources, however, is hugely asymmetric,[3] which means that the combination in which they are brought together varies widely across countries. The world's unskilled labour is concentrated in developing countries, while its capital and skills are concentrated in developed countries. Globally, the poorer a country, the greater is its supply of unskilled labour and the smaller is its supply of capital and skills. This pattern of distribution of productive resources is the fundamental reason why productive employment is so much more scarce in the developing than in the developed world. From a global perspective, this is also a source of inefficiency in the use of global productive resources (including unskilled labour).[4]

Improvement in the global employment situation requires faster growth of productive employment, and hence faster growth of capital and skills, in poorer countries.[5] It thus both implies and requires reducing the existing asymmetries in the cross-country distribution of productive resources.

As it stands today, the pattern of demographic change across countries militates against such reduction. The poorer a country, the higher is its rate of labour force growth. For the asymmetries even to remain unchanged at their present levels, therefore, the poorer a country, the faster must be the growth

---

[3] This asymmetry is of course a result of uneven development over a long period in history.
[4] The volume of productive employment in the world would be much larger than it is if labour, capital and skills were distributed in exactly the same proportions across countries.
[5] This effectively means that the enormity of the task for national policies varies inversely with level of development.

in the supply of capital and skills; yet, the poorer a country, the lower is its ability to achieve growth in the supply of these productive resources. It is easy to see, then, that the prevailing pattern of demographic change actually generates a tendency for the asymmetries to increase over time.

The other force with potential to change the distribution of productive resources across countries is globalization. The increasingly free cross-border flow of capital – a core element of globalization – has the potential for altering the distribution of the world's capital between developed and developing countries. And international migration – which has not been a core element of globalization but has nevertheless been influenced by it – has the potential for altering the distribution of the world's labour and skills. The long-term impact of globalization on productive employment in the world depends on whether and to what extent these effects help reduce the asymmetries in resource distribution.

With this perspective in view, this chapter considers, first, the current pattern of cross-country distribution of productive resources and the change in this distribution since 1990, and, second, the impact that cross-border flows of capital and labour have had on the distribution during the same period.

3.1 Asymmetric distribution of productive resources

The huge asymmetry in the distribution of the world's productive resources across countries is quite evident from table 3.1: in a sample of 99 countries, in 2000 (the latest date for which data on education are available) developed countries accounted for less than 2 per cent of the unskilled labour force but 57 per cent of the high-skilled labour force and 54 per cent of investment; in contrast, developing countries (medium-income developing and least developed countries combined) accounted for 95 per cent of the unskilled labour force but only 36 per cent of the high-skilled labour force and 39 per cent of investment.

The implication is that an average worker in a developed country can be employed with far higher levels of capital and skills than an average worker in a developing country. In 2000, investment per worker (defined as the ratio of total fixed capital formation to the total labour force) in a developed country was 22.5 times that in a least developed country and skill per worker (defined as the ratio of the labour force with tertiary education to the total labour force) in a developed country was 17.6 times that in a least developed country (table 3.2). We need hardly any other information to conclude that the volume of productive employment was proportionately far higher in a developed than in a least developed country.

Has there been any tendency for the asymmetries to decline? Generally speaking, yes. In the 1990s, the concentration of the world's labour force in

Table 3.1 Distribution of productive resources by country group, 1990–2000 (percentages)

Country group	Labour force		GDP[a]		Fixed capital formation[a]		Labour force with tertiary education		Labour force with no education	
	1990	2000	1990	2000	1990	2000	1990	2000	1990	2000
Developed	19.5	18.0	65.7	59.3	64.8	54.0	63.0	57.0	1.8	1.8
CEE	2.1	1.7	2.5	2.0	2.3	2.0	2.0	1.8	0.2	0.3
Other high-income	1.3	1.3	2.2	2.7	3.2	3.6	2.2	3.1	0.4	0.5
Petroleum exporter developing	1.8	2.2	1.9	1.8	1.5	1.8	1.3	2.0	2.5	2.6
excluding the Islamic Rep. of Iran	*1.0*	*1.3*	*1.0*	*0.9*	*0.9*	*0.8*	*0.9*	*1.3*	*1.1*	*1.2*
Medium-income developing	69.0	69.9	26.5	33.2	27.4	37.7	30.4	34.8	81.8	79.5
excluding China and India	*20.1*	*22.0*	*15.2*	*15.2*	*12.8*	*13.3*	*15.1*	*18.7*	*21.3*	*22.7*
Least developed	6.3	6.9	1.2	1.0	0.8	0.9	1.1	1.2	13.3	15.3
excluding Bangladesh	*4.0*	*4.5*	*0.7*	*0.5*	*0.5*	*0.4*	*0.4*	*0.5*	*8.2*	*10.0*
World (excluding CIS countries)	100.0	100.0	100.0	100.0	100.0	100.0	100.0	100.0	100.0	100.0

Note: Based on data for the following 99 countries and territories: **Developed**: Australia, Austria, Belgium, Canada, Denmark, Finland, France, Germany, Greece, Iceland, Ireland, Italy, Japan, Netherlands, New Zealand, Norway, Portugal, Spain, Sweden, Switzerland, United Kingdom, United States. **CEE**: Bulgaria, Croatia, Hungary, Poland, Romania, Slovakia. **Other high-income**: Barbados, Hong Kong (China), Israel, Korea (Rep.), Singapore. **Petroleum exporter developing**: Algeria, Bahrain, Congo, Iran, Syria, Trinidad and Tobago, Venezuela. **Medium-income developing**: Bolivia, Botswana, Brazil, Cameroon, Chile, China, Colombia, Costa Rica, Dominican Republic, Ecuador, Egypt, El Salvador, Fiji, Ghana, Guatemala, Guyana, Honduras, India, Indonesia, Jamaica, Jordan, Kenya, Malaysia, Mauritius, Mexico, Nicaragua, Pakistan, Panama, Paraguay, Peru, Philippines, South Africa, Sri Lanka, Swaziland, Thailand, Tunisia, Turkey, Uruguay, Zimbabwe. **Least developed**: Bangladesh, Benin, Central African Republic, Congo (Democratic Rep.), Gambia, Guinea-Bissau, Haiti, Lesotho, Malawi, Mali, Mozambique, Nepal, Niger, Rwanda, Senegal, Sierra Leone, Tanzania, Togo, Uganda, Zambia.

[a] Measured in PPP$.

Sources: Derived from ILO (LABORSTA/KILM) database (http://laborsta.ilo.org/), Barro and Lee (2000) and World Bank, World Development Indicators database (CD-ROM, 2005).

Table 3.2 Investment per worker and skill per worker: Developed versus developing countries, 1990–2000

Country group	Ratio between developed and developing countries			
	Investment per worker		Skill per worker	
	1990	2000	1990	2000
Medium-income developing countries	8.4	5.5	7.3	6.4
excluding China and India	*4.4*	*4.9*	*4.3*	*3.7*
Least developed countries	25.5	22.5	20.0	17.6
excluding Bangladesh	*27.7*	*32.0*	*34.2*	*28.8*

Sources: Derived from ILO (LABORSTA/KILM) database (http://laborsta.ilo.org/), Barro and Lee (2000) and World Bank, World Development Indicators database (CD-ROM, 2005).

developing countries was growing, but the shares of these countries in global investment and skilled labour force were growing somewhat faster. Thus the gap between developed and developing countries in terms of investment per worker and skill per worker declined. Investment per worker in a developed country, for example, was 25.5 times that in a least developed country in 1990 and 22.5 times in 2000. Similarly, skill per worker in a developed country was 20 times that in a least developed country in 1990 and 17.6 times in 2000. A process of convergence appears to have been under way.

In the case of investment per worker, however, this process of catching up was confined to a small select group of developing countries. This is evident from the fact that exclusion of just a few countries from the groups of developing countries transforms a converging trend into a diverging one. Exclusion of just Bangladesh from the group of least developed countries, for example, changes the picture dramatically: investment per worker in developed countries was 27.7 times that in least developed countries excluding Bangladesh in 1990 and 32 times in 2000, showing divergence. Similarly, though with less dramatic results, when China and India are excluded from the medium-income developing country group, the trend is transformed towards divergence.

In the case of skill per worker, the trend towards convergence seems to have been more substantive: exclusion of Bangladesh from the group of least developed countries and of China and India from the group of medium-income developing countries no longer transforms a converging trend into a diverging one. Inspection of the detailed data shows, however, that a substantial number of countries in each of the groups have been falling behind.

Overall, therefore, no systematic tendency for the asymmetries in the distribution of productive resources across countries to decline is discernible. It would seem, then, that globalization has not countered the effects of demographic developments to any significant extent. The analysis presented in the two following sections shows that thus far globalization has not been a substantial force in reducing the asymmetries in the distribution of productive resources across countries.

3.2 Capital flows and investment in developing countries

Certain facts about recent trends in capital flows are by now well known.[6] In the 1990s, there was very sharp growth of private capital flows globally, including to developing countries, while official flows (bilateral and multilateral loans and grants) stagnated. Thus aggregate capital flows grew sharply while the share of official flows in aggregate flows dwindled. Of the various types of private capital flows, foreign direct investment (FDI) showed the sharpest growth and became the dominant form of capital flow.

In theory, the growth of capital flows across countries should have led to a substantial transfer of capital from developed countries, where it is in abundant supply, to developing countries, where it is scarce.[7] The reality has been rather different. The data presented in table 3.3 show that overall net inflow of foreign capital was significant only in the case of least developed countries, but the inflow was entirely based on foreign aid. In the case of medium-income developing countries, which received little foreign aid (on a net basis), net capital inflow was rather small.

During the period under review, FDI clearly represented the most important form of inflow of foreign private capital into medium-income developing countries. Indeed, net FDI inflow was fairly significant. The overall net inflow was not so significant because the net inflow of private loans was negative. However, net FDI inflow was concentrated in a few countries, as can be seen from the fact that exclusion of just three countries – Brazil, China and Mexico – from the group substantially reduces its magnitude.

The rapid growth of cross-border private capital flows in the 1990s thus did not generally result in significant inflow of foreign private capital into developing countries. Moreover, even the inflow that did go into some medium-income developing countries does not seem to have added to the investment rate in many of them. This can be seen from the following facts: the investment rate in many of these countries was in fact lower than the

---

[6] See, for example, Ghose (2004b, 2005b).

[7] In developed countries, savings are abundant but return to investment is low because capital per worker is already high. In developing countries, on the other hand, return to investment is high because capital per worker is low but savings are scarce. Therefore, freer cross-border movement of capital should lead to investment of a part of the savings of developed countries in developing countries.

The global employment challenge

Table 3.3 Net foreign capital inflow as share of GDP, selected countries, 1990–2003 (percentages)

Country group	Foreign direct investment (FDI)[a] (1)	Portfolio equity[b] (2)	Private loan[c] (3)	Official inflow[d] (4)	Total (5)
Medium-income developing	2.2	0.4	–1.3	–0.1	1.2
excluding Brazil, China and Mexico	1.4	0.3	–1.3	0.0	0.4
Least developed	1.0	0.0	–0.9	7.4	7.5
excluding Bangladesh and Bhutan	0.8	0.0	–1.3	10.0	9.5

Note: Based on data for the following 71 countries: **Medium-income developing:** Argentina, Bolivia, Botswana, Brazil, Cameroon, Chile, China, Colombia, Costa Rica, Côte d'Ivoire, Dominican Republic, Ecuador, Egypt, El Salvador, Ghana, Guatemala, Honduras, India, Indonesia, Jamaica, Jordan, Kenya, Lebanon, Malaysia, Mauritius, Mexico, Morocco, Nicaragua, Pakistan, Panama, Paraguay, Peru, Philippines, Sri Lanka, Swaziland, Thailand, Tunisia, Turkey, Uruguay, Zimbabwe. **Least developed:** Bangladesh, Belize, Benin, Bhutan, Burkina Faso, Burundi, Cape Verde, Central African Republic, Chad, Comoros, Ethiopia, Gambia, Guinea, Guinea Bissau, Haiti, Lesotho, Madagascar, Malawi, Mali, Mauritania, Mozambique, Nepal, Niger, Rwanda, Samoa, Senegal, Sierra Leone, Tanzania, Togo, Uganda, Yemen, Zambia.

[a] Net FDI inflow is defined as inflow minus outflow.
[b] Portfolio equity flow includes country funds, depository receipts and direct purchase of shares by foreign investors, inflow minus outflow.
[c] Net inflow of private loan is new debt to private creditors minus principal and interest payments on past debt.
[d] Net official inflow is new debt to official creditors (excluding IMF) plus official grants minus principal and interest payments on past debt to official creditors.

Sources: Col. 1: UNCTAD, Foreign Direct Investment database (http://www.unctad.org/Templates/page.asp?intItemID =3199&lang=1); Cols 2, 3 and 4: World Bank, Global Development Finance database (CD-ROM, 2005); data on GDP are from World Bank, World Development Indicators database (CD-ROM, 2005).

domestic saving rate and the excess of domestic saving over aggregate investment actually increased in the 1990s (table 3.4). The developments look quite striking if we consider medium-income developing countries excluding Brazil, China and Mexico. The investment rate was higher than the domestic saving rate in the early 1990s, but lower than the domestic saving rate by the early 2000s; meanwhile, the domestic saving rate itself had declined.

The fact that the investment rate was lower than the domestic saving rate even while there was positive net inflow of foreign private capital is clearly rather intriguing: it suggests that foreign private capital tended to crowd out domestic capital.[8] There are several possible reasons why crowding out could have occurred. In some cases, foreign capital went mainly into mergers and acquisitions associated with privatization of state enterprises, the revenue from

---

[8] A consequence of crowding out is an accumulation of foreign currency reserves. The fact that the foreign currency reserves of developing countries have been growing rather rapidly in the 1990s is thus another indication of crowding out. See Ghose (2004b, 2005a) for a detailed analysis of the phenomenon of crowding out.

Globalization in an unequal world

Table 3.4 Saving and investment as share of GDP, selected countries, 1990–2003 (percentages)

Country group	Saving[a]			Investment[b]		
	1990–92	2001–03	1990–2003	1990–92	2001–03	1990–2003
Medium-income developing	24.2	27.3	25.8	24.0	25.4	24.8
excluding Brazil, China and Mexico	22.1	21.3	21.6	25.6	19.3	22.8
Least developed	6.2	11.6	9.4	16.3	21.1	19.1
excluding Bangladesh and Bhutan	3.9	8.1	6.3	15.9	19.6	18.0

Note: Based on data for the following 71 countries: **Medium-income developing:** Argentina, Bolivia, Botswana, Brazil, Cameroon, Chile, China, Colombia, Costa Rica, Côte d'Ivoire, Dominican Republic, Ecuador, Egypt, El Salvador, Ghana, Guatemala, Honduras, India, Indonesia, Jamaica, Jordan, Kenya, Lebanon, Malaysia, Mauritius, Mexico, Morocco, Nicaragua, Pakistan, Panama, Paraguay, Peru, Philippines, Sri Lanka, Swaziland, Thailand, Tunisia, Turkey, Uruguay, Zimbabwe. **Least developed:** Bangladesh, Belize, Benin, Bhutan, Burkina Faso, Burundi, Cape Verde, Central African Republic, Chad, Comoros, Ethiopia, Gambia, Guinea, Guinea Bissau, Haiti, Lesotho, Madagascar, Malawi, Mali, Mauritania, Mozambique, Nepal, Niger, Rwanda, Samoa, Senegal, Sierra Leone, Tanzania, Togo, Uganda, Yemen, Zambia.

[a] Saving refers to gross domestic saving.
[b] Investment refers to gross fixed capital formation.

Source: World Bank, World Development Indicators database (CD-ROM, 2005).

which may have been used to finance government consumption or debt repayment. In other cases, domestic interest rates were raised to high levels to attract foreign capital, thereby discouraging domestic investment.[9] In still other cases, serious problems of macroeconomic management were encountered. Significant net inflow of foreign private capital generates pressures for appreciation of the recipient country's currency. Since such appreciation hurts exports, it is rational for the recipient country to prevent this, but preventing currency appreciation requires large expansion in money supply, which threatens to generate inflation. The standard remedy is sterilization (reduction of money supply through sale of securities by the central bank), but sterilization either reduces the availability or increases the cost of finance for domestic investors and hence restrains domestic investment.[10]

Overall, it is quite clear that the very sharp growth of cross-border flows of private capital in the 1990s did not have the anticipated effect: it did not

---

[9] It is hard to see any rationale for this policy. High interest rates can at best attract short-term capital flows, which are highly volatile.
[10] FDI is the overwhelmingly dominant form of capital flow and it is this that has grown rapidly through the 1990s. There is little evidence to show that FDI is attracted by high interest rate in a country. From a country's point of view, inflow of FDI is essentially autonomous. This is why the problem of currency appreciation cannot be remedied by lowering the interest rate.

significantly raise investment rates in developing countries. In contrast, net inflow of official resources (i.e., foreign aid) to the least developed countries was not only substantial but also financed new investment. Since these countries had (and continue to have) very low domestic saving rates, their much higher rates of investment could not have been achieved had foreign aid not been used for investment purposes.

Two conclusions follow: (1) the impressive growth of private capital flows across national frontiers has done little to increase investment per worker in developing countries; and (2) foreign aid has been quite effective in augmenting investment in the least developed countries so that the current scepticism about the effectiveness of foreign aid is not really justified (see box 3.1).

Box 3.1   Does foreign aid help poor countries?

In the economic literature, the issue of whether or not foreign aid contributes to investment and economic growth in poor countries remains mired in controversy. Many empirical studies have failed to find any robust positive impact of foreign aid on economic growth (a review is available in Rajan and Subramanian, 2005a). A variety of explanations for this "observed ineffectiveness" of foreign aid have been proposed (see Rajan and Subramanian, 2005b). One is that bad policies (including corruption and mismanagement) in the countries that receive foreign aid undermine its effectiveness. Another is that foreign aid can only bring material resources but not the incentives and institutions needed to promote economic growth. A third is that availability of foreign aid relaxes the need for governments to focus on mobilization of domestic resources for investment. A fourth is that inflow of foreign aid leads to appreciation of real exchange rates and this has adverse consequences for the traded goods sector: such developments undermine the impact of aid on economic growth.

But is ineffectiveness of foreign aid an established fact? The answer is no. The empirical studies have tried to examine the links between growth and overall volumes of aid, which include not just aid for investment but also technical assistance (costs of consultants from donor countries or multilateral agencies), administrative costs of running aid programmes, emergency aid and debt relief. A recent study (Clemens et al., 2004) considers only the component of aid that translates into investment and finds that this kind of aid contributes significantly to economic growth.

However, aid-financed investments may well have been wasteful to a certain extent and as such may not have had the expected effect on economic growth. It is widely recognized now that aid efforts in the past were not well coordinated, lacked clear developmental goals and were often driven by donor objectives (UNMP, 2005). Addressing these problems would be a worthwhile endeavour.

3.3 Labour flows and supply of labour and skills in developing countries

Widespread liberalization of international trade and capital flows since the mid-1980s stands in sharp contrast to the total lack of liberalization of international migration. Movement of people across national frontiers remains severely restricted. Indeed, the restrictions are arguably stronger today than they were in pre-globalization times (in the 1960s and 1970s, for example).

The available empirical evidence (see box 3.2 for observations on the nature and limitations of the evidence) suggests that, viewed over a long period, the stock of migrant population as a percentage of world population has changed little (table 3.5). The percentage actually declined slightly between 1960 and 1985, then increased sharply between 1985 and 1990, and remained stable between 1990 and 2005. But the marked increase between 1985 and 1990 is almost entirely explained by the sudden increase in migrant population in CIS countries, due to a re-classification of citizens of the former Soviet Union into citizens of a number of independent States.

Box 3.2   Data on international migration

The UN (Population Division of the Department of Economic and Social Affairs) database on migration provides estimates of stock of migrant population in each country of the world for the years 1960, 1965, 1970, 1975, 1980, 1985, 1990, 1995, 2000 and 2005. The estimates refer to persons born in a country other than the one in which they currently live and thus include refugees. Estimates of refugee population in each of the countries are also available from the same source. We have used the estimates that include refugees after checking that exclusion of refugees changed the numbers but not the trends and patterns.

Data on stocks of migrants in developed countries are available from the OECD's "Database on immigrants and expatriates". These data refer to persons aged 15 years or more who were not born in the developed country in which they currently live and work. Estimates of the number of migrants by country of origin are available. The estimates we use refer to persons who were born in medium-income developing and least developed countries. For the year 2000, detailed data on the distribution of migrants by level of education are also available. These are used together with the Barro–Lee database (Barro and Lee, 2000) on the distribution of the adult population in individual countries by level of education to derive estimates of emigration rates by level of education.

The global employment challenge

Table 3.5   Migrants as share of total population, 1960–2005 (percentages)

Country group	1960	1965	1970	1975	1980	1985	1990	1995	2000	2005
Developed	4.1	4.3	4.6	5.0	5.5	6.1	7.1	8.3	9.3	10.3
CEE	3.6	3.2	2.9	2.5	2.2	2.0	2.5	3.3	3.1	2.9
CIS	1.4	1.3	1.3	1.2	1.2	1.2	10.4	9.8	9.5	9.3
Other high-income	10.2	9.6	9.3	9.3	9.7	9.7	9.9	10.6	11.5	12.9
Petroleum exporter developing	2.3	2.2	2.5	3.5	4.7	5.4	6.2	5.1	5.2	5.4
Medium-income developing	1.8	1.5	1.3	1.1	1.0	1.0	1.0	0.8	0.8	0.7
Least developed	2.6	2.5	2.3	1.9	2.3	2.0	2.1	2.0	1.5	1.4
World	2.5	2.3	2.2	2.1	2.2	2.3	2.9	2.9	2.9	2.9
	(75.0)	(77.9)	(80.7)	(86.1)	(98.5)	(110.2)	(154.0)	(163.8)	(175.3)	(188.9)

Notes: The term "migrants" as used in this table refers to persons born in a country other than that in which they currently live and thus includes refugees.
Figures in parentheses show world totals in millions.

Source: Derived from UN Department of Economic and Social Affairs, Population Division, *Trends in total migrant stock: The 2005 revision* (CD-ROM, 2006).

Significantly, however, the share of migrants in total population in developed countries increased steadily throughout the period 1960–2005. This reflects a decelerating rate of natural increase in population in these countries, on the one hand, and accelerating growth of migrant population, on the other. The average annual rate of growth of the stock of migrants in these countries was 2.2 per cent during 1960–70, 2.6 per cent during 1970–80, 3.2 per cent during 1980–90, 3.4 per cent during 1990–2000 and 2.6 per cent during 2000–05.

The global picture for the post-1990 period is thus one of stability of international migration combined with growth of migration to developed countries.[11] The latter fact, however, should not be interpreted to mean that migration from developing to developed countries was growing. Estimates of migration to developed countries include migrants from developed, CEE and CIS

---

[11] Migration to other high-income countries was also growing during the period. For lack of information, however, we cannot do much more than note the fact. This is an area for future research.

Table 3.6 Adult migrants from developing to developed countries as share of adult population of developing countries,[a] 2000 (percentages)

Country group	All migrants	Migrants by level of education[b]		
		Low	Medium	High
Medium-income developing	1.06	0.62	2.33	8.09
Least developed	0.59	0.25	4.19	14.80
Developing countries	*1.01*	*0.57*	*2.40*	*8.38*

[a] "Developing countries" refers to medium-income developing and least developed countries taken together.
[b] Level of education: low – up to lower secondary; medium – above lower secondary and up to higher secondary; high – tertiary.

Sources: Derived from database on immigrants and expatriates in the OECD website (http://www.oecd.org/) and Barro and Lee (2000).

countries as well, and it is known that the 1990s saw accelerating growth in the number of migrants from these countries. Other evidence suggests that the rate of migration from developing to developed countries recorded a very small rise in the 1990s and that this is accounted for basically by increased migration from Central American and Caribbean countries to the United States.[12]

What is of greater interest in the present context is the effect that international migration may have had on the labour force and its skill intensity in developing countries. The latest year for which evidence on migration from developing to developed countries by level of education is available is 2000 (table 3.6). This evidence shows that just 1 per cent of the adult population of less developed countries lived and worked in developed countries. Of course, there are countries for which the percentage is high, but these are typically countries with small populations (table 3.7).[13] It is also worth noting that migration from least developed countries has generally been very low.

It is clear that for most developing countries international migration has had no significant effect on the size and growth of the total labour force. Moreover, the effect of international migration on the low-skilled labour force

---

[12] See Docquier and Marfouk (2004) and Dumont and Lemaître (2004). In economic theory, international migration is governed by the gap in labour incomes (wages, working conditions and social security arrangements) between countries and the costs (transportation, communication and search costs) of migration. Given the huge gap in labour incomes between developed and developing countries, both skilled and unskilled labour have strong incentives to move from the latter group. By substantially reducing the costs of migration, recent technological changes have strengthened the incentives. The very small growth of migration from the developing world can therefore be explained only by the growing severity of restrictions in place in developed countries.

[13] The exception is Mexico, which has for some time served as the major source of migrant workers for the United States, with which it shares a border.

Table 3.7 Distribution of countries by incidence of migration[a] to developed countries, 2000

Percentage group	Country group			
	Other high-income	Petroleum exporter developing	Medium-income developing	Least developed
>20%	Barbados, Cyprus		Guyana, Jamaica	
10–20%		Trinidad and Tobago	Dominican Rep., El Salvador, Fiji, Mexico, Panama	
5–10%	Hong Kong (China)	Algeria, Congo, Kuwait	Cuba, Ecuador, Guatemala, Honduras, Jordan, Mauritius, Nicaragua, Tunisia	Gambia, Guinea-Bissau, Haiti
2–5%	Israel, Singapore	Iraq	Colombia, Costa Rica, Philippines, Sri Lanka, Swaziland, Turkey, Uruguay	Mali, Mozambique, Rwanda, Senegal, Togo
1–2%		Bahrain, Venezuela	Argentina, Bolivia, Chile, Papua New Guinea, Peru, Zimbabwe	Sierra Leone, Liberia, Lesotho
<1%	Korea (Rep.)	Iran, Syria	Brazil, Botswana, China, Cameroon, Egypt, Ghana, India, Indonesia, Kenya, Malaysia, Pakistan, Paraguay, South Africa, Thailand	Afghanistan, Bangladesh, Benin, Central African Republic, Congo (Dem. Rep.), Malawi, Myanmar, Nepal, Niger, Sudan, Tanzania, Uganda, Zambia

[a] Incidence of migration is the stock of adult migrants as percentage of adult population in the country of origin.

Source: Derived from appendix table A3.1.

has been negligible for the most part. At the same time, migration of high-skilled workers from developing to developed countries was very substantial, which obviously restrained the growth of skill per worker in the former. As regards medium-income developing countries, in 2000 about 8 per cent of the adult population with tertiary education was working in developed countries, while in the case of least developed countries the figure was about 15 per cent.

Therefore, migration from developing to developed countries has largely meant brain drain. Of course, the incidence of brain drain (the stock of adult migrants with tertiary education as a percentage of adult population with tertiary education in the country of origin) has not been equally significant for all developing countries. Indeed, it was not significant for important emerging economies such as China, Brazil or India, but it was very substantial for a fairly large number of poor countries (table 3.8). The incidence of brain drain exceeded 20 per cent for 17 (from a sample of 39) medium-income developing countries (mainly from Central America and the Caribbean) and 14 (from a sample of 24) least developed countries (all from sub-Saharan Africa). In short, limited as it was, international migration served to restrain the growth of skill intensity of the labour force in quite a large number of developing countries, and particularly in the least developed countries.[14]

There is evidence to suggest, moreover, that the outward migration of skilled workers from many developing countries increased in the 1990s (Docquier and Marfouk, 2004): the countries include Mexico, some countries of Central America and the Caribbean, and some of the poorest countries of sub-Saharan Africa (Angola, Burundi, Equatorial Guinea, Ghana, Guinea-Bissau, Liberia, Mauritania, Rwanda, Sao Tome and Principe, Sierra Leone and Somalia). Globalization, it appears, has been associated not so much with increased overall migration from developing countries as with increased migration of high-skilled workers.

On reflection, this does not appear particularly surprising. Technological change has been skill-biased in all lines of production in developed countries, and growth in trade with developing countries has prompted specialization in skill-intensive goods and services in developed countries. The two factors together caused fairly sharp growth in demand for skilled labour (see Chapter 6), inducing governments in developed countries to adopt measures, including amendments of migration legislation, to encourage migration of skilled labour into these countries (Dumont and Lemaître, 2004; OECD, 2001, 2004).

While international migration has restrained the growth in skill supply in developing countries, it could conceivably have brought them compensatory

---

[14] It has been argued that the possibility of emigration may encourage skill acquisition so that it is theoretically possible for skill gain to exceed skill loss (see Commander et al., 2003 for a review of the relevant literature). For this argument to be valid, however, the following condition must hold: skill generation is constrained by demand, i.e., there is excess capacity in the education system. There are not many developing countries where this condition holds.

Table 3.8 Distribution of countries by incidence of brain drain,[a] 2000

Percentage group	Country group			
	Other high-income	Petroleum exporter developing	Medium-income developing	Least developed
>80%			Guyana, Jamaica	Guinea-Bissau
70–80%		Trinidad and Tobago	Mauritius	Haiti
50–70%	Barbados		Fiji	Gambia, Mozambique
40–50%	Hong Kong (China)	Congo	Ghana, Kenya, Papua New Guinea, Sri Lanka	Sierra Leone
30–40%	Cyprus, Singapore	Algeria	Cuba, El Salvador	Liberia, Uganda
20–30%		Iran	Dominican Republic, Guatemala, Honduras, Malaysia, Nicaragua, Tunisia, Zimbabwe	Benin, Malawi, Mali, Rwanda, Senegal, Tanzania, Zambia
10–20%	Israel	Bahrain, Iraq, Kuwait	Botswana, Cameroon, Colombia, Ecuador, Indonesia, Mexico, Pakistan, Panama, Philippines, South Africa, Uruguay	Afghanistan, Central African Republic, Congo (Democratic Rep.), Niger, Sudan, Togo
<10%	Korea (Rep.)	Venezuela, Syria	Argentina, Bolivia, Brazil, Chile, China, Costa Rica, Egypt, India, Jordan, Paraguay, Peru, Swaziland, Thailand, Turkey	Bangladesh, Lesotho, Myanmar, Nepal

[a] Incidence of brain drain is the stock of adult migrants with tertiary education as a percentage of adult population with tertiary education in the country of origin.

Source: Derived from appendix table A3.1.

Globalization in an unequal world

benefits through another channel, as migrants send remittances to their countries of origin. Evidence suggests that the flow of remittances was growing in the 1990s (World Bank, 2006). For quite a number of developing countries, remittances became an increasingly important source of foreign exchange earnings and may have helped increase investment and reduce poverty.

Unfortunately, the available data on remittances[15] suffer from serious limitations arising from non-reporting by some countries, misclassification of categories in some cases and general non-availability of information on remittances sent through informal channels. Because of this, studies based on these data have produced only inconclusive results about the economic effects of remittances in recipient countries (World Bank, 2006; IMF, 2005).[16] In other words, there is as yet no convincing evidence to suggest that remittances have had either positive or negative effects on investment and growth in recipient developing countries.

It is intuitively obvious that only remittances from low-skilled migrants (who generally come from low-income households) could directly reduce poverty, while remittances from high-skilled migrants (who generally come from well-off households and are able to send higher remittances per capita) are most likely to increase inequality. If we assume that all migrants are equally likely to send remittances, given the observed pattern of migration we should expect remittances both to reduce poverty and to increase inequality. However, there are good reasons to believe that low-skilled migrants are much more likely to send remittances than high-skilled migrants. The households left behind by low-skilled migrants need regular support and the desire to provide such support is what motivated these people to migrate in the first place. The households left behind by high-skilled migrants, on the other hand, are well off and do not need regular support. On balance, therefore, remittances can be expected to reduce poverty rather than increase inequality.

By the same reasoning, however, the amount of remittances received by a country can be expected to depend on the skill composition of its migrants: the higher the incidence of outward migration of skilled workers, the smaller is the flow of remittances. The experience of South Asian countries illustrates this point. A large proportion of the remittances received by these countries comes from the Gulf States rather than from the United States or other developed countries, but most migrants to the Gulf States are low skilled while

---

[15] Data on remittances come from the World Bank's World Development Indicators database (CD-ROM, 2005).

[16] The estimates represent the sum of workers' remittances, compensation of employees and migrants' transfers. Workers' remittances are current transfers from migrant workers who have been resident in their host countries for at least one year. Compensation of employees is the income of temporary migrants, i.e., those who have been residents in host countries for less than one year (normally referred to as factor income). Migrants' transfers refer to the net worth of migrants that are transferred from one country to another at the time of migration (for at least one year).

Box 3.3 High-skilled migrants and remittances

It is reasonable to expect that, across countries, a higher incidence of migration means higher remittances to the economy. If high-skilled migrants are as likely to send remittances as low-skilled migrants, we should also expect the following: the higher the share of high-skilled migrants in total migrants, the higher is the amount of remittances to the economy (given that high-skilled migrants are expected to earn higher incomes than low-skilled migrants, so that remittances per migrant should be higher for the high skilled).

This is the hypothesis we test through a simple cross-country regression exercise. For the year 2000, we have data on incidence of migration to developed countries, incidence of high-skilled migration to developed countries and remittances as percentage of GDP for a sample of 54 medium-income developing and least developed countries. However, the estimates of remittances refer to remittances from all countries and not just from developed countries (according to the World Bank, between 30 and 45 per cent of the remittances received by developing countries originate in developing countries; see World Bank, 2006, Chapter 4). As we cannot separate out remittances originating in developed countries, we focus on a selection of countries. We know that certain countries receive much of their remittances from other developing countries: countries such as Bangladesh, Egypt, India, Jordan, Pakistan, Philippines, Sri Lanka and Sudan receive large remittances from the Gulf States; countries such as Botswana, Lesotho and Swaziland receive large remittances from South Africa; countries such as Indonesia and Philippines receive large remittances from East Asian countries; and Nepal receives remittances from India and the Gulf States. By excluding these countries, we get a sample of 41 countries.[1] We can be fairly certain that remittances to this set of countries come mainly from developed countries.

A simple cross-country regression yields the following result:

remgdp = 0.032 + 0.392 *migpop* − 0.060 *hsmhsp*
            (0.020)   (0.000)   (0.109)
R^2 = 0.527, number of observations = 41
(The figures in parentheses indicate levels of statistical significance.)

Where:
remgdp represents remittances received as percentage of GDP,
migpop represents stock of adult migrants as percentage of population, and
hsmhsp represents adult high-skilled migrants as percentage of adult high-skilled population.

> The coefficients are statistically significant, but the coefficient of *hsmhsp* has the wrong sign. If we exclude one outlier – Turkey – from the sample, the result improves substantially:
>
> *remgdp* = 0.037 + 0.375 *migpop* – 0.072 *hsmhsp*
>   (0.012)   (0.000)   (0.067)
> R^2 = 0.539, number of observations = 40
> (The figures in parentheses indicate levels of significance.)
>
> These results clearly reject the hypothesis that high-skilled migrants are as likely to send remittances as low-skilled migrants. They suggest that low-skilled migrants are much more likely to send remittances than high-skilled migrants.
>
> [1] Argentina, Benin, Bolivia, Brazil, Cameroon, China, Colombia, Costa Rica, Dominican Republic, Ecuador, El Salvador, Gambia, Ghana, Guatemala, Guinea-Bissau, Haiti, Honduras, Jamaica, Kenya, Malawi, Malaysia, Mali, Mauritius, Mexico, Mozambique, Nicaragua, Niger, Panama, Papua New Guinea, Paraguay, Peru, Rwanda, Senegal, Sierra Leone, South Africa, Tanzania, Thailand, Togo, Tunisia, Turkey, Uganda.

most migrants to developed countries are high skilled. More direct evidence for Latin American countries is also available. Results of a recent survey show that most of the migrants from Latin America working in the United States and sending remittances are low skilled (see IADB, 2006). Cross-country comparisons also suggest that remittances are sent more by low-skilled than by high-skilled migrants (see box 3.3). Across countries that receive substantial remittances, remittance as percentage of GDP varies directly with the overall incidence of migration and inversely with the share of high-skilled migrants in all migrants.

From the point of view of developing countries, therefore, low-skilled migration brings benefits through several channels: it reduces surplus labour (it is low-skilled labour that is in surplus in developing countries), generates foreign exchange earnings in the form of remittances, and reduces poverty. In contrast, high-skilled migration means loss of human capital for which there is inadequate compensation in the form of remittances. Since in reality migration from developing to developed countries has basically meant brain drain, it cannot be said to have been beneficial for the originating countries; it has actually tended to increase rather than reduce the asymmetry in the cross-country distribution of skills. The skill gap between developed and developing countries has nevertheless been narrowing (as observed earlier), but the narrowing would clearly have been faster in the absence of brain drain.

Appendix table A3.1 Migration from developing to developed countries, 2000

Country	Number of migrants				As percentage of adult population			
	Low skilled	Medium skilled	High skilled	All	Low skilled	Medium skilled	High skilled	All
Afghanistan	17 843	12 933	8 600	39 376	0.12	2.73	3.09	0.25
Algeria	297 287	87 982	44 020	429 289	1.70	3.39	9.45	2.09
Argentina	18 566	28 528	25 624	72 718	0.10	0.48	1.22	0.27
Bahrain	265	745	872	1 882	0.08	0.90	5.02	0.43
Bangladesh	23 037	22 421	33 784	79 242	0.03	0.47	2.77	0.09
Barbados	5 885	11 180	4 485	21 550	3.50	25.38	26.44	9.40
Benin	1 160	1 432	2 163	4 755	0.04	1.70	9.81	0.14
Bolivia	8 594	17 003	8 268	33 865	0.21	2.79	2.85	0.67
Botswana	172	1 066	632	1 870	0.02	1.00	4.30	0.19
Brazil	105 960	150 154	86 428	342 542	0.10	1.44	1.88	0.28
Cameroon	6 818	9 400	12 745	28 963	0.08	3.02	10.20	0.33
Central African Rep.	1 469	1 231	1 116	3 816	0.07	1.88	6.92	0.18
Chile	19 957	31 440	21 657	73 054	0.24	1.52	2.71	0.66
China	257 017	199 377	384 189	840 583	0.03	0.13	1.87	0.09
Colombia	94 354	124 459	71 255	290 068	0.43	3.43	5.79	1.09
Congo	9 937	11 714	9 747	31 398	0.68	7.87	22.35	1.91
Congo, Dem. Rep.	10 929	13 317	9 654	33 900	0.04	1.05	5.67	0.13
Costa Rica	15 618	17 221	7 238	40 077	0.78	4.71	3.24	1.55
Cuba	164 729	109 420	49 947	324 096	2.42	6.07	9.82	3.55
Cyprus	2 942	10 610	7 220	20 772	0.78	6.38	11.19	3.43
Dominican Republic	237 744	126 645	34 095	398 484	4.83	15.65	9.52	6.55
Ecuador	85 006	76 084	24 534	185 624	1.29	5.79	3.71	2.17
Egypt	13 495	20 728	35 706	69 929	0.04	0.30	1.82	0.16
El Salvador	409 640	142 741	26 843	579 224	10.57	31.52	15.60	12.87
Fiji	12 007	12 086	4 893	28 986	2.61	9.52	20.28	4.74

Globalization in an unequal world

Gambia	2 667	3 173	1 529	7 369	0.36	19.76	33.52	0.96
Ghana	13 230	25 561	16 349	55 140	0.12	7.02	22.47	0.49
Guatemala	239 335	86 311	19 790	345 436	3.57	19.53	11.42	4.72
Guinea-Bissau	13 116	3 242	1 356	17 714	1.86	39.89	66.02	2.48
Guyana	35 652	41 536	14 239	91 427	6.23	37.54	56.18	12.91
Haiti	112 285	92 080	29 974	234 339	2.45	24.59	55.61	4.67
Honduras	125 917	55 966	14 156	196 039	3.72	11.40	13.99	4.93
Hong Kong, China	28 934	38 372	38 651	105 957	1.03	1.98	10.96	2.08
India	150 968	134 860	476 114	761 942	0.02	0.24	3.08	0.11
Indonesia	12 049	39 100	39 045	90 194	0.01	0.21	5.04	0.06
Iran	39 955	60 667	70 169	170 791	0.11	0.79	5.84	0.39
Iraq	46 519	27 702	23 042	97 263	0.39	2.21	5.16	0.71
Israel	9 357	18 189	19 520	47 066	0.37	1.26	4.11	1.06
Jamaica	93 687	123 513	46 643	263 843	5.54	38.78	60.09	12.65
Jordan	4 795	7 331	8 670	20 796	0.18	0.97	3.17	0.57
Kenya	3 828	14 373	15 583	33 784	0.02	5.23	15.22	0.19
Korea, Rep.	21 027	41 086	55 418	117 531	0.18	0.20	1.23	0.32
Kuwait	2 711	6 265	7 088	16 064	0.33	2.12	6.66	1.32
Lesotho	36	80	109	225	0.00	0.19	0.98	0.02
Liberia	6 344	12 159	7 276	25 779	0.34	16.06	23.94	1.32
Malawi	173	614	677	1 464	0.00	0.58	3.34	0.02
Malaysia	15 693	24 484	41 662	81 839	0.13	1.06	9.05	0.56
Mali	23 615	5 079	2 693	31 387	0.36	7.12	11.93	0.47
Mauritius	9 259	5 061	3 271	17 591	1.57	1.79	29.59	2.00
Mexico	4 636 930	1 397 663	267 472	6 302 065	8.48	8.54	8.20	8.48
Mozambique	4 153	2 089	1 163	7 405	0.04	2.75	9.93	0.07
Myanmar	4 755	4 724	7 530	17 009	0.02	0.20	1.75	0.05
Nepal	2 655	5 233	6 500	14 388	0.02	0.52	4.26	0.10
Nicaragua	68 356	53 910	17 034	139 300	2.57	20.91	11.97	4.56
Niger	498	577	783	1 858	0.01	1.28	4.49	0.03
Pakistan	58 081	49 941	73 425	181 447	0.08	0.37	5.04	0.20

Appendix table A3.1 Migration from developing to developed countries, 2000 (continued)

Country	Number of migrants				As percentage of adult population			
	Low skilled	Medium skilled	High skilled	All	Low skilled	Medium skilled	High skilled	All
Panama	9 905	21 995	9 717	41 617	0.82	3.71	4.76	2.08
Papua New Guinea	1 351	826	1 289	3 466	0.05	0.93	8.04	0.12
Paraguay	2 591	3 127	1 413	7 131	0.09	0.60	0.90	0.21
Peru	49 051	96 346	48 630	194 027	0.42	2.27	2.78	1.09
Philippines	131 319	242 140	278 266	651 725	0.51	1.49	4.66	1.35
Rwanda	1 840	2 536	2 178	6 554	0.04	4.81	12.65	0.13
Senegal	26 009	10 564	8 708	45 281	0.50	7.31	12.88	0.84
Sierra Leone	4 209	7 087	4 243	15 539	0.15	13.54	23.07	0.55
Singapore	3 988	9 493	18 166	31 647	0.21	2.46	17.44	1.34
South Africa	10 133	22 747	38 748	71 628	0.04	0.92	4.99	0.24
Sri Lanka	40 471	27 739	23 118	91 328	0.35	1.16	16.99	0.64
Sudan	5 395	6 632	7 215	19 242	0.03	1.05	5.32	0.10
Swaziland	111	135	214	460	0.02	0.45	2.03	0.08
Syria	13 799	11 676	12 269	37 744	0.18	0.96	2.54	0.40
Tanzania	1 823	3 965	4 509	10 297	0.01	5.03	3.86	0.05
Thailand	57 786	41 934	39 150	138 870	0.15	1.13	1.21	0.30
Togo	2 442	3 007	3 222	8 671	0.10	4.74	10.02	0.33
Trinidad and Tobago	31 165	56 589	21 911	109 665	3.58	31.51	51.46	10.03
Tunisia	84 100	30 412	14 910	129 422	1.49	3.50	6.40	1.92
Turkey	258 797	74 710	34 985	368 492	0.65	1.47	2.49	0.80
Uganda	1 803	3 435	4 607	9 845	0.01	1.59	8.42	0.08
Uruguay	4 967	6 314	3 890	15 171	0.26	1.58	2.18	0.61
Venezuela	16 607	28 823	32 445	77 875	0.14	0.94	3.70	0.49
Zambia	790	1 974	2 680	5 444	0.02	0.26	6.20	0.09
Zimbabwe	1 424	4 751	6 613	12 788	0.02	1.77	4.90	0.18

PRODUCTIVE EMPLOYMENT IN DEVELOPING COUNTRIES 4

4.1 The nature of employment and unemployment in developing countries

Three important structural features characterize developing economies, distinguishing them from developed economies. The first is dualism.[17] A typical developing economy is composed of two radically distinct parts – a formal segment, which employs a small proportion of the labour force, and a non-formal segment (i.e., the rest of the economy), which employs the bulk of the labour force (see box 4.1). In schematic terms, the differences between the two segments are as follows. Production in the formal segment involves the use of reproducible capital (often embodying advanced technology) together with labour (skilled and unskilled), while production in the non-formal segment involves the use of labour (basically unskilled) together with natural resources and/or simple tools and implements. In the formal segment, entrepreneurs (including governments) organize production for profit, save a part of the profit and use this for new investment; in the non-formal segment, producers are subsistence oriented and do not save or invest. In the formal segment, workers are engaged as regular, full-time wage employees; in the non-formal segment, workers are either self-employed or engaged as casual/irregular wage workers.

The second distinguishing feature is surplus labour. In most developing economies, a substantial proportion of the workers in the non-formal segment could be withdrawn (either out of the labour force or into the formal segment)

---

[17] There is a large literature on the structure and characteristics of a dual economy. See Basu (1984) for an insightful analysis.

The global employment challenge

> **Box 4.1 Formal and non-formal segments**
>
> Throughout this book, the terms "formal segment" and "non-formal segment" are used in the sense defined above. It is worth noting that the "formal segment", as defined here, has roughly the same meaning as "modern sector" or "formal sector", though we make the simplifying assumption that in the formal segment there is no casual/irregular wage employment. The "non-formal segment", however, is to be distinguished from the "informal sector", which normally refers to the non-modern part of the urban or the non-agricultural economy. On the other hand, the notion of the "non-formal segment" is very similar to that of the "informal economy", which is defined by the ILO as "all economic activities by workers and economic units that are – in law or in practice – not covered or insufficiently covered by formal arrangements" (ILO, 2002). We choose to use the term "non-formal segment" in this book for two reasons. First, the word "segment" makes it obvious that we are talking about a part of a national economy. Second, the use of the word "non-formal" underlines the fact that we are talking about a residual category.

without affecting the labour input actually used in production in that segment (see box 4.2). This is possible because in the non-formal segment under-employment is widespread. The system of casual wage employment allows sharing of a given amount of wage-paid work by a varying number of wage workers, just as self-employment allows sharing of a given amount of work in household enterprises by a varying number of family workers. These modes of employment accommodate surplus labour by ensuring that no individual worker is wholly unemployed.

The third feature characterizing developing economies relates to the near-total absence of institutionalized social security. In a few relatively advanced countries, a section of the workers in the formal segment receive limited benefits on loss of employment or on retirement, and in some poor countries, where extended family and kinship ties still remain strong, individuals in the non-formal segment have some protection against indigence. As a rule, however, the vast majority of people in developing countries do not have access to any organized social protection system.

These structural features need to be reckoned with in defining a framework for analysing the employment situation in developing countries, and they also have important implications for interpretation and use of available statistical data. Data collection systems in developing countries happen to be modelled on those established in developed countries. As a result, the available statistical indicators of employment and labour markets are the same for both developed and developing economies. Yet, given the structural differences

> **Box 4.2 Surplus labour**
>
> The notion of surplus labour, i.e., the idea that only a part of the available labour supply is used in the production of goods and services in developing countries, was developed by Arthur Lewis in a celebrated paper (Lewis, 1954), although other economists (e.g. Rosenstein-Rodan, 1943; Nurkse, 1953) had previously asserted the existence of surplus labour in Eastern and South-eastern Europe, as well as in the Soviet Union. Lewis's formulation attracted widespread attention and aroused much controversy. Many economists (e.g., Schultz, 1964; Viner, 1957) believed that the existence of surplus labour required the marginal productivity of labour to be zero, which they found unacceptable. In a well-known paper, Sen (1966) showed that, in the context of self-employment, surplus labour could exist without requiring marginal labour productivity to be zero. However, surplus labour can also exist in wage employment when this is casual or irregular, i.e., when labour hiring occurs on a daily or periodic basis. In situations where self-employment and casual wage employment predominate, therefore, the amount of labour actually used in production can be invariant to the number of workers ready to supply it (Ghose, 2006).
>
> Surplus labour typically arises in agriculture and is often associated with scarcity of arable land in relation to population. However, it can also be artificially created. Even in situations of land abundance, for example, high concentration of landholdings creates surplus labour, such as can be found in some Latin American and African countries. In these circumstances, surplus labour is often found in non-agricultural

between the two types of economies, the same indicator does not necessarily point to the same thing.[18] Furthermore, information on important features such as dualism or forms of wage labour is often missing. All this makes empirical assessment of the employment situation in developing countries rather difficult and requires careful interpretation and imaginative use of available data.

In the absence of institutionalized social security systems, only persons from relatively well-off households can really be in unemployment. Most people have to work to survive, even if the work found is not full time and does not generate anything more than bare subsistence. Thus, in the context of developing countries, the unemployment rate usually reflects the extent of queuing by young persons (often with secondary or higher education) from relatively well-off households for "good" jobs in the formal segment. While

---

[18] The unemployment rate is much lower in China and India than in France and Germany, yet nobody would claim that labour market conditions are much better in China and India than in France and Germany.

surplus labour is a basic feature of these economies, its existence is indicated by widespread prevalence of self-employment and casual wage employment rather than by a high level of unemployment (box 4.3).

> **Box 4.3 How does the labour market work in a dual economy?**
>
> An analytical view of how the labour market works in a typical developing economy helps to clarify the various points. As noted above, in the non-formal segment wage labour is employed primarily on a casual, daily basis, while in the formal segment it is employed on a regular, full-time basis.
>
> How are wages determined? The wage in the formal segment is determined by government regulations and collective bargaining. It is usually set without any reference to, and far above, the average earning in the non-formal segment. This is possible because labour productivity in the formal segment, where reproducible capital is used, is much higher than that in the non-formal segment. The large wage gap makes it worthwhile for all workers in the non-formal segment to seek employment in the formal segment; the potential supply of labour to the formal segment is, in this sense, unlimited. The actual level of employment in the formal segment is thus determined solely by the demand for labour at the given wage. Those unable to find employment in the formal segment must either engage in self-employment and casual wage employment in the non-formal segment or join the queue for jobs in the formal segment. However, the latter option is available only to those persons who have access to means of survival through family support during the period of waiting (which can be long). Obviously, only households that are relatively well off can provide such support.
>
> In the non-formal segment, self-employment and casual wage employment are alternatives. Wage income from casual labour is thus closely linked to earning from self-employment. The level of underemployment of casual wage workers provides the critical link between the daily wage rate for casual labour and the income of an average self-employed person over a certain period. It is the average wage income from casual wage employment over a certain period which tends to equal the average earning from self-employment over the same period. This means that there is no unique equilibrium wage rate. But any arbitrary wage rate, once established, tends to remain stable because the level of underemployment can adjust to maintain rough equality between earning from self-employment and that from casual wage employment. A rise in earning from self-employment, for example, induces some casual wage workers to shift to self-employment, thereby reducing underemployment among those who continue to seek casual wage employment. Even without a change in the wage rate, therefore, earning from casual wage employment rises and rough parity with earning from self-employment is restored.

In a situation where most people must work to survive, total employment – conventionally measured as the number of persons observed to be engaged in some kind of gainful activity – is a very poor indicator of the quantity of productive work carried out in the economy. Many persons are under-employed, and many of the activities engaged in represent survival strategies rather than productive work. Hence the observed growth in total employment says little about the growth of productive jobs in the economy. In fact, in the non-formal segment of the economy, labour force growth automatically translates into "employment" growth but may mean nothing more than increased underemployment. Only in the context of the formal segment can growth in the number of workers in employment be interpreted as growth of productive jobs.[19]

4.2 Assessing the employment situation in a developing country

Methodology and indicators

It should be clear from what has been said above that making a factual assessment of the employment situation in developing countries is not an easy task. Apart from the problem posed by the paucity of statistical data, the available data cannot be used in a straightforward manner. Unemployment cannot be taken as a straightforward measure of excess supply of labour in the economy, nor can employment be taken as a straightforward measure of the volume of productive jobs available in the economy. Given that dualism and surplus labour are defining characteristics of these economies, the standard indicators need to be carefully reinterpreted and new indicators have to be found. The problem reflected in queuing for jobs in the formal segment has to be distinguished from that of underemployment of the employed. It is also important to distinguish between jobs in the formal segment – which are not only regular, full time and wage paid, but are also regulated through legislations and collective agreements – and self-employment and casual wage employment in the non-formal segment, which conceal surplus labour and reflect survival strategies.

In searching for appropriate indicators, it is useful to ask what constitutes an improvement in the employment situation in an economy characterized by

---

[19] The following implication is worth noting. Estimates of employment elasticity (the degree of responsiveness of employment to a change in output) – a standard tool used to study effects of economic growth on employment – are meaningful only in the context of the formal segment. Estimates of employment elasticity for the non-formal segment or for the economy as a whole, though often used, are in effect devoid of meaning.

dualism and surplus labour. The answer: an increase in the share of the formal segment in total employment combined with stability or decline in underemployment in the non-formal segment. Movement of some workers from poor jobs in the non-formal segment to regular, full-time wage employment in the formal segment obviously implies an improvement in the employment situation, provided that underemployment in the non-formal segment does not increase.

Can a steadily rising share of the formal segment in total employment guarantee by itself that underemployment in the non-formal segment will not increase? In the literature on development it has been implicitly assumed that rapid growth of employment in the formal segment can in fact reduce the labour force in the non-formal segment in absolute terms; output and labour use per worker in the non-formal segment increase as a result (since the aggregate labour input as well as the aggregate output remain unchanged). On this view, an exclusive focus on rapid growth of output in the formal segment can be regarded as a viable strategy for improving the overall employment situation. Growth strategies in developing countries tended to be based on such a presumption.

It is easy to show, however, that such a strategy can work only in situations in which labour force growth is close to zero. Even in an economy where the share of the formal segment in total employment is 30 per cent and the labour force is growing at 2 per cent per annum, employment in the formal segment has to grow at 6.7 per cent per annum for there to be zero growth of labour force in the non-formal segment.[20] In most developing countries, the share of the formal segment in total employment is much less than 30 per cent (as we shall see below) and the labour force is growing at much more than 2 per cent per annum (as we saw in Chapter 2). In other words, impossibly high rates of growth of employment in the formal segment are required to even ensure zero growth of underemployment in the non-formal segment if there is no output growth in the latter.

Thus a strategy of rapid growth of the formal segment alone can conceivably ensure a steadily rising share of the formal segment in total employment but cannot make labour force growth in the non-formal segment negative or even zero. Underemployment, therefore, can only increase if nothing is done to increase the aggregate output in the non-formal segment. So a steady process of improvement in the overall employment situation can only result from simultaneous processes of rapid growth of employment in the formal segment

---

[20] If a is the current share of the formal segment in total employment, r_f is the rate of growth of employment in the formal segment in the next period, r_m is the rate of growth of labour force in the non-formal segment in the next period and r is the rate of growth of labour force in the economy, then the condition $a.r_f + (1-a) r_m = r$ has to be satisfied if the incremental labour force is to be in employment. If $r_m = 0$, the condition reduces to $r_f = r/a$. In other words, employment in the formal segment has to grow at a rate of (r/a) if the labour force in the non-formal segment is to remain unchanged.

(a rate of growth in excess of that of labour force in the economy) and of a rate of output growth in the non-formal segment that equals or exceeds the rate of labour force growth in that segment.

This perspective suggests two basic indicators – share of the formal segment in total employment and output per worker in the non-formal segment – as most relevant to assessing the overall employment situation in developing countries. Should the unemployment rate be regarded as a relevant indicator, too? It will be argued below that, given the method of its measurement, the reported unemployment rate for any given country actually represents the sum of chronic and transient unemployment rates. While chronic unemployment (unemployment of duration of one year or more) reflects queuing for jobs in the formal segment, transient unemployment (unemployment of very short duration) reflects the fact that a casual wage worker does not find employment on every day of any given period. The transient unemployment rate, therefore, is really a measure of underemployment of casual wage workers in the non-formal segment. But it is only a partial measure since it does not take account of underemployment of those casual wage workers that are reported as employed. Nevertheless, because the reported unemployment rate incorporates a partial measure of underemployment of casual wage workers, it would be inappropriate to disregard it. In fact, it would also be inappropriate to ignore queuing even though it is to an extent voluntary and involves workers from relatively well-off households. Other things being equal, a shorter job queue in the formal segment is surely better than a longer one.

We thus have three indicators that need to be considered together for a proper assessment of the employment situation in developing countries:

(1) share of the formal segment in total employment,

(2) output per worker in the non-formal segment, and

(3) unemployment rate.

Other things being equal,

- the larger the share of the formal segment in total employment, the better is the employment situation;

- the higher the output per worker in the non-formal segment, the better is the employment situation;

- the higher the employment ratio[21] (i.e., the lower the unemployment rate), the better is the employment situation.

---

[21] Employment ratio = 1 – (unemployment rate) / 100.

The global employment challenge

An empirical view of dualism

Available statistical data provide direct estimates of only one indicator (employment ratio) of the three identified above. Neither national accounts statistics nor labour force surveys distinguish between formal and non-formal segments as defined above. Underemployment, moreover, is inherently difficult to measure, and very few labour force surveys even attempt to gather information on this. Despite these problems, however, it is possible to use the available statistical data to construct imperfect but still meaningful statistical measures for the other two indicators. Based on the fact that dualism is reflected in a large gap in output per worker between formal and non-formal segments, it is possible to identify formal and non-formal economic sectors of national economies and to develop a measure of the degree of dualism. Similarly, by recognizing the fact that the existence of surplus labour is only made possible by the existence of certain forms of employment – namely, self-employment and casual wage employment – indicators of the extent of surplus labour can be developed.

The relevant statistical data that are available for a fairly large number of countries relate to estimates of output and employment shares of three broad sectors – agriculture, industry and services. We use these data to identify formal and non-formal segments in individual economies (see box 4.4 for a description of the methodology).

The estimates presented in table 4.1 are admittedly crude. Each of the broad sectors – agriculture, industry and services – actually contains both formal and non-formal segments (see box 4.5), such that the sectors identified

---

Box 4.4   Identifying formal and non-formal segments

We focus on the data on industrial distribution of employment and GDP. Suppose, in any given developing economy, E, E_j and E_k are, respectively, total employment, employment in sector j and employment in sector k, and Y, Y_j and Y_k are, respectively, total output (GDP), output in sector j and output in sector k. Then $(Y_j/Y) / (E_j/E) = (Y_j/E_j) / (Y/E)$ is the ratio of output per worker in sector j to output per worker in the economy as a whole. The same ratio for sector k is $(Y_k/Y) / (E_k/E) = (Y_k/E_k) / (Y/E)$. We identify sector j as predominantly non-formal if the ratio is less than unity, i.e., if the output per worker in the sector is lower than that in the economy. If, by using this method, sector j is identified as predominantly non-formal and sector k as predominantly formal, the gap in output per worker between the sectors can be derived by dividing the ratio for sector j by that for sector k. This gives us $(Y_j/E_j) / (Y_k/E_k)$, which is the ratio of output per worker in sector j to that in sector k.

Productive employment in developing countries

Box 4.5 Dualism within sectors: Brazil and India

As the following illustrative examples show, none of the three broad sectors – agriculture, industry and services – is either purely formal or purely non-formal.

Distribution of employment by status, Brazil, 2004 (percentages)

Worker category	Agriculture	Non-agriculture
Entrepreneurs	3.3	4.5
Wage employees with social security registration	9.8	49.9
Other wage employees	20.1	21.8
Self-employed and unpaid family workers	66.8	23.8

Source: Data supplied by the Brazilian Institute of Geography and Statistics (IBGE), Government of Brazil.

At the risk of some exaggeration, entrepreneurs and wage employees with social security registration can be counted as working in the formal segment. On this reckoning, 87 per cent of all agricultural workers are in the non-formal segment while some 46 per cent of all non-agricultural workers are in the non-formal segment.

In India, agriculture is almost wholly non-formal while industry and services have non-formal sub-sectors.

Distribution of employment by status, India, 2000 (percentages)

Worker category	Agriculture	Industry	Services
Regular wage employees	1.5	27.4	44.1
In organized sector establishments	0.6	16.7	18.4
In unorganized sector establishments	0.9	10.7	25.7
Casual wage labourers	43.6	35.8	10.8
Self-employed and unpaid family workers	54.9	36.8	45.1

Source: Ghose (2004a).

Organized sector establishments are defined to include all public sector establishments and those private sector establishments that employ at least ten workers. Only regular wage employees in organized sector establishments can properly be counted as working in the formal sub-sector of each of the sectors (entrepreneurs account for an insignificant percentage). Regular wage employees in unorganized sector establishments rely on informal contracts and should really be regarded as irregular. Thus while agriculture is overwhelmingly non-formal, even industry and services contain sizeable non-formal sub-sectors.

The global employment challenge

Table 4.1   Dual economy indicators, ca. 2003

Country	Year	Non-formal segment	Output per worker, non-formal versus formal segment*	Formal segment
Petroleum exporter developing				
Algeria	2001	Agriculture & services	28.6	Industry
Trinidad and Tobago	2002	Agriculture & services	50.0	Industry
Venezuela	2003	Agriculture & services	23.3	Industry
Medium-income developing				
Argentina	2003	Services	6.8	Agriculture & industry
Bolivia	2000	Services	20.4	Agriculture & industry
Botswana	2001	Agriculture & services	33.3	Industry
Brazil	2002	Agriculture & services	45.5	Industry
Chile	2003	Agriculture & services	43.5	Industry
China	2002	Agriculture	6.0	Industry & services
Costa Rica	2003	Agriculture	53.3	Industry & services
Cuba	2000	Agriculture	9.6	Industry & services
Dominican Republic	2002	Agriculture & services	55.6	Industry
Ecuador	2003	Services	77.8	Agriculture & industry
Egypt	2002	Agriculture	23.3	Industry & services
El Salvador	2003	Agriculture	21.7	Industry & services
Ghana	2000	Agriculture	21.7	Industry & services
Guatemala	2002	Agriculture	23.3	Industry & services
Honduras	2002	Agriculture	13.0	Industry & services
India	2000	Agriculture	23.3	Industry & services
Indonesia	2003	Agriculture	8.0	Industry & services
Jamaica	2003	Agriculture	10.0	Industry & services
Kenya	1999	Services	32.3	Agriculture & industry
Malaysia	2003	Agriculture & services	50.0	Industry
Mauritius	2003	Agriculture & industry	66.7	Services
Mexico	2003	Agriculture	10.8	Industry & services
Mongolia	2003	Agriculture	16.7	Industry & services
Namibia	2000	Agriculture	10.4	Industry & services
Nicaragua	2001	Agriculture	28.2	Industry & services
Pakistan	2002	Agriculture	22.2	Industry & services

Productive employment in developing countries

Country	Year	Non-formal segment	Output per worker, non-formal versus formal segment*	Formal segment
Panama	2003	Agriculture	22.2	Industry & services
Papua New Guinea	2000	Agriculture	14.1	Industry & services
Paraguay	2003	Agriculture & services	58.7	Industry
Peru	2003	Services	4.8	Agriculture & industry
Philippines	2001	Agriculture	12.8	Industry & services
South Africa	2003	Agriculture	15.9	Industry & services
Sri Lanka	2003	Agriculture	22.2	Industry & services
Thailand	2003	Agriculture	6.5	Industry & services
Turkey	2003	Agriculture	16.1	Industry & services
Viet Nam	2003	Agriculture	9.5	Industry & services
Uruguay	2003	Services	21.3	Agriculture & industry
Least developed				
Bangladesh	2000	Agriculture	9.1	Industry & services
Belize	1999	Agriculture	28.6	Industry & services
Ethiopia	1999	Agriculture	14.1	Industry & services
Myanmar	1998	Agriculture	47.6	Industry & services
Nepal	1995	Agriculture	9.2	Industry & services
Tanzania	2001	Agriculture	6.3	Industry & services
Uganda	2003	Agriculture	9.8	Industry & services

* Value added per worker in non-formal segment as percentage of value added in formal segment.

Sources: Derived from World Bank, World Development Indicators database (CD-ROM, 2005) and ILO LABORSTA/KILM database (http://www.laborsta.ilo.org/).

as non-formal contain parts of the formal segment, just as the sectors identified as formal contain parts of the non-formal segment. In other words, we have succeeded only in identifying "predominantly formal" and "predominantly non-formal" segments. As it happens, the gap in output per worker is actually underestimated as a result. Since, within any given sector, output per formal worker is substantially higher than output per non-formal worker, our methodology leads to overestimation of output per worker in the non-formal segment and underestimation of output per worker in the formal segment.

In development theory, agriculture is generally assumed to be the core of the non-formal segment and the reservoir of surplus labour. The data in

The global employment challenge

table 4.1 show that this is not an unreasonable assumption; in a large majority of developing countries, agriculture indeed makes up the core of the non-formal segment. However, it is also important to note that in a few developing countries (mainly in Latin America and the Caribbean) it is the services sector rather than agriculture that constitutes the core of the non-formal segment, while in a few others (again mainly in Latin America and the Caribbean), services together with agriculture constitute the non-formal segment. In these countries, agriculture is either part of the formal segment (e.g., in Argentina or Peru) or is itself dualistic (e.g., in Brazil), comprising both large commercial farms and subsistence-oriented household farms.

The estimates unambiguously suggest that dualism remains a central feature of contemporary developing economies. The gap in output per worker between formal and non-formal segments is typically large, in some cases even astonishingly large. In Peru, for example, output per worker in the non-formal segment is less than 5 per cent of that in the formal segment, and in several other countries (Argentina, Bangladesh, China, Cuba, Indonesia, Nepal, the United Republic of Tanzania, Thailand, Uganda and Viet Nam) it is less than 10 per cent. In a majority of developing countries output per worker in the non-formal segment is less than 25 per cent of that in the formal segment. And these figures, it should not be forgotten, underestimate the gap.

This large gap in output per worker between the two segments implies large gaps in capital and skills per worker, although empirical evidence of these gaps is not easy to find (see, however, box 4.6). It also reflects another fact: while most workers employed in the formal segment are in full-time productive jobs, those in the non-formal segment tend to be underemployed (by time criterion) and often engaged in intrinsically low-productivity activities (underemployed by productivity criterion).

Employment in formal and non-formal segments

Table 4.2 presents estimates of percentage distribution of workers by type of employment for a sample of countries. Data on self-employment are available for quite a large number of countries, although not always on an annual basis. The category "self-employed" in the table includes the categories "own-account workers" as well as "unpaid family workers". It also includes the category "employers", which typically accounts for a very small percentage of the workforce.[22] Data on wage employment in formal and non-formal segments are not directly available. However, by adopting a particular

---

[22] In the case of China, self-employment refers to those working under "responsibility systems" in agriculture and those engaged in "individual businesses" in urban and rural areas (Ghose, 2005a).

Productive employment in developing countries

Box 4.6   The skill gap between formal and non-formal segments

Lack of data makes it impossible to empirically examine the skill gap for any sizeable sample of countries. However, the following examples illustrate the point.

The table below shows the level of education of different categories of workers in India in 2000. The category "regular employees" in the table includes salaried employees in the non-formal segment (e.g. shop assistants or domestic employees) who should really be regarded as irregular employees since their employment conditions are not determined by government regulations or collective bargaining. Thus the level of education of employees in the formal segment is actually being understated: regular employees in the formal segment have a substantially higher level of education than irregular salaried employees in the non-formal segment. It is quite clear, then, that the skill gap between formal and non-formal segments is very large.

Worker category	Average years of education	Percentage with:	
		No education	Tertiary education
Regular employees	7.8	12.7	22.0
Casual wage labourers	1.8	60.3	0.3
Self-employed	3.7	41.6	4.4
All employed	3.7	43.4	5.8

Source: Ghose (2004a).

The table below shows average years of education of workers in formal and non-formal employment in Brazil in 2004. The categories "wage employees with social security registration" and "entrepreneurs" can be regarded as persons in employment in the formal segment. Once again, it is clear that the skill gap between the two segments is wide.

Worker category	All	In agriculture	In non-agriculture
Entrepreneurs	9.5	9.0	6.6
Wage employees with social security registration	5.5	6.0	4.1
Other wage employees	3.2	3.3	10.1
Self-employed	9.3	7.2	7.0

Source: Data supplied by the Brazilian Institute of Geography and Statistics (IBGE), Government of Brazil.

The global employment challenge

Table 4.2 Distribution of total employment by employment status, ca. 2003 (percentages)

Country	Year	Regular wage employment	Self-employment	Casual/irregular wage employment
Petroleum exporter developing				
Algeria	2003	–	35.0	–
Trinidad and Tobago	2002	–	21.8	–
Venezuela	2002	34.7	–	–
Medium-income developing				
Argentina	2003	44.1	28.2	27.7
Bolivia	2000	–	50.1	–
Botswana	2000	50.3	30.3	19.4
Brazil	2003	32.5	37.9	29.6
Cameroon	2001	–	77.5	–
Chile	2003	45.9	31.8	22.3
China	2003	14.0	61.0	25.0
Colombia	2003	20.3	50.0	29.7
Costa Rica	2003	30.7	30.5	38.8
Dominica	2001	–	30.9	–
Dominican Rep.	1997	–	47.7	–
Ecuador	2003	24.8	38.7	36.5
Egypt	1998	8.6	38.6	52.8
El Salvador	2003	29.9	29.4	40.7
Ghana	1999	–	86.3	–
Guatemala	2002	–	60.4	–
Honduras	2001	19.6	54.5	25.9
India	2000	7.3	50.0	42.7
Indonesia	2002	26.8	–	–
Jamaica	2002	13.2	39.6	47.2
Madagascar	2002	–	84.3	–
Malaysia	2003	–	23.8	–
Mauritius	1995	63.2	19.1	17.7
Mexico	2003	21.7	37.6	40.7
Mongolia	2000	–	57.8	–
Morocco	2003	–	58.4	–

Country	Year	Regular wage employment	Self-employment	Casual/irregular wage employment
Namibia	2000	–	35.8	–
Nicaragua	2002	16.8	–	–
Pakistan	2002	–	60.2	–
Panama	2003	32.9	35.1	32.0
Paraguay	2004	14.2	–	–
Philippines	2003	–	49.1	–
South Africa	2000	33.0	15.0	52.0
Sri Lanka	2003	11.7	29.2	59.1
Thailand	2003	–	59.4	–
Tunisia	2003	–	35.6	–
Turkey	2003	–	49.4	–
Uruguay	2003	30.8	29.8	39.4
Viet Nam	2003	–	77.3	–
Zimbabwe	1999	26.9	–	–
Least developed				
Bangladesh	2003	–	63.5	–
Cambodia	2001	–	83.7	–
Ethiopia	1999	–	91.3	–
Malawi	1998	–	87.1	–
Maldives	2000	–	53.6	–
Myanmar	1998	6.4	–	–
Rwanda	1996	–	92.6	–
Tanzania	2001	–	87.9	–
Uganda	2000	–	86.6	–
Yemen	1999	–	33.5	–

– = data not available.

Sources: For the Latin American countries, special tabulations of data from household surveys were done. Data for China are derived (by using the methodology outlined in Ghose, 2005a) from National Bureau of Statistics (Government of the People's Republic of China), China Statistical Yearbook (CD-ROM, 2004 and 2005). Data for India are from Ghose (2004a). For the remaining countries, the estimates are based on data available from ILO-LABORSTA database (http://laborsta.ilo.org/).

definition whereby employment in the formal segment is taken to be the sum of wage employment in the public sector and wage employment in those private sector establishments that employ at least ten wage workers, we are able to derive rough estimates of employment in the formal segment for a number of developing countries.[23] Whenever information on both self-employment and regular wage employment (i.e., wage employment in the formal segment) is available, casual/irregular wage employment is estimated as a residual. Employment in the non-formal segment obviously equals the sum of self-employment and casual/irregular wage employment.[24]

The estimates show that there are a few developing countries (Argentina, Botswana, Chile and Mauritius in our sample) where the share of the formal segment in total employment is quite high (greater than 40 per cent). But in most developing countries this share is very small and an overwhelming majority of workers are engaged in self-employment and casual wage employment, forms of employment that conceal surplus labour and survival strategies. In the group of 19 medium-income developing countries for which full information is available (and presented in table 4.2), only 14 per cent of the employed are in regular full-time wage employment in the formal segment; 86 per cent are employed outside the formal segment.[25]

The general picture, then, is as follows. The bulk of the workforce in developing countries is either underemployed or in low-productivity jobs in the non-formal segment, while a small part is in full-time employment in relatively high-productivity jobs in the formal segment. In other words, labour is concentrated in the non-formal segment where capital is scarce, and the available capital is concentrated in the formal segment. The formal segment is also where the available skills are concentrated. In these respects, the differences between formal and non-formal segments within developing countries are strikingly similar to those between developed and developing countries at the global level.

Output per worker in the non-formal segment

The data on employment in the non-formal segment in table 4.2 cannot be used to estimate output per worker in the segment, as corresponding estimates of output are not available. To estimate output per worker we therefore have to use the information in table 4.1; the non-formal segment in each country has to be taken as that identified therein. The estimates derived on this basis

---

[23] This methodology is inapplicable in the case of China, given the nature of its database. The estimates for employment in the formal segment in China are derived by adding up the employment in state-owned enterprises, in collective-owned enterprises and in private large-scale enterprises. This follows the methodology developed in Ghose (2005a) except that employment in township and village industries is now regarded as irregular wage employment.

[24] This measure differs from the measure proposed by the ILO (see Hussmanns, 2005) only in that the ILO measure leaves open the possibility that there may be some casual/irregular wage employment in the formal segment.

[25] It is worth noting that the 19 countries concerned account for more than 60 per cent of the labour force in developing countries but do not include any of the "least developed" countries. The share of the formal segment in total employment would be even lower if the whole group of developing countries were considered.

are presented in table 4.3. In order to ensure cross-country comparability, the estimates are made in terms of Purchasing Power Parity dollars (PPP$). These are admittedly rather crude estimates; indeed, as already noted, they are actually overestimates and the degree of overestimation varies from country to country. Moreover, for some of the countries included in table 4.3, data on industrial distribution of employment for the year 2003 were missing. In such cases, we took the values available for the year closest to 2003.

Despite the limitations, however, the estimates are good enough to highlight a central aspect of the employment problem in developing countries. A glance at the estimates of value added per employed worker per day makes it obvious that in many developing countries workers in the non-formal segment are either seriously underemployed or engaged in low-productivity activities (which often represent little more than survival strategies), or both. On plausible assumptions about the share of labour in value added, the distribution of earnings among workers and the average dependency ratio, the observed values of value added per worker per day imply a large incidence of extreme poverty in many of the countries. If, for example, we conservatively suppose labour's share to be 0.8, the coefficient of variation of (logarithms of) earnings to be 0.67 and a dependency ratio of 3, a value added per worker per day of PPP$40 implies that approximately 16 per cent of the workers have incomes that are insufficient to ensure PPP$1.08 per household member per day.[26] In only seven out of the 41 countries does output per worker per day exceed PPP$40. It falls short of PPP$10 in 15 of the countries. Moreover, it should not be forgotten that these figures are actually overestimates.

Unemployment rate

Available data on rates of unemployment in developing countries for the most recent period are assembled in table 4.4. The unemployment rate is high in many countries: in 33 of the 54 countries for which we have information it is higher than 5 per cent, and in 20 of these it exceeds 10 per cent. This seems rather puzzling; one cannot help but wonder how such a large percentage of the labour force could be surviving without earnings from work in countries where institutionalized social security systems do not exist. Things become clear, however, once we realize that, given the method of estimation, these rates represent the sum of chronic and transient unemployment rates (see box 4.7). While the chronic unemployment rate indicates the extent of queuing for jobs in the formal segment, the transient unemployment rate is a partial

---

[26] The implicit assumption is that the distribution of workers' earnings is lognormal. PPP$1.08 per person per day is widely regarded as the line of extreme poverty (see Chapter 5).

Table 4.3   Value added per worker in non-formal segment, ca. 2003 (PPP$)

Country	Value added per worker (PPP$)	
	Per annum	Per day
Petroleum exporter developing		
Algeria	12 383.9	33.9
Trinidad and Tobago	18 235.1	50.0
Venezuela	7 886.6	21.6
Medium-income developing		
Argentina	35 958.7	98.5
Bolivia	5 104.8	14.0
Botswana	20 800.8	57.0
Brazil	13 359.3	36.6
Chile	21 306.5	58.4
China	2 605.6	7.1
Costa Rica	13 669.3	37.5
Dominican Republic	18 041.0	49.4
Ecuador	7 525.0	20.6
Egypt	8 980.7	24.6
El Salvador	6 461.2	17.7
Ghana	3 442.5	9.4
Guatemala	7 875.7	21.6
Honduras	2 652.1	7.3
India	3 251.1	8.9
Indonesia	2 712.4	7.4
Jamaica	2 887.0	7.9
Malaysia	17 532.4	48.0
Mexico	5 515.2	15.1

measure of underemployment of casual/irregular wage workers. A high overall rate of unemployment could thus reflect either a long queue for jobs in the formal segment or a high incidence of casual/irregular wage employment in the non-formal segment, or both.

To the extent that the reported unemployment rate captures a part of the underemployment of casual wage workers (and no part of the underemployment of the self-employed), we should expect the rate to be high wherever casual wage employment is the dominant form of employment in

Productive employment in developing countries

Country	Value added per worker (PPP$)	
	Per annum	Per day
Mongolia	2 360.6	6.5
Morocco	4 603.9	12.6
Namibia	11 181.4	30.6
Nicaragua	6 890.2	18.9
Pakistan	3 532.1	9.7
Panama	7 778.4	21.3
Paraguay	10 434.9	28.6
Philippines	3 818.0	10.5
South Africa	12 347.7	33.8
Sri Lanka	5 365.6	14.7
Thailand	3 155.9	8.7
Turkey	9 046.7	24.8
Uruguay	15 668.7	42.9
Viet Nam	1 859.3	5.1
Least developed		
Bangladesh	1 397.2	3.8
Cambodia	2 355.1	6.5
Madagascar	713.7	2.0
Tanzania	728.9	2.0
Uganda	1 650.4	4.5

Note: For definition of respective countries' non-formal segment, see table 4.1.

Sources: Derived from World Bank, World Development Indicators database (CD-ROM, 2005) and ILO LABORSTA/KILM database (http://www.laborsta.ilo.org/).

the non-formal segment. By implication, we should expect the unemployment rate to be low wherever self-employment is the dominant form of employment in the non-formal segment. Figure 4.1 shows that this expectation is indeed borne out by the data: across countries, the rate of unemployment is inversely related to the incidence of self-employment.

Thus, the larger the incidence of casual wage employment, the higher is the reported unemployment rate. The exceptionally high rate of unemployment observed in South Africa, for example, reflects the fact that casual wage

The global employment challenge

Table 4.4   Unemployment rate, 2003* (percentages)

Country	Total
Petroleum exporter developing	
Algeria	23.7
Trinidad and Tobago (2002)	10.5
Venezuela	16.8
Medium-income developing	
Argentina	15.2
Bolivia (2002)	5.4
Botswana (2000)	15.7
Brazil	9.7
Cameroon (200	7.6
Chile	9.8
China	2.5
Colombia	14.3
Costa Rica	6.6
Cuba (2002)	3.3
Dominican Republic	16.7
Ecuador	9.3
Egypt	11.0
El Salvador	6.9
Ghana (1999)	3.5
Guatemala	2.7
Honduras	5.2
India	3.1
Indonesia	9.6
Jamaica	10.9
Jordan	14.5
Malaysia	3.6
Mexico	2.4
Mongolia	3.5
Morocco	11.9
Namibia (2001)	30.8

Country	Total
Nicaragua	10.3
Pakistan	7.7
Panama	13.1
Papua New Guinea (2000)	2.9
Paraguay	7.9
Philippines (2001)	9.7
South Africa	27.9
Sri Lanka	8.8
Thailand	1.5
Tunisia	14.3
Turkey	10.5
Uruguay	13.0
Viet Nam	2.3
Least developed	
Bangladesh (2000)	3.2
Belize (2002)	10.1
Cambodia (2001)	1.8
Haiti (1999)	7.1
Madagascar (2002)	4.5
Maldives (2000)	2.0
Myanmar (1999)	4.1
Nepal (1999)	1.2
Samoa (2001)	4.4
Tanzania (2001)	1.2
Uganda (2000)	0.9
Yemen (1999)	11.3

* Unless otherwise indicated in parentheses.

Sources: ILO LABORSTA/KILM database (http://laborsta.ilo.org/); special tabulations of household survey data; China Statistical Yearbook (CD-ROM, 2004 and 2005); National Sample Survey Organisation (Government of India), *Employment and Unemployment Situation, 1999–2000* (New Delhi, 2001); Collier (2006); Ghose (2005a).

Box 4.7   Unemployment rate: Nature of the data

The standard method of collection of employment and unemployment data uses a reference period of one week. A person who worked for at least one hour in the reference week is counted as employed while a person who did not work but was seeking or available for work is counted as unemployed.

Given these criteria, it is most unlikely that a self-employed person would ever be found to be unemployed. It is hard to think of a self-employed person who cannot find work for even an hour in any given week. Yet it is perfectly possible that the person concerned works for only one or two days each week. In other words, underemployment of the self-employed is not at all captured by the reported unemployment rate.

On the other hand, a casual wage worker who is found to have been unemployed in the reference week may well have been employed in the preceding or the following week. In the case of these workers, therefore, what is being measured is transient unemployment or, more precisely, underemployment. At the same time, the full extent of underemployment of these workers is not being captured since a casual wage worker found to have worked at least one hour in the reference week is being counted as employed even though it is perfectly possible that he/she actually worked for only a day and could not find work for the rest of the week. In other words, many of the casual wage workers counted as employed could have been seriously underemployed, but the reported unemployment rate does not capture this.

What the reported unemployment rate represents, therefore, is chronic unemployment combined with a part of the underemployment of the employed. The available data from India provide helpful illustrations. In Indian surveys of employment and unemployment, three different reference periods are used: last year, last week and each half-day of last week. We thus get three different unemployment rates: usual principal status (UPS), current weekly status (CWS) and current daily status (CDS). The UPS rate indicates chronic unemployment; the CWS rate indicates a combination of chronic unemployment and transient unemployment of casual/irregular wage workers; and the CDS rate indicates a combination of chronic unemployment, transient unemployment of casual/irregular wage workers and underemployment of all types of workers during the period of employment. In 2000, the three unemployment rates were found to be 2.8 per cent, 4.1 per cent and 7.2 per cent, respectively. We can deduce that the rate of queuing for jobs in the formal segment was 2.8 per cent, the transient unemployment rate was 1.3 per cent and the rate of underemployment of the employed was 3.1 per cent. The CWS unemployment rate is what is available for most countries and the data presented in table 4.4 refer to this.

Productive employment in developing countries

Figure 4.1 Unemployment rate and incidence of self-employment, ca. 2003

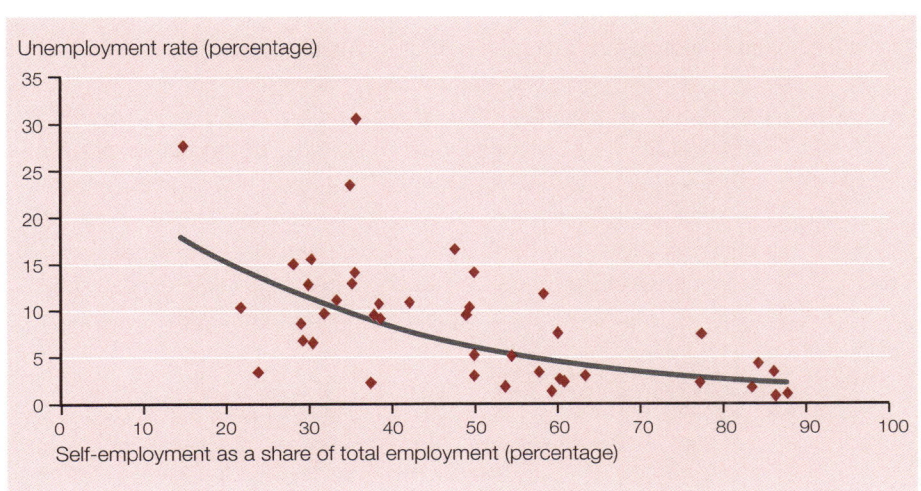

Notes: The regression equation is: Ln (Y) = 3.343 – 0.030 X, R^2 = 0.465. The coefficient is significant at less than 1 per cent.

Based on data for the following 42 countries: Algeria, Argentina, Bangladesh, Bolivia, Botswana, Brazil, Cambodia, Cameroon, Chile, China, Colombia, Costa Rica, Dominican Republic, Ecuador, Egypt, El Salvador, Ghana, Guatemala, Honduras, India, Jamaica, Madagascar, Malaysia, Maldives, Mexico, Mongolia, Morocco, Namibia, Pakistan, Panama, Philippines, South Africa, Sri Lanka, Tanzania, Thailand, Trinidad and Tobago, Tunisia, Turkey, Uganda, Uruguay, Viet Nam, Yemen.

Sources: Derived from tables 4.2 and 4.4.

workers constitute 78 per cent of all workers in the non-formal segment (see box 4.8 in this context). On the other hand, the exceptionally low rates of unemployment observed in the United Republic of Tanzania and Uganda reflect the fact that casual wage employment is quite insignificant in the non-formal segment; in these countries, around 87 per cent of all workers are self-employed.

To what extent, then, do the reported unemployment rates reflect chronic unemployment or queuing for jobs in the formal segment? Since only persons from relatively well-off households can afford to queue for jobs in the formal segment, we can expect the extent of queuing to be directly related to the share of relatively well-off households in all households (see box 4.9). And since this share can plausibly be supposed to vary directly with level of economic development, we can expect the chronic unemployment rate to vary directly with per capita GDP (in PPP$). In so far as the reported unemployment rate incorporates the chronic unemployment rate, therefore,

The global employment challenge

> **Box 4.8   Unemployment in South Africa**
>
> In recent periods, the reported unemployment rate in South Africa has been persistently high, in excess of 25 per cent. This has puzzled many observers and inspired a considerable amount of investigative work. In a recent paper, Kingdon and Knight (2004) argue that queuing for jobs in the formal segment is not the main explanation for the high observed rate of unemployment. They show that "urban informal" employment constitutes a rather small percentage of total non-agricultural employment and that most of the unemployed are in fact poor. They therefore argue that the explanation lies in the existence of serious barriers to entry into informal employment in the urban sector – legacies of the apartheid regime. Rodrik (2006) makes a very similar argument.
>
> The argument appears convincing, particularly since unemployment is known to be heavily concentrated among the young, the unskilled and the black population (Banerjee et al., 2006), but it can be carried a little further. The incidence of casual wage employment in South Africa is very high and, correspondingly, the incidence of self-employment is very low. Thus the high rate of unemployment really reflects the high rate of transient unemployment. The question is, then, why is the incidence of self-employment so low? The answer implied by Kingdon and Knight as well as by Rodrik is that there are serious barriers to entry into self-employment in the urban economy. But it is also possible that the extremely poor resource position of the workers outside the formal segment prevents them from being self-employed and forces them to seek casual wage employment.

we should expect the former to vary directly with per capita GDP (in PPP$). This is indeed the case, as shown in figure 4.2.

Thus there are good grounds, both theoretical and empirical, for supposing that higher reported rates of unemployment reflect either higher rates of transient unemployment of casual wage workers or longer queues for jobs in the formal segment, or both. Arguably, because queuing is to some extent voluntary and involves persons from relatively well-off households, it can be viewed as a less serious problem than transient unemployment. However, long queues could discourage acquisition of education or cause social unrest, so both queuing and transient unemployment need to be treated as problems. Hence, other things being equal, a higher rate of reported unemployment should be taken as indicating a worse employment situation.

Productive employment in developing countries

Figure 4.2 Unemployment rate and level of economic development, ca. 2003

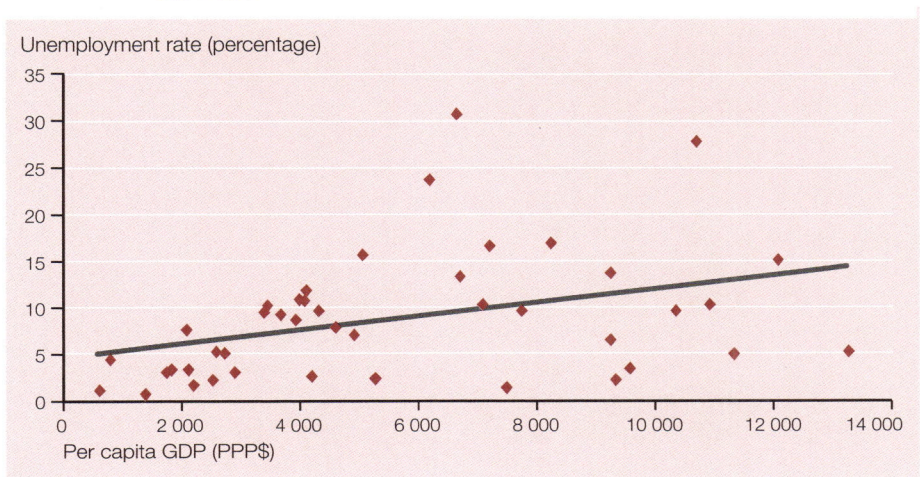

Notes: The regression equation is: $Y = 4.726 + 0.746\,X$, $R^2 = 0.135$. The coefficient is significant at 1.6 per cent.
Based on data for the following 43 countries: Algeria, Argentina, Bangladesh, Bolivia, Botswana, Brazil, Cambodia, Chile, China, Costa Rica, Dominican Republic, Ecuador, Egypt, El Salvador, Ghana, Guatemala, Honduras, India, Indonesia, Jamaica, Madagascar, Malaysia, Mauritius, Mexico, Mongolia, Morocco, Namibia, Nicaragua, Pakistan, Panama, Paraguay, Philippines, Saudi Arabia, South Africa, Sri Lanka, Tanzania, Thailand, Trinidad and Tobago, Turkey, Uganda, Uruguay, Venezuela, Viet Nam.

Sources: Derived from table 4.4 and World Bank, World Development Indicators database (CD-ROM, 2005).

Box 4.9 Chronic unemployment rate as a measure of queuing: India and Brazil

Unemployment rates by years of education, India, 2000 (percentages)

Years of education	Usual principal status (UPS)	Current weekly status (CWS)
0	0.3	2.8
1–5	1.6	3.1
6–8	3.8	5.1
9–10	6.5	7.1
10–12	9.1	9.1
12+	11.3	9.6

Note: See box 4.7 for explanation of employment status.

Source: Ghose, 2004a.

(continued)

The global employment challenge

> **Box 4.9** **Chronic unemployment rate as a measure of queuing: India and Brazil (continued)**
>
> Indian data provide a good illustration of the fact that only chronic unemployment reflects queuing for jobs in the formal segment.
>
> Both rates rise as the level of education rises but the gap between the two narrows, indicating declining importance of transient unemployment and growing importance of queuing. For persons with little or no education, transient unemployment (or underemployment) is significant, indicating that they work mainly as casual wage workers. At the other end, persons with 12 or more years of education are unemployed only in a chronic sense; they are clearly waiting for jobs in the formal segment. Indeed, the fact that the UPS rate exceeds the CWS rate for persons with the highest level of education indicates that these persons actually do occasional work even while they are waiting for jobs in the formal segment.
>
> In the case of Brazil, separate estimates for chronic and transient unemployment are not available. However, the data suggest that both types of unemployment rise with rising level of education for persons with up to ten years of education and that transient unemployment is non-existent for persons with more than ten years of education.
>
> **Unemployment rate by years of education, Brazil, 2004 (percentages)**
>
> | Years of education | Current weekly status (CWS) |
> |:---:|:---:|
> | 0 | 4.8 |
> | 1–7 | 8.0 |
> | 8 | 10.8 |
> | 9–10 | 17.7 |
> | 11–12 | 10.7 |
> | 12+ | 12.5 |
>
> **Source:** Data supplied by the Brazilian Institute of Geography and Statistics (IBGE), Government of Brazil.

4.3 The current state of employment

Overall employment situation

When viewed together, the evidence on the three indicators (tables 4.2, 4.3 and 4.4) presents a rather dismal picture of the current employment situation in developing countries. An overwhelming majority of workers are in the non-formal segment where capital and skills are scarce. These workers are either self-employed or in irregular wage employment. In both forms of employment, they face serious underemployment and low productivity.

It is clear that the employment problem in developing countries is really one of underemployment and low-productivity employment of a large section of the labour force. In 2003, for a group of 19 countries[27] the unemployment rate was less than 4 per cent while 54 per cent of the employed were self-employed and 32 per cent were in casual/irregular wage employment. What is more, the group does not include any least developed countries, where the unemployment rate is even lower and the share of self-employment and casual/irregular wage employment in total employment even higher.

Of course, the seriousness of the employment problem varies across countries and it is of some interest to compare the overall employment situation in one country with that in another. One way of doing this is to combine the three indicators to develop a ranking of countries with reference to the overall employment situation. The method used here to develop such rankings in a particular year is simple: first, each of the indicators is used separately to rank countries, a higher rank showing a better state of employment. Thus, the higher the ratio of employment in the formal segment to total employment, the higher is the rank; the higher the output per worker in the non-formal segment, the higher is the rank; and the higher the ratio of total employment to total labour force (i.e., the lower the rate of unemployment), the higher is the rank. Second, a simple average of the separate ranks for each country gives an overall rank. The higher this rank, the better is the employment situation.

Given the limitations imposed by non-availability of data, this exercise can only be carried out for a set of 21 countries and for the year 2003. The results are presented in table 4.5. These estimates are useful for studying the relationship between the level of development and employment situation, as we shall see below. What we note here is that a higher unemployment rate, in and of itself, does not necessarily imply a worse overall employment situation

---

[27] The countries for which we have the full set of required data are: Argentina, Botswana, Brazil, Chile, China, Colombia, Costa Rica, Ecuador, Egypt, El Salvador, Honduras, India, Jamaica, Mauritius, Mexico, Panama, South Africa, Sri Lanka and Uruguay. See tables 4.2 and 4.4.

The global employment challenge

Table 4.5 Ranking by employment situation, selected countries, 2003

Country	Ranking by formal segment share in total employment (1)		Ranking by value added per worker per day in non-formal segment (2)		Ranking by total employment as percentage of labour force (3)		Average rank
Petroleum exporter developing							
Venezuela	18	(34.7)	12	(21.6)	2	(83.2)	10.67
Medium-income developing							
Argentina	19	(44.1)	21	(98.5)	4	(84.8)	14.67
Botswana	21	(50.3)	19	(57.0)	3	(84.3)	14.33
Brazil	15	(32.5)	16	(36.6)	11	(90.3)	14.00
Chile	20	(45.9)	20	(58.4)	10	(90.2)	16.67
China	5	(14.0)	1	(7.1)	20	(97.5)	8.67
Costa Rica	13	(30.7)	17	(37.5)	17	(93.4)	15.67
Ecuador	10	(24.8)	10	(20.6)	13	(90.7)	11.00
Egypt	2	(8.6)	13	(24.6)	7	(89.0)	7.33
El Salvador	12	(29.9)	8	(17.7)	16	(93.1)	12.00
Honduras	8	(19.6)	2	(7.3)	18	(94.8)	9.33
India	1	(7.3)	5	(8.9)	19	(96.9)	8.33
Indonesia	11	(26.8)	3	(7.4)	12	(90.4)	8.67
Jamaica	4	(13.2)	4	(7.9)	8	(89.1)	5.33
Mexico	9	(21.7)	7	(15.1)	21	(97.6)	12.33
Nicaragua	7	(16.8)	9	(18.9)	9	(89.7)	8.33
Panama	16	(32.9)	11	(21.3)	5	(86.9)	10.67
Paraguay	6	(14.2)	14	(28.6)	15	(92.1)	11.67
South Africa	17	(33.0)	15	(33.8)	1	(72.1)	11.00
Sri Lanka	3	(11.7)	6	(14.7)	14	(91.2)	7.67
Uruguay	14	(30.8)	18	(42.9)	6	(87.0)	12.67

Note: Figures in parentheses show actual values. In each case, a higher value means a higher rank. A higher average rank indicates a better overall employment situation.

Sources: Col. 1: table 4.2; Col. 2: table 4.3; Col. 3: table 4.4, where employment as percentage of labour force = 100 − unemployment rate.

in the context of developing countries. Mexico has a much lower unemployment rate than Brazil, but also a worse overall employment situation. South Africa has a much higher unemployment rate than India, but also a better overall employment situation.

Gender disparity in employment

Two of the major ways in which gender disparity in employment can arise in a developing country are the following.[28] First, there can be disparity in terms of opportunities for employment; this would show up in inequality of unemployment rates. Second, there can be disparity in terms of quality of employment; this would show up in differences in the distribution of total employment by type. If the percentage of the employed with jobs in the formal segment is found to be lower for women than for men, for example, it can be said that the average quality of women's employment is worse than men's.

Table 4.6 presents estimates of two simple ratios (the background data are presented in appendix table A4.4). The first is the ratio of the unemployment rate for women to that for men. In most countries, the value of this ratio exceeds unity as women's unemployment rate is generally higher than that of men. The second ratio is the ratio of the percentage of employed women holding jobs in the formal segment to the percentage of employed men holding jobs in the formal segment. For reasons of data availability, this ratio could be estimated only for 20 countries. The value of the ratio exceeds unity in the case of 11 countries and is less than unity in the case of eight (for one country, Uruguay, the ratio turns out to be exactly equal to unity). Thus we do not observe any systematic tendency for the average quality of women's employment to be better or worse than that of men's employment.

Broadly speaking, therefore, gender disparity in employment is observed to arise mainly in terms of opportunities for employment. This is a broad view because it is possible, indeed likely, that within each of the segments women workers are concentrated in relatively lower-quality jobs. This is suggested by the widely noted fact that average wage earnings of female workers tend to be lower than those of male workers in both formal and non-formal segments. These, however, are aspects that need to be studied at the level of national economies.

What explains the general tendency for the female unemployment rate to be higher than the male? The reported unemployment rates, we may recall,

---

[28] A third way in which gender inequality can arise is in terms of differential rates of labour force participation. However, in the context of developing countries, the observed difference in participation rate does not carry an unambiguous meaning, as the analysis in Chapter 2 has shown. Both within and across developing countries, labour force participation of both men and women declines as income level rises. But women's participation declines faster than men's so that the ratio of women's participation rate to men's participation rate declines as income level rises.

The global employment challenge

Table 4.6   Gender disparity in employment

Country	Year	Ratio of female to male unemployment rate	Ratio of female to male share of employment in formal segment
Petroleum exporter developing			
Algeria	2003	1.09	–
Iran	1996	1.58	–
Venezuela	2003	1.41	1.12
Medium-income developing			
Argentina	2003	1.16	1.19
Bolivia	2000	1.56	–
Botswana	1998	1.27	0.91
Brazil	2003	1.58	0.95
Cameroon	2001	0.82	–
Chile	2003	1.48	0.92
Colombia	2004	1.59	1.14
Costa Rica	2004	1.57	1.09
Dominican Republic	2004	2.93	–
Ecuador	2004	1.83	0.80
Egypt	1998	3.90	0.76
El Salvador	2004	0.44	1.15
Guatemala	2002	1.44	–
Honduras	2004	1.74	1.44
India	2000	0.93	0.63
Indonesia	1996	1.52	–
Jamaica	2004	1.94	–
Malaysia	2002	1.15	–
Mauritius	1995	1.80	1.18
Mexico	2004	1.23	1.12
Morocco	2003	1.13	–
Namibia	2000	1.38	–
Nicaragua	1998	1.65	1.90
Pakistan	2002	2.65	–
Panama	2004	1.82	1.21
Paraguay	2004	1.60	0.89
Philippines	2001	1.10	–

Productive employment in developing countries

Country	Year	Ratio of female to male unemployment rate	Ratio of female to male share of employment in formal segment
South Africa	2002	1.30	–
Sri Lanka	2003	2.37	2.16
Thailand	2004	0.88	–
Trinidad and Tobago	2002	1.86	–
Turkey	2004	0.92	–
Uruguay	2003	1.54	1.00
Viet Nam	2004	1.31	–
Zimbabwe	1999	0.63	0.33
Least developed			
Bangladesh	2000	1.03	–
Cambodia	2001	1.43	–
Madagascar	2002	1.60	–
Malawi	1998	0.50	–
Maldives	2000	1.69	–
Rwanda	1996	0.38	–
Yemen	1999	0.66	–

– = data not available.

Source: Derived from appendix table A4.4.

incorporate both chronic and transient unemployment rates. This suggests two possible explanations. The first is that, compared to men, proportionately more women workers are in irregular wage employment in the non-formal segment; in this case, the transient unemployment rate would be higher for women than for men. The second is that women may be more willing and able to queue for jobs in the formal segment than men; in this case, the chronic unemployment rate would be higher for women than for men.

To the extent that the first explanation holds, we should expect the ratio of female to male unemployment rates to vary, across countries, directly with another ratio – the ratio of the percentage of female workers in irregular wage employment in the non-formal segment to the percentage of male workers in irregular wage employment in the non-formal segment. Figure 4.3 shows the nature of this relationship for a sample of 15 countries for which we have the required statistical data. The relationship is positive, as expected, but rather weak (statistically not significant).

The global employment challenge

Figure 4.3 Gender disparity in unemployment and in irregular wage employment, ca. 2003

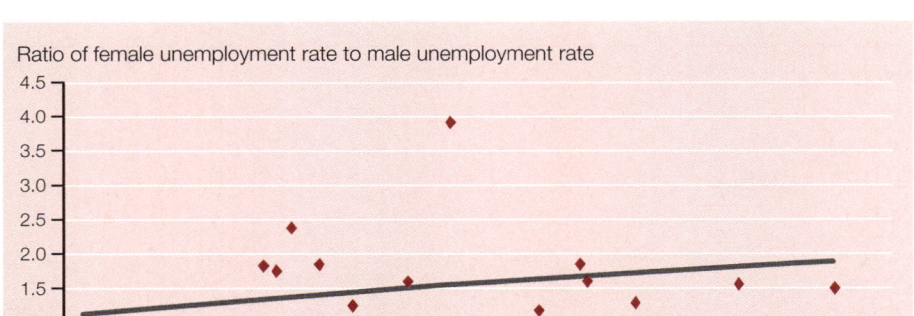

Notes: The regression equation is: Ln (Y) = 0.167 + 0.483 Ln (X), R² = 0.088. The coefficient is significant only at 28.4 per cent.
Based on data for the following 15 countries: Argentina, Brazil, Botswana, Chile, Costa Rica, Ecuador, Egypt, El Salvador, Honduras, India, Mauritius, Mexico, Panama, Sri Lanka, Uruguay.

Source: Derived from appendix table A4.4.

There is another way of empirically verifying the hypothesis. We can plausibly suppose that, for both male and female workers, there would be an inverse relation between the percentage of self-employed and the percentage of casual/irregular wage workers. On this basis, it can also be said that the ratio of female to male unemployment would be expected to vary, across countries, inversely with the ratio of the percentage of female workers in self-employment to the percentage of male workers in self-employment. This relationship can be studied for a larger sample of countries. Figure 4.4 shows that the relationship is negative, as expected, and statistically significant.

Overall, the evidence seems to suggest that only a small part of the gender gap in unemployment rates is explained by the fact that proportionately more women workers (compared to men) tend to be in irregular wage employment. A large part is to be explained by the phenomenon of queuing for jobs in the formal segment; compared to men, a larger proportion of women tend to be in the queue for jobs in the formal segment (see box 4.10 on page 90). This could indicate the existence of discrimination (i.e., preference for male workers among employers) in the formal segment, but not necessarily. Indeed, it is also possible that proportionately more women workers seek specific types of jobs

Figure 4.4   Gender disparity in unemployment and in self-employment, ca. 2003

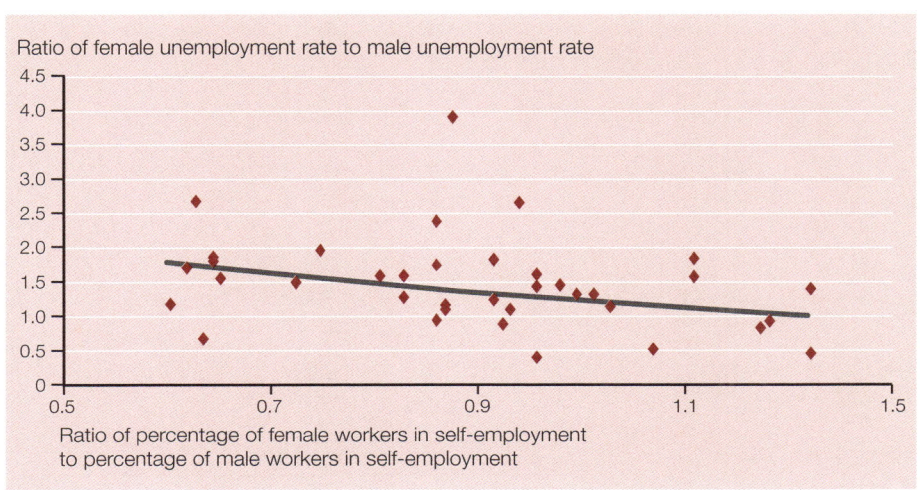

Notes: The regression equation is: Ln (Y) = 1.049 – 0.774 X, R² = 0.125. The coefficient is significant at 3 per cent. Based on data for the following 38 countries: Algeria, Argentina, Bolivia, Botswana, Brazil, Cambodia, Cameroon, Chile, Costa Rica, Dominican Republic, Ecuador, Egypt, El Salvador, Guatemala, Honduras, India, Iran, Jamaica, Madagascar, Malawi, Malaysia, Maldives, Mauritius, Mexico, Morocco, Namibia, Pakistan, Panama, Philippines, Rwanda, South Africa, Sri Lanka, Thailand, Trinidad and Tobago, Turkey, Uruguay, Viet Nam, Yemen.

Source: Derived from appendix table A4.4.

in the formal segment and have access to means of survival while waiting in the queue. On the one hand, women are likely to seek jobs mainly in services; on the other, given social norms, they are more likely than men to receive family support while waiting in the queue.

What emerges from this analysis is that gender disparity in employment exists mainly in terms of employment opportunities in the formal segment, which tend to be somewhat more restricted for women than for men. This is reflected in higher chronic unemployment rates for women. It is not clear to what extent this disparity results from discrimination, however, as there is some evidence to suggest that proportionately more women than men are willing and able to wait for "suitable" jobs in the formal segment.

4.4   Recent trends

For an assessment of change in the overall employment situation in individual countries in the 1990s, we need to take an integrated view of the trends in the three indicators. For the purpose, a simple tool – the Employment Situation

The global employment challenge

> **Box 4.10 Job queuing and gender: India and Brazil**
>
> Evidence from India and Brazil illustrates the point that the incidence of queuing tends to be higher among women than among men.
>
> Chronic unemployment rate by years of education, India, 2000 (percentages)
>
> | Years of education | Male | Female |
> |---|---|---|
> | 0 | 0.4 | 0.1 |
> | 1–5 | 1.7 | 1.3 |
> | 6–8 | 3.7 | 4.9 |
> | 9–10 | 5.4 | 15.8 |
> | 11–12 | 7.6 | 21.1 |
> | 12+ | 8.5 | 27.0 |
>
> Source: Ghose (2004a).
>
> For workers with up to five years of education, the unemployment rate is generally insignificant for both males and females, but the female unemployment rate is even lower than the male rate. For workers with higher education, on the other hand, the female unemployment rate is far higher than the male, indicating greater incidence of queuing among females.
>
> Unemployment rate by years of education, Brazil, 2004 (percentages)
>
> | Years of education | Male | Female |
> |---|---|---|
> | 0 | 6.2 | 4.0 |
> | 1–7 | 36.0 | 30.6 |
> | 8 | 12.7 | 11.8 |
> | 9–10 | 14.2 | 15.0 |
> | 11 | 23.2 | 29.7 |
> | 12+ | 6.6 | 7.8 |
>
> Source: Data supplied by the Brazilian Institute of Geography and Statistics (IBGE), Government of Brazil.
>
> Here the unemployment rates represent the sum of chronic and transient unemployment rates. For workers with up to eight years of education the male unemployment rate is higher than the female rate, indicating higher incidence of irregular employment among males. For workers with higher education the female unemployment rate is higher than the male rate, indicating greater incidence of queuing among females.

Index (ESI) – is developed. The methodology used to construct this index is as follows. First, time-series estimates of the values of each of three indicators – share of the formal segment in total employment, real output per worker in the non-formal segment and employment ratio – are assembled. Second, these values are transformed into index numbers by setting the value for the initial year in each case equal to unity. Finally, a simple average of the three indices for each of the years is estimated and it is this average that is designated as the ESI.[29] A rising (declining) trend in ESI indicates improvement (deterioration) in the overall employment situation.

The full set of ESI estimates is presented in appendix table A4.3. Given the limitations of data, they could be made for only 19 countries. Even so, time-series estimates for the full period (1990–2003) could not be made for all of them. For a few countries, time-series estimates were not possible at all, so estimates were derived only for two or three years. These are important limitations that unfortunately cannot be remedied. However, some satisfaction can be derived from the fact that the 19 countries in the sample actually cover a majority of the labour force of the developing world.

Estimates of average annual rate of change in each of the three indicators and in the ESI are presented in table 4.7. A first observation that can be made is that in the 1990s the overall employment situation improved in a majority of the sample countries: the ESI showed a rising trend in 12 countries, a declining trend in five countries and no trend in two countries.

A second observation qualifies the first: the rate of improvement in the employment situation has generally been rather low. The explanation lies in the remarkable fact that in none of the countries do all three indicators show simultaneous positive trends. Moreover, in only one country (Chile) do the two main indicators – share of the formal segment in total employment and output per worker in the non-formal segment – show simultaneously rising trends. In general, simultaneous processes of labour transfer from non-formal to formal segment and of declining underemployment in the non-formal segment are not observed. Indeed, if we leave Chile out of account, we observe an intriguing pattern: the countries where underemployment in the non-formal segment declined are also those where the share of the formal segment in total employment failed to rise, and the countries where the share of the formal segment in total employment rose are also those where underemployment in the non-formal segment failed to decline.

A few other related facts are worthy of note. First, the share of the formal segment in total employment generally declined (it rose in only five countries

---

[29] Note that the three indicators are being accorded equal weights. It would be useful to experiment by assigning unequal and varying weights. This exercise is left for the future when more data become available.

Table 4.7 Trends in employment situation, selected countries

Country	Period	Average annual rate of change (%)			
		Share of formal segment in total employment (1)	Output per worker in non-formal segment (2)	Employment ratio (3)	Employment Situation Index (ESI) (4)
Petroleum exporter developing					
Venezuela	1994–2002	−4.68	−3.87	−0.84	−3.07
Medium-income developing					
Argentina	1998–2003	−1.84	−8.80	−1.03[b]	−3.66
Botswana	1995–2001	−0.21[a]	3.33[a]	1.53[a]	1.60[a]
Brazil	1992–2002	0.26[b]	2.09	−0.47	0.68
Chile	1990–2003	1.27	3.06	−0.40	1.46
China	1990–2002	−3.95	5.07	−0.18	0.86
Costa Rica	1990–2003	1.43	−0.06[b]	−0.18	0.44
Ecuador	2000–2003	1.00[b]	6.75	−0.72	2.44
Egypt	1990–1998	−2.72	4.10	0.04[b]	0.71
El Salvador	1993–2003	2.38	−0.75[b]	0.24	0.61
Honduras	1990–2002	−1.03[b]	−3.63	0.00[b]	−1.55
India	1990–2000	−1.25	2.19	−0.03[b]	0.38
Jamaica	1998–2002	−3.00	−4.43	0.34	−2.31
Mexico	1991–2003	1.42	−1.03	0.17	0.30[b]
Nicaragua	1993–2001	1.57	−5.66	0.99	−0.47[b]
Panama	1991–2003	0.24[b]	3.04	0.18	1.22
Paraguay	1998–2003	−3.09	−1.24[b]	−0.80	−1.71
Sri Lanka	1990–2003	0.50[b]	2.09	0.61	1.15
Least developed					
Myanmar	1990–1998	−2.62[a]	3.41[a]	0.02[a]	0.43[a]

[a] Estimated by using values for initial and terminal years (no series available).
[b] Statistically not significantly different from zero.

Source: Derived from appendix table A4.3.

while it declined in nine and remained unchanged in another five); the rate of job growth in the formal segment was generally lower than that of labour force growth in the economy. Second, the unemployment rate showed no general trend: the employment ratio showed a rising trend in eight countries, a declining trend in seven countries and no trend in four countries. Data for a larger set of 39 countries (table 4.8) show a similar picture: the employment ratio showed a rising trend in 15 countries, a declining trend in 15 countries and no trend in nine countries. Third, underemployment in the non-formal segment declined in about half the countries. Output per worker in the non-formal segment showed a rising trend in ten of the 19 countries (in table 4.7), a declining trend in six countries and no trend in three countries. Once again, data for a larger set of 39 countries (table 4.8) show a similar picture: output per worker showed a rising trend in 21 countries, a declining trend in eight countries and no trend in ten countries.[30]

There was another positive development: gender disparity in employment showed a general tendency to decline. As the data in table 4.9 (see page 96) show, disparity in terms of employment opportunities in the formal segment (as indicated by the ratio of female to male unemployment rates) increased in some countries but declined in a larger number of countries. The same can be said about the disparity in terms of job quality: the ratio of the percentage of women holding jobs in the formal segment to the percentage of men holding jobs in the formal segment declined in some countries but increased in a larger number of countries.

The conclusion, then, is that in the 1990s the overall employment situation improved, albeit rather slowly, in a majority of the sample countries. This slow progress is attributable to the fact that simultaneous processes of rapid job creation in the formal segment and of reduction in underemployment in the non-formal segment were not in evidence. The fact that underemployment in the non-formal segment was declining in a significant number of countries suggests that government policies did focus on ensuring a flow of investment into the segment.[31] But there was a fairly general failure

---

[30] One qualification needs to be added. Wherever agriculture is identified as the core of the non-formal segment, the estimates of the rate of change in output per worker could conceivably be biased upward. The reason is that growth of employment in agriculture has been slower than that of the labour force in national economies in virtually all cases. Yet, given that the growth of employment in the formal segment has generally been slower than that of the labour force in national economies, the growth of employment in the non-formal segment must have been higher than that of the labour force. So the observed rate of growth of output per worker in agriculture could well be overstating the growth of output per worker in the non-formal segment as a whole. (The problem does not arise in cases where services alone or agriculture and services together constitute the core of the non-formal segment.) However, it is arguable that persons who move out of agriculture into non-formal industrial or service activities expect to earn an income that is roughly equal to what they could have earned in agriculture. Thus there are grounds for expecting output per worker in non-formal industrial and service activities to remain roughly comparable to that in agriculture. The observed rate of growth of output per worker in agriculture is then a fairly good measure of the unobservable rate of growth of output per worker in the non-formal segment.

[31] The fact of substantial growth of output in the non-formal segment indicates that there was significant investment in the segment. Since saving and entrepreneurship are concentrated in the formal segment, significant investment in the non-formal segment is unlikely to have occurred without government intervention. This intervention can mean public investment as well as facilitation of investment by those working in the non-formal segment through measures such as extension services, credit supply, training, etc.

Table 4.8 Trends in two employment indicators, selected countries

Country	Period	Output per worker in non-formal segment (1)	Employment ratio (2)
Petroleum exporter developing			
Algeria	1997–2001	0.59[a]	−0.65[a]
Trinidad and Tobago	1990–2002	0.24[b]	1.03
Venezuela	1994–2002	−3.87	−0.84
Medium-income developing			
Argentina	1998–2003	−8.80	−1.03[b]
Botswana	1995–2001	3.33[a]	1.53[a]
Brazil	1992–2002	2.09	−0.47
Chile	1990–2003	3.06	−0.40
China	1990–2002	5.07	−0.18
Costa Rica	1990–2003	−0.06[b]	−0.18
Cuba	1994–2000	2.34[b]	0.31
Dominican Republic	1996–2002	2.92	0.05[b]
Ecuador	2000–2003	6.75	−0.72
Egypt	1990–2002	4.39	0.04[b]
El Salvador	1993–2003	−0.75[b]	0.24
Ghana	1992–2000	1.00[a]	−0.04[a]
Guatemala	1998–2002	−1.36[b]	0.05[b]
Honduras	1990–2002	−3.63	0.00[b]
India	1990–2000	2.19	−0.03[b]
Indonesia	1995–2002	−2.48	−0.44
Jamaica	1992–2003	−1.47	0.31
Malaysia	1990–2003	1.71	0.06[b]
Mexico	1991–2003	−1.03	0.17
Mongolia	1992–2003	−3.85	0.45[a]
Namibia	1997–2001	7.37	0.45
Nicaragua	1990–2001	−6.90	0.36
Pakistan	1990–2002	1.29	−0.35
Panama	1991–2003	3.04	0.18
Paraguay	1998–2003	−1.24[b]	−0.80
Philippines	1990–2001	−0.94	−0.13
South Africa	1999–2003	10.32[b]	−1.30[b]

Country	Period	Average annual rate of change (%)	
		Output per worker in non-formal segment (1)	Employment ratio (2)
Sri Lanka	1990–2003	2.09	0.61
Thailand	1990–2003	3.43	−0.03[b]
Turkey	1990–2003	2.69	−0.08[b]
Viet Nam	1998–2003	1.72[b]	0.52
Least developed			
Bangladesh	1996–2000	3.35[a]	−0.18[a]
Belize	1993–1999	−2.84[b]	−0.60
Myanmar	1990–1998	3.41[a]	0.02
Tanzania	1991–2001	0.11[a]	−0.12[a]
Uganda	1992–2003	3.66[a]	0.11[a]

[a] Estimated by using values for initial and terminal years (no time series available).
[b] Statistically not significantly different from zero.

Sources: Col. 1: derived from appendix table A4.2; Col. 2: derived from ILO LABORSTA/KILM database (http://laborsta.ilo.org/); special tabulations of household survey data; China Statistical Yearbook (CD-ROM, 2004 and 2005); National Sample Survey Organisation (Government of India), *Employment and Unemployment Situation, 1999–2000* (New Delhi, 2001); Collier (2006); Ghose (2005a).

in the area of job creation in the formal segment; employment growth in the segment lagged behind labour force growth in most countries. What underlies this failure?

Table 4.10 presents estimates of growth in output and employment in the formal segment of 17 countries. In estimating output growth, the formal segment in each country is taken to be as indicated by the data in table 4.1. In the case of Brazil, industry alone is regarded as the formal segment; in the case of China, the formal segment is taken to be composed of industry and services, and so on. Hence the estimates of output contain a part that should be attributed to the non-formal segment but also leave out a part that should be attributed to the formal segment. The two parts, we assume, are roughly equal so that the estimates of output growth are free of serious biases. The estimates of employment in the formal segment are the same as those of regular wage employment as defined in table 4.2.

The estimates show that in a few of the countries (Argentina, Ecuador, Jamaica, Paraguay and Venezuela), growth crisis was a major cause of stagnation or decline in employment in the formal segment. In these countries, underemployment in the non-formal segment also tended to rise

Table 4.9 Trends in gender disparity, 1990s

Country	Period	Change in female to male ratio	
		Unemployment rate	Employment in formal segment as percentage of total employment
Petroleum exporter developing			
Venezuela	1995–2003	–0.12	–0.06
Medium-income developing			
Argentina	1998–2003	–0.04	0.23
Cameroon	1996–2001	0.14	–
Chile	1998–2003	0.23	–0.01
Costa Rica	1990–2004	0.13	–0.19
Dominican Republic	1996–2004	0.26	–
El Salvador	1995–2004	–0.25	0.06
Honduras	1996–2004	0.72	0.05
India	1994–2000	0.09	0.10
Jamaica	1998–2004	–0.27	–
Malaysia	1995–2002	–0.21	–
Mexico	1991–2004	–0.45	–0.15
Nicaragua	1993–1998	–5.28	0.21
Pakistan	1995–2002	–1.13	
Panama	1992–2004	–0.25	–0.26
Paraguay	1999–2004	0.37	0.05
Sri Lanka	1990–2003	–0.22	0.39
Thailand	1990–2004	–0.32	–
Trinidad and Tobago	1990–2002	0.51	–
Turkey	1998–2004	–0.07	–
Viet Nam	1996–2004	0.57	–
Least developed			
Bangladesh	1996–2000	0.22	–
Maldives	1995–2000	–0.48	–

– = data not available.

Source: Derived from appendix table A4.4.

Table 4.10 Growth of output and employment in formal segment, 1990s

Country	Period	Average annual rate of growth (%)	
		Output[a]	Employment[b]
Petroleum exporter developing			
Venezuela	1994–2002	1.72[a]	–1.73[a]
Medium-income developing			
Argentina	1998–2003	2.90[c]	–1.07
Brazil	1992–2002	0.73[c]	1.97
Chile	1990–2003	5.73	3.20
China	1990–2002	11.46	–2.94
Costa Rica	1990–2003	5.49	5.41
Ecuador	1990–2003	2.61	2.44
Egypt	1990–1998	4.46	0.06
El Salvador	1993–2003	4.04	5.40
Honduras	1990–2002	4.05	3.41
India	1990–2000	6.95	0.65
Jamaica	1998–2002	1.57	–2.50
Mexico	1991–2003	3.31	4.24
Nicaragua	1993–2001	5.13	5.83
Panama	1991–2003	4.02	3.42
Paraguay	1994–2003	0.53	1.97
Sri Lanka	1990–2003	5.50[c]	2.09[c]

Notes: [a] Refers to output in the segment(s) other than the one(s) identified as non-formal in table 4.1.
[b] Refers to regular wage employment as defined in table 4.2.
[c] Statistically not different from zero.

Sources: Output: derived from World Bank, World Development Indicators database (CD-ROM, 2005); Employment: derived from appendix table A4.1.

(table 4.7). The most interesting fact, however, relates to the contrasting experiences of two sets of countries – one set comprising China, India and Egypt and the other comprising Latin American countries (Brazil, Costa Rica, Ecuador, El Salvador, Honduras, Mexico, Nicaragua, Panama and Paraguay).

In the first set, employment growth in the formal segment was small or negative while output growth was high. Evidently, growth in the formal segment was driven by rising capital per worker and technological innovations.

The global employment challenge

> **Box 4.11 Formal employment in China in the 1990s**
>
> Employment in the formal segment in China declined from 149 million in 1995 to 105 million in 2003. This resulted from the fact that job losses in the public sector (state-owned and collective-owned enterprises) were much larger than job gains in the emerging private sector. Employment in the public sector declined from 140 million in 1995 to 76 million in 2003 while employment in emerging large-scale private enterprises increased from 9 million to 29 million.
>
> The explanation lies in the growing difficulties encountered by the public sector enterprises in carrying the huge stocks of surplus labour that they had accumulated over the years as a result of past policies of job allocation through administrative methods. The transition to a market economy and openness required reforms of the employment system and the labour market. When such reforms were introduced and public enterprises were allowed to shed labour, employment in these enterprises declined very sharply. Thus efforts to correct imbalances carried over from the past resulted in a sharp decline in employment in the formal segment.
>
> **Source:** Ghose (2005a).

In the case of China there was an additional factor, namely correction of imbalances carried over from the past (see box 4.11).[32]

In the second set of countries the developments seem rather intriguing: except in Brazil and Paraguay, output growth in the formal segment was reasonably rapid, but the rate of employment growth equalled or exceeded the rate of output growth; employment growth in the formal segment was apparently associated with stagnant or declining output per worker. What does this signify? It is possible to imagine that governments, faced with lengthening queues for jobs in the formal segment, ignored considerations of productivity and created jobs in the public sector. However, there is evidence to show that this was not the case; the share of the public sector in total employment in the formal segment was declining in all the countries. The only plausible explanation seems to be that there was a change in the composition of output: the share of low-value-added, labour-intensive products in total output of the formal segment increased. In other words, output growth in the formal segment was driven by growth of labour-intensive activities.

---

[32] To a lesser extent, this factor was also relevant in the case of India. See Ghose (2005c).

To sum up, two types of restructuring appear to have occurred in the formal segment in the 1990s. Some countries restructured capital and technology rather than output; in these cases, labour productivity increased rapidly while employment showed zero or negative growth. Other countries restructured output rather than capital or technology; there it was employment that increased rapidly while labour productivity showed zero or negative growth. On the whole, the evidence suggests the existence of a strong employment–productivity trade-off in the formal segment.

To what extent can the results be generalized to all developing countries? Given the problems of data availability, we have been forced to use samples that cannot be called representative. In particular, least developed countries and countries of sub-Saharan Africa are underrepresented in the samples.[33] On the other hand, the samples do cover a majority of workers in developing countries.

Our judgement is that the following general conclusions can be drawn. First, the overall employment situation improved for a substantial section of the workers, though only in a minority of the countries, in the developing world. Second, in most cases the improvement derived from output growth in the non-formal segment. Third, in terms of employment generation the formal segment performed poorly in most countries. Fourth, rapid growth of employment in the formal segment, wherever this occurred, was associated with output restructuring that increased the share of labour-intensive products in total output. Finally, in very few countries did a growing "formality of employment" (i.e., rising share of the formal segment in total employment) go hand in hand with falling underemployment in the non-formal segment.

4.5   Economic growth and employment

The empirical evidence for recent periods does suggest that economic growth is generally associated with improvement in the employment situation. One piece of evidence is the relationship between the ranking of countries in terms of employment situation as established in table 4.5, and the same countries' rankings in terms of per capita GDP in PPP$ (the lowest per capita GDP is made equal to unity and the figures for the rest of the countries are expressed as multiples of this). The relationship, shown in figure 4.5, is positive and surprisingly strong, given the small number of observations on which it is based. Higher-income countries do have a better overall employment situation and this suggests that the improvement is due to past economic growth.

---

[33] There are studies that indicate a worsening employment situation in many countries of sub-Saharan Africa (Collier, 2006). The trends in poverty, discussed in Chapter 5, also indicate that the employment situation is deteriorating in many countries of the region.

The global employment challenge

Figure 4.5 Employment situation and level of economic development, ca. 2003

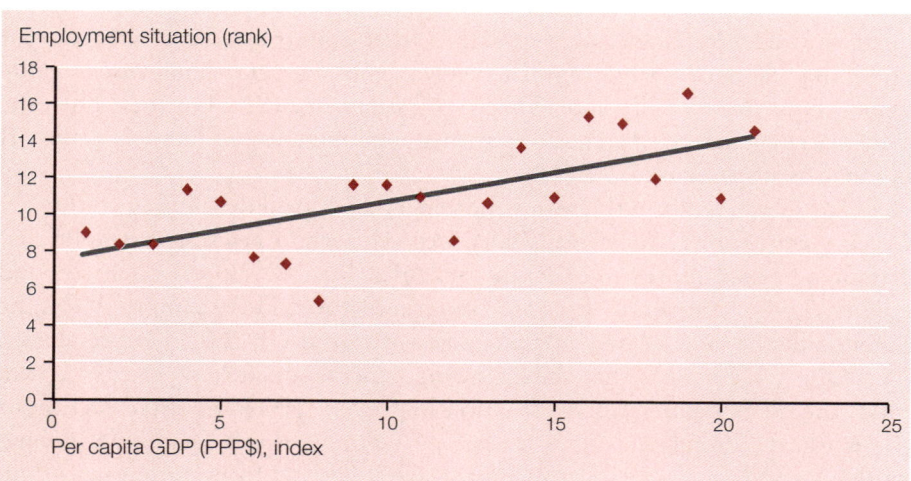

Notes: The regression equation is: Y = 7.414 + 0.326 X, R^2 = 0.481. The coefficient is significant at less than 1 per cent. Lowest per capita GDP is set equal to unity and the figures for the rest are expressed as multiples of this. Based on data for the following 21 countries: Argentina, Botswana, Brazil, Chile, China, Costa Rica, Ecuador, Egypt, El Salvador, Honduras, India, Indonesia, Jamaica, Mexico, Nicaragua, Panama, Paraguay, South Africa, Sri Lanka, Uruguay, Venezuela.

Sources: Derived from table 4.5 and World Bank, World Development Indicators database (CD-ROM, 2005).

This is confirmed by another, more direct piece of evidence which concerns the relationship between the average annual rates of change in the ESI, presented in table 4.7, and those in real per capita GDP over the same periods. This relationship, shown in figure 4.6, is also positive and surprisingly strong. Faster pace of economic growth does seem to have led to faster pace of improvement in the employment situation in the 1990s.

Thus, as a broad generalization, it can be said that economic growth generally improved the employment situation in the 1990s. Figure 4.6 suggests a much more nuanced view, however. It is clear that very low or negative growth was necessarily associated with a worsening employment situation, as was the case for two low-growth countries (Honduras and Jamaica) and three negative-growth countries (Argentina, Paraguay and Venezuela). But it is also clear that similar rates of positive economic growth generated very different rates of improvement in the employment situation in different countries. Mexico's growth rate was slightly higher than that of Brazil, yet the employment situation improved in Brazil and failed to improve in Mexico. India's growth rate was similar to that of Chile, yet the improvement in the

Figure 4.6   Economic growth and employment situation, 1990s

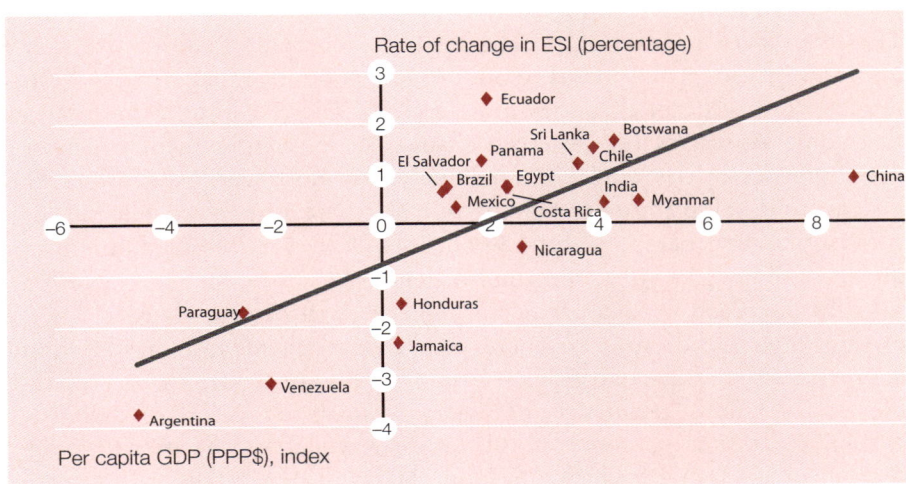

Notes: The regression equation is: Y = − 0.820 + 0.426 X, R² = 0.546. The coefficient is significant at less than 1 per cent.
Based on data for the following 19 countries: Argentina, Botswana, Brazil, Chile, China, Costa Rica, Ecuador, Egypt, El Salvador, Honduras, India, Jamaica, Mexico, Myanmar, Nicaragua, Panama, Paraguay, Sri Lanka, Venezuela.

Sources: Derived from table 4.7 and World Bank, World Development Indicators database (CD-ROM, 2005).

employment situation was far larger in Chile than in India. China's growth rate was much higher than that of Chile, yet the improvement in the employment situation was significantly larger in Chile than in China.

The basic conclusions are as follows. Lack of economic growth necessarily worsens the employment situation in developing countries while economic growth generally, but not universally, improves it. Most importantly, economic growth certainly does not improve the employment situation to the same extent everywhere.

The reasons why the effect of positive economic growth on the overall employment situation tends to be so varied are also quite clear. As Chile's experience shows, economic growth has the most favourable impact on employment when it generates simultaneous processes of rapid growth of employment in the formal segment and rising output per worker in the non-formal segment. However, except in Chile, economic growth did not in fact generate such simultaneous processes. Even rapid economic growth was usually associated with either rising share of the formal segment in total employment or rising output per worker in the non-formal segment, but not both.

4.6 Employment effects of capital inflow and trade growth

The 1990s were a period of globalization, i.e., a period of substantive change in the international division of labour brought about by rapid growth of cross-border flows of capital, goods and services. There is thus a presumption that some aspects of the observed changes in the employment situation in developing countries could be attributable to globalization. It is of some interest to develop an understanding of what these aspects are. Globalization is a continuing process and future policies will need to be based on a proper understanding of its effects on employment.

As discussed in Chapter 3, the rapid growth of cross-border flows of private capital did little to increase the investment rate in developing countries.[34] There are two main reasons for this. First, the sharp growth of cross-border flows resulted in only a fairly small net inflow of capital into developing countries; moreover, this inflow was highly concentrated in a few dynamic, high-saving countries. Second, the investment rate quite often failed to increase even in those developing countries that received substantial net inflow because capital inflow tended to crowd out domestic investment.

The fact that foreign private capital has had little effect on investment in developing countries does not mean that it has had no effect on employment. Even when it does not add to aggregate investment in the economy (because of crowding out of domestic investment), inflow of foreign private capital can still affect employment in the formal segment, to which it flows, in two possible ways: by directly promoting labour-intensive, export-oriented manufacturing industries (often in special economic zones) and by facilitating technology upgrading in existing import-substitution industries (some of which may begin to develop as export industries). In the first case, growth of employment in the formal segment is stimulated as labour-intensive industries expand at a faster pace than capital-intensive industries, raising employment per unit of output. In the second case, there is in effect displacement of labour-intensive industries by capital- and skill-intensive industries so that employment growth in the formal segment is restrained while growth of labour productivity is stimulated.

These employment effects of foreign capital cannot in reality be isolated from the employment effects of trade growth (rise in trade–GDP ratio), which are also confined to the formal segment as this is the main producer of tradable goods and services. Therefore, observed employment effects of trade growth should really be interpreted as the combined effects of capital inflow and trade

---

[34] This is also reflected in the fact that inflow of foreign capital has not had any discernible effect on economic growth in developing countries. See Kose et al. (2006) for a review of the evidence.

growth. It is the increased openness to trade that creates the basic stimulus for structural change in the formal segment and thus defines the role of foreign capital in a given country. The need to expand exports brings comparative advantage in labour-intensive industries into play and competition from imports generates pressures for technological change in import-substitution industries.

In theory, trade growth can also affect employment in the formal segment through its effect on output growth. It is widely believed that increased trade orientation has a stimulating effect on economic growth in developing countries. The theoretical arguments are well known: increased trade leads to higher labour productivity by promoting specialization, inducing realization of economies of scale and facilitating technological innovations. Empirically, however, the alleged positive effect of trade on growth has proved hard to establish. The evidence in fact suggests that increased trade has had quite varied effects on economic growth.[35]

Both trade growth and foreign capital inflow appear to have affected employment in the formal segment primarily by altering output structure and/or technology.[36] This leads us to expect the overall effect of trade growth (reflecting the combined effects of foreign capital and trade) on employment in the formal segment to have been varied across countries. In countries where trade growth mainly altered the output structure, we can expect the employment effect to have been positive; in countries where it mainly altered the technology, we can expect the employment effect to have been insignificant or negative.

The available empirical evidence does suggest that in the 1990s the effect of trade growth on employment in the formal segment was indeed varied rather than systematic. Figure 4.7 demonstrates the absence of a cross-country relationship (in the sample of countries represented in table 4.10) between change in trade–GDP ratio and change in employment in the formal segment. Figure 4.8 shows a positive but statistically insignificant relationship between change in trade–GDP ratio and change in the share of the formal segment in total employment.[37]

A comparison of the experiences of China and India with those of three Latin American countries (Costa Rica, El Salvador and Mexico) is illuminating. As seen above, during 1990–2003 the share of the formal segment in total employment declined in China and India while it increased in the three Latin American countries (table 4.7). On the other hand, labour productivity

---

[35] See Ghose (2003) and Jansen and Lee (2007) for reviews of the evidence.
[36] Technological change can sometimes result from within-industry restructuring set off by trade growth. Within an industry, enterprises that use advanced technology grow as they successfully enter export markets and survive competition from foreign firms in the domestic market, while low-productivity enterprises decline or close down. At the industry level, the effects of this type of restructuring are technological change and productivity growth.
[37] The few country-level studies that exist also show that the effect of trade liberalization on the degree of formality of employment has been varied. See Jansen and Lee (2007).

The global employment challenge

Figure 4.7   Trade growth and formal employment, 1990s

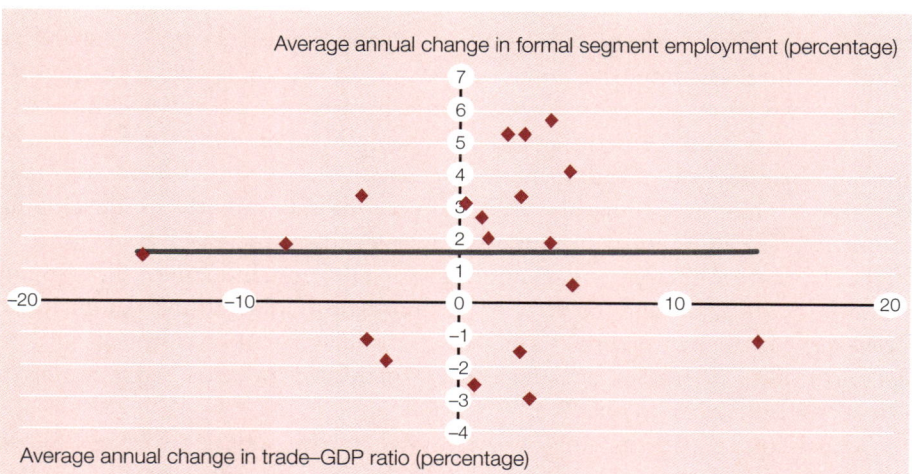

Sources: Derived from appendix table A4.1 and World Bank, World Development Indicators database (CD-ROM, 2005).

Figure 4.8   Trade growth and formal segment's share of total employment, 1990s

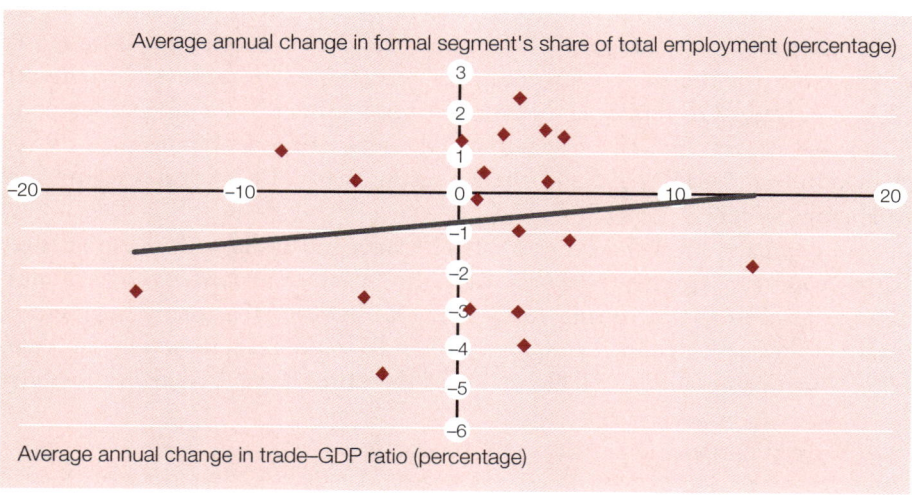

Sources: Derived from appendix table A4.1 and World Bank, World Development Indicators database (CD-ROM, 2005).

104

Table 4.11 Trade performance, selected economies, 1990s

Country	Exports as share of GDP		Agricultural exports as share of merchandise exports		Manufactured exports as share of merchandise exports		Net manufactured exports as share of total trade in manufactures	
	1990–92	2001–03	1990–92	2001–03	1990–92	2001–03	1990–92	2001–03
China	20.9	25.8	14.9	5.7	75.3	89.7	1.9	10.2
India	8.3	14.6	18.7	13.4	72.0	75.5	8.8	14.2
Costa Rica	34.5	43.6	65.1	34.6	25.3	63.8	−59.0	−26.6
El Salvador	17.3	26.3	54.6	34.5	41.9	56.8	−58.5	−58.1
Mexico	16.7	27.4	11.9	5.7	55.1	83.6	−23.0	−4.1

Sources: Derived from UNCTAD Handbook of Statistics online (http://stats.unctad.org/handbook/) and World Bank, World Development Indicators database (CD-ROM, 2005).

in the formal segment showed rapid growth in China and India, little change in Costa Rica, and decline in El Salvador and Mexico (table 4.10). All the countries rapidly expanded their export–GDP ratio as well as manufactured exports; Costa Rica and El Salvador actually transformed themselves from exporters of agricultural products into exporters of manufactures.

The striking difference between the Asian and the Latin American countries considered relates to the balance of trade in manufactures. This was positive for the former and negative for the latter (table 4.11), indicating that exports from the Latin American countries were far more import-intensive than those from the Asian countries. The most likely explanation is that while China and India have been increasing exports of final products, the three Latin American countries have been increasing exports of either intermediate products or final products that are assembled rather than produced. This suggests that while the growth of manufactured exports has been driven predominantly by domestic capital in China and India, in the three Latin American countries it has been driven largely by foreign capital.[38] At the same time, rapid growth of labour productivity in China and India, combined with stagnating employment, suggests capital deepening and technological change, while the stagnation of labour productivity in the Latin American countries, together with rapid growth of employment, suggests substantial change in

---

[38] In other words, the growth of export-oriented labour-intensive industries in Latin American countries seems to be linked to the growing phenomenon of slicing up the value chain. This involves slicing up the production of goods traditionally viewed as skill, capital, or technology intensive for the purpose of locating labour-intensive slices in low-wage economies.

The global employment challenge

output structure. Increased trade and capital inflow thus brought technological innovations and economies of scale to the two Asian countries and new labour-intensive industries to the three Latin American countries.

The non-formal segment in developing countries essentially produces non-tradable goods and services and does not receive inflows of foreign capital. As such, neither capital inflow nor trade growth has a direct impact on output and employment in the segment. However, trade growth is associated with a reallocation of investment from sectors producing non-tradable goods and services into sectors producing tradable goods and services, and this effectively means a reallocation of investment from the non-formal to the formal segment. The effect of this reallocation on investment in the non-formal segment depends on what happens to aggregate investment in the economy: if the latter remains unchanged or declines, investment (and hence output growth) in the non-formal segment declines. As it happens, trade growth in the 1990s tended to be associated with a decline in investment rate in a fairly large number of developing countries.[39] Thus trade growth appears to have been associated with a fall in investment in the non-formal segment in many cases, which leads us to expect that trade growth had an adverse effect on output per worker in the non-formal segment in many countries. The empirical evidence bears out the expectation. Figure 4.9 shows the cross-country relationship between change in trade–GDP ratio and change in output per worker in the non-formal segment. The relationship is inverse and statistically significant: trade growth appears to have had the effect of slowing down the growth of output per worker in the non-formal segment. The validity of the finding is further tested in Chapter 5. Here it needs to be emphasized that the adverse impact is attributable not to trade growth *per se* but to the failure of investment to rise along with trade growth. It seems that many governments adopted policies for trade promotion without paying much attention to investment in the economy, perhaps because they expected trade growth itself to lead to higher investment.

To sum up, the rapid growth of trade and capital flows in the 1990s produced rather mixed effects on employment in developing countries. In some countries they stimulated employment growth in the formal segment; in others they stimulated productivity growth rather than employment growth. On the other hand, trade growth was often accompanied by reduced investment in

---

[39] World Bank data (World Development Indicators database, CD-ROM, 2005) for 40 medium-income developing countries show that in about half of them the rate of investment declined between 1990–92 and 2001–03. The 40 countries are: Argentina*, Bolivia, Botswana*, Brazil*, Cameroon, Chile, China, Colombia*, Costa Rica*, Côte d'Ivoire, Dominican Republic, Ecuador, Egypt*, El Salvador, Ghana, Guatemala, Honduras, India, Indonesia*, Jamaica, Jordan*, Kenya*, Lebanon*, Malaysia*, Mauritius*, Mexico, Morocco, Nicaragua, Pakistan*, Panama, Paraguay*, Peru, Philippines*, Sri Lanka*, Swaziland*, Thailand*, Tunisia*, Turkey*, Uruguay* and Zimbabwe* (the countries that witnessed a decline in investment rate are marked with an asterisk).

Productive employment in developing countries

Figure 4.9 Trade growth and output per worker in non-formal segment, 1990s

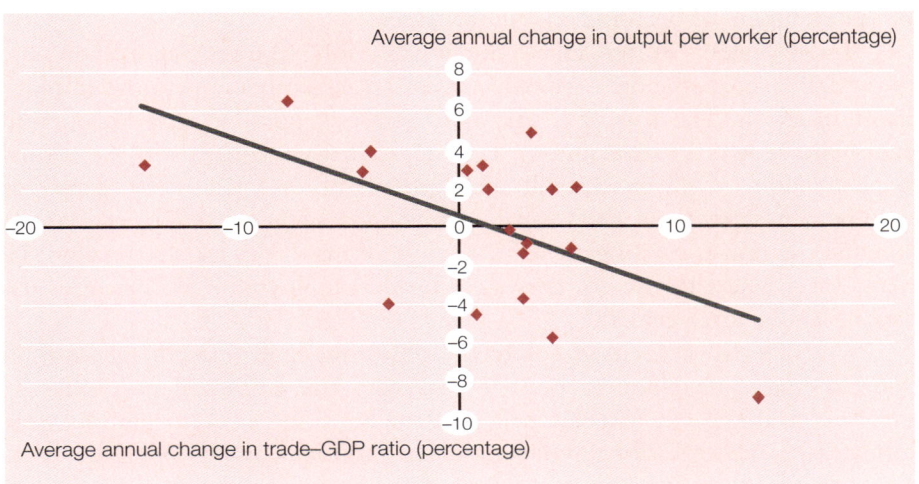

Notes: The regression equation is: Y = 0.627 − 0.398 X, R^2 = 0.330. The coefficient is significant at 1 per cent.
Based on data for the following 19 countries: Argentina, Botswana, Brazil, Chile, China, Costa Rica, Ecuador, Egypt, El Salvador, Honduras, India, Jamaica, Mexico, Myanmar, Nicaragua, Panama, Paraguay, Sri Lanka, Venezuela (Bolivarian Rep.).

Sources: Derived from table 4.8 and World Bank, World Development Indicators database (CD-ROM, 2005).

the economy and thus had an adverse effect on labour productivity (and hence on employment) in the non-formal segment.

4.7 Policy challenges

The challenge facing developing countries is not just one of productively absorbing the incremental labour force; it is also one of transferring masses of workers from less-than-full-time engagement in low-productivity activities to full-time employment in higher-productivity activities. Given the high rate of labour force growth with which they must contend, the challenge looks truly formidable.

Yet the experience of the 1990s shows that, with the right policies, the challenge can be met. It also suggests what these right policies are. Steady improvement in the employment situation in economies that are characterized by dualism and surplus labour requires simultaneous processes of rapid growth of employment in the formal segment and rapid decline in underemployment in the non-formal segment. Such simultaneous processes were rarely in evidence in developing countries in the 1990s. The employment situation improved where it did either because employment in the formal segment grew faster than the labour force or because underemployment in the non-formal segment declined; both developments occurred only in rare cases.

Improvement in the employment situation requires rapid economic growth, but rapid economic growth does not necessarily improve the employment situation. The reason is that it is perfectly possible to achieve rapid economic growth by focusing on labour productivity growth in the formal segment alone. Only rarely will such growth be associated with a rate of employment growth in the formal segment sufficient to reduce the labour force in the non-formal segment in absolute terms. Indeed, there may not be many cases where the rate of growth of formal employment even exceeds the rate of labour force growth.

Thus, policies focused solely on achieving high growth will not in general enable developing countries to meet the employment challenge. Growth strategies themselves will need to be designed with employment objectives in view. National policies will have to focus on achieving two basic employment objectives. First, the rate of employment growth in the formal segment must exceed the rate of labour force growth in the economy. This is necessary to ensure a steady process of movement of labour from the non-formal to the formal segment. Second, labour productivity in the non-formal segment must grow at a reasonable rate. This is necessary to ensure a steady decline in underemployment (and engagement in intrinsically low-productivity activities).

These imperatives define the policy challenges. In the first place, macroeconomic policies have to be concerned with ensuring adequate growth of investment in the economy. Monetary, fiscal and exchange rate policies need to be geared towards encouraging domestic investment and facilitating absorption of foreign capital without generating crowding-out effects. Neither trade growth nor foreign capital inflow can be seen as objectives in and of themselves. Moreover, merely freeing trade and capital flow does not stimulate investment. Trade growth and capital inflow can serve as effective instruments for bringing about beneficial structural change in output and employment only when they can be supported by domestic policies that stimulate investment.

Second, macroeconomic policies must also be concerned with ensuring an appropriate allocation of investment between formal and non-formal segments. Given the concentration of savings, skills and entrepreneurship in the formal segment, promotion of investment in the non-formal segment usually involves public investment as well as active efforts by governments to build institutions for channelling investment. Indeed, it requires defining explicit growth strategies for the non-formal segment together with plans for

Productive employment in developing countries

public investment in physical infrastructure and for creating or strengthening institutions for supplying credit to and upgrading technology and skills in small, micro- and household enterprises.[40]

The third important policy challenge is that of ensuring an appropriate combination of output growth and employment elasticity in the formal segment so that the rate of growth of formal employment exceeds the rate of labour force growth. Given the experience of the 1990s, when employment growth in the formal segment exceeded labour force growth in very few countries and there was "jobless growth" in the formal segment of a number of countries, ensuring fairly high employment elasticity in the formal segment must be a matter of prime concern. This, as past experience suggests, requires emphasis on restructuring of output in the formal segment designed to increase the share of labour-intensive products in total output.[41] Trade growth can obviously help, provided that policies for stimulating investment are in place. The question of appropriateness of the existing labour market regulations and institutions also becomes relevant in this context. It is necessary to ensure that they provide protection to workers without generating strong incentives for investment in capital- or technology-intensive products or for substitution of capital for labour.

The fact that substantial investment is required in both formal and non-formal segments implies that, in any given country, a minimum level of aggregate investment is required to implement a growth strategy that improves the employment situation. This minimum depends on the rate of labour force growth as well as on the initial distribution of workers between formal and non-formal segments.[42] Obviously, there is no reason to suppose that each individual developing country has the ability to finance this minimum level of aggregate investment. The least developed countries in particular have very low domestic saving rates (precisely because they are poor) and are not in a position to ensure a rate of investment required to improve the employment situation without external help.[43]

---

[40] It needs to be emphasized that a focus on household enterprises is critically important since it is the growth of productivity in self-employment that improves the employment situation of casual/irregular wage workers either by reducing underemployment or by increasing wages, or by doing both.

[41] For a given level of investment, there is a trade-off between employment growth and productivity growth in the formal segment. The required employment growth is well defined: it must exceed the labour force growth by a substantive margin. The productivity growth that can be achieved thus depends on the level of investment that is feasible.

[42] Ghose (2006) suggests a method of defining the minimum level of investment that is required to achieve the twin objectives of increasing the share of the formal segment in total employment and of increasing output per worker in the non-formal segment simultaneously.

[43] Data from the World Bank (World Development Indicators database, CD-ROM, 2005) show that the following 24 least developed countries had domestic saving rates of less than 10 per cent in 2003: Benin, Burkina Faso, Burundi, Cape Verde, Comoros, Congo (Dem. Rep.), Eritrea, Ethiopia, Guinea, Guinea-Bissau, Haiti, Lesotho, Liberia, Madagascar, Malawi, Mauritania, Niger, Rwanda, Sao Tome and Principe, Senegal, Sierra Leone, Tanzania (United Rep.), Timor-Leste and Togo. Ten of these countries actually had negative domestic saving rates.

This underlines the importance of international policy in enabling the poorer developing countries to meet the employment challenge. The growth of cross-border flows of private capital has not resulted in significant net resource flow to poorer countries. On the other hand, there is evidence to show that foreign aid did enable the poorer countries to sustain investment rates much above their domestic saving rates. If these countries are to meet the formidable employment challenge, therefore, international policy must ensure flows of adequate official aid for investment to them. It also needs to be emphasized that debt relief and humanitarian aid, important as they are, cannot be seen as substitutes for aid for investment.

The other issue of international policy relates to the problem of brain drain that restrains the growth of skill supply in a sizeable number of developing countries, particularly the poorer ones. It is hard for national governments to deal with this problem without arousing concerns about human rights. In this context, a framework international agreement is required. The basic objective here should be to transform brain drain into brain circulation that benefits both developing and developed countries. A possible way of achieving this objective is to develop a transparent system of fixed-term migration of high-skilled labour. For developing countries, this would mean temporary loss of high-skilled labour that would be compensated for when the migrants return with enhanced skills. And it would help developed countries to meet the growing demand for high-skilled labour without undermining the growth prospects of poorer developing countries.

Appendix table A4.1   Employment in formal segment, 1990–2003 (millions)

Country	1990	1991	1992	1993	1994	1995	1996	1997	1998	1999	2000	2001	2002	2003
Venezuela														
Total	–	–	–	–	3.61	3.79	3.78	4.21	4.18	3.28	3.34	3.51	3.33	3.27
					(49.5)	(49.1)	(47.9)	(49.6)	(47.4)	(37.5)	(37.3)	(36.3)	(34.1)	(32.7)
Male	–	–	–	–	2.33	2.42	2.41	2.69	2.65	1.99	2.03	2.11	1.98	1.92
					(46.5)	(46.3)	(45.5)	(48.4)	(46.7)	(35.6)	(35.4)	(35.2)	(32.8)	(31.3)
Female	–	–	–	–	1.28	1.37	1.37	1.53	1.53	1.28	1.31	1.40	1.35	1.35
					(56.3)	(54.7)	(52.6)	(51.8)	(48.6)	(41.0)	(40.6)	(38.0)	(36.0)	(35.0)
Argentina														
Total	–	–	–	–	–	–	–	–	4.10	4.07	4.00	3.93	3.95	3.89
									(49.8)	(49.5)	(48.5)	(48.3)	(49.0)	(44.1)
Male	–	–	–	–	–	–	–	–	2.54	2.48	2.42	2.34	2.21	2.07
									(50.6)	(50.0)	(49.0)	(48.6)	(47.2)	(40.8)
Female	–	–	–	–	–	–	–	–	1.56	1.60	1.58	1.58	1.74	1.81
									(48.6)	(48.8)	(47.8)	(47.9)	(51.5)	(48.4)
Botswana														
Total	0.21	0.23	0.22	0.23	0.23	0.23	0.24	0.23	0.24	0.26	0.27	0.27	0.28	–
					(50.9)	(50.4)			(48.9)		(50.3)	(49.8)		
Male	0.14	0.15	0.15	–	–	0.14	–	0.14	0.15	0.15	–	0.16	0.16	–
						(53.7)			(50.8)					
Female	0.07	0.08	0.08	–	–	0.09	–	0.09	0.09	0.10	–	0.11	0.12	–
						(46.0)			(46.3)					
Brazil														
Total	–	–	20.70	21.01	21.10	21.20	21.04	21.27	21.48	21.41	23.10	24.79	26.18	26.29
			(33.4)	(33.3)	(32.6)	(32.0)	(32.2)	(31.9)	(31.8)	(31.0)	(32.4)	(33.7)	(34.3)	(33.9)
Male	–	–	13.23	13.35	–	13.33	13.01	13.28	13.22	13.05	–	15.11	15.84	15.68
			(35.1)	(34.8)		(33.6)	(32.9)	(33.0)	(32.5)	(31.7)		(34.8)	(35.5)	(34.7)
Female	–	–	7.46	7.66	–	7.87	8.02	7.98	8.27	8.37	–	9.68	10.34	10.61
			(30.8)	(30.9)		(29.6)	(31.0)	(30.1)	(30.8)	(29.9)		(32.2)	(32.6)	(32.8)

Appendix table A4.1 Employment in formal segment, 1990–2003 (millions) (continued)

Country	1990	1991	1992	1993	1994	1995	1996	1997	1998	1999	2000	2001	2002	2003
Chile														
Total	1.75	1.88	2.00	2.07	2.15	2.26	2.27	2.38	2.48	2.50	2.51	2.59	2.66	2.73
	(39.8)	(40.4)	(41.0)	(41.7)	(42.3)	(43.7)	(43.0)	(44.8)	(46.5)	(46.3)	(46.2)	(46.1)	(46.0)	(45.9)
Male	1.22	–	1.41	–	1.48	–	1.52	–	1.63	–	1.66	–	–	1.77
	(40.9)		(42.9)		(43.6)		(43.6)		(47.7)		(47.7)			(47.4)
Female	0.53	–	0.59	–	0.67	–	0.75	–	0.84	–	0.86	–	–	0.96
	(37.4)		(37.1)		(39.8)		(42.0)		(44.3)		(43.5)			(43.4)
China														
Total	140.70	145.10	147.90	148.30	148.40	149.10	148.40	146.70	123.50	117.70	112.60	107.90	105.60	104.90
	(21.7)	(22.2)	(22.4)	(22.2)	(22.1)	(22.0)	(21.6)	(21.1)	(17.6)	(16.6)	(15.7)	(14.8)	(14.4)	(14.1)
Male	–	–	–	–	–	–	–	–	–	–	–	–	–	–
Female	–	–	–	–	–	–	–	–	–	–	–	–	–	–
Costa Rica														
Total	0.26	0.24	0.28	0.28	0.28	0.29	0.27	0.28	0.30	0.31	0.33	0.49	0.49	0.52
	(25.8)	(24.4)	(27.1)	(25.7)	(24.8)	(25.4)	(23.7)	(23.4)	(23.7)	(24.3)	(25.6)	(31.6)	(31.0)	(31.8)
Male	0.17	0.16	0.18	0.18	0.18	0.19	0.17	0.18	0.19	0.20	0.21	0.30	0.31	0.32
	(23.8)	(22.8)	(25.5)	(24.0)	(22.9)	(23.8)	(21.5)	(21.6)	(21.6)	(23.1)	(24.0)	(30.0)	(30.0)	(30.4)
Female	0.09	0.08	0.09	0.10	0.10	0.10	0.10	0.10	0.11	0.11	0.12	0.19	0.18	0.20
	(30.6)	(28.3)	(31.1)	(29.9)	(29.3)	(29.0)	(29.1)	(27.4)	(28.0)	(26.9)	(29.2)	(34.8)	(32.9)	(34.5)
Ecuador														
Total	0.88	1.05	1.04	1.02	1.00	1.08	1.10	1.12	1.14	1.14	1.22	1.26	1.26	1.30
											(24.0)	(22.3)	(23.1)	(24.5)
Male	0.60	0.73	–	–	0.67	0.73	–	–	0.75	0.77	0.79	0.82	0.85	0.85
											(24.3)	(24.0)		(25.8)
Female	0.28	0.33	–	–	0.33	0.36	–	–	0.39	0.37	0.43	0.44	0.42	0.45
											(23.5)	(19.7)		(22.6)
Egypt														
Total	1.60	1.63	1.65	1.68	1.70	1.73	1.61	1.51	1.45	–	–	–	–	–
	(10.6)	(11.2)	(11.1)	(11.3)	(11.0)	(11.1)	(10.0)	(9.1)	(8.6)					
Male	1.39	–	–	–	–	1.49	1.39	1.30	1.24	–	–	–	–	–
	(12.0)					(11.9)		(9.7)	(9.0)					
Female	0.21	–	–	–	–	0.23	0.22	0.21	0.21	–	–	–	–	–
	(6.0)					(7.7)		(6.8)	(6.8)					

	1	2	3	4	5	6	7	8	9	10	11	12	13	14
El Salvador														
Total	0.33	0.36	0.42	0.44 (23.8)	0.46 (23.3)	0.48 (23.6)	0.49 (24.2)	0.51 (25.2)	0.61 (28.2)	0.62 (28.1)	0.62 (27.2)	0.63 (26.9)	0.69 (29.2)	0.76 (31.0)
Male	0.22	0.23	0.27	—	0.29 (22.9)	0.30 (22.9)	—	0.32 (25.6)	0.37 (28.9)	0.37 (28.4)	0.37 (27.7)	0.38 (27.1)	0.37 (27.0)	0.41 (29.2)
Female	0.11	0.13	0.15	—	0.18 (24.0)	0.18 (24.9)	—	0.19 (24.5)	0.23 (27.2)	0.25 (27.6)	0.25 (26.5)	0.26 (26.7)	0.32 (32.2)	0.34 (33.4)
Honduras														
Total	0.28 (19.6)	0.30 (20.7)	0.34 (21.4)	0.35 (21.1)	0.35 (20.9)	0.36 (20.9)	0.39 (20.4)	0.41 (20.4)	0.42 (21.0)	0.43 (20.4)	0.46 (21.2)	0.48 (22.1)	0.35 (15.8)	0.44 (18.7)
Male	0.19 (18.6)	0.19 (18.9)	0.22 (20.0)	—	—	0.22 (18.8)	0.23 (18.0)	0.23 (18.0)	0.25 (18.5)	0.25 (18.3)	—	0.28 (19.0)	0.20 (13.0)	0.25 (16.4)
Female	0.09 (22.0)	0.11 (24.9)	0.13 (24.7)	—	—	0.13 (25.6)	0.16 (25.1)	0.17 (25.1)	0.18 (26.0)	0.19 (23.9)	—	0.20 (28.2)	0.16 (21.7)	0.19 (23.4)
India														
Total	26.35 (9.1)	26.73 (9.1)	27.06 (9.0)	27.18 (8.8)	27.38 (8.8)	27.53 (8.5)	27.94 (8.5)	28.25 (8.4)	28.17 (8.4)	28.11 (8.2)	27.96 (8.0)	27.79 (7.7)	27.21 (7.4)	27.00 (7.2)
Male	22.71 (10.5)	22.95 (10.4)	23.15 (10.3)	23.15 (10.1)	23.22 (9.9)	23.30 (9.6)	23.51 (9.5)	23.61 (9.4)	23.39 (9.3)	23.28 (9.1)	23.04 (8.8)	22.84 (8.5)	22.27 (8.1)	22.03 (7.9)
Female	3.64 (5.1)	3.78 (5.1)	3.91 (5.2)	4.03 (5.2)	4.15 (5.3)	4.23 (5.2)	4.43 (5.3)	4.64 (5.5)	4.77 (5.6)	4.83 (5.6)	4.92 (5.6)	4.95 (5.4)	4.94 (5.3)	4.97 (5.2)
Indonesia														
Total	—	—	—	—	—	—	—	—	—	—	—	26.58 (28.7)	25.05 (26.9)	24.15
Male	—	—	—	—	—	—	—	—	—	—	—	—	—	—
Female	—	—	—	—	—	—	—	—	—	—	—	—	—	—
Jamaica														
Total	—	—	—	—	—	—	—	—	0.15 (14.8)	0.14 (14.3)	0.14 (13.8)	0.13 (13.4)	0.13 (13.2)	—
Male	—	—	—	—	—	—	—	—	—	—	—	—	—	—
Female	—	—	—	—	—	—	—	—	—	—	—	—	—	—

Appendix table A4.1   Employment in formal segment, 1990–2003 (millions) (continued)

Country	1990	1991	1992	1993	1994	1995	1996	1997	1998	1999	2000	2001	2002	2003
Kenya														
Total	1.41	1.44	1.46	1.48	1.51 (13.2)	1.56	1.61	1.65	1.66	1.67	1.68	–	–	–
Male	1.10	1.12	1.11	1.13	1.13 (18.1)	1.15	1.15	1.14	–	–	–	–	–	–
Female	0.31	0.32	0.35	0.34	0.38 (7.3)	0.41	0.46	0.50	–	–	–	–	–	–
Mexico														
Total	5.71	5.88 (19.6)	7.21 (23.1)	7.39 (22.8)	7.28 (22.1)	7.18 (21.3)	7.63 (21.8)	8.35 (22.5)	9.59 (25.3)	9.92 (25.6)	10.38 (26.2)	10.27 (25.7)	10.34 (25.3)	8.93 (21.7)
Male	3.74	3.81 (18.2)	4.70	4.80 (21.5)	–	4.57 (20.5)	4.82 (20.8)	5.31 (22.0)	6.08	6.31	6.55 (25.8)	6.41 (25.2)	6.46 (24.9)	5.59 (21.3)
Female	1.97	2.06 (23.0)	2.52	2.59 (25.8)	–	2.61 (24.0)	2.81 (25.1)	3.04 (24.4)	3.51	3.60	3.83 (29.1)	3.86 (29.0)	3.88 (28.6)	3.34 (24.0)
Nicaragua														
Total	–	–	–	0.19 (16.5)	0.19 (15.9)	0.19 (15.3)	0.19 (14.6)	0.19 (13.7)	0.21 (14.5)	0.24 (16.3)	0.32 (20.7)	0.26 (16.6)	0.27 (16.8)	0.47
Male	–	–	–	0.12	–	0.11	0.11	0.11	0.12	0.14	0.19	0.14	0.15	0.28
Female	–	–	–	0.08	–	0.07 (12.9) (21.1)	0.08 (12.3) (20.6)	0.08 (11.2) (19.8)	0.09 (11.6) (22.1)	0.10	0.14	0.12	0.12	0.19
Panama														
Total	–	0.24 (32.9)	0.28 (36.1)	0.30 (37.2)	0.32 (38.4)	0.32 (37.3)	0.32 (36.8)	0.34 (37.7)	0.35 (37.5)	0.36 (37.5)	0.35 (37.0)	0.38 (36.8)	0.39 (34.7)	0.39 (32.2)
Male	–	0.14 (27.6)	0.17 (31.6)	0.18 (32.3)	0.19 (34.2)	0.20 (33.6)	0.19 (32.8)	0.21 (34.1)	0.21 (34.0)	0.22 (34.0)	0.21 (33.1)	0.23 (33.)	0.23 (31.2)	0.23 (30.8)
Female	–	0.10 (44.5)	0.11 (46.3)	0.12 (47.9)	0.13 (47.3)	0.13 (45.1)	0.13 (45.2)	0.14 (44.7)	0.14 (44.4)	0.14 (44.4)	0.14 (44.8)	0.15 (44.6)	0.16 (41.5)	0.16 (40.6)
Paraguay														
Total	–	–	–	–	0.28	0.30 (14.2)	0.31 (14.9)	0.33 (15.9)	0.34 (16.9)	0.37 (17.7)	0.37 (16.7)	0.36 (15.8)	0.32 (15.1)	0.34 (15.1)
Male	–	–	–	–	0.18	0.21 (16.4)	0.20	–	0.23 (17.2)	0.25 (18.8)	–	0.22 (15.7)	0.20 (14.8)	0.21 (15.4)
Female	–	–	–	–	0.10	0.10 (11.1)	0.11	–	0.12 (16.3)	0.12 (15.8)	–	0.14 (15.9)	0.12 (15.6)	0.13 (14.6)

Productive employment in developing countries

South Africa															
Total	–	–	–	–	–	–	–	5.14 (34.9)	5.24 (36.5)	5.16 (36.0)	4.97 (35.1)	4.87 (34.2)	4.72 (33.0)	–	–
Male	0.76 (11.7)	–	–	–	–	–	–	–	–	–	–	–	–	–	–
	0.43 (9.4)														
	0.34 (16.8)														
Female	–	–	–	–	–	–	–	–	–	–	–	–	–	–	–
Sri Lanka															
Total	0.80 (12.1)	0.65 (9.6)	0.73 (10.7)	0.79 (11.6)	0.95 (13.5)	1.09 (15.1)	0.84 (11.5)	0.99 (13.2)	0.87 (11.4)	1.03 (13.3)	1.01 (12.9)	0.82 (10.5)	0.92 (11.7)		
Male	0.45 (9.9)	0.35 (7.5)	0.38 (8.0)	0.41 (8.6)	0.49 (10.0)	0.57 (11.4)	0.47 (9.2)	0.55 (10.5)	0.47 (8.9)	0.53 (9.9)	0.53 (9.7)	0.48 (8.8)	0.49 (8.8)		
Female	0.35 (16.9)	0.30 (14.2)	0.35 (16.5)	0.38 (18.4)	0.46 (21.7)	0.52 (23.8)	0.37 (16.9)	0.44 (19.3)	0.39 (17.1)	0.50 (21.2)	0.47 (20.4)	0.34 (14.7)	0.43 (19.0)		
Swaziland															
Total	0.09 (36.2)	0.09 (35.2)	0.09 (34.3)	0.09 (33.1)	0.09 (31.5)	0.09 (30.6)	0.09 (31.0)	–	–	–	–	–	–	–	–
Male	–	–	–	0.07 (37.9)	0.06 (34.5)	0.06 (34.0)	0.06 (34.0)	–	–	–	–	–	–	–	–
Female	–	–	–	0.03 (28.0)	0.03 (26.3)	0.03 (24.4)	0.03 (25.6)	–	–	–	–	–	–	–	–
Uruguay															
Total	–	–	–	–	–	–	–	0.55	0.59	0.57	0.56	0.50	0.47	0.46 (42.9)	
Male	–	–	–	–	–	–	–	0.34	0.36	0.35	0.34	0.29	0.27	0.26 (42.9)	
Female	–	–	–	–	–	–	–	0.21	0.23	0.23	0.23	0.20	0.20	0.20 (42.9)	
Zimbabwe															
Total	1.19 (28.0)	1.24 (28.2)	1.24 (27.0)	1.24 (26.3)	1.26 (26.1)	1.24 (25.0)	1.27 (25.1)	1.32 (25.6)	1.35 (25.9)	1.32 (25.2)	1.24 (23.2)	1.18 (29.7)	1.07 (19.5)	–	–
Male	0.98 (43.5)	1.02 (43.4)	1.01 (41.6)	1.00 (39.7)	1.01 (39.1)	0.98 (37.1)	1.00 (36.9)	1.04 (37.3)	1.05 (37.4)	1.02 (36.0)	0.95 (32.3)	0.90 (29.7)	0.82 (26.6)	–	–
Female	0.21 (10.7)	0.23 (11.0)	0.22 (10.5)	0.24 (11.1)	0.25 (11.3)	0.26 (11.1)	0.27 (11.5)	0.29 (12.0)	0.30 (12.4)	0.29 (12.4)	0.29 (12.1)	0.29 (11.7)	0.26 (10.5)	–	–

Appendix table A4.1 Employment in formal segment, 1990–2003 (millions) (continued)

Country	1990	1991	1992	1993	1994	1995	1996	1997	1998	1999	2000	2001	2002	2003
Madagascar														
Total	0.28 (5.2)	0.29 (5.1)	–	0.32 (5.3)	0.32 (5.3)	0.34 (5.4)	–	–	–	–	–	–	–	–
Male	–	–	–	–	–	–	–	–	–	–	–	–	–	–
Female	–	–	–	–	–	–	–	–	–	–	–	–	–	–
Malawi														
Total	0.47 (10.5)	0.56 (12.2)	0.55 (11.7)	0.58 (12.3)	0.65 (13.6)	0.70 (14.5)	–	–	–	–	–	–	–	–
Male	0.39 (17.6)	0.46 (20.4)	0.45 (19.3)	0.48 (20.4)	0.51 (21.1)	0.55 (22.8)	–	–	–	–	–	–	–	–
Female	0.08 (3.5)	0.10 (4.2)	0.09 (4.0)	0.10 (4.2)	0.14 (5.9)	0.15 (6.1)	–	–	–	–	–	–	–	–
Mali														
Total	–	–	–	–	–	–	–	–	0.05 (1.0)	0.06 (1.1)	0.06 (1.2)	–	–	–
Male	–	–	–	–	–	–	–	–	–	–	–	–	–	–
Female	–	–	–	–	–	–	–	–	–	–	–	–	–	–
Myanmar														
Total	1.51 (7.9)	–	–	–	–	1.25 (6.4)	1.33 (6.3)	1.41 (6.4)	–	–	–	–	–	–
Male	–	–	–	–	–	0.83	0.86	0.91	–	–	–	–	–	–
Female	–	–	–	–	–	0.42	0.47	0.50	–	–	–	–	–	–

Note: Figures in parentheses show formal employment as percentage of total employment.
– = data not available.
Sources: ILO–LABORSTA database (http://laborsta.ilo.org/); data supplied by ILO–SIAL (Panama); China Statistical Yearbook (CD-ROM, 2004 and 2005); Ghose (2005a); Collier (2006).

Appendix table A4.2   Value added[a] per worker in non-formal segment, 1990–2003

Country	1990	1991	1992	1993	1994	1995	1996	1997	1998	1999	2000	2001	2002	2003
Algeria	–	–	–	–	–	–	–	18.9	–	–	18.3	19.4	–	–
Iran	–	–	–	–	–	–	70.2	–	–	–	–	–	–	–
Saudi Arabia	–	–	–	–	–	–	–	–	–	62.3	55.0	57.7	54.9	–
Trinidad and Tobago	75.6	77.2	77.5	75.8	67.0	68.7	67.9	70.9	81.5	79.1	72.6	74.6	79.7	–
Venezuela	27.1	31.5	34.0	35.2	37.5	38.8	32.3	32.5	35.7	32.3	29.3	31.1	25.7	–
Argentina	–	–	–	–	–	–	–	–	30.9	30.0	29.4	28.8	21.1	20.1
Bolivia	–	–	–	–	–	–	–	–	–	–	5.4	–	–	–
Botswana	–	–	–	–	–	17.4	–	–	18.7	–	19.7	21.2	–	–
Brazil	7.3	7.3	6.5	6.4	6.8	7.2	8.4	8.4	8.5	8.4	8.6	7.4	7.5	–
Chile	796.1	847.2	938.3	1 031.1	1 057.6	1 151.0	1 221.7	1 221.1	1 267.2	1 212.4	1 231.0	1 228.4	1 211.1	1 183.2
China	1.5	1.4	1.4	1.5	1.8	2.0	2.2	2.2	2.2	2.2	2.2	2.3	2.5	–
Costa Rica	0.6	0.5	0.5	0.5	0.6	0.6	0.6	0.6	0.6	0.6	0.5	0.5	0.5	0.6
Cuba	–	–	–	–	1.2	1.2	1.4	1.3	1.2	1.4	1.5	–	–	–
Dominican Republic	–	–	–	–	–	–	28.4	29.3	30.1	30.8	31.9	33.0	33.6	–
Ecuador	–	–	–	–	–	–	–	–	–	–	2.5	2.7	2.9	3.1
Egypt	4.3	5.1	4.0	4.6	4.6	4.9	5.4	5.6	6.2	6.5	6.4	6.7	7	–
El Salvador	–	–	–	1.5	1.6	1.8	1.8	1.9	1.8	1.7	1.6	1.5	1.5	1.6
Ghana	–	–	0.8	–	–	–	–	–	–	–	0.9	–	–	–
Guatemala	–	–	–	–	–	–	–	–	0.9	0.9	0.9	0.9	0.8	–
Honduras	1.5	2.0	1.8	1.9	2.1	1.9	1.8	2.0	1.7	1.3	1.4	1.3	1.1	–
India	13.4	13.4	13.6	14.0	14.5	14.1	15.5	15.3	16.2	16.3	15.7	–	–	–
Indonesia	4 261.5	–	–	–	–	6 616.6	6 419.8	6 337.7	6 003.6	6 625.4	5 161.4	5 554.6	5 844.5	–
Jamaica	–	–	75.4	73.2	81.5	88.5	84.4	85.3	83.1	81.1	73.3	72.7	70.0	63.3
Malaysia	12.5	13.8	14.9	16.2	17.6	18.1	18.5	19.3	17.2	17.0	16.3	17.0	17.3	17.5
Mexico	–	11.6	10.3	9.5	10.0	9.5	10.7	10.2	10.8	9.6	9.7	9.5	9.0	9.5
Mongolia	–	–	825.4	848.6	866.9	950.2	1 107.6	904.1	928.6	926.3	754.1	637.4	566.2	586.3

Appendix table A4.2 Value added[a] per worker in non-formal segment, 1990–2003 (continued)

Country	1990	1991	1992	1993	1994	1995	1996	1997	1998	1999	2000	2001	2002	2003
Namibia	–	–	–	–	–	–	–	10.6	–	–	13.1	–	–	–
Nicaragua	15.9	15.8	15.9	15.4	9.2	10.0	10.6	9.7	9.1	8.3	8.3	7.9	–	–
Pakistan	37.0	42.7	44.9	42.7	41.9	47.5	47.1	51.4	48.5	48.0	46.2	42.7	47.4	–
Panama	–	3.2	3.3	3.4	3.8	3.6	3.5	3.8	4.3	4.1	4.4	4.4	4.4	4.5
Paraguay	–	–	–	–	–	451.8	–	–	492.6	486.5	458.7	438.5	471.7	464.1
Philippines	16.2	15.1	15.2	14.9	15.7	15.7	16.1	15.7	14.0	15.0	14.8	13.3	–	–
South Africa	–	–	–	–	–	–	–	–	–	20.2	14.5	24.8	24.4	25.5
Sri Lanka	48.0	58.1	54.8	61.8	57.1	64.9	68.1	65.3	57.7	60.7	63.2	65.0	72.5	72.7
Thailand	12.9	14.9	15.4	12.6	14.6	17.4	18.6	17.8	18.2	17.5	17.1	18.4	19.6	23.1
Turkey	1 657.4	1 390.3	1 516.0	1 910.7	1 596.9	1 709.4	1 905.6	1 854.3	2 301.2	1 934.7	2 271.4	1 684.0	2 004.0	2 271.2
Uruguay	–	–	–	–	–	–	–	–	–	–	–	–	–	0.1
Viet Nam	–	–	–	–	–	–	2 407.8	2 589.7	2 758.9	2 784.1	2 645.4	2 684.6	2 854.4	3 053.3
Bangladesh	–	–	–	–	–	–	13.3	–	–	–	15.2	–	–	–
Belize	–	–	–	14.2	14.9	12.9	12.0	11.0	13.0	12.5	–	–	–	–
Myanmar	2.6	2.6	2.6	2.8	3.0	3.0	3.0	3.3	3.4	3.7	–	–	–	–
Tanzania	–	60.7	–	–	–	–	–	–	–	–	–	61.4	–	–
Uganda	–	–	332.6	365.0	367.7	–	–	–	–	–	–	–	–	443.5

– = data not available.

Sources: Derived from ILO-LABORSTA/KILM database (http://laborsta.ilo.org/) and World Bank, World Development Indicators database (CD-ROM, 2005).

Appendix table A4.3 Employment Situation Index (ESI), 1990–2003

Country	1990	1991	1992	1993	1994	1995	1996	1997	1998	1999	2000	2001	2002	2003
Venezuela	–	–	–	–	1.00	1.01	0.93	0.96	0.97	0.86	0.83	0.85	0.77	0.84
Argentina	–	–	–	–	–	–	–	–	1.00	0.98	0.97	0.95	0.86	–
Botswana	–	–	–	–	–	1.00	–	–	1.02	–	1.07	1.01	–	–
Brazil	–	–	1.00	0.99	1.00	1.02	1.08	1.07	1.07	1.05	1.08	1.04	1.05	–
Chile	1.00	1.03	1.08	1.12	1.13	1.19	1.21	1.21	1.25	1.22	1.23	1.23	1.22	1.21
China	1.00	1.00	1.00	1.02	1.07	1.12	1.15	1.15	1.10	1.09	1.07	1.08	1.10	–
Costa Rica	1.00	0.90	0.97	0.97	0.99	1.00	0.96	0.96	0.98	0.94	0.92	1.07	1.05	1.10
Ecuador	–	–	–	–	–	–	–	–	–	–	1.00	1.00	1.03	1.07
Egypt	1.00	1.08	0.99	1.03	1.02	1.05	1.06	1.06	1.09	–	–	–	–	–
El Salvador	–	–	–	1.00	1.05	1.09	1.09	1.12	1.13	1.11	1.09	1.06	1.09	1.13
Honduras	1.00	1.13	1.11	1.13	1.18	1.11	1.10	1.13	1.07	0.97	1.00	0.99	0.83	–
India	1.00	1.00	1.00	1.01	1.02	1.00	1.03	1.03	1.04	1.04	1.02	–	–	–
Jamaica	–	–	–	–	–	–	–	–	1.00	0.98	0.94	0.93	0.91	–
Mexico	–	1.00	1.02	0.99	0.99	0.96	1.01	1.01	1.07	1.05	1.06	1.05	1.03	0.98
Nicaragua	–	–	–	1.00	0.85	0.85	0.86	0.83	0.84	0.86	0.95	0.85	–	–
Panama	–	1.00	1.05	1.07	1.13	1.09	1.07	1.12	1.16	1.14	1.15	1.18	1.17	1.18
Paraguay	–	–	–	–	–	–	–	–	1.00	1.01	0.97	0.93	0.93	0.94
Sri Lanka	1.00	1.08	0.99	1.07	1.06	1.18	1.25	1.13	1.13	1.10	1.18	1.18	1.16	1.19
Myanmar	1.00	–	–	–	–	0.99	0.98	–	1.04	–	–	–	–	–

– = data not available.

Sources: Derived from tables A4.1 and A4.2, ILO-LABORSTA database (http://laborsta.ilo.org/), data supplied by ILO-SIAL (Panama), China Statistical Yearbook (CD-ROM, 2004 and 2005), Ghose (2005a) and Collier (2006).

Appendix table A4.4 Employment and unemployment by gender

Country	Year	Unemployment rate		Structure of employment						
				Male			Female			
		Male	Female	Formal wage employment as percentage of total employment	Self-employment as percentage of total employment	Casual/irregular wage employment as percentage of total employment	Formal wage employment as percentage of total employment	Self-employment as percentage of total employment	Casual/irregular wage employment as percentage of total employment
Algeria	2003	23.4	25.4	–	35.19	–	–	33.83	–
Iran	1996	8.5	13.4	–	45.24	–	–	41.35	–
Trinidad and Tobago	1990	17.9	24.2	–	26.09	–	–	22.54	–
	2002	7.8	14.5	–	24.71	–	–	16.83	–
Venezuela	1995	8.7	13.3	46.32	–	–	54.74	–	–
	2003	14.4	20.3	31.28	–	–	34.97	–	–
Argentina	1998	11.8	14.2	50.61	30.03	19.36	48.59	24.42	26.99
	2003	14.2	16.5	40.83	33.52	25.65	48.43	21.04	30.53
Bolivia	2000	3.6	5.6	–	44.81	–	–	56.72	–
Botswana	1998	18.5	23.5	50.80	27.79	21.41	46.30	25.19	28.51
Brazil	2003	7.8	12.3	34.66	39.90	25.44	32.83	35.15	32.02
Cameroon	1996	9.5	6.5	–	74.79	–	–	93.03	–
	2001	8.2	6.7	–	66.50	–	–	88.89	–
Chile	1998	9.1	11.3	47.70	32.59	19.71	44.30	27.25	28.45
	2003	8.3	12.2	47.39	34.30	18.31	43.43	26.82	29.75
Colombia	2004	11.4	18.1	21.42	–	–	24.46	–	–
Costa Rica	1990	4.0	5.8	23.83	32.93	43.24	30.62	22.34	47.04
	2004	5.4	8.4	31.49	32.19	36.32	34.28	29.37	36.35
Dominican Republic	1996	10.4	27.8	–	45.20	–	–	29.72	–
	2004	10.4	30.6	–	–	–	–	–	–
Ecuador	2004	5.8	10.6	26.76	37.77	35.47	21.54	47.72	30.74

Productive employment in developing countries

Country	Year								
Egypt	1998	5.1	19.9	9.02	40.44	50.54	6.83	39.34	53.83
El Salvador	1995	8.1	5.6	22.91	38.97	38.12	24.91	48.85	26.24
	2004	8.7	3.9	27.55	34.33	38.12	31.71	48.10	20.19
Guatemala	2002	1.6	2.3	–	58.35	–	–	63.96	–
Honduras	1996	4.3	4.4	17.99	54.20	27.81	25.09	52.09	22.82
	2004	4.8	8.3	18.54	52.88	28.58	26.72	50.02	23.26
India	1994	3.7	3.1	9.93	52.60	37.47	5.26	49.00	45.74
	2000	4.2	3.9	8.84	50.90	40.26	5.56	48.30	46.14
Indonesia	1996	3.3	5.0	–	–	–	–	–	–
Jamaica	1998	10.0	22.1	–	45.10	–	–	33.97	–
	2004	8.1	15.7	–	41.98	–	–	34.06	–
Malaysia	1995	2.8	3.8	–	27.51	–	–	27.06	–
	2002	3.3	3.8	–	23.59	–	–	22.74	–
Mauritius	1995	4.0	7.2	59.57	21.20	19.23	70.37	14.46	15.17
Mexico	1991	2.5	4.2	18.16	47.13	34.71	23.02	38.40	38.58
	2004	2.6	3.2	21.58	37.16	41.26	24.23	37.95	37.82
Morocco	2003	11.5	13.0	–	56.00	–	–	65.01	–
Namibia	2000	28.3	39.0	–	30.11	–	–	42.18	–
Nicaragua	1993	4.9	33.7	13.83	–	–	23.33	–	–
	1998	8.8	14.5	11.58	–	–	22.06	–	–
Pakistan	1995	3.7	14.0	–	64.58	–	–	75.21	–
	2002	6.2	16.4	–	59.68	–	–	62.88	–
Panama	1992	10.8	22.3	31.60	43.07	25.33	46.34	16.50	37.16
	2004	9.0	16.4	32.97	39.02	28.01	39.77	25.11	35.12
Paraguay	1999	6.1	7.5	18.80	–	–	15.80	–	–
	2004	5.9	9.5	14.86	–	–	13.23	–	–
Philippines	2001	9.4	10.3	–	50.25	–	–	52.09	–
South Africa	2002	26.9	35.1	–	18.03	–	–	20.64	–
Sri Lanka	1990	9.1	23.6	9.44	–	–	16.75	–	–
	2003	6.2	14.7	8.77	42.60	48.63	18.98	40.40	40.62

Appendix table A4.4 Employment and unemployment by gender (continued)

Country	Year	Unemployment rate		Structure of employment					
		Male	Female	Male			Female		
				Formal wage employment as percentage of total employment	Self-employment as percentage of total employment	Casual/irregular wage employment as percentage of total employment	Formal wage employment as percentage of total employment	Self-employment as percentage of total employment	Casual/irregular wage employment as percentage of total employment
Thailand	1990	2.0	2.4	–	69.02	–	–	74.44	–
	2004	1.6	1.4	–	55.37	–	–	56.90	–
Turkey	1998	6.9	6.8	–	49.39	–	–	69.17	–
	2004	10.5	9.7	–	44.99	–	–	60.71	–
Uruguay	2003	10.2	16.6	42.89	34.48	22.63	42.92	23.65	33.43
Viet Nam	1996	3.1	2.3	–	79.42	–	–	86.13	–
	2004	1.9	2.4	–	70.22	–	–	78.84	–
Zimbabwe	1999	7.3	4.6	38.84	–	–	12.95	–	–
Bangladesh	1996	2.7	2.2	–	17.48	–	–	77.47	–
	2000	3.2	3.3	–	10.36	–	–	73.30	–
Cambodia	2001	1.4	2.0	–	80.83	–	–	86.31	–
Madagascar	2002	3.5	5.6	–	81.34	–	–	87.35	–
Malawi	1998	1.2	0.6	–	78.78	–	–	95.19	–
Maldives	1995	0.6	1.3	–	61.66	–	–	50.74	–
	2000	1.6	2.7	–	60.69	–	–	39.59	–
Rwanda	1996	0.8	0.3	–	88.94	–	–	95.56	–
Yemen	1999	12.5	8.2	–	36.48	–	–	24.32	–

– = data not available.

Sources: Derived from table A4.1, ILO-LABORSTA database (http://laborsta.ilo.org/), data supplied by ILO-SIAL (Panama), China Statistical Yearbook (CD-ROM, 2004 and 2005), Ghose (2005a) and Collier (2006)

THE EMPLOYMENT–POVERTY INTERFACE IN DEVELOPING COUNTRIES

5

5.1 Reducing global poverty

Poverty in developing countries has become a global concern and poverty reduction is now a recognized objective of international policy. In 2000, meeting at the Millennium Summit organized by the United Nations, world leaders set the goal of halving by 2015 the 1990 level of poverty in the developing world. World Bank estimates showed that in 1990 nearly 30 per cent of the population of the developing world (around 1.3 billion people) lived in poverty.[44] Accordingly, the objective set at the Millennium Summit was to bring this proportion down to 15 per cent by the year 2015.

But how is poverty to be reduced? The Millennium Development Goal of halving poverty does not incorporate policy recommendations, either for the international community or for national governments.[45] It would be wildly optimistic to suppose that poverty could be rapidly reduced simply through international transfers. In the first place, foreign aid resources that are currently available are much too inadequate to make possible substantial transfers to the poor,[46] and it is far from certain that we can expect a dramatic increase in

---

[44] For the purpose of this estimate, developing world included other high-income as well as CEE and CIS countries. Poverty means "extreme poverty" defined as a level of expenditure per person per day of 1 Purchasing Power Parity dollar (PPP$) in 1985 prices. Subsequently, "extreme poverty" was redefined by the World Bank as a level of expenditure per person per day of PPP$1.08 in 1993 prices (Chen and Ravallion, 2004a). This was found to be representative of the national poverty lines actually used by some of the lowest-income countries of the world.

[45] A more recent document (UNMP, 2005) proposes a wide-ranging set of programmes that need to be implemented through collaborative efforts by national and local governments, civil society organizations and international donor agencies.

[46] Besley and Burgess (2003) show that foreign aid and debt forgiveness on offer are woefully inadequate for poverty reduction on any significant scale.

these resources in the near future. Second, if poverty is to be reduced through this route, foreign aid resources would need to be committed for years to come (since transfers must be recurrent) and it is hard to see such commitments forthcoming. Third, even if aid were substantially augmented and committed for an indefinite period, distributing internationally available resources to poor persons would be an undertaking whose enormity defies imagination.

In debates and discussions on poverty, the dominant proposition is that economic growth reduces poverty. The proposition is attractive for obvious reasons. If it were valid, then all attention could be focused on promoting growth. International policy debates could thus simply focus on how developing countries could achieve growth, and international resources could be used to promote economic growth in countries with a high incidence of poverty.

The arguments and evidence cited in support of the proposition are as follows. It is tautologically true that if the average income in a country rises while distributional inequality remains unchanged, poverty will decline. Many economists have concluded from the evidence of past experiences that growth does not have any systematic effect on distributional inequality. It follows that, on average, growth reduces poverty. And many economists claim to have shown empirically that poverty indeed declines with economic growth.

These findings can be questioned on methodological and empirical grounds, as we shall see below. What is important to note here is that the proposition itself does not imply a denial of growth being associated with rising distributional inequality, and hence with unchanging or rising poverty, in some instances. This means that unless we know the specificities of situations in which growth might or might not be associated with rising distributional inequality, we are not in a position to argue that promoting growth will reduce poverty in any particular developing country. Thus the proposition does not in fact provide a good basis for contemplating poverty reduction policies.

To put it differently, in thinking about policy it is not enough to know that, more often than not, growth reduces poverty; we need to know why growth can be expected to reduce it. In other words, we need to know the channels and mechanisms through which growth reduces poverty, if it indeed does reduce it. These questions have yet to be asked and answered. Yet in current debates the poverty-reducing attribute of growth is taken for granted so that the focus is on what nurtures or obstructs economic growth in developing countries. It is precisely with respect to this approach that some of the established ideas are being challenged. One part of the traditional view – namely, that growth occurs through accumulation of physical and human capital – is not in dispute. It is the other part – that a stable macroeconomic

The employment–poverty interface in developing countries

> **Box 5.1   Strategies for poverty reduction: The shift in focus**
>
> The contrasting perspectives presented in the two Reports on poverty produced by the World Bank (1990, 2000) reflect the shift in views. The 1990 Report proposes a strategy of poverty reduction that has two elements: "The first element is to promote the productive use of the poor's most abundant asset – labour. ... The second is to provide basic social services to the poor" (World Bank, 1990, p. 3). In the 2000 Report, issues of governance take centre stage: creation of a "sound business environment" for all types of private entrepreneurs (including poor households), ensuring "good quality service delivery through institutional action involving sound governance and the use of markets and multiple agents", "a range of institutional and participatory approaches" aimed at "getting infrastructure and knowledge to poor areas", "transparent institutions, with democratic and participatory mechanisms for making decisions and monitoring their implementation, backed up by legal systems that foster economic growth and promote legal equity", creation of "public administrations that foster growth and equity", promotion of "inclusive decentralization and community development", and so on, are now listed as main recipes for poverty reduction (World Bank, 2000, pp. 8–11).

environment is what nurtures accumulation – that is being questioned. Indeed, factors traditionally viewed as manifestations of underdevelopment – flawed social and political institutions, unfavourable "climate" for establishing and running modern businesses, widespread corruption and so on – are now regarded as primary obstacles to accumulation and growth in developing countries. The corollary is that developing countries, irrespective of their level of development, need to acquire a certain (undefined) level of "governance capability" before they can hope to achieve growth and thus begin to reduce poverty (see box 5.1). It also follows that international resources cannot be of much help until and unless these conditions are met. So we reach a conundrum.

This being the context, it is of some importance to refocus attention on channels and mechanisms through which growth affects poverty. This chapter attempts to do this by arguing that poverty is rooted in the employment problem typical of developing countries and that economic growth reduces poverty only in so far as it addresses the employment problem. Intuitively, these propositions would appear to be self-evidently valid.[47] In situations

---

[47] The surprise is that these arguments have received such scant attention in the very large literature on poverty. It has been argued, of course, that growth needs to be employment intensive if it is to reduce poverty. But what exactly is employment-intensive growth? How do we measure it? And how can it be achieved?

where institutionalized social security systems do not exist and some people have abysmally low incomes, it follows that this must be because they have low-quality employment or no employment at all. If in these circumstances economic growth reduces poverty, then it must do so either by improving the quality of employment of the poor or by generating fresh employment opportunities for them.

These growth–employment–poverty linkages are not very easy to verify empirically, however, as we cannot look for straightforward empirical regularities linking the three. The problem is that satisfactory statistical indicators of employment in developing countries are not readily available (as shown in Chapter 4). Given the inadequacies of statistical data currently available, even imperfect indicators can at present be developed for only a small number of countries. Under the circumstances, conclusive results are beyond our reach; we can hope only to establish a framework for analysis and use this to examine some illustrative evidence.

In the discussion that follows, the focus is on extreme poverty, i.e., the percentage of the population living on less than 1.08 Purchasing Power Parity dollars (PPP$) (in 1993 prices) per person per day.[48] We also choose to focus only on medium-income developing and least developed countries.[49] The analysis proceeds in four steps. In the first step, an effort is made to assess the trends in the incidence of poverty in the 1990s. The next step is to ascertain whether the observed trends are related to the trends in real GDP per capita. The third step discusses the specific sense in which employment can be regarded as a key link between growth and poverty in developing countries, and examines the relevant empirical evidence. Finally, in the light of these discussions, we explore the following issue of current interest. In an era of globalization, the idea that growth reduces poverty has also led naturally to the idea that increased trade openness is poverty reducing, since there are reasons to believe that increased trade openness stimulates growth. Yet many commentators have expressed concern that trade-led growth at best leaves the poor behind and at worst causes them harm. Such contrasting views call for a probe into whether the growing trade orientation of developing economies has consequences for poverty and its alleviation.

---

[48] It is by now well recognized that poverty is a multidimensional phenomenon. As such, it is difficult to find a fully satisfactory measure for it. Discussions of the issues involved and the measures proposed are available in Sen (1993) and World Bank (2000). Kakwani and Son (2006) have attempted to define more appropriate poverty lines and have provided alternative estimates of global poverty. For our analysis in this chapter, however, we choose to use World Bank estimates (though they have well-known limitations) as these are the most widely used.

[49] Other high-income countries and most of the petroleum exporter developing countries have insignificant levels of extreme poverty. It also seems sensible, from an analytical perspective, not to lump these as well as CEE and CIS countries together with medium-income developing and least developed countries, as there are important structural differences between them.

5.2 Did poverty decline in the 1990s?

According to World Bank estimates, in the developing world extreme poverty was on the decline in the 1990s (table 5.1). Overall (in medium-income developing and least developed countries taken together), the incidence of poverty declined from 31 per cent in 1990 to 23 per cent in 2001, and even the absolute number of persons living in poverty declined by 141 million. Much of the decline, however, is accounted for by what happened in China, where the incidence of poverty fell from 33 per cent to around 17 per cent and the number of persons in poverty declined by 163 million. In sub-Saharan Africa both the incidence of poverty and the number in poverty increased. Moreover, the depth of poverty (the distance between

Table 5.1   Poverty in the developing world, 1990s

Region	Number of people living below the poverty line (millions)		Proportion of population living below the poverty line (%)		Mean daily income of poor persons (PPP$)	
	1990	2001	1990	2001	1990	2001
East Asia (excluding China)	97.4	59.7	21.2	10.9	0.83	0.87
China	374.8	211.6	33.0	16.6	0.79	0.82
Latin America and the Caribbean	49.3	49.8	11.3	9.5	0.73	0.70
Middle East and North Africa	5.5	7.1	2.3	2.4	0.85	0.87
South Asia (excluding India)	104.9	72.5	38.8	21.1	0.79	0.92
India	357.4	358.6	42.1	34.7	0.79	0.86
Sub-Saharan Africa	226.8	315.8	44.6	46.9	0.62	0.61
Developing world	1 216.1	1 075.1	31.1	22.9	0.76	0.78
Developing world (excluding China)	841.3	863.5	30.3	25.2	0.75	0.77
Developing world (excluding China and India)	483.9	504.9	25.1	21.2	0.71	0.70

Notes: The poverty line is PPP$1.08 at 1993 prices.

Source: Derived from Chen and Ravallion (2004a).

the poverty line and the mean income of persons below the poverty line), which showed a decline in the developing world as a whole, increased in two regions – Latin America and the Caribbean, and sub-Saharan Africa. So while there was progress, it was very uneven.

The data in table 5.1 do not tell us if poverty was declining in a majority or a minority of the countries. The country groups for which poverty estimates are given can also be regarded as "not quite appropriate" since each group includes countries with little "dollar-a-day" poverty as well as countries where this type of poverty is widespread. In addition, the regional aggregates are estimates based on rather sketchy country-level data and many assumptions (see box 5.2). It is important, therefore, to consider the trends at the level of individual countries.

The limited nature of country-level data is quite evident from a glance at appendix table A5.1, which presents the available survey-based estimates of the incidence of "dollar-a-day" poverty in medium-income developing and least developed countries. Only those countries for which survey-based estimates for at least two periods are available are represented in the table. It is clear from the omissions that for a significant number of countries survey-based estimates are either not available at all or available for just one period.

The estimates of incidence of poverty, presented in appendix table A5.1, suffer from a number of well-known weaknesses. One is due to the fact that the survey method is not uniform across countries. This clearly makes

---

Box 5.2   Counting the poor

The critical assumptions used to derive regional aggregates are as follows (for details, see Chen and Ravallion, 2004a):

- The percentage of population below the poverty line in a region is the same as that for the group of countries in the region for which at least one household survey is available.

- When there is only one survey for a country, the survey mean income or consumption is assumed to grow at the same rate as private consumption expenditure per capita (available from the national accounts) and distributional inequality is assumed to remain unchanged at the level shown by the survey.

- When two or more surveys are available for a country, data on private consumption expenditure from the national accounts, on mean income or consumption from the surveys and on distributional inequality from the surveys are used together to derive estimates for the periods in between two survey periods.

cross-country comparisons difficult, but not much can be done about it. A second weakness arises from the fact that the estimates are derived from consumption surveys for some countries and from income surveys for others. This also makes cross-country comparison of levels of poverty problematic: with the same poverty line, we are likely to get different estimates of poverty incidence for any given country depending on whether we use the data on consumption distribution or the data on income distribution. Fortunately, the distortions arising from this are minimized if for cross-country comparison we consider time trends rather than poverty levels; it is reasonable to suppose that in any particular country the time trend given by consumption-survey-based estimates would not be radically different from that given by income-survey-based estimates.

However, given that the available survey-based estimates are for discrete time periods, time trends at the country level can only be observed by comparing the estimates for initial and terminal periods, which happen to be different for different countries. This creates a number of problems. Evidently, time trends for different countries cannot be observed over the same period of time. Moreover, a comparison of initial and terminal values will almost always show a trend, but it is perfectly possible that the incidence was in fact fluctuating without showing any real trend. It is also possible that the trend would have been quite different from what we observe had different initial and terminal periods been chosen. Finally, trends should ideally be observed over a reasonably long period; yet, for some countries, data are available only for two periods with a short interval in between.

Unfortunately, not much can be done to fix these problems. We can only try to minimize chances of error by (1) leaving out the cases where the gap between the initial and terminal periods is less than four years; (2) choosing, wherever data for more than two periods are available, initial and terminal periods in such a way as to minimize the possibility of deriving misleading trends; (3) choosing a single time period or "spell" for each country even though multiple "spells" could have been chosen for some; and (4) leaving out the cases in which the incidence has been and remains very low (2 per cent or less). The resulting sample of 43 countries is shown in appendix table A5.2. The analysis in this chapter is based on this sample.

Figure 5.1 shows the scatter of the sample countries along a 45° line with the horizontal axis representing the poverty rate in the initial year and the vertical axis representing the poverty rate in the terminal year. The points to the right of the 45° line represent countries where the poverty rate showed a trend decline and the points to the left of the 45° line represent those where the poverty rate showed a trend increase. It is evident that the number of countries in which poverty declined is much larger than the number of countries in which it increased. Poverty declined in 30 of the 43 countries

Figure 5.1 Trends in incidence of poverty in developing countries, 1990s

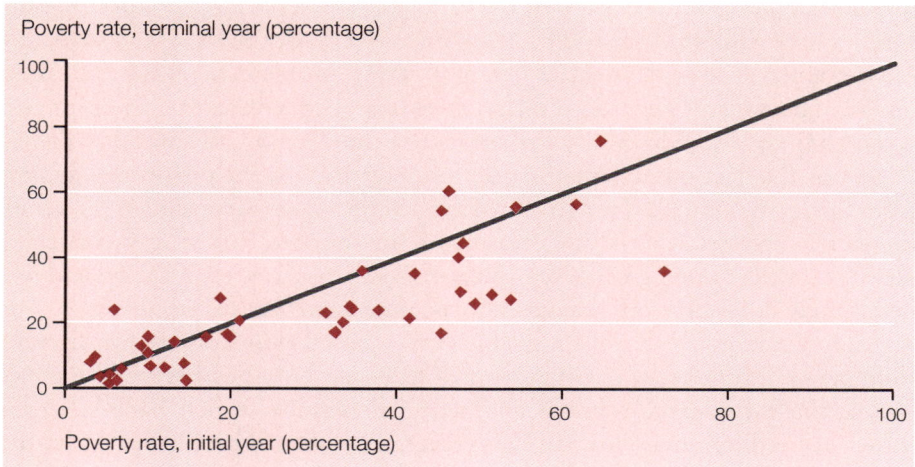

Note: Poverty rate is defined as proportion of population living on less than PPP$1.08 (1993 prices) per person per day.

Source: Derived from appendix table A.5.2.

listed. It declined in 10 out of the 16 least developed countries and in 20 of the 27 medium-income developing countries represented in the sample. Declining poverty was clearly the dominant trend in the 1990s.

5.3 Economic growth and poverty reduction

As already noted, the proposition that growth reduces poverty lacks a clear theoretical underpinning; there is no coherent and widely accepted explanation of why growth should reduce poverty. The proposition is derived from a particular reading of the available empirical evidence consisting of estimates of incidence of poverty, distribution of consumption or income and mean consumption or income – all derived from the same household surveys. The methodology usually employed to study growth–distribution and growth–poverty relationships is as follows (see, however, box 5.3 on page 132). For the set of countries for which household surveys exist for at least two points in time, change in each of the variables (incidence of poverty, distributional inequality and mean consumption/income) over discrete time periods is estimated (whenever feasible, multiple time periods or "spells" for a single country are included). Empirical exercises then involve studying cross-country relationships among these change variables. The general results of such exercises are that change in mean consumption/income bears no systematic relation to change in the distribution of consumption/income, while change in the incidence of poverty is strongly and negatively related to change in mean consumption/income.[50] On the basis of these results, it is claimed that economic growth reduces poverty.

Is the claim justified? Not really. Typically, survey-based estimates of consumption (or of income) per capita are substantially lower than estimates of private consumption expenditure (or of personal disposable income) per capita that are available from national accounts statistics. The well-known reason for the discrepancy is that richer households tend to be poorly represented in household surveys.[51] This does not seriously affect estimates of poverty incidence but results in serious underestimation of mean consumption/income and of distributional inequality; the degree of this underestimation can clearly vary across surveys undertaken in different countries, as well as at different points in time in any given country. All this means that the observed change in survey-based expenditure (income) per person can be quite different from the observed change in private consumption expenditure (personal disposable income) per capita derived from national accounts statistics. Furthermore, change in private consumption expenditure (personal disposable income) per capita can be quite different from change in per capita GDP in any given country, since tax rates and saving behaviour can change. The upshot is that change in survey-based mean consumption/income is not a good indicator of economic growth, just as change in distributional inequality, derived from household surveys, is not a good indicator of distributional change in the economy. Thus the observed inverse relation between change in survey-based estimates of poverty incidence and change in survey-based estimates of mean expenditure/income does not in fact constitute a proper basis for claiming that economic growth is distribution neutral and poverty reducing.

The point is that it is necessary to demonstrate a robust inverse relationship between change in poverty incidence and change in per capita GDP if it is to be argued, purely on empirical grounds, that economic growth is generally poverty reducing. But this relationship has yet to be empirically established even though no great methodological difficulties arise in studying it (since the limitations of household surveys do not seriously affect poverty estimates).

Figure 5.2 shows the cross-country relationship between change in poverty incidence and change in per capita GDP for the set of 43 countries in

---

[50] Cf. Fields (1989); Ravallion (1995, 2001); Bruno et al. (1998); Dollar and Kray (2002); and Chen and Ravallion (2004a). It is worth noting, however, that one study – Lundberg and Squire (2003) – has found a tendency for economic growth to be associated with rising inequality.

[51] In a few of the least developed countries, mean consumption (income) derived from surveys is found to be higher than private consumption expenditure (personal disposable income) per capita derived from national accounts data (see UNCTAD, 2002). In these countries, it seems, it is the poorer households that tend to be under-represented in household surveys. In such cases there is serious underestimation not just of distributional inequality but also of poverty incidence. On the other hand, there is serious overestimation of average consumption/income.

Figure 5.2 Poverty and GDP, 43 countries, 1990s

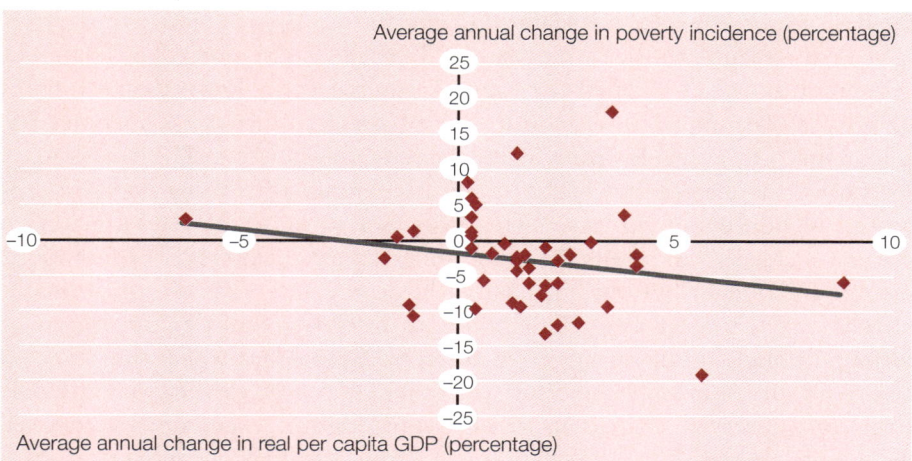

Notes: The regression equation is: $Y = -1.671 - 0.660 X$, $R^2 = 0.045$. The coefficient is significant only at 17.1 per cent. Based on data for the following 43 countries: Bangladesh, Bolivia, Brazil, Burkina Faso, Burundi, Cameroon, China, Colombia, Costa Rica, Côte d'Ivoire, Ecuador, Egypt, El Salvador, Ethiopia, Gambia, Ghana, Guatemala, Honduras, India, Kenya, Lao PDR, Madagascar, Malawi, Mali, Mauritania, Mexico, Nepal, Nicaragua, Pakistan, Panama, Paraguay, Peru, Philippines, Senegal, South Africa, Sri Lanka, Tanzania, Thailand, Uganda, Viet Nam, Yemen, Zambia, Zimbabwe.

Source: Derived from appendix table A5.3.

Box 5.3 Economic growth and poverty: Some other evidence

Some studies try out somewhat different exercises but do not really overcome the problem of mismatch between empirical evidence and analytical statements. Chen and Ravallion (2004a) examine the relationship between the change in poverty incidence and that in personal disposable income per capita (derived from national accounts data). The relationship shows up to be inverse but weaker in terms of statistical significance. Furthermore, it is not quite appropriate to interpret the observed change in per capita personal disposable income as economic growth. Dollar and Kray (2002) use survey-based estimates of distributive shares together with GDP to infer mean income of the poorest quintile and study the cross-country relationship between this mean income and per capita GDP. The results show that the elasticity of the mean income of the poorest quintile with respect to per capita GDP is unity, suggesting that growth has the same impact on the incomes of the poor and the non-poor. This amounts to showing that the income share of the poorest quintile is uncorrelated with GDP per capita across a large set of countries – developing, transition and developed.

The employment–poverty interface in developing countries

Figure 5.3 Poverty and growth of mean expenditure/income, 43 countries, 1990s

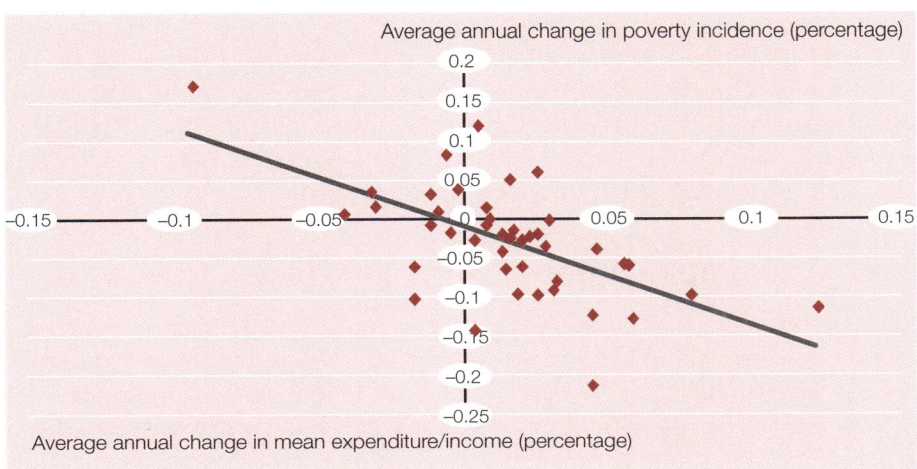

Notes: The regression equation is: $Y = -0.009 - 1.272\,X$, $R^2 = 0.374$. The coefficient is significant at less than 1 per cent. Based on data for the following 43 countries: Bangladesh, Bolivia, Brazil, Burkina Faso, Burundi, Cameroon, China, Colombia, Costa Rica, Côte d'Ivoire, Ecuador, Egypt, El Salvador, Ethiopia, Gambia, Ghana, Guatemala, Honduras, India, Kenya, Lao PDR, Madagascar, Malawi, Mali, Mauritania, Mexico, Nepal, Nicaragua, Pakistan, Panama, Paraguay, Peru, Philippines, Senegal, South Africa, Sri Lanka, Tanzania, Thailand, Uganda, Viet Nam, Yemen, Zambia, Zimbabwe.

Source: Derived from appendix table A5.3.

(A much simpler exercise would actually have shown this.) Apart from the fact that the choice of a sample that includes all types of countries cannot really be regarded as appropriate, there remains the fact that the estimates of income share of the poorest quintile are derived from household survey data and hence are not reliable, at least in the case of the developing countries in the sample.

Besley and Burgess (2003) employ the fixed-effect regression method to estimate the elasticity of poverty incidence with respect to per capita national income. The estimated elasticity turns out to be negative. The reliability of such an estimate is open to question, however, given the nature of the database used. This consists of the World Bank's survey-based estimates of the incidence of "dollar-a-day" poverty for those countries for which surveys for at least two periods are available. As already noted, some of these estimates are derived from consumption surveys while others are derived from income surveys. In addition, the number of observations per country and the length of period between observations vary widely across countries. Moreover, the sample is not confined to developing countries.

our sample, while figure 5.3 shows, for the same set of countries, the cross-country relationship between change in poverty incidence and change in survey mean expenditure/income (appendix figure A5.1 shows the same relationship when change is represented by log difference). Figure 5.2 shows an inverse relationship, but it is statistically insignificant. Figure 5.3, on the other hand, shows a strong and statistically significant inverse relationship. Clearly, the second relationship does not imply the first. And figure 5.2 really suggests that economic growth has rather varied effects on poverty.

5.4 The employment–poverty interface

There are good reasons to think that, in the context of developing countries, economic growth should indeed be expected to have varied effects on poverty. As observed in Chapter 4, developing economies are labour-surplus dual economies. The poor work in the non-formal segment of these economies, either as self-employed in low-productivity activities or as casual wage labourers. In both types of employment, they face serious underemployment as well as low returns to labour. In this setting, poverty reduction requires either a decline in underemployment or a shift into higher-productivity activities (resulting either from increases in productivity in existing activities or from the emergence of new employment opportunities). An indicator of such changes is the change in output per worker in the non-formal segment. Thus it is the growth of output per worker in the non-formal segment that can be expected to reduce poverty.

There are two possible situations in which output per worker in the non-formal segment can rise. One is rapid growth of employment in the formal segment. In theory, a combination of rapid output growth and high employment elasticity in the formal segment can generate a process of transfer of workers from the non-formal to the formal segment that is rapid enough to reduce the labour force in the non-formal segment. In this case, output per worker rises even while there is no change in total output in the non-formal segment. In practice, this is a very remote possibility; as shown in Chapter 4, the required rate of employment growth in the formal segment is generally too high to be attainable. The other way, indeed the only way that output per worker in the non-formal segment can increase, is through output growth (higher than labour force growth) in the non-formal segment itself.

In short, it is growth in the non-formal segment that reduces poverty, while growth in the formal segment has little or no effect on it.[52] It is easy to see, then,

---

[52] Arguably, growth in the formal segment can reduce poverty through what might be called a spill-over effect: a part of the incremental income generated in the formal segment might serve to generate demand for goods and services produced in the non-formal segment. Growth in demand for services helps to reduce poverty as it directly reduces underemployment in the non-formal segment. Growth in demand for goods produced in the non-formal segment,

The employment–poverty interface in developing countries

Figure 5.4   Poverty and output per worker in non-formal segment, 20 countries, 1990s

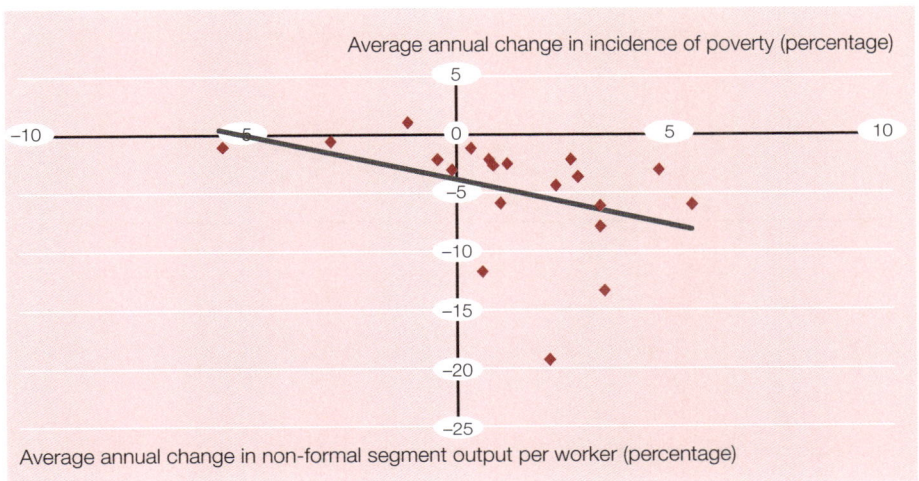

Notes: The regression equation is: Y = – 3.785 - 0.801 X, R² = 0.168. The coefficient is significant at 7.2 per cent. Based on data for the following 20 countries: Brazil, China, Costa Rica, Egypt, El Salvador, Ghana, Guatemala, Honduras, India, Mexico, Nicaragua, Pakistan, Panama, Paraguay, Philippines, Sri Lanka, Tanzania, Thailand, Uganda, Viet Nam.

Source: Derived from appendix table A5.3.

why we should not expect any well-defined relationship between poverty and economic growth: there is no necessary relationship between growth of an economy, defined as growth of per capita GDP, and growth of output per worker in its non-formal segment; the former can conceivably result, primarily or entirely, from growth in the formal segment alone. Thus a positive rate of growth of per capita GDP can, in principle, be associated with negative, zero or positive growth of output per worker in the non-formal segment; accordingly, it can be associated with rising, constant or falling incidence of poverty.

It also follows that the relationship between poverty and employment is not as straightforward as it is usually thought to be. An improvement in the overall employment situation in a developing economy does not imply anything definite about the change in output per worker in the non-formal

---

however, is unlikely to help because in labour-surplus dual economies lack of capital (and skills) constitutes a binding constraint on output growth. The effect of growth in demand, therefore, is likely to be a rise in prices rather than in output. And such price increases tend to hurt the poor, who are often buyers rather than sellers of commodities. Overall, output growth in the formal segment is likely to have a rather small spill-over effect on poverty.

The global employment challenge

Figure 5.5 Output per worker in non-formal segment and per capita GDP, 20 countries, 1990s

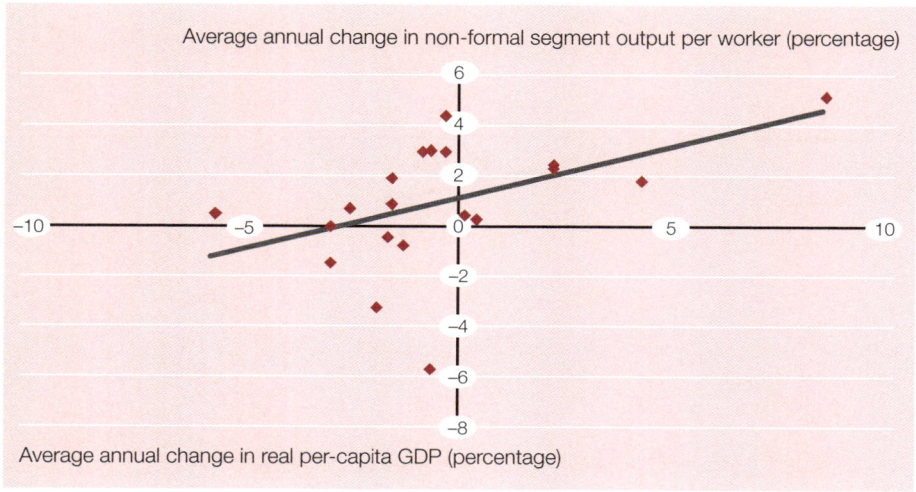

Notes: The regression equation is: Y = − 0.219 + 0.558 X, R^2 = 0.230. The coefficient is significant at 3.2 per cent. Based on data for the following 20 countries: Brazil, China, Costa Rica, Egypt, El Salvador, Ghana, Guatemala, Honduras, India, Mexico, Nicaragua, Pakistan, Panama, Paraguay, Philippines, Sri Lanka, Tanzania, Thailand, Uganda, Viet Nam.

Source: Derived from appendix table A5.3.

---

segment (see Chapter 4 for the arguments and evidence). This means that change in a country's overall employment situation has no unambiguous implication for change in poverty. If, for example, the share of the formal segment in total employment has increased while output per worker in the non-formal segment has remained constant, we would conclude that the overall employment situation has improved but we do not expect poverty to have declined. Similarly, if output per worker in the non-formal segment has increased but the share of the formal segment in total employment has declined, we would expect poverty to have declined even though there is no unambiguous improvement in the overall employment situation.

Thus it is employment in the non-formal segment that provides the key link between economic growth and poverty. Figure 5.4 shows the relationship between the rate of change in the incidence of poverty and the rate of change in output per worker in the non-formal segment, over the same period, for a small set of countries for which we have the required data. The relationship is inverse and statistically significant; growth of output per worker in the non-formal segment reduces poverty. Figure 5.5 shows, for the same set of

Figure 5.6   Poverty and GDP, 20 countries, 1990s

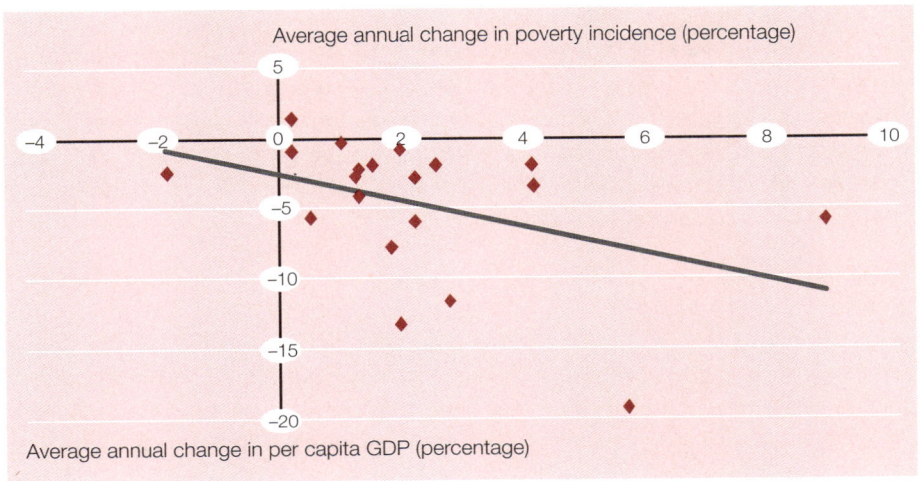

Notes: The regression equation is: Y = – 2.458 – 0.956 X, R² = 0.177. The coefficient is significant at 6.5 per cent. Based on data for the following 20 countries: Brazil, China, Costa Rica, Egypt, El Salvador, Ghana, Guatemala, Honduras, India, Mexico, Nicaragua, Pakistan, Panama, Paraguay, Philippines, Sri Lanka, Tanzania, Thailand, Uganda, Viet Nam.

Source: Derived from appendix table A5.3.

countries, the relationship between the rate of change in per capita GDP and the rate of change in output per worker in the non-formal segment. The relationship turns out to be positive and statistically significant; for the set of countries in question, economic growth was associated with significant improvements in employment conditions in the non-formal segment. This suggests that economic growth in this set of countries was poverty reducing. Figure 5.6 shows this to be the case: the relationship between the rate of change in poverty incidence and the rate of change in per capita GDP is inverse and statistically significant.

This evidence, although not conclusive, is sufficiently suggestive. Economic growth reduces poverty when it is associated with substantial growth of the non-formal segment (see also box 5.4). But economic growth is not always associated with substantial growth of the non-formal segment and hence is not always poverty reducing.

Box 5.4 Poverty and output per worker in the non-formal segment

The idea that economic growth reduces poverty only when associated with substantial growth of output per worker in the non-formal segment can be further empirically explored as follows. We can suppose that the higher the rate of growth of output per worker in the non-formal segment in relation to the growth of per capita GDP, the greater is the magnitude of decline in poverty incidence. For a set of 20 countries, the following cross-country relationship is found:

$rpov = -4.460 - 1.377\ RT$, $R^2 = 0.196$, number of observations: 20
$\qquad\quad\ (0.000)\quad\ (0.051)$

where $rpov$ = average annual rate of change in poverty incidence, RT = ratio of average annual growth rate of output per worker in the non-formal segment to average annual growth rate of per capita GDP, and the figures in parentheses are P-values (indicating the level of significance). The equation tells us that, for any given growth rate of per capita GDP, the higher the rate of growth of output per worker in the non-formal segment, the higher is the rate of poverty reduction.

In econometric terms, however, the significance of the relationship between $rpov$ and RT could be spurious because RT, being the ratio of two growth rates, is not normally distributed. One way of checking for this is to transform RT into Rt such that Rt is normally distributed. This can be done by using the formula:

$$Rt = (RT^k - 1)/k$$

where k is a transformation factor that makes skewness (of Rt) approximate 0 and kurtosis approximate 3. The following cross-country relationship is then found:

$rpov = -1.391 - 0.013\ Rt$, $R^2 = 0.146$, number of observations: 20
$\qquad\quad\ (0.522)\quad\ (0.096)$

where the figures in parentheses are P-values (indicating the level of significance). These results confirm that the relationship between $rpov$ and RT is not spurious.

5.5 Trade growth and the poor

There is some concern that the growing trade orientation of developing countries may have had an adverse impact on the level of poverty.[53] At first sight, the concern appears to be misplaced since most existing studies conclude that trade growth reduces poverty; on close scrutiny, however, it turns out that their claim that trade growth reduces poverty is based on evidence and methodologies that are very much open to question (see box 5.5). The basic argument presented in these studies is as follows: trade growth stimulates economic growth and economic growth reduces poverty; therefore trade growth reduces poverty. The first two propositions, however, are not empirically well founded and hence the third cannot be taken as established in any sense. Also, there are good reasons to suspect that trade growth may have affected poverty in developing countries through a reallocation effect rather than through a growth effect.

As argued in Chapter 4, growing trade orientation means growing share of tradable goods and services in the total output of an economy. This in turn implies a shift in investment from the sectors producing non-tradable products to those producing tradable products. In the context of a developing

---

Box 5.5   Trade orientation, economic growth and poverty

In the existing studies it is taken for granted that growth reduces poverty and that trade stimulates growth. It is then asked whether trade-induced growth is any less or any more poverty reducing than growth induced by other factors. The studies generally find no convincing reasons for either proposition. They therefore argue that growth of trade orientation helps poverty reduction because it stimulates economic growth. See, in particular, Berg and Krueger (2003), Dollar and Kray (2004) and Winters et al. (2004).

However, what is taken for granted in these studies cannot in fact be taken for granted. As we have seen, the proposition that growth reduces poverty is not empirically well founded, and the proposition that increased trade orientation stimulates growth has also proved difficult to establish empirically. The relevant literature is reviewed in Ghose (2003) and Jansen and Lee (2007).

Thus the validity of the argument that trade growth reduces poverty remains to be established. Some recent studies (Harrison, 2006; Ravallion, 2007) show that there are no theoretical or empirical grounds for the claim that trade growth reduces poverty in all circumstances.

---

[53] See Aisbett (2005) on the critics and their concerns.

economy, it can be plausibly assumed that tradable products are produced mainly in the formal segment and non-tradable products mainly in the non-formal segment. Trade growth then implies a reallocation of investment from the non-formal to the formal segment. If unaccompanied by an increase in the level of aggregate investment in the economy, such a reallocation implies an acceleration of output growth in the formal segment and a deceleration of output growth in the non-formal segment. The likely result is a slowdown in the growth of output per worker in the non-formal segment, which amounts to a slowdown in poverty reduction.

In so far as it is appropriate to assume that the formal segment is the producer of tradable products in developing countries, we can therefore expect trade growth to slow down the process of poverty reduction in certain circumstances. How appropriate is this assumption? It is obviously appropriate when a country's trade is mainly in minerals, manufactures or services. It is not necessarily inappropriate even in the case of countries that rely mainly on agricultural exports since these often consist of processed products and processing is usually done by enterprises in the formal segment. Even unprocessed export products tend to be produced by large commercial farms which really belong to the formal segment. There are exceptions to the rule, of course: in some African countries, for example, small household farms often engage in the production of export crops such as coffee, cocoa or cotton. Even then, exports of these commodities are handled either by state trading agencies or by commercial establishments, both belonging to the formal segment. Overall, there is no great difficulty in accepting, as a stylized fact, that the formal segment is the producer of tradable goods and services in developing economies.

The concern that trade growth has been bad for the poor thus cannot be dismissed lightly. There are good theoretical reasons to believe that it may indeed be the case in countries where trade growth is accompanied by stagnation or decline in the level of investment. In order to argue that trade growth has been good for the poor, we need to show that growth of investment (and, by implication, acceleration in the growth of per capita GDP) generally accompanied trade growth. This, unfortunately, cannot be shown.

We have already seen (in Chapter 4) some evidence suggesting that trade growth (i.e., growth of trade–GDP ratio) in the 1990s tended to be associated with a slowdown in the growth of output per worker in the non-formal segment. Here we examine some more evidence. Figure 5.7 shows the relationship between trade growth and change in output per worker in the non-formal segment for a sample of 32 countries. The relationship is inverse and statistically significant. It confirms the finding reported in Chapter 4 that trade growth does appear to have had the effect of slowing down the growth of output per worker in the non-formal segment in the 1990s.

Figure 5.7 Trade growth and output per worker in non-formal segment, 1990s

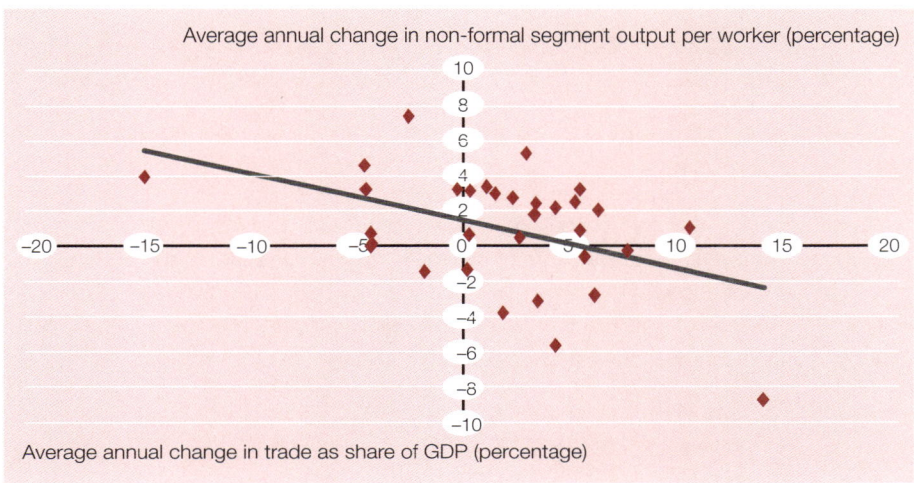

Notes: The regression equation is: Y = 1.371 – 0.277 X, R² = 0.196. The coefficient is significant at 1.1 per cent.
Based on data for the following 32 countries: Argentina, Belize, Botswana, Brazil, Chile, China, Costa Rica, Cuba, Dominican Republic, Egypt, El Salvador, Fiji, Ghana, Guatemala, Honduras, India, Jamaica, Malaysia, Mexico, Mongolia, Myanmar, Namibia, Nicaragua, Pakistan, Panama, Paraguay, Philippines, Sri Lanka, Tanzania, Thailand, Uganda, Viet Nam.

Source: Derived from appendix table A5.4.

The analysis can be carried a little further. For the set of countries represented in figure 5.7, it can be shown that the change in output per worker in the non-formal segment is positively related to change in per capita GDP and negatively related to change in trade–GDP ratio. Thus a rise in trade–GDP ratio alone depresses the rate of growth of output per worker in the non-formal segment, thereby slowing down the pace of poverty reduction. But simultaneous increases in trade–GDP ratio and in growth of per capita GDP have an ambiguous effect: depending on the magnitude of the changes, the pace of poverty reduction could either decline, remain unchanged or increase (see box 5.6 for the technical details of the argument and box 5.7 for an illustration). The evidence (figure 5.7) seems to suggest, therefore, that growth of trade orientation in the 1990s was not generally accompanied by significant growth acceleration. This is another way of saying that trade growth in the 1990s did not in general go hand in hand with investment growth.[54]

---

[54] For the 32 countries represented in figure 5.7, World Bank (World Development Indicators database, CD-ROM, 2005) data show that the rate of investment increased in 12 countries, declined in 12 others and remained unchanged in eight.

Box 5.6 Trade growth and output per worker in non-formal segment

For the sample of 32 countries represented in figure 5.7, a regression equation that incorporates change in per capita GDP as an explanatory variable yields the following result:

$$ropwnf = 0.302 - 0.234\ rtdr + 0.727\ rgdppc,\ R^2 = 0.475,\ \text{number of observations: 32}$$
$$ (0.631)\ \ (0.009)\ \ \ \ \ \ \ \ \ \ (0.000)$$

where *ropwnf* is average annual change in output per worker in the non-formal segment, *rtdr* is average annual rate of change in trade–GDP ratio, *rgdppc* is average annual rate of change in per capita GDP and the figures in parentheses are P-values (indicating the level of significance). There is no significant correlation between *rtdr* and *rgdppc*. The intercept is statistically insignificant and can be dropped:

$$ropwnf = -0.247\ rtdr + 0.665\ rgdppc,\ R^2 = 0.471,\ \text{number of observations: 32}$$
$$ (0.004)\ \ \ \ \ \ \ \ \ \ (0.000)$$

This equation can be used to depict the relationship between *ropwnf* and *rtdr*, with *rgdppc* as a shift factor:

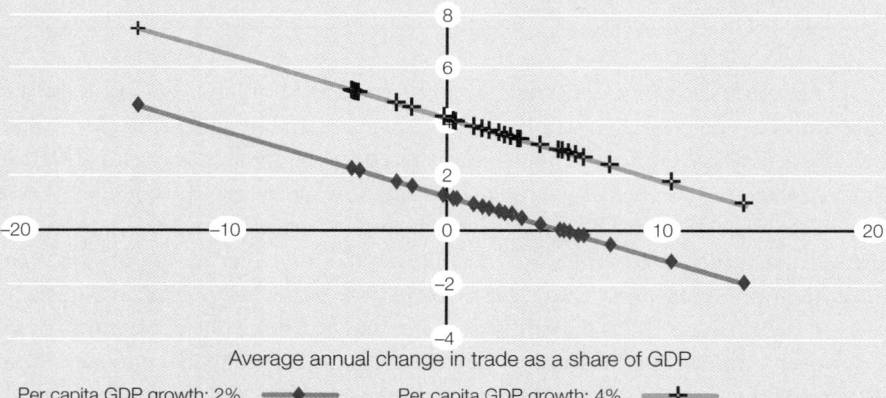

Average annual change in non-formal segment output per worker

Average annual change in trade as a share of GDP

Per capita GDP growth: 2% ◆ Per capita GDP growth: 4% ✛

The figure shows that rising trade orientation, when unaccompanied by growth acceleration, depresses the growth of output per worker in the non-formal segment and hence slows down the pace of poverty reduction. However, if GDP growth accelerates with trade growth, the pace of poverty reduction could (depending on the extent of growth acceleration) accelerate, remain unchanged or decelerate.

> **Box 5.7   Trade growth and poverty reduction: China's experience**
>
> The experience of China, the country that has since 1980 achieved the sharpest reduction in poverty as well as the sharpest increase in trade orientation and the highest rate of economic growth within the developing world, actually provides a good illustration of the point being made here. A recent study (Ravallion, 2007) shows that the incidence of poverty (estimated by using the national poverty line):
>
> - fell from 53 per cent in 1981 to 18 per cent in 1985,
>
> - remained virtually unchanged between 1985 and 1994 (with fluctuations in between), and
>
> - fell again by about nine percentage points between 1994 and 2000.
>
> Trade growth (i.e., growth of trade–GDP ratio) began in 1985, was rapid until 1994 and was virtually zero after 1994. Per capita GDP grew by 10.6 per cent per annum in the first period, by 8.3 per cent per annum in the second period and by 7.6 per cent per annum in the third period.
>
> On a simple view, trade growth, despite being accompanied by rapid economic growth, appears to have halted the process of poverty reduction. Econometric exercises show, however, that trade growth had no effect on poverty. The time trend in poverty is explained entirely by domestic policies that are quite unrelated to trade. In the early 1980s, land redistribution, revival of household farming systems and increases in prices of agricultural products hugely boosted output per worker in agriculture, leading to rapid reduction in poverty. During 1985–94, agricultural growth decelerated and there was high inflation, both of which contributed to halting the process of poverty reduction.

It is perhaps useful to underline that slowdown in poverty reduction means rising poverty only in those cases where poverty had been stable or rising even before trade orientation started growing. In other words, our result does not show that growth of trade orientation increased poverty. In fact, poverty was declining in a majority of developing countries in the 1990s (as shown above) and output per worker in the non-formal segment also showed a rising trend in a majority of developing countries (as shown in Chapter 4). What our result suggests is that the decline in global poverty would have been larger had trade growth been accompanied by a rise in investment rate in all or at least a majority of the countries considered.

The global employment challenge

5.6 Policies for poverty reduction

Poverty is rooted in poor employment conditions in the non-formal segment of developing economies. For it to be reduced, therefore, steady improvement in these conditions is required. In general, employment conditions in the non-formal segment cannot improve in the absence of output growth in the segment. This is why it is misleading to argue that economic growth – i.e., growth of GDP per capita – reduces poverty. Indeed, economic growth can mean output growth in the formal segment together with stagnation in the non-formal segment and can therefore leave poverty unaffected or even increase it. For similar reasons, it would also be misleading to argue that improvement in the overall employment situation reduces poverty: such an improvement can mean a combination of employment growth in the formal segment and stagnation of output per worker in the non-formal segment.

The correct argument is that poverty reduction requires economic growth and improvement in the overall employment situation. Here economic growth must mean simultaneous growth of output in formal and non-formal segments. And improvement in the overall employment situation must mean simultaneous growth of employment in the formal segment and of output per worker in the non-formal segment.

Trade growth, when it is not associated with growth acceleration, tends to slow down the pace of poverty reduction. Since there are no strong empirical grounds for supposing that trade growth itself induces growth acceleration, efforts to promote trade must always be accompanied by efforts to promote growth. In other words, if governments seek to promote trade, they must seek to accelerate growth (by promoting investment) at the same time.[55]

Policies for poverty reduction, then, are essentially the same as those required to address the employment problem in developing countries: they are policies aimed at stimulating investment and output growth in the non-formal segment and ensuring employment-intensive growth in the formal segment. The relevant issues have already been discussed in Chapter 4 and need not be repeated here. However, a few additional observations are in order.

First, developing countries have often attempted to reduce poverty by implementing special public works programmes or employment guarantee schemes. In principle, these programmes can constitute investment programmes for the non-formal segment. In practice, they often function as mechanisms for transfer payments to the poor. Transfer payments are important since the desperately poor need immediate relief, but they should complement and not

---

[55] In the mass media, it is routinely asserted that globalization has lifted millions out of poverty. This is quite misleading. In truth, it is national policies in some of the globalizing countries that have lifted millions out of poverty.

substitute for investment in the non-formal segment. Use of public works programmes or employment guarantee schemes as mechanisms for transfer payments obscures the perspective. A clear distinction needs to be maintained between programmes for transfer payments and programmes for investment.

Second, programmes for delivery of primary education and primary health care to the poor are sometimes proposed as anti-poverty programmes. Delivery of these services to the entire population, poor and non-poor, must be a central objective of policy in all developing countries. But it is hard to see how these services can be delivered to the poor alone, and even if special programmes aimed exclusively at the poor could be designed and implemented, they would not be substitutes for programmes of investment in the non-formal segment. Delivery of primary education to the poor can at best help prevent direct transmission of poverty across generations but it cannot ensure a lower incidence of poverty for the next generation. As for delivery of primary health care to the poor, it brings benefits to today's poor children as well as today's poor adults (by reducing the frequency of illness, for example) but it cannot generate additional employment opportunities for them. Consequently, programmes for delivery of primary education and primary health care are better viewed as imperatives for development rather than as programmes for poverty alleviation.

Appendix table A5.1 Proportion of population living on less than PPP$1.08 (1993 prices) per person per day, 1990–2004 (percentages)

Country	1990	1991	1992	1993	1994	1995	1996	1997	1998	1999	2000	2001	2002	2003	2004
Medium-income developing															
Argentina (urban)	–	–	0.1	–	–	–	1.1	–	1.2	–	–	3.3	7.5	7.3	–
Bolivia	5.7	–	–	–	–	–	–	20.4	–	26.2	–	–	24.0	–	–
Botswana	–	–	–	32.1	–	–	–	–	–	–	–	–	–	–	–
Brazil	14.0	–	10.1	8.3	–	10.5	6.9	9.0	8.0	8.0	–	8.2	6.7	7.4	7.6
Cameroon	–	–	–	–	–	–	32.5	–	–	–	–	17.1	–	–	–
Chile	6.2	–	1.2	–	0.8	–	0.0	–	–	–	1.0	–	–	–	–
China	32.6	–	29.1	27.7	24.3	21.3	16.9	16.2	16.2	17.8	–	16.9	–	–	–
Colombia	–	2.8	–	–	–	3.1	5.3	–	8.3	8.2	8.7	–	–	7.6	–
Costa Rica	5.2	–	–	4.1	–	–	3.6	1.9	1.4	–	2.0	1.4	–	–	–
Côte d'Ivoire	–	–	–	9.9	–	12.3	–	–	15.5	–	–	–	15.7	–	–
Dominican Republic	–	–	1.6	–	–	–	1.8	–	–	–	1.1	–	–	1.9	–
Ecuador	–	–	–	–	16.8	–	–	–	15.8	–	–	–	–	–	–
Egypt	4.0	–	–	–	–	2.6	–	–	–	3.1	–	–	–	–	–
El Salvador	–	–	–	–	–	20.8	25.3	21.4	21.4	–	18.9	–	20.4	–	–
Ghana	–	47.2	–	–	–	–	–	–	40.5	–	–	–	–	–	–
Guatemala	–	–	–	–	–	–	–	–	13.2	–	10.7	–	14.0	–	–
Honduras	37.8	–	28.3	–	23.7	–	25.0	–	23.8	20.7	–	–	–	14.1	–
India	42.0	–	51.1	42.1	45.1	50.6	–	44.3	–	35.5	–	–	–	–	–
Indonesia	–	–	–	17.4	–	–	14.1	–	26.3	8.0	7.2	–	7.5	–	–
Jamaica	0.6	4.1	6.7	4.9	–	–	2.3	–	–	1.7	0.0	–	–	–	–
Jordan	–	–	0.6	–	–	–	–	–	–	–	–	–	0.1	–	–

The employment–poverty interface in developing countries

Country														
Kenya	—	33.5	—	26.5	—	—	20.1	—	—	—	—	—	—	—
Malaysia	—	0.4	—	—	—	—	0.2	—	—	—	—	—	—	—
Mexico	—	5.2	—	—	8.4	7.8	—	8.8	—	5.9	—	4.3	—	—
Mongolia	—	—	—	—	13.9	—	—	27.0	—	—	—	10.8	—	—
Morocco	0.1	—	—	—	—	—	—	0.6	—	—	—	—	—	—
Namibia	—	—	34.9	—	—	—	—	—	—	—	—	—	—	—
Nicaragua	—	—	47.9	—	—	—	—	44.7	—	—	45.1	—	—	—
Pakistan	47.8	33.9	—	—	29.5	—	—	—	—	7.2	9.4	6.1	—	—
Panama	—	—	—	—	7.4	7.9	3.2	—	—	—	—	—	—	—
Paraguay	4.9	—	—	—	19.4	—	15.9	—	14.9	—	—	16.4	—	—
Peru	1.4	—	—	9.4	—	8.9	—	—	—	18.1	15.5	12.8	—	—
Philippines	—	19.8	—	18.4	—	—	14.4	—	—	15.5	—	—	—	—
South Africa	—	—	10.0	—	6.3	—	—	—	—	10.7	—	—	—	—
Sri Lanka	3.8	—	—	—	6.6	—	—	—	7.6	—	—	5.8	—	—
Swaziland	—	—	—	8.0	—	—	—	—	—	—	—	—	—	—
Thailand	—	6.0	—	—	—	2.2	—	0.0	2.0	1.9	—	1.0	—	—
Tunisia	1.3	—	—	—	1.0	—	—	—	—	0.3	—	—	—	—
Uruguay	—	—	—	—	—	0.6	—	0.6	—	0.2	0.0	—	0.0	—
Viet Nam	—	—	14.6	—	—	—	—	3.8	—	—	—	2.2	—	0.0
Zimbabwe	54.4	—	—	—	56.1	—	—	—	—	—	—	—	—	—
Least developed														
Bangladesh	—	35.9	—	—	28.6	—	—	—	—	36.0	—	—	—	—
Benin	—	—	—	—	—	—	—	—	—	—	—	—	30.9	—
Burkina Faso	—	—	—	51.4	—	—	—	44.9	—	—	—	—	28.7	—
Burundi	—	—	45.2	—	—	—	—	54.6	—	—	—	—	—	—
Cambodia	—	—	—	—	—	—	34.1	—	—	—	—	—	—	—
Central African Republic	—	—	66.6	—	—	—	—	—	—	—	—	—	—	—

Appendix table A5.1   Proportion of population living on less than PPP$1.08 (1993 prices) per person per day, 1990–2004 (percentages) (continued)

Country	1990	1991	1992	1993	1994	1995	1996	1997	1998	1999	2000	2001	2002	2003	2004
Ethiopia	–	–	–	–	–	31.2	–	–	–	–	23.0	–	–	–	–
Gambia	–	–	53.7	–	–	–	–	–	27.1	–	–	–	–	–	–
Haiti	–	–	–	–	–	–	–	–	–	–	–	52.9	–	–	–
Lao PDR	–	–	18.6	–	–	–	–	26.4	–	–	–	–	27.4	–	–
Lesotho	–	–	–	43.1	–	36.4	–	–	–	–	–	–	–	–	–
Madagascar	–	–	–	46.3	–	–	–	49.8	–	66.0	–	61.0	–	–	–
Malawi	–	–	–	–	–	–	–	41.7	–	–	–	–	–	–	21.3
Mali	–	–	–	–	72.3	–	–	–	–	–	–	–	–	–	–
Mauritania	–	–	–	49.4	–	28.6	–	–	–	–	25.9	36.4	–	–	–
Mozambique	–	–	–	–	–	–	37.9	–	–	–	–	–	–	–	–
Nepal	–	–	–	–	–	34.4	–	–	–	–	–	–	–	25.3	–
Niger	–	–	41.7	–	54.8	–	–	–	–	–	–	–	–	–	–
Rwanda	–	–	–	–	–	–	–	–	–	51.8	–	–	–	–	–
Senegal	–	45.4	–	–	24.0	–	–	–	–	–	–	17.0	–	–	–
Tanzania	–	61.5	–	–	–	–	–	–	–	–	57.0	–	–	–	–
Uganda	–	–	34.5	–	–	–	26.6	–	–	26.8	–	–	24.4	–	–
Yemen	–	–	3.4	–	–	–	–	–	9.4	–	–	–	–	–	–
Zambia	–	64.6	–	73.6	–	–	72.6	–	65.7	–	–	–	76.4	–	–

Notes: For China and India, estimates of poverty rates were available separately for rural and urban areas. The overall rates are estimated by using data on rural and urban populations as weights. In the case of China, no estimate of urban poverty was available for 1990 and no estimate of rural poverty was available for 1991. The overall figure for 1990 is estimated by assuming that the incidence of urban poverty was the same in 1990 as in 1991.
– = data not available.
Source: World Bank, PovcalNet 2006 database (http://iresearch.worldbank.org/PovcalNet/jsp/index.jsp).

Appendix table A5.2 Proportion of population living on less than PPP$1.08 (1993 prices) per person per day, selected sample (percentages)

Country	Period	Initial year	Final year
Medium-income developing			
Bolivia	1990–2002	5.68	24.01
Brazil	1992–2002	10.09	6.66
Cameroon	1996–2001	32.45	17.11
China	1990–2001	32.55	16.88
Colombia	1991–2003	2.82	7.64
Costa Rica	1990–2001	5.24	1.35
Côte d'Ivoire	1993–2002	9.88	15.72
Ecuador	1994–1998	16.78	15.78
Egypt	1990–1999	3.97	3.09
El Salvador	1995–2002	20.80	20.44
Ghana	1991–1998	47.24	40.51
Guatemala	1998–2002	13.19	13.97
Honduras	1990–1998	37.83	23.84
India	1990–1999	42.06	35.54
Kenya	1992–1997	33.54	20.13
Mexico	1992–2002	5.19	4.31
Nicaragua	1993–2001	47.88	45.06
Pakistan	1990–1996	47.76	29.49
Panama	1991–2002	11.81	6.06
Paraguay	1995–2002	19.36	16.37
Peru	1996–2002	8.88	12.83
Philippines	1991–2000	19.77	15.48
South Africa	1993–2000	10.02	10.71
Sri Lanka	1995–2002	6.56	5.75
Thailand	1992–2000	6.02	1.93
Viet Nam	1993–2002	14.63	2.15
Zimbabwe	1990–1995	54.39	56.12
Least developed			
Bangladesh	1991–2000	35.86	36.03
Burkina Faso	1994–2003	51.41	28.65
Burundi	1992–1998	45.24	54.56
Ethiopia	1995–2000	31.25	22.97

Appendix table A5.2 Proportion of population living on less than PPP$1.08 (1993 prices) per person per day, selected sample (percentages) (continued)

Country	Period	Initial year	Final year
Gambia	1992–1998	53.69	27.07
Lao PDR	1992–2002	18.57	27.37
Madagascar	1993–2001	46.31	61.04
Malawi	1997–2004	41.66	21.30
Mali	1994–2001	72.29	36.35
Mauritania	1993–2000	49.37	25.94
Nepal	1995–2003	34.42	25.27
Senegal	1991–2001	45.38	17.01
Tanzania	1991–2000	61.51	56.99
Uganda	1992–2002	34.46	24.36
Yemen	1992–1998	3.38	9.42
Zambia	1991–2002	64.64	76.43

Source: Appendix table A5.1.

Appendix table A5.3 Average annual rate of change in some key variables, selected countries, 1990s

Country	Period	Average annual rate of growth (%)			
		Incidence of poverty (1)	Mean expenditure/ income (2)	GDP per capita (in constant local currency unit) (3)	Output per worker in non-formal segment (4)
Bangladesh	1991–2000	0.053	0.930	3.084	–
Bolivia	1990–2002	12.764	0.498	1.396	–
Brazil	1992–2002	–4.069	1.330	1.379	2.087
Burkina Faso	1994–2003	–6.290	1.574	2.008	–
Burundi	1992–1998	3.171	–1.138	–6.215	–
Cameroon	1996–2001	–12.015	6.082	2.336	–
China	1990–2001	–5.795	5.962	8.834	5.310
Colombia	1991–2003	8.660	–0.535	0.245	–
Costa Rica	1990–2001	–11.599	4.602	2.823	0.396
Côte d'Ivoire	1993–2002	5.296	1.596	0.407	–
Ecuador	1994–1998	–1.524	1.856	0.825	–
Egypt	1990–1999	–2.746	0.375	2.294	4.534
El Salvador	1995–2002	–0.249	3.033	1.110	–3.172
Ethiopia	1995–2000	–5.971	–1.644	1.672	–
Gambia	1992–1998	–10.786	13.000	–1.015	–
Ghana	1991–1998	–2.172	2.361	1.389	1.004
Guatemala	1998–2002	1.447	0.823	0.337	–1.364
Honduras	1990–1998	–5.608	5.756	0.626	0.851
India	1990–1999	–1.853	1.406	4.139	2.458
Kenya	1992–1997	–9.707	–1.576	0.422	–
Lao PDR	1992–2002	3.955	–0.103	3.792	–
Madagascar	1993–2001	3.512	–3.093	0.324	–
Malawi	1997–2004	–9.138	1.876	–1.098	–
Mali	1994–2001	–9.354	8.298	3.475	–
Mauritania	1993–2000	–8.784	3.200	1.261	–
Mexico	1992–2002	–1.841	–0.341	1.604	–0.622
Nepal	1995–2003	–3.789	4.777	1.694	–
Nicaragua	1993–2001	–0.756	–1.020	2.037	–5.656
Pakistan	1990–1996	–7.721	3.375	1.908	3.149
Panama	1991–2002	–5.885	2.050	2.293	3.144
Paraguay	1995–2002	–2.368	1.638	–1.653	0.620

Appendix table A5.3 Average annual rate of change in some key variables, selected countries, 1990s (continued)

Country	Period	Average annual rate of growth (%)			
		Incidence of poverty (1)	Mean expenditure/ income (2)	GDP per capita (in constant local currency unit) (3)	Output per worker in non-formal segment (4)
Peru	1996–2002	6.325	2.584	0.345	–
Philippines	1991–2000	–2.681	2.052	1.330	–0.335
Senegal	1991–2001	–9.347	2.641	1.443	–
South Africa	1993–2000	0.956	–0.880	0.373	–
Sri Lanka	1995–2002	–1.865	2.567	2.624	0.591
Tanzania	1991–2000	–0.844	0.843	0.331	0.110
Thailand	1992–2000	–13.255	0.386	2.040	3.197
Uganda	1992–2002	–3.409	2.896	4.169	2.652
Viet Nam	1993–2002	–19.190	4.592	5.682	1.949
Yemen	1992–1998	18.628	–8.877	3.597	–
Zambia	1991–2002	1.535	–2.978	–0.961	–
Zimbabwe	1990–1995	0.628	–4.043	–1.339	–

Note: The growth rates are estimated by using the compound interest formula with initial and terminal values in the case of poverty rate and mean expenditure/income, and by using regression equations in the case of output per worker in the non-formal segment.
– = data not available.

Sources: Cols. 1 and 2: World Bank, PovcalNet 2006 database (http://iresearch.worldbank.org/PovcalNet/jsp/index.jsp); Col. 3: World Bank, World Development Indicators database (CD-ROM, 2005); Col. 4: Chapter 4 (appendix table A.4.2).

Appendix table A5.4 Average annual rate of change in growth indicators, selected countries, 1990s (percentages)

Country	Period	Average annual rate of growth (%)		
		GDP per capita (in constant local currency unit) (1)	Output per worker in non-formal segment (2)	Trade as share of GDP (percentage)
Argentina	1998–2003	–4.051	–8.796	13.667
Belize	1996–2000	3.699	–2.838	5.997
Botswana	1995–2001	3.980	3.330	1.060
Brazil	1992–2002	1.379	2.087	4.234
Chile	1990–2003	4.061	3.060	0.318
China	1990–2001	8.834	5.310	2.873
Costa Rica	1990–2001	2.823	0.396	2.570
Cuba	1994–2000	3.712	2.345	3.315
Dominican Republic	1996–2002	4.753	2.918	1.480
Egypt	1990–1999	2.294	4.534	–4.506
El Salvador	1995–2002	1.110	–3.172	3.413
Fiji	1992–1998	1.561	–0.090	–4.244
Ghana	1991–1998	1.389	1.004	10.288
Guatemala	1998–2002	0.337	–1.364	0.193
Honduras	1990–1998	0.626	0.851	5.338
India	1990–1999	4.139	2.458	5.083
Jamaica	1992–2003	–0.160	–1.466	–1.788
Malaysia	1990–2003	3.430	1.709	3.262
Mexico	1992–2002	1.604	–0.622	5.584
Mongolia	1992–2003	–1.063	–3.848	1.847
Myanmar	1990–1999	4.872	3.887	–14.498
Namibia	1997–2000	0.334	7.375	–2.515
Nicaragua	1993–2001	2.037	–5.656	4.188
Pakistan	1990–1996	1.908	3.149	–0.295
Panama	1991–2002	2.293	3.144	–4.413
Paraguay	1995–2002	–1.653	0.620	–4.195
Philippines	1991–2000	1.330	–0.335	7.493
Sri Lanka	1995–2002	2.624	0.591	0.245
Tanzania	1991–2000	0.331	0.110	–4.161
Thailand	1992–2000	2.040	3.197	5.359
Uganda	1992–2002	4.169	2.652	2.284
Viet Nam	1993–2002	5.682	1.949	6.164

Note: The growth rates are estimated by using regression equations.

Sources: Cols. 1 and 3: World Bank, World Development Indicators database (CD-ROM, 2005); Col. 2: Chapter 4 (appendix table A4.2).

Appendix figure A5.1 Poverty (log difference) and mean expenditure/income (log difference)

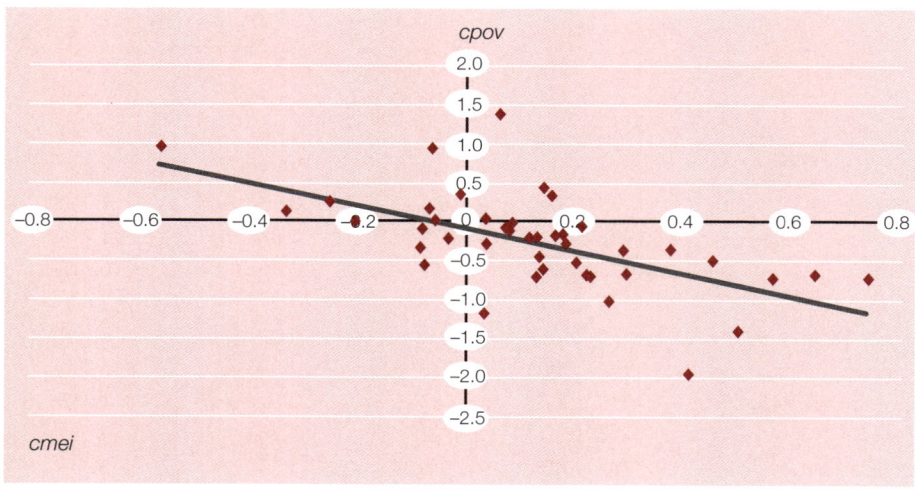

Note: The estimated regression equation is:
$cpov = -0.0391 - 1.459\ cmei$, $R^2 = 0.355$, number of observations: 43
      (0.645) (0.000)
where *cpov* is change (log difference) in the incidence of poverty, *cmei* is change (log difference) in mean expenditure/income and the figures in parentheses are P-values (indicating the level of significance).

Source: World Bank, PovcalNet 2006 database (http://iresearch.worldbank.org/PovcalNet/jsp/index.jsp).

PERSISTENT EMPLOYMENT PROBLEMS IN DEVELOPED COUNTRIES   6

The story of the emergence of employment problems in the developed world is by now well known. In the 1960s, near-full employment prevailed in most of the developed countries; the rate of unemployment exceeded 5 per cent in only four of them – Canada, Greece, Ireland and the United States (appendix table A6.1). Following the first oil shock in 1973, the unemployment rate started rising, reaching a high level by the early 1980s. It remained stable at a high level until the mid-1990s and showed a downward trend thereafter. Despite the recent decline, however, unemployment still remains high in a majority of the countries belonging to this group. This is the general picture. In a few countries the pattern of change was somewhat different: in Germany, Japan and Switzerland the rise in the unemployment rate has been slow but steady and the trend is yet to be reversed. Also, in Austria, Iceland, Japan, Luxembourg, Norway and Switzerland unemployment never really reached very high levels.

Rising unemployment, however, is only one part of the story: the other part has been the growing incidence of non-standard jobs. The share of part-time employment[56] in total employment started rising in most countries in the early 1980s (appendix table A6.2) and – unlike the trend in the unemployment rate – persists to this day. In some European developed countries, where the level of employment protection has traditionally been high, there has also been significant growth of temporary employment[57] (appendix table A6.2). In other words, both underemployment and job insecurity have grown.

---

[56] Part-time employment involves usual working hours of less than 30 hours per week.
[57] Temporary employees include workers on fixed-term contracts, temporary agency workers, workers on contracts for a specific task, workers on replacement contracts, seasonal workers, on-call workers, daily workers, trainees or apprentices without guarantee of permanent contract and workers employed under job creation schemes.

Although much research has been done and many policy changes have been introduced, it cannot be claimed that the causes behind the persistence of the employment problem are well understood. Moreover, it does not appear that the policy changes have been particularly successful in dealing with the problem. This is the backdrop against which this chapter undertakes a fresh analysis of the issue and of the appropriateness of policy responses.

6.1 Employment and unemployment in developed countries

The current employment situation

The basic facts about employment, unemployment and labour force participation in the developed world in the current period are set out in tables 6.1 and 6.2. Data are presented for 2003, as more recent information on indicators other than the unemployment rate was not available for several countries when work on this book began. At any rate, more recent data on unemployment rates do not show substantial changes since 2003 (appendix table A6.3). The observations that can be derived from the data in table 6.1 are as follows:

- The unemployment rate is high: in 14 of the 23 countries making up the developed world it exceeds 5 per cent, and in eight of those 14 countries it is higher than 7 per cent.

- Remarkably, however, the rate of long-term unemployment (duration: one year or more) is low in most of the countries; it exceeds 2 per cent in only eight of the 22 countries for which the relevant data are available. In contrast, the rate of short-term unemployment (duration: less than one year) exceeds 4 per cent in 14 countries. As a rule, a high level of overall unemployment now reflects a high level of short-term unemployment.

- The incidence of part-time employment is high in most countries. Its share in total employment exceeds 15 per cent in 13 countries; in eight of these it is higher than 20 per cent.

- Substantial sections of the employed workforce are in insecure jobs. The share of temporary employment in total employment exceeds 10 per cent in eight of the 18 European countries belonging to this category.

- Temporary employment is relevant only in the case of those seeking wage employment, of course, and it can be argued that the same is true of part-time employment (part-time self-employment is not very meaningful as a notion and is in any case hard to measure). If we consider the shares of

Table 6.1   Employment and unemployment, 2003 (percentages)

Country	Unemployment rate	Short-term unemployment rate	Long-term unemployment rate	Part-time employment as share of total employment	Temporary employment as share of total employment	Part-time employment as share of total wage employment	Temporary employment as share of total wage employment
Australia	5.71	4.42	1.29	26.47	–	30.55	–
Austria	4.21	3.08	1.13	13.18	6.09	15.09	6.80
Belgium	7.68	4.13	3.55	17.64	7.15	20.49	8.29
Canada	7.60	6.87	0.73	18.92	–	20.97	–
Denmark	5.40	4.34	1.06	15.79	8.40	17.29	9.07
Finland	9.05	6.93	2.12	11.24	14.28	12.89	16.24
France	9.73	5.93	3.80	12.46	11.31	13.65	12.08
Germany	9.27	4.40	4.86	19.61	10.85	22.12	12.13
Greece	9.34	4.09	5.26	5.63	6.91	8.11	9.72
Iceland[a]	3.35	–	–	20.10	4.87	24.02	5.52
Ireland	4.38	2.80	1.58	18.87	4.28	22.85	5.17
Italy	8.65	3.54	5.12	11.95	7.25	16.40	9.77
Japan	5.22	3.48	1.74	25.42	–	29.96	–
Luxembourg	3.68	2.75	0.92	13.26	3.21	14.83	3.57
Netherlands	4.20	3.16	1.04	35.01	12.67	39.33	14.29
New Zealand	4.64	4.11	0.53	22.02	–	27.20	–
Norway	4.42	4.14	0.28	20.81	8.72	22.44	9.20
Portugal	6.37	4.35	2.02	10.02	15.89	13.63	20.46
Spain	11.30	7.11	4.19	7.83	26.08	9.60	32.92
Sweden	5.77	4.78	0.99	13.78	13.41	15.22	14.59
Switzerland	4.13	3.07	1.06	25.11	10.06	28.73	11.20
United Kingdom	4.84	3.71	1.13	23.80	5.18	27.37	5.84
United States	5.99	5.28	0.71	11.74	–	12.70	–

Notes: [a] Data on part-time employment refer to 2002.
– = data not available.

Source: OECD OLISNET database (http://stats.oecd.org/WBOS/default.aspx).

Table 6.2　Labour force participation rate in developed countries, 2003 (percentages)

Country	Participation rate (%)
Australia	62.71
Austria	58.93
Belgium	51.31
Canada	65.51
Denmark	65.37
Finland	60.55
France	55.83
Germany	56.12
Greece	51.36
Iceland[a]	73.20
Ireland	59.13
Italy	49.24
Japan	60.76
Luxembourg	53.17
Netherlands	63.36
New Zealand	65.48
Norway	64.94
Portugal	61.63
Spain	52.42
Sweden	62.19
Switzerland	67.04
United Kingdom	60.12
United States	63.62

[a] Refers to 2002.

Source: Derived from OECD OLISNET database (http://stats.oecd.org/WBOS/default.aspx).

part-time and temporary employment in total wage employment, we see that non-standard wage employment is now a major feature of labour markets in developed countries.

The employment problem facing developed countries today thus has two defining characteristics: high short-term unemployment and high incidence of non-standard wage employment. There is, of course, some degree of heterogeneity across countries – the long-term unemployment rate is high in a few countries (e.g., Germany, Greece and Italy) and the incidence of non-standard

Figure 6.1 Short-term unemployment and temporary employment, 2003

Note: The regression equation is: $Y = 2.595 + 0.140\ X$, $R^2 = 0.550$. The coefficient is significant at less than 1 per cent.
Based on data for the following 18 countries: Austria, Belgium, Denmark, Finland, France, Germany, Greece, Iceland, Ireland, Italy, Luxembourg, Netherlands, Norway, Portugal, Spain, Sweden, Switzerland, United Kingdom.

Source: Derived from table 6.1.

wage employment is low in a few (e.g. Greece) – but the general picture is clear enough.

There are reasons to think that the level of unemployment and the incidence of non-standard employment are in fact interrelated. When many people are in temporary jobs, flows in and out of employment are large, so that frictional or short-term unemployment is likely to be high. And when many people are in part-time jobs, whether permanent or temporary, there is substantial work-sharing so that long-term unemployment should be low.

Figure 6.1 shows the cross-country relationship between the rate of short-term unemployment and the share of temporary employment in total wage employment. The relationship is positive and significant: a country with a higher incidence of temporary employment also has a higher rate of short-term unemployment. Figure 6.2 shows the cross-country relationship between the rate of long-term unemployment and the share of part-time employment in total employment. The relationship is negative and significant: a country with a higher incidence of part-time employment also has a lower rate of long-term unemployment.

Much of the part-time employment, however, is reported to be voluntary. This suggests that at least some of those who are currently in part-time

The global employment challenge

Figure 6.2   Long-term unemployment and part-time employment, 2003

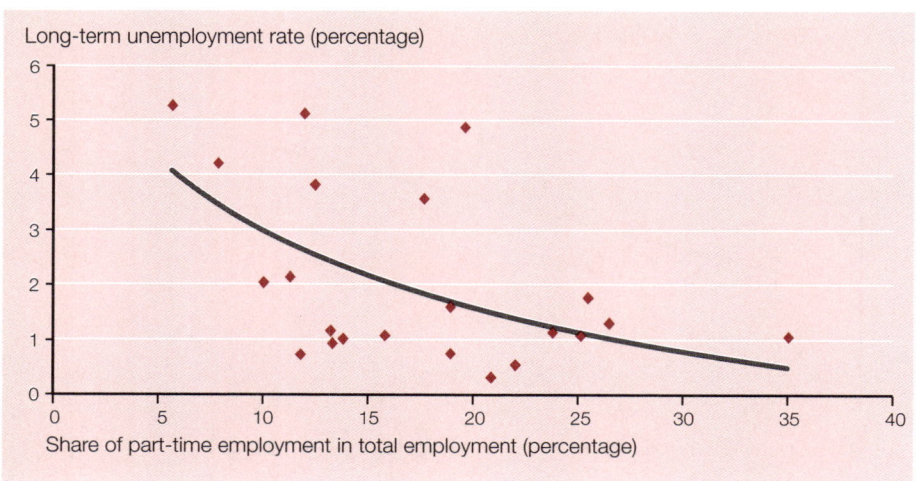

Note: The regression equation is: $Y = 7.510 - 1.974 \ln(X)$, $R^2 = 0.287$. The coefficient is significant at 1 per cent. Based on data for the following 22 countries: Australia, Austria, Belgium, Canada, Denmark, Finland, France, Germany, Greece, Ireland, Italy, Japan, Luxembourg, Netherlands, New Zealand, Norway, Portugal, Spain, Sweden, Switzerland, United Kingdom, United States.

Source: Derived from table 6.1.

employment might not have entered the labour force at all had part-time jobs not been available. In other words, availability of part-time jobs induced some economically inactive persons to enter the labour force and hence increased the labour force participation rate. Figure 6.3 shows that this is indeed the case: countries with higher incidences of part-time employment tend to have higher labour force participation rates.

What emerges from all this is that labour markets in developed countries today are flexible in that they offer ample opportunities for establishing non-standard employment contracts. Such flexibility helps keep labour force participation at a high level and long-term unemployment at a low level. However, it also generates underemployment and insecurity for a substantial section of the workers.

It is arguable that, in view of the high incidence of non-standard employment, the overall unemployment rate can no longer be regarded as an adequate indicator of the overall employment situation in developed countries. When employment is associated with varying degrees of underemployment and insecurity, a binary classification of the labour force into "employed" and "unemployed" does not seem very appropriate or informative. It is worthwhile, therefore, to try to construct what might be called a Composite Employment Indicator (CEI)

Figure 6.3 Labour force participation and part-time employment, 2003

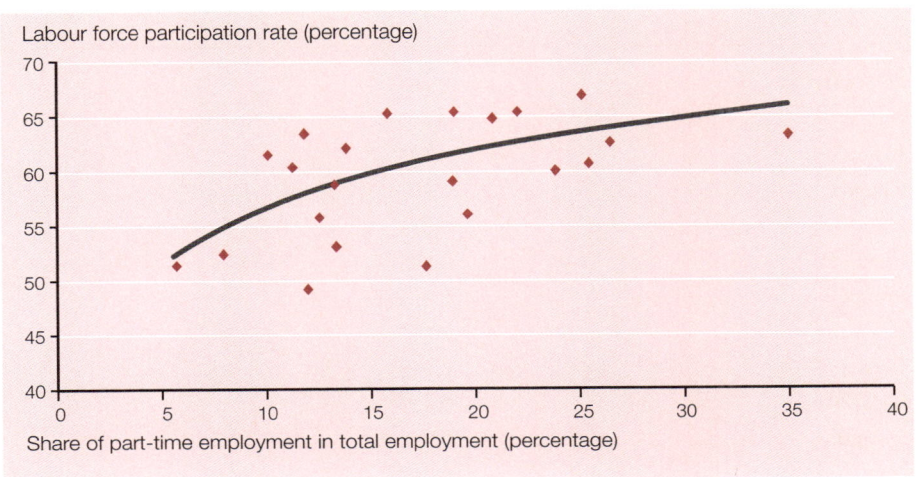

Note: The regression equation is: Y = 39.373 + 7.495 Ln(X), R² = 0.292. The coefficient is significant at less than 1 per cent. Based on data for the following 22 countries: Australia, Austria, Belgium, Canada, Denmark, Finland, France, Germany, Greece, Ireland, Italy, Japan, Luxembourg, Netherlands, New Zealand, Norway, Portugal, Spain, Sweden, Switzerland, United Kingdom, United States.

Sources: Derived from tables 6.1 and 6.2.

that incorporates both the extent of unemployment and the extent of non-standard employment. A simple way of constructing this is as follows:

$$CEI = [(LF/WAP) + (E/LF) + (FTE/E)] / 3$$

where LF is labour force, WAP is working-age population, E is total employment and FTE is full-time employment.

It is easy to see that the CEI attains the maximum value of unity when labour force participation is at 100 per cent and there is no unemployment or part-time employment. This can be regarded as the "ideal" employment situation, which may never be attained in reality but nevertheless serves as a useful benchmark. The larger the distance of the actual CEI value from unity (i.e., the smaller the actual value of the CEI), the worse is the employment situation.

Two observations are in order. First, one type of non-standard employment that is being left out of account in the formulation of the CEI is temporary employment. Currently we do not have separate data for temporary part-time and temporary full-time employment. Also, scant data are available for non-European developed countries. If and when such data become available, the formula for the CEI can be easily modified to incorporate the aspect of temporary employment. Second, the formulation accords equal weights to the

Table 6.3 Composite Employment Indicator (CEI) estimates, 2003

Country	CEI
Australia	0.768
Austria	0.805
Belgium	0.753
Canada	0.797
Denmark	0.814
Finland	0.802
France	0.779
Germany	0.757
Greece	0.788
Iceland[a]	0.833
Ireland	0.786
Italy	0.762
Japan	0.767
Luxembourg	0.787
Netherlands	0.747
New Zealand	0.796
Norway	0.799
Portugal	0.817
Spain	0.778
Sweden	0.809
Switzerland	0.795
United Kingdom	0.772
United States	0.820

[a] Refers to 2002.

Source: Authors' calculations based on data in tables 6.1 and 6.2

CEI's three components. At present we do not have very good arguments for assigning different weights to them: more research is required to see if there are solid grounds for assigning different weights to the different components.

Table 6.3 presents CEI estimates for the year 2003. Judged by these estimates, Iceland, the United States, Portugal and Denmark appear to have the best overall employment situation while Belgium, Germany and the Netherlands appear to have the worst. Figure 6.4 depicts the cross-country relationship between the CEI and the unemployment rate. It shows that there is no significant relation between the two.

Figure 6.4 Unemployment rate and overall employment situation, 2003

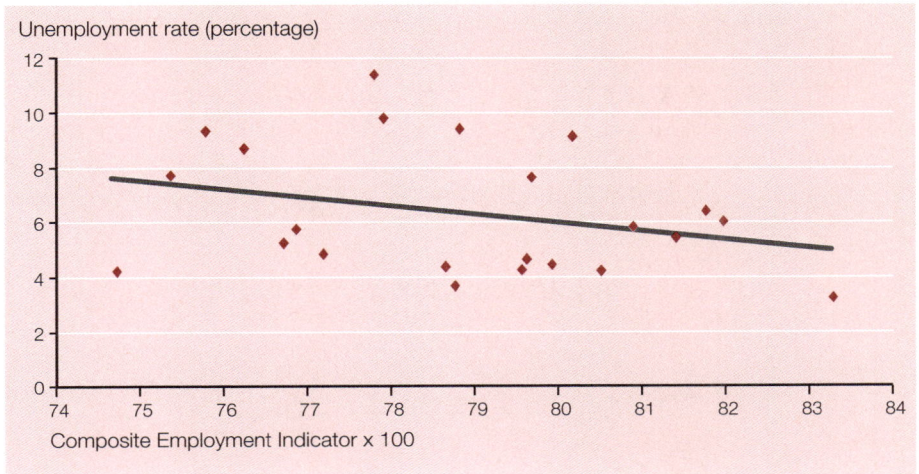

Note: The regression equation is: Y = 30.078 − 0.302 X, R² = 0.091. The coefficient is significant only at 16.2 per cent. Based on data for the following 23 countries: Australia, Austria, Belgium, Canada, Denmark, Finland, France, Germany, Greece, Iceland, Ireland, Italy, Japan, Luxembourg, Netherlands, New Zealand, Norway, Portugal, Spain, Sweden, Switzerland, United Kingdom, United States.

Sources: Derived from tables 6.1 and 6.3.

The CEI, as constructed above, really shows the rate of utilization of the available labour and implicitly assumes that all workers in part-time employment would prefer full-time employment. However, some of the workers in part-time employment are known to have voluntarily chosen it and would not have entered the labour market if part-time jobs had not been available. This needs to be taken into account in judging the employment situation. Modifying the CEI as follows can do this:

$$MCEI = [(MLF/WAP) + (ME/MLF) + (MFTE/ME)] / 3$$

where MCEI is modified CEI, MLF (= $ME + U$) is modified labour force, ME (= $FTE + 0.5\ PTE$) is modified total employment, U (= $LF - E$) is total unemployment, $MFTE$ (= $FTE + 0.5\ VPTE$) is modified full-time employment and $VPTE$ is voluntary part-time employment.

Several qualifying remarks are in order. First, the MCEI cannot be computed for two countries – Finland and the United States – as no data on voluntary/involuntary part-time employment are available. Second, the available estimates of voluntary part-time employment are generally thought to be overestimates. Some persons understandably find it difficult to admit that they have not found the jobs they were looking for. Thus some of those

Table 6.4 Key employment indicators by gender, 2003 (percentages)

Country	Male					Female				
	PR	UR	URS	URL	PTE	TEMP	PR	UR	URS	URL	PTE	TEMP
Australia	82.69	5.61	4.09	1.52	15.67	–	66.73	5.84	4.84	1.00	39.89	–
Austria	80.09	4.28	3.05	1.23	3.04	6.14	64.66	4.12	3.11	1.01	25.74	6.00
Belgium	73.07	7.44	4.12	3.32	5.86	5.20	56.16	8.00	4.14	3.85	33.28	9.72
Canada	84.87	7.97	7.10	0.88	11.07	–	74.05	7.18	6.62	0.56	27.86	–
Denmark	85.36	5.09	4.00	1.10	10.52	7.17	75.67	5.75	4.73	1.02	21.91	9.79
Finland	76.70	9.19	6.77	2.41	7.89	10.60	72.37	8.90	7.11	1.80	14.86	18.24
France	75.50	8.70	5.29	3.41	4.52	9.81	63.73	10.94	6.68	4.26	22.02	13.10
Germany	78.96	9.63	4.73	4.90	5.96	10.48	65.06	8.82	4.00	4.82	36.28	11.30
Greece	80.24	6.02	3.07	2.94	2.87	5.84	52.79	14.33	5.60	8.72	10.17	8.64
Iceland[a]	94.15	3.60	–	–	10.24	4.15	86.70	3.08	–	–	31.18	5.28
Ireland	80.31	4.76	2.78	1.98	7.58	3.37	58.23	3.85	2.83	1.03	34.37	5.55
Italy	76.15	6.74	2.85	3.89	4.86	5.74	48.83	11.62	4.60	7.02	23.63	9.72
Japan	91.74	5.47	3.33	2.14	14.37	–	64.31	4.86	3.69	1.17	41.26	–
Luxembourg	75.88	3.00	2.03	0.96	1.63	2.73	54.70	4.63	3.77	0.87	30.06	3.90
Netherlands	84.74	4.10	3.06	1.04	14.99	10.98	68.38	4.34	3.29	1.05	60.50	14.79
New Zealand	85.40	4.34	3.76	0.58	10.70	–	70.33	4.99	4.53	0.47	35.40	–
Norway	84.54	4.85	4.51	0.34	9.77	6.85	77.16	3.95	3.73	0.22	33.15	10.76
Portugal	83.88	5.55	3.93	1.62	5.85	14.42	69.40	7.33	4.84	2.49	14.98	17.64
Spain	81.63	8.17	5.58	2.58	2.46	23.86	56.00	15.91	9.36	6.55	16.44	29.63
Sweden	82.63	6.31	5.12	1.19	7.72	10.73	77.69	5.18	4.40	0.78	20.35	16.29
Switzerland	88.55	3.94	3.11	0.84	8.14	9.53	74.13	4.59	3.20	1.39	45.81	10.70
United Kingdom	85.44	5.46	3.96	1.50	10.03	4.33	70.22	4.10	3.41	0.69	39.85	6.17
United States	85.09	6.27	5.49	0.78	6.87	–	71.88	5.66	5.04	0.62	17.28	–

[a] Data on PTE refer to 2002.

PR – labour force participation rate. UR – unemployment rate. URS – short-term unemployment rate. URL – long-term unemployment rate. PTE – share of part-time employment in total employment. TEMP – share of temporary employment in total employment.
– = data not available.

Source: Derived from OECD OLISNET database (http://stats.oecd.org/WBOS/default.aspx).

claiming to have voluntarily chosen part-time employment might in fact be prepared to accept full-time employment if available. The MCEI therefore tends to show the employment situation as better than it really is. Finally, in so far as the degree of overestimation of voluntary part-time employment varies across countries, some problems of cross-country comparability also arise.

The MCEI is thus a better indicator of employment situation than the CEI in conceptual terms but not necessarily so in empirical terms. At any rate, its use alters the ranking of the countries somewhat: Iceland, Portugal and Denmark still turn out to have the best employment situation but Greece, Italy and Belgium now turn out to have the worst (see appendix table A6.4). Moreover, there is a fairly strong inverse relation between the MCEI and the rate of unemployment (see appendix figure A6.1), suggesting that unemployment rate is an imperfect but not misleading indicator of the employment situation.

Gender disparity in employment

Given the nature of the labour markets, gender disparity in employment can arise from three different sources: differential labour force participation rates, differential unemployment rates and differential incidences of non-standard employment. The relevant data for the year 2003 are put together in table 6.4. The following observations can be made on the basis of these data:

- The labour force participation rate is systematically lower for women than for men.

- The overall unemployment rate for women is not systematically different from that for men. Women's unemployment rate is higher than that of men in 12 of the 23 countries and lower in the remaining 11 countries.

- The short-term unemployment rate tends to be higher for women while the long-term unemployment rate tends to be higher for men.

- The incidence of part-time employment is much higher for women than for men. The share of involuntary part-time employment in total part-time employment is also generally higher for women than for men (see appendix table 6.5). In other words, the incidence of involuntary part-time employment is significantly higher for women than for men. This explains why the long-term unemployment rate is, more often than not, lower for women than for men.

- The incidence of temporary employment is also higher for women, although not by a wide margin. This explains why the short-term unemployment rate is, more often than not, higher for women than for men.

The global employment challenge

It is clear that gender disparity in employment arises essentially from differences in labour force participation and in incidence of part-time employment. A simple way of representing this disparity is to estimate first the CEI separately for men and women and then the ratio of the value for women to the corresponding value for men. The higher the value of this ratio, the lower is the gender disparity.

Table 6.5 presents the estimates of the degree of gender disparity in employment, while figure 6.5 shows the cross-country relationship between gender disparity and overall employment situation. The basic result that

Table 6.5 Gender disparity in employment, 2003[a]

Country	Ratio of CEIs: female to male
Australia	0.841
Austria	0.846
Belgium (2002)	0.816
Canada	0.892
Denmark	0.907
Finland	0.938
France	0.867
Germany	0.820
Greece (1999)	0.835
Iceland (2002)	0.886
Ireland	0.818
Italy	0.805
Japan	0.929
Luxembourg	0.805
Netherlands	0.751
New Zealand	0.846
Norway	0.872
Portugal	0.899
Spain	0.825
Sweden	0.923
Switzerland	0.791
United Kingdom	0.831
United States	0.915

[a] Unless otherwise indicated in parentheses.

Source: Authors' estimates based on data in table 6.4.

Persistent employment problems in developed countries

Figure 6.5 Gender disparity and overall employment situation, 2003

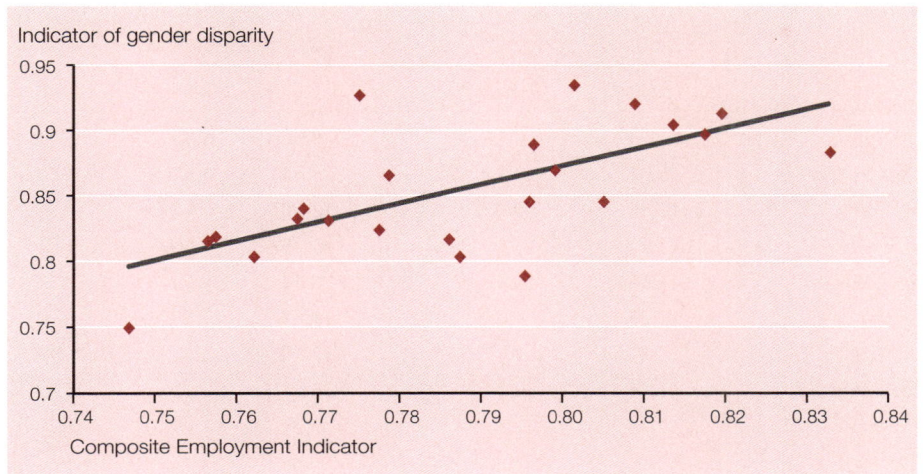

Note: The regression equation is: $Y = -0.283 + 1.444\,X$, $R^2 = 0.442$. The coefficient is significant at less than 1 per cent. Based on data for the following 23 countries: Australia, Austria, Belgium, Canada, Denmark, Finland, France, Germany, Greece, Iceland, Ireland, Italy, Japan, Luxembourg, Netherlands, New Zealand, Norway, Portugal, Spain, Sweden, Switzerland, United Kingdom, United States.

Sources: Derived from tables 6.1 and 6.5.

emerges is that the better the overall employment situation, the lower is the degree of gender disparity in employment. Interestingly, this result does not change if we measure gender disparity by using MCEI estimates instead of CEI estimates (see appendix table A6.6 and appendix figure A6.2).

Skills and employment

The existence of a skills mismatch is an important characteristic of the labour market in developed countries; this is underlined by the fact that the average level of education of the unemployed is significantly lower than that of the employed (table 6.6). In fact, in most countries the rate of unemployment steadily declines as the level of education rises. In broad terms, low-skilled workers (and medium-skilled workers in some cases) have a significantly higher probability of being unemployed than high-skilled workers; indeed, it would be only a slight distortion to say that unemployment is a serious problem only for the low skilled.[58] There is also evidence to suggest that low-skilled workers have a

---

[58] In the analysis, we focus particularly on the low skilled and the high skilled. It should be said, however, that much of what is said about the low skilled also applies to a section of the medium skilled.

The global employment challenge

Table 6.6 Employment, unemployment and level of education,[a] 2003

Country	Average years of education		Rate of unemployment (%) Level of education		
	Employed	Employed	Low	Medium	High
Australia	10.54	9.11	9.56	5.43	3.59
Austria	10.61	9.38	8.30	3.62	2.01
Belgium	10.86	9.45	12.50	8.40	4.39
Canada	11.77	10.60	13.75	7.50	5.39
Denmark	11.15	10.46	8.31	4.55	4.74
Finland	11.25	9.89	14.88	10.88	4.31
France	10.47	9.47	13.90	8.62	6.84
Germany	11.11	10.07	16.08	10.17	5.11
Greece	9.74	9.83	7.69	11.97	6.34
Iceland	–	–	–	–	–
Ireland	10.54	9.28	7.26	4.01	3.00
Italy	9.26	8.67	10.65	8.77	5.45
Japan	11.54	11.02	6.51	5.83	4.07
Luxembourg	10.30	9.92	4.00	2.72	3.11
Netherlands	10.38	9.12	4.98	2.46	1.98
New Zealand	11.08	10.35	7.16	4.01	3.92
Norway	11.59	10.83	6.96	4.72	2.65
Portugal	7.59	7.49	6.29	6.96	5.10
Spain	9.57	8.95	12.73	11.32	8.79
Sweden	11.34	10.41	9.07	5.79	3.86
Switzerland	11.33	10.33	8.58	3.89	2.99
United Kingdom	11.51	10.46	9.67	5.19	2.58
United States	11.71	10.33	13.00	6.81	3.38

[a] Level of education: low – up to lower secondary (assumed average years of education: 6); medium – above lower secondary and up to higher secondary (assumed average years of education: 11); high – tertiary (assumed average years of education: 14.5).
– = data not available.
Source: Derived from OECD OLISNET database (http://stats.oecd.org/WBOS/default.aspx).

significantly higher probability of being in non-standard jobs (see box 6.1). The employment problem in developed countries today reflects, to a very large extent, a shortfall in the demand for low-skilled labour in relation to its supply.

Significantly, labour force participation of low-skilled persons is also low, suggesting the presence of a fairly strong "discouraged worker effect" (table 6.7). The participation rate of persons with up to lower secondary level

Box 6.1 Level of education and non-standard employment

The table below shows that temporary jobs are held mainly by low- and medium-skilled workers.

Incidence and distribution of temporary employment by level of education, 2000

Country	Temporary employment as share of total wage employment by level of education (%)			Distribution of temporary workers by level of education (%)		
	Low	Medium	High	Low	Medium	High
Austria	21.9	4.2	5.7	54.4	35.3	10.3
Belgium	10.3	9.7	8.1	35.5	34.3	30.2
Canada	15.4	14.5	10.6	4.0	51.8	44.2
Denmark	18.9	8.5	5.9	40.9	44.6	14.5
Finland	17.9	20.5	13.9	21.7	50.6	27.7
France	16.3	15.2	13.0	32.8	45.2	22.1
Germany	29.5	9.2	9.1	41.1	42.1	16.8
Greece	17.7	12.1	9.4	41.0	40.5	18.5
Iceland	5.3	5.8	5.0	44.0	36.1	19.9
Ireland	11.5	8.4	8.1	42.5	30.8	26.7
Italy	10.2	9.6	11.3	43.0	43.5	13.6
Luxembourg	3.2	3.7	2.9	32.6	50.0	17.4
Netherlands	17.1	11.7	10.2	40.0	40.0	20.0
Norway	11.1	9.4	9.7	14.3	53.0	32.7
Portugal	19.4	24.0	20.6	70.3	17.5	12.3
Spain	36.6	29.5	26.2	57.9	17.9	24.2
Sweden	17.9	14.0	13.4	23.8	47.6	28.6
Switzerland	30.0	5.9	8.6	54.5	28.9	16.7
United Kingdom	5.3	6.0	8.9	10.0	51.4	38.6
United States	6.1	4.1	3.3	18.4	51.1	30.5

Note: Level of education: low – up to lower secondary (assumed average years of education: 6); medium – above lower secondary and up to higher secondary (assumed average years of education: 11); high – tertiary (assumed average years of education: 14.5).

Source: OECD (2002).

It should be noted that most of the low- and medium-skilled temporary workers usually hold work contracts of less than one year. They thus tend to be ineligible for non-wage benefits, besides earning substantially lower wages than the permanent workers engaged in similar work. In contrast, high-skilled temporary workers usually

(continued)

> **Box 6.1   Level of education and non-standard employment (continued)**
>
> hold work contracts of more than one year. They tend to be eligible for the same non-wage benefits as permanent workers and earn the same wages as permanent workers engaged in similar work. The probability of their moving to permanent jobs is also high (OECD, 2002; Booth et al., 2002; Holmlund and Storrie, 2002; Dolado et al., 2002).
>
> Information on the nature and characteristics of part-time employment is scarce. However, the rather dated information available from EC (1997) and OECD (1999) reveals the following:
>
> - Part-time workers have lower levels of education, on average, than full-time workers.
> - Across countries, the average hourly earning of part-time workers ranges between 55 and 90 per cent of the average hourly earning of full-time workers.
> - In many cases, non-wage benefits received by part-time workers are lower, even on a pro rata basis, than those received by full-time workers.
> - The occupations in which the share of part-time workers in all workers is high are also occupations where the average wage is low for all workers.
>
> These facts certainly suggest that a majority of part-time workers are low skilled. Admittedly, however, more research and up-to-date information are required to confirm the validity of this conclusion.

of education tends to be lower than that of persons with tertiary education by as much as 30–35 percentage points. The gap is larger among women than among men.

It is worth underlining that these labour market disadvantages of low-skilled workers are observed in all the countries even though labour market institutions vary across them. The unemployment rate of low-skilled workers is 4.1 times that of high-skilled workers in Austria, the United Kingdom and the United States, 2.6 times in Australia and Norway, 2.4 times in Ireland and Sweden, and 1.8 times in Denmark and New Zealand (see table 6.6). The participation rate of low-skilled persons is lower than that of high-skilled persons by 35 percentage points in both Finland and the United States, by 33 percentage points in both Austria and the United Kingdom, and by 27 percentage points in both Denmark and France (see table 6.7).

It is clear that the employment problem facing the developed world today is rooted in serious labour market disadvantages of low-skilled workers, reflected in a combination of low labour force participation, high

Persistent employment problems in developed countries

Table 6.7 Labour force[a] participation by gender and level of education,[b] 2003 (percentages)

Country	Participation rate (percentage) Level of education								
	Male			Female			All		
	Low	Medium	High	Low	Medium	High	Low	Medium	High
Australia	73.19	87.91	90.99	55.58	72.99	80.95	63.43	81.71	85.70
Austria	61.95	83.34	88.21	46.78	69.83	82.75	53.04	76.90	86.09
Belgium	58.18	77.96	89.47	35.45	61.06	82.65	47.10	69.78	85.94
Canada	67.49	85.60	89.89	50.64	74.01	82.60	59.52	80.08	85.98
Denmark	69.22	86.39	91.50	54.69	78.23	87.18	62.25	82.54	89.29
Finland	54.58	78.49	90.78	51.21	74.03	87.05	53.01	76.37	88.74
France	62.85	81.71	86.79	48.85	70.73	79.26	55.56	76.55	82.85
Germany	59.74	82.75	90.30	44.17	71.10	83.17	51.07	76.94	87.42
Greece	71.73	78.50	89.18	38.84	53.87	82.91	54.70	65.91	86.19
Iceland	–	–	–	–	–	–	–	–	–
Ireland	67.35	85.40	91.90	35.37	64.32	82.80	52.53	74.11	87.16
Italy[c]	67.44	79.17	90.38	32.45	62.73	82.38	49.87	70.99	86.41
Japan	80.49	84.12	87.40	51.87	59.20	64.54	66.59	71.23	76.35
Luxembourg	62.53	77.03	87.21	42.83	56.00	74.25	52.85	67.18	82.78
Netherlands[c]	74.25	86.93	92.80	50.00	75.19	84.41	61.50	81.22	89.01
New Zealand	70.85	86.46	89.59	53.90	72.36	79.58	62.16	79.82	84.05
Norway	65.71	82.91	92.50	53.81	76.00	87.51	59.91	79.65	89.87
Portugal	78.92	69.16	91.93	62.19	64.27	89.02	70.69	66.60	90.14
Spain	79.07	77.19	89.60	43.51	58.57	81.87	61.54	67.80	85.75
Sweden	64.83	86.53	87.42	56.57	81.49	85.58	62.28	84.10	86.44
Switzerland	52.21	88.60	95.21	47.70	74.86	84.59	49.75	81.12	92.14
United Kingdom	64.95	84.77	92.06	46.99	74.21	86.73	55.63	79.83	89.58
United States	56.98	82.09	90.05	41.69	70.80	80.15	49.74	76.32	84.90

[a] Labour force is defined as population in age group 15–64. [b] Level of education: low – up to lower secondary (assumed average years of education: 6); medium – above lower secondary and up to higher secondary (assumed average years of education: 11); high – tertiary (assumed average years of education: 14.5). [c] Data refer to 2002.
– = data not available.

Source: Derived from OECD OLISNET database (http://stats.oecd.org/WBOS/default.aspx).

Box 6.2 Earnings inequality

In many of the developed countries where unemployment declined during 1991–2003, earnings inequality is known to have risen. Unfortunately, the available empirical evidence on earnings relates to full-time, permanent workers only. Even these data, presented in the table below, show a large and widening gap in earnings between high-skilled and low-skilled labour.

Ratio of gross earnings of the lowest- to the highest-paid workers, selected countries, 1990–2001

Country	1990–94	1995–99	2000–01
Australia	2.82	2.94	3.07
Finland	2.39	2.36	2.41
France	3.21	3.07	–
Germany	2.79	2.87	–
Japan	3.07	2.99	–
Netherlands	2.60	2.85	–
New Zealand	3.06	3.28	–
Sweden	2.11	2.23	2.30
United Kingdom	3.39	3.45	3.40
United States	4.39	4.59	4.64

Notes: The figures refer to the ratio of the gross earnings per full-time employee in the top 10 per cent to that in the bottom 10 per cent.

– = data not available.

Source: OECD (2004).

As estimates of earnings inequality these are serious underestimates, and the degree of underestimation is likely to have increased over time. The reason is that data on earnings of part-time and temporary workers (who tend to have lower earnings than full-time, permanent workers) are not included and the share of these workers in total employed workforce has been increasing over time. Moreover, the estimates are of inequality of earnings per worker, which is expected to be substantially lower than the inequality of earnings per person in worker households. The data on participation rates by level of education (table 6.7) suggest that a low-earning worker has more dependants to support than a high-earning worker.

Persistent employment problems in developed countries

unemployment and high incidence of non-standard employment. The high and growing earnings inequality observed in developed countries is largely due to the high and persistent "employment inequality" between high-skilled and low-skilled labour (box 6.2). The dwindling share of labour in national income also reflects the serious labour market disadvantages of low-skilled workers.[59] These features are common to all developed countries even though they do not have the same labour market institutions and policies.

6.2 Persisting trends

Trends in overall employment situation

There are five important trends that can be discerned from the empirical evidence over the last decade and a half. First, the unemployment rate declined between 1991 and 2003. In figure 6.6, the average rate of unemployment for the period 2001–03 is plotted against the average for the period 1991–93 with a 45° line passing through the origin. The figure shows that in most countries the unemployment rate in 2001–03 was lower than that in 1991–93.

Figure 6.6   Average rate of unemployment, 1991–93 versus 2001–03

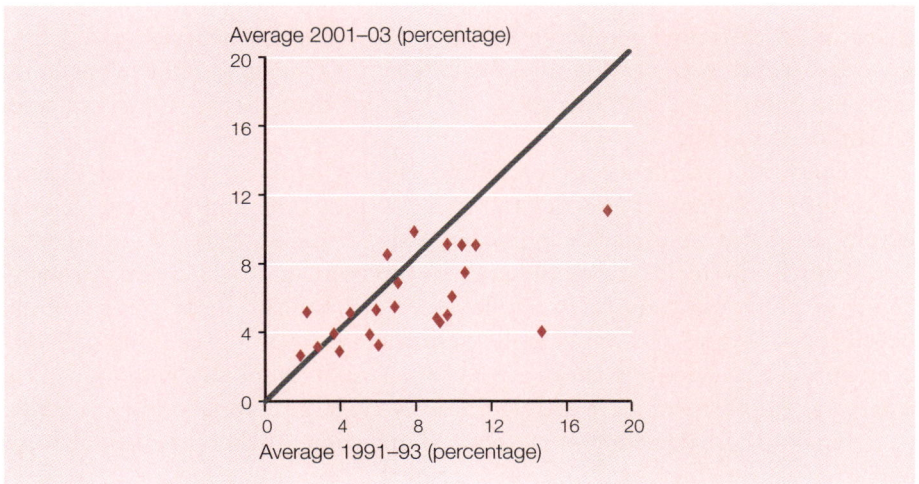

Source: Derived from OECD OLISNET database (http://stats.oecd.org/WBOS/default.aspx).

---

[59] A recent study (IMF, 2007) shows that the share of labour in national income in developed countries has been declining since 1980. It also finds that "... most of the decline in the labour share can be attributed to the fall in unskilled sectors ... The income share of labour in skilled sectors, on the other hand, has been on the rise ..." (p. 168).

Figure 6.7   Average share of short-term unemployed in all unemployed, 1991–93 versus 2001–03

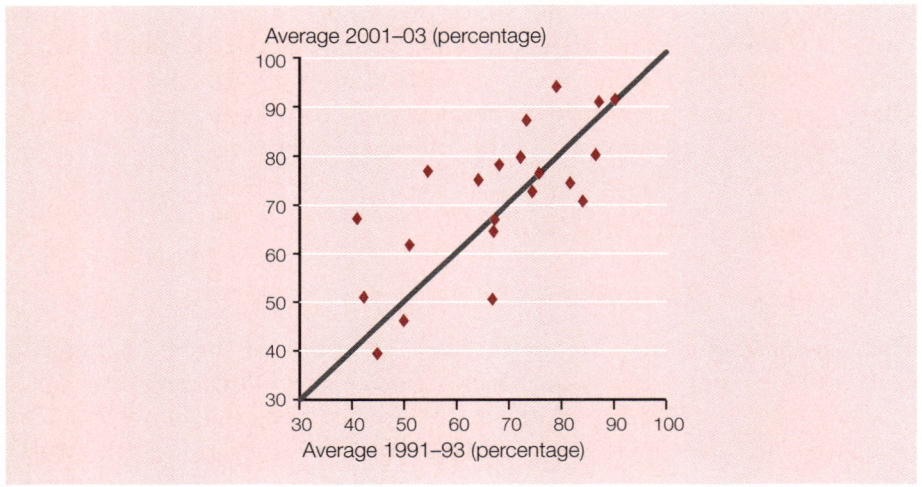

Note: Data for Austria and Iceland are not available.

Source: Derived from OECD OLISNET database (http://stats.oecd.org/WBOS/default.aspx).

Second, there was a change in the character of unemployment: the share of short-term unemployment in total unemployment increased in a majority of the countries (figure 6.7). This means that the decline in the long-term unemployment rate was generally sharper than that in the short-term unemployment rate.

Third, the incidence of part-time employment increased: in a large majority of developed countries the share of part-time employment in total employment was significantly higher in 2001–03 than in 1991–93 (figure 6.8).

Fourth, the incidence of temporary employment also increased in many countries. Data on temporary employment are available only for European developed countries and only for the period 1995–2003. Figure 6.9 shows that even during that relatively short period the share of temporary employment in total wage employment increased significantly in a large number of the countries.

Finally, these developments occurred in a context where the labour force participation rate increased in a majority of the countries (figure 6.10).

The overall picture emerging from these trends can be summed up as follows. The fact that unemployment showed a declining trend even while growth of labour supply accelerated (because of rising labour force participation) appears to suggest a rather remarkable improvement in the employment situation in most countries. However, the improvement looks

Figure 6.8   Incidence of part-time employment, 1991–93 versus 2001–03

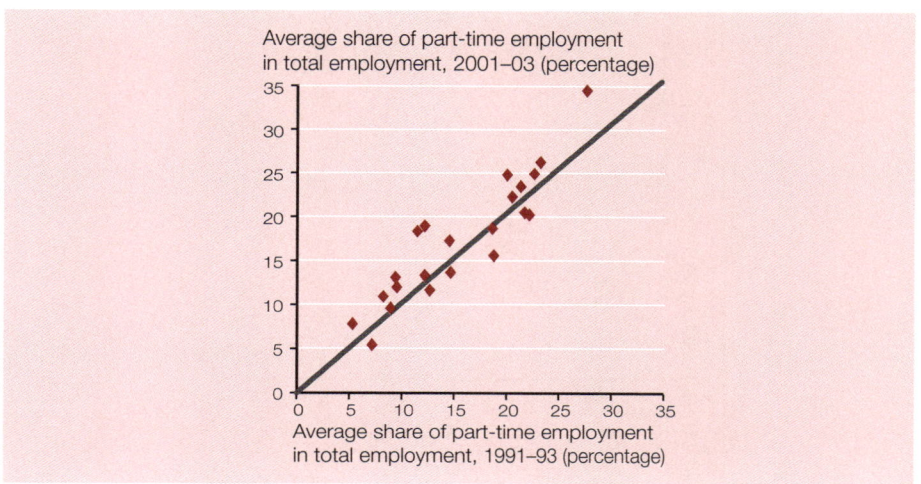

Note: Data for Austria are not available.

Source: Derived from OECD OLISNET database (http://stats.oecd.org/WBOS/default.aspx).

Figure 6.9   Incidence of temporary employment, 1995–97 versus 2001–03

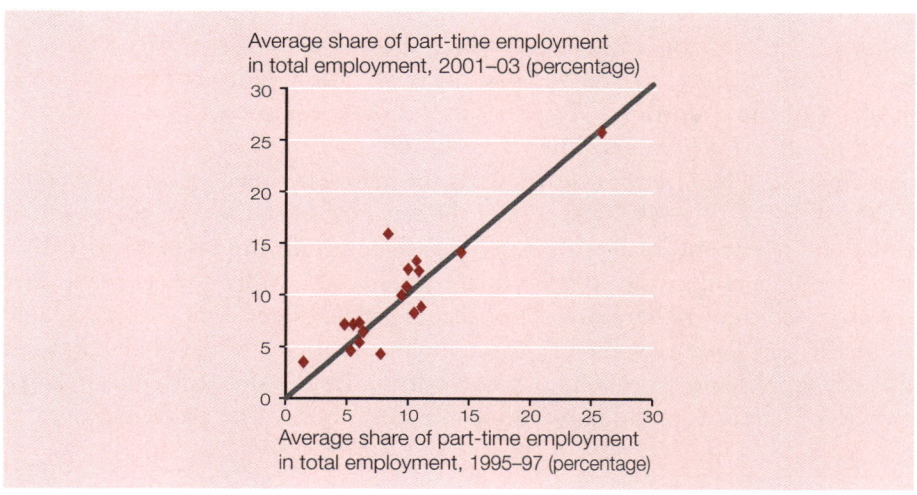

Note: Data for Australia, Canada, Japan, New Zealand and United States are not available.

Source: Derived from OECD OLISNET database (http://stats.oecd.org/WBOS/default.aspx).

Figure 6.10 Labour force participation, 1991–93 versus 2001–03

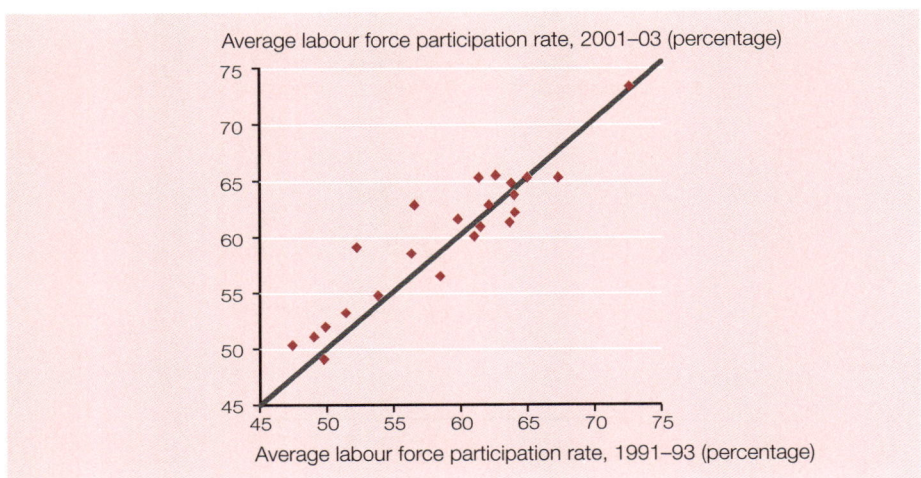

Source: Derived from OECD OLISNET database (http://stats.oecd.org/WBOS/default.aspx).

much less remarkable once it is recognized that the decline in unemployment was associated with growth of part-time and temporary employment. In fact, the growth of part-time employment has clearly been instrumental both in reducing unemployment and in increasing the participation rate.

It is not entirely clear, therefore, to what extent the observed decline in the unemployment rate actually indicates improvement in the overall employment situation. Figure 6.11, which shows the trends in the CEI, seems to confirm that the overall employment situation indeed improved in a majority of the countries.[60] A further probe shows, however, that the upward trend in the CEI is explained largely by the increase in labour force participation. This emerges clearly from the fact that when CEI is replaced by CEI* $(= [(E/LF) + (FE/E)] / 2)$ as the measure of the overall employment situation, it cannot really be said that the overall employment situation improved in a majority of the countries (figure 6.12). The correct reading of the observed trends, therefore, is not that unemployment declined (it declined at least in part because some of the unemployed moved to part-time jobs) but that the employment problem did not worsen despite the acceleration in the growth of labour supply (resulting from rising labour force participation).

---

[60] Time-series estimates of the MCEI could not be derived, as the data on voluntary/involuntary part-time employment are sketchy. It is highly unlikely, however, that the CEI and the MCEI would move in opposite directions in any given country. However, even the sketchy data suggest that the share of voluntary part-time employment in total part-time employment tended to decline in many countries. To the extent that this is true, the unobserved trend increase in the MCEI can be expected to have been lower than the observed trend increase in the CEI.

Figure 6.11 Composite Employment Indicator (CEI), 1991–93 versus 2001–03

Note: Data for Austria are not available.

Source: Derived from appendix table A6.8.

Figure 6.12 Adjusted Composite Employment Indicator (CEI*), 1991–93 versus 2001–03

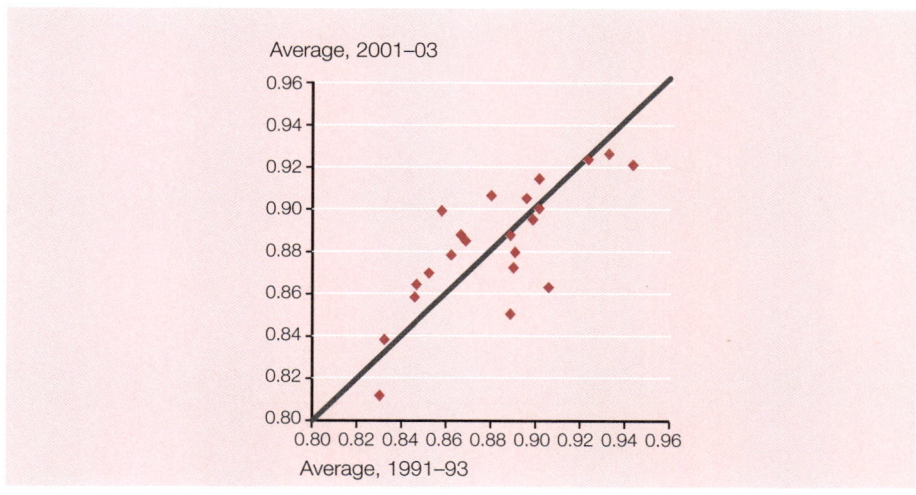

Note: Data for Austria are not available.

Source: Derived from appendix table A6.9.

The global employment challenge

Trends in gender disparity

Gender disparity declined in a majority of the countries during 1991–2003, as figure 6.13 shows. A close inspection of the evidence reveals, however, that the decline is attributable almost entirely to the growing feminization of labour force and employment. This is seen from the fact that when disparity is defined in terms of CEI* rather than CEI, it is not so clear that gender disparity in employment declined in most of the countries (figure 6.14). Thus what declined is the gender disparity in labour force participation. The increase in the overall participation rate in most of the countries during 1991–2003 is almost wholly attributable to the increase in women's labour force participation; men's labour force participation generally remained stable (table 6.8 on page 180).

On the other hand, the trends in the unemployment rate were similar for men and women, as were the trends in the incidence of part-time employment. On the whole, it can be said that the "true" incidence of unemployment changed in much the same manner for men and women, declining unemployment being associated with rising incidence of part-time employment for both. But since the growth of the female labour force was faster than that of the male labour force, the unchanging unemployment situation for both men

Figure 6.13 Gender disparity (in terms of Composite Employment Indicator), 1991–93 versus 2001–03

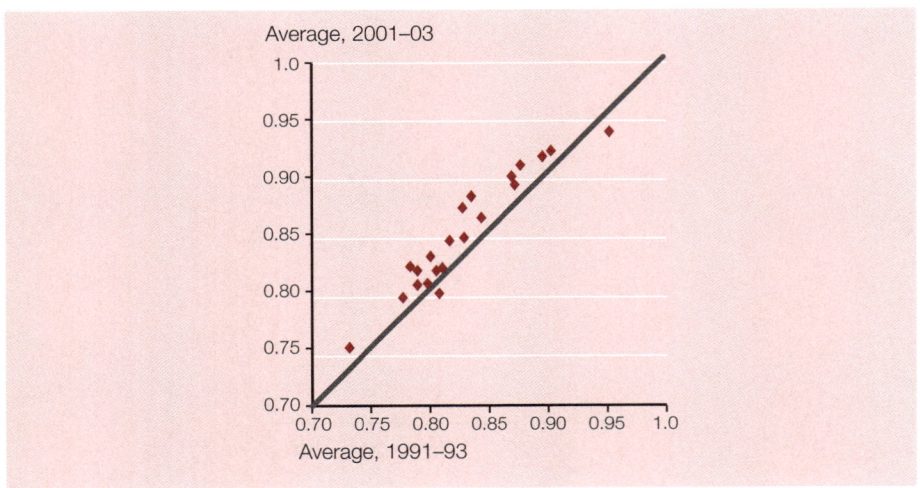

Note: Data for Austria and Greece are not available.

Source: Derived from appendix table A6.8.

Figure 6.14 Gender disparity (in terms of adjusted Composite Employment Indicator), 1991–93 versus 2001–03

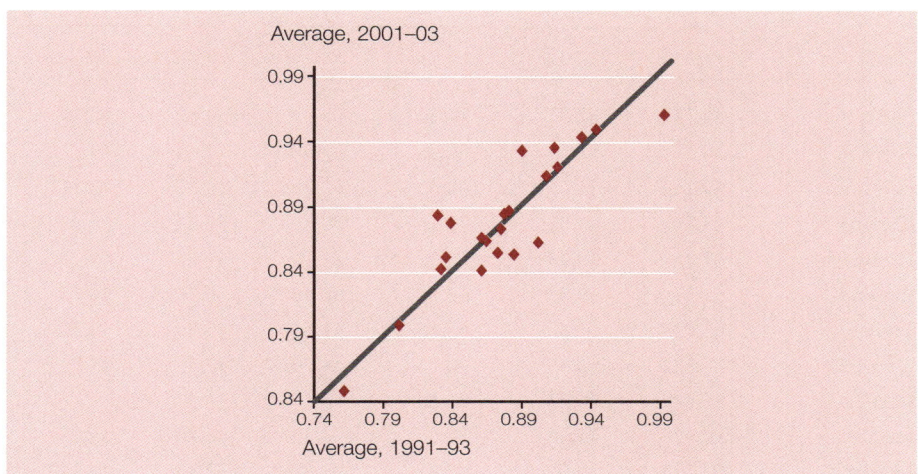

Note: Data for Austria and Greece are not available.

Source: Derived from appendix table A6.8.

and women implies faster growth of employment for women. In other words, much of the incremental employment generated in the 1990s went to women, some of whom were moving from inactivity into the labour force. This is why improvement in the overall employment situation was associated with declining gender inequality (figure 6.15).

Trends in employment by skill category

There is evidence to suggest that the change in unemployment in the 1990s was mainly about change in unemployment of low-skilled labour (see table 6.9 on page 182). For high-skilled workers, the rate of unemployment had not been high even in the mid-1990s (when the overall unemployment rate was still at its peak in most of the countries) and showed negligible change during 1997–2003.[61] Wherever the rate of unemployment declined significantly in the second half of the 1990s, it declined mainly for low- and medium-skilled labour, and in the few countries where it increased (as in Germany, Japan and Switzerland), it increased mainly for low- and medium-skilled labour.

---

[61] There are, of course, exceptions to the rule. In Finland, France, Greece, Italy and Spain, the unemployment rate for the high skilled had been high in 1997 and declined fairly sharply during 1997–2003.

The global employment challenge

Table 6.8   Labour force participation rate by gender, 1991–93 and 2001–03 (percentages)

Country	All		Male		Female	
	1991–93	2001–03	1991–93	2001–03	1991–93	2001–03
Australia	62.14	62.83	73.02	70.81	51.52	55.09
Austria	56.37	58.51	69.36	67.98	44.63	49.77
Belgium	49.11	51.04	60.32	60.25	38.60	42.11
Canada	63.84	64.81	71.75	70.83	56.22	58.99
Denmark	67.36	65.33	73.32	71.10	61.65	59.79
Finland	61.51	60.97	67.08	65.46	56.36	56.75
France	53.93	54.67	62.68	61.66	45.84	48.23
Germany	58.52	56.49	70.63	64.79	47.43	48.72
Greece	47.48	50.23	61.69	–	33.93	–
Iceland	72.69	73.37	78.65	78.23	66.76	68.57
Ireland	52.27	59.09	67.82	70.20	37.18	48.31
Italy	49.86	48.96	65.37	62.10	35.49	36.75
Japan	63.74	61.29	77.76	74.72	50.46	48.67
Luxembourg	51.49	53.11	67.28	64.48	36.52	42.27
Netherlands	56.65	62.90	69.08	72.05	44.69	54.07
New Zealand	62.71	65.48	72.47	73.23	53.47	58.20
Norway	61.42	65.28	68.50	70.64	54.60	60.13
Portugal	59.87	61.58	71.42	69.88	49.55	53.99
Spain	49.99	51.90	66.54	64.20	34.44	40.25
Sweden	64.14	62.14	68.54	66.22	59.93	58.19
Switzerland	65.04	65.25	76.37	73.80	54.44	57.23
United Kingdom	61.09	60.05	71.69	67.36	51.31	53.23
United States	64.09	63.74	72.64	70.06	56.14	57.75

– = data not available.

Source: Derived from OECD OLISNET database (http://stats.oecd.org/WBOS/default.aspx).

However, the supply of low-skilled labour was actually declining rather rapidly in all countries except three – Germany, Iceland and the Netherlands (table 6.10 on page 183). Clearly the demand for low-skilled labour was also declining. The decline in unemployment of low-skilled labour, therefore, is explained partly by the decline in supply and partly by the fact that some of the unemployed found part-time jobs. The contrast with the developments relating to high-skilled labour is stark. The supply of high-skilled labour

Figure 6.15 Change in gender disparity and in overall employment situation, 1991–2003

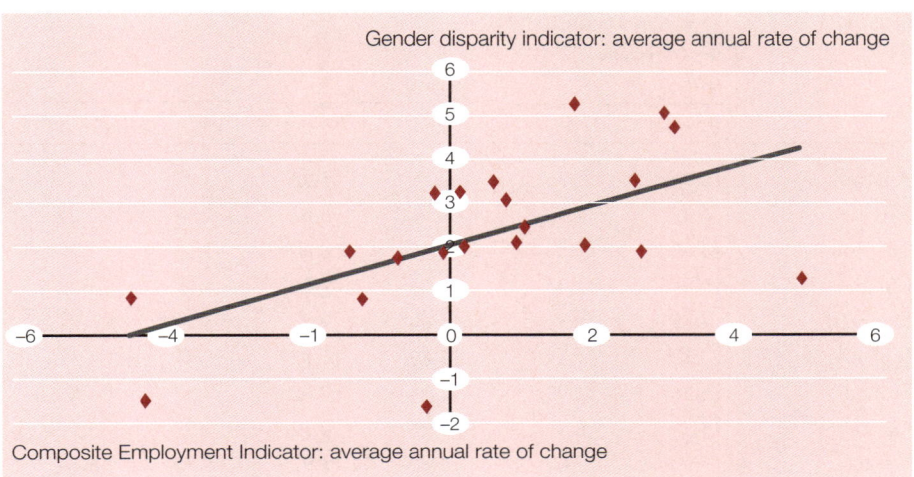

Notes: The regression equation is: Y = 2.040 + 0.451 X, R² = 0.322. The coefficient is significant at less than 1 per cent.

Source: Derived from appendix table A6.8.

increased at a rapid rate in all countries except Germany and the Netherlands, yet the unemployment rate for the high skilled declined in 14 of the 21 countries for which data are available (table 6.10). Clearly the demand for high-skilled labour also increased at a rapid rate.

Overview

The central feature of labour market developments in the period since 1990 is not the decline in unemployment but the persistence of a wide gap between the low skilled and the high skilled in terms of employment situation. The substantial shortfall in demand for low-skilled labour in relation to its supply, already existing at the beginning of the 1990s, persisted throughout the period. Since the supply of low-skilled labour actually declined at a fairly rapid rate, it is evident that the observed decline in the unemployment rate of low-skilled labour occurred either because the decline in the supply of low-skilled labour was faster than the decline in demand or because some of the low-skilled unemployed moved to part-time jobs, or both. In sharp contrast, unemployment of high-skilled labour was low even at the beginning of the 1990s and remained low throughout the period despite a rapid growth in supply. Thus the persistence of the employment problem since 1990 is attributable not to a lack of growth in demand for labour as such (indeed, rising participation rates

Table 6.9 Rate of unemployment by level of education, 1997 and 2003 (percentages)

Country	Unemployment rate (%) Level of education[a]					
	Low		Medium		High	
	1997	2003	1997	2003	1997	2003
Australia	12.46	9.56	7.79	5.43	3.95	3.59
Austria	6.87	8.30	3.61	3.62	2.55	2.01
Belgium	14.00	12.50	8.40	8.40	3.66	4.39
Canada	15.54	13.75	9.03	7.50	5.69	5.39
Denmark	7.33[b]	8.31	4.68[b]	4.55	3.34[b]	4.74
Finland	17.62	14.88	13.66	10.88	6.83	4.31
France	16.56	13.90	11.14	8.62	7.57	6.84
Germany	14.79	16.08	9.94	10.17	5.57	5.11
Greece	7.60	7.69	14.80	11.97	8.53	6.34
Iceland	–	–	–	–	–	–
Ireland	15.72	7.26	8.30	4.01	4.75	3.00
Italy	13.22[b]	10.65[d]	12.01[b]	8.77[d]	7.11[b]	5.45[d]
Japan	3.98	6.51	3.81	5.83	2.72	4.07
Luxembourg	–	4.00	–	2.72	–	3.11
Netherlands	6.24[c]	4.98[d]	2.73[c]	2.46[d]	1.57[c]	1.98[d]
New Zealand	11.22	7.16	5.64	4.01	4.47	3.92
Norway	5.85	6.96	4.25	4.72	1.94	2.65
Portugal	4.85[b]	6.29	7.00[b]	6.96	2.95[b]	5.10
Spain	21.95	12.73	21.83	11.32	17.13	8.79
Sweden	13.94	9.07	10.76	5.79	5.32	3.86
Switzerland	6.29	8.58	2.97	3.89	4.43	2.99
United Kingdom	13.51	9.67	7.26	5.19	3.16	2.58
United States	13.47	13.00	5.45	6.81	2.24	3.38

[a] Level of education: low – up to lower secondary (assumed average years of education: 6); medium – above lower secondary and up to higher secondary (assumed average years of education: 11); high – tertiary (assumed average years of education: 14.5).
[b] Refers to 1998.
[c] Refers to 1999.
[d] Refers to 2002.
– = data not available.

Source: Derived from OECD OLISNET database (http://stats.oecd.org/WBOS/default.aspx).

Table 6.10 Growth of labour force[a] by level of education,[b] 1997–2003

Country	Average annual rate of growth (%) Level of education		
	Low	Medium	High
Australia	−2.2	2.6	5.2
Austria	−2.2	0.3	4.9
Belgium	−2.1	1.7	2.8
Canada	−1.7	1.6	4.0
Denmark[c]	−3.6	−0.8	5.1
Finland	−3.5	1.5	2.1
France	−1.2	1.7	3.5
Germany	1.7	−0.4	0.6
Greece	−2.0	3.1	3.4
Iceland	–	–	–
Ireland	−2.0	7.4	4.4
Italy[d]	−1.3	2.0	5.4
Japan	−3.8	−1.2	2.6
Luxembourg	–	–	–
Netherlands[d]	1.8	3.3	1.2
New Zealand	−1.9	0.9	3.9
Norway	−3.6	0.3	3.9
Portugal[c]	−0.3	4.9	6.0
Spain	−0.3	6.0	6.6
Sweden	−4.2	0.5	3.9
Switzerland	−7.6	0.7	3.9
United Kingdom	−4.0	0.3	4.0
United States	−0.1	0.2	3.0

[a] Labour force is defined as population in age group 15–64.
[b] Level of education: low – up to lower secondary; medium – above lower secondary and up to higher secondary; high – tertiary.
[c] Growth over five years (1998–2003).
[d] Growth over four years (1998–2002).
– = data not available.

Source: Derived from OECD OLISNET database (http://stats.oecd.org/WBOS/default.aspx).

indicate rising demand for labour) but to a rapid shift in labour demand away from the low skilled to the high skilled. The fact that such a shift occurred in all developed countries suggests, moreover, that it was not strongly influenced by labour market institutions.

6.3 Finding explanations

The emergence and persistence of unemployment in developed countries have attracted wide attention from economists and there exists a large literature seeking to explain these phenomena. The explanatory framework that came to acquire wide acceptability saw unemployment as resulting from interactions between macroeconomic shocks and labour market institutions (box 6.3). The emergence of the employment problem in the 1970s was thus attributed to the institutional rigidities in the labour markets in the face of macroeconomic shocks, namely the two successive oil shocks (1973 and 1979). However, the persistence of unemployment in many developed countries in the period since the mid-1980s, when there were no macroeconomic shocks, brought the role of labour market institutions into focus. A highly influential OECD study (OECD, 1994) argued that inappropriate labour market institutions were largely responsible for the persistence of high unemployment and advocated wide-ranging reforms of these institutions as the means to reduce it (box 6.4). These ideas proved attractive to governments and significant reforms of labour market institutions were implemented in most developed countries in the second half of the 1990s.

> **Box 6.3 Explaining unemployment: Macroeconomic shocks and labour market institutions**
>
> Bruno and Sachs (1985) developed the basic analytical framework that attributed the rise in unemployment in developed countries to macroeconomic shocks interacting with nominal and real-wage rigidities. According to this view, the effect of macroeconomic shocks on unemployment depends on the flexibility with which nominal and real wages can be adjusted. Real-wage rigidity makes it difficult for firms to sustain profitability when there is a shock in the form of sharp deceleration in productivity growth, leading to downward adjustment in output and hence in employment. Nominal-wage rigidity allows policy-makers to use monetary policy to limit the decline in aggregate demand when there is a shock in the form of sharp rises in the prices of non-labour factors of production, thereby limiting the rise in unemployment. These rigidities, however, are short-run phenomena: in the long run, increased unemployment brings about the required adjustments in both nominal and real wages. This is why the framework is appropriate for understanding rises in unemployment following macroeconomic shocks but not its persistence over a long period.

The persistence of unemployment drew attention to labour market institutions that might pre-empt wage flexibility in the long run. Lindbeck and Snower (1989) focused on collective bargaining and developed the notion of the *insider–outsider* problem. The basic idea is simple: since only the employed are engaged in wage bargaining, there is no good reason to suppose that rising unemployment brings about wage flexibility in the long run. This view led to the notion of hysteresis, that is, the tendency of unemployment, once pushed to a high level by shocks, to persist at that level. Pissarides (1990) developed a more general framework for analysing the role of labour market institutions – collective bargaining, employment protection legislation, unemployment benefit systems – in the determination of wages and labour market flows and hence of unemployment. This is the framework that is elaborated and used in OECD (1994) to explain the persistence of high unemployment in many countries long after macroeconomic shocks.

A review of the evolution of these ideas is available in Blanchard (2005).

Box 6.4 OECD recommendations for labour market reforms

The relevant recommendations for labour market reforms, made by OECD (1994), are as follows:

- Increase flexibility of working time (both short-term and lifetime) voluntarily sought by workers and employers.

- Make wage and labour costs more flexible by removing restrictions that prevent wages from reflecting local conditions and individual skill levels, in particular of younger workers.

- Reform employment security provisions that inhibit the expansion of employment in the private sector.

- Reform unemployment and related benefit systems – and their interactions with the tax system – such that society's fundamental equity goals are achieved in ways that impinge far less on the efficient functioning of labour markets.

- Strengthen the emphasis on active labour market policies and reinforce their effectiveness.

- Improve labour force skills and competencies through wide-ranging changes in education and training systems.

Source: OECD (2006).

The global employment challenge

A basic problem with the entire literature is its exclusive concern with explaining the behaviour of the overall unemployment rate across countries and over time. Our analysis in this chapter shows that this is not the right focus. The problem is not just persistence of high unemployment but also growing incidence of non-standard employment. Besides, even the problem of high unemployment is quite particular: it is a problem for low-skilled labour and not for all labour, and it persisted through the period since 1990 despite a rapid decline in the supply of low-skilled labour.

What needs to be explained, therefore, is not the behaviour of the overall unemployment rate but the dwindling demand for low-skilled labour. There is no easy explanation available in the form of poor economic growth or functioning of labour markets. During 1991–2003, economic growth in the developed world was neither poor nor jobless (table 6.11). The average annual rate of growth of GDP was below 2 per cent in only four of the countries (Germany, Italy, Japan and Switzerland); in 14 countries it was above 2.5 per cent. The estimates of employment elasticity clearly show that, in general, economic growth was fairly employment intensive. The demand for labour showed negligible growth in only five countries (Austria, Germany, Italy, Japan and Sweden), but economic growth itself was low in three of these (Germany, Italy and Japan). Growth can be said to have been jobless in only two countries – Austria and Sweden – but the growth of Sweden's labour force was also zero.

As a matter of fact, the growth of labour demand was higher than that of labour supply in 14 of the 23 developed countries. It should be remembered that the growth of labour supply itself was actually accelerating because of rising labour force participation rates. In aggregate terms, employment growth was quite rapid.

But an important process of structural change was under way. In most of the countries, employment was declining in agriculture and manufacturing while increasing in the services sector (table 6.12). Job gains in services, however, were generally much larger than combined job losses in agriculture and manufacturing (appendix table A6.7). In the group of developed countries as a whole, agriculture and manufacturing shed 11 million jobs (nearly 8 million in manufacturing alone) while services created 41 million jobs (in addition, non-manufacturing industries created about 3 million jobs). The net increase in employment was 33 million against a labour force increase of 32 million. In the sub-group of European developed countries, agriculture, manufacturing and non-manufacturing industries together shed about 6 million jobs, while services created 17 million jobs. The net increase in employment was 11 million against a labour force increase of 9 million.

It is clear that, had there been no skill bias in labour demand, unemployment would have disappeared for all categories of labour. What appears to have

Table 6.11   Economic growth and the labour market, 1991–2003

Country	Average annual growth of real GDP[a] (%)	Employment elasticity		Average annual rate of growth	
		Estimate A[b]	Estimate A[c]	Labour demand[d] (%)	Labour supply[e] (%)
Australia	3.82	0.46	0.42	1.60	1.48
Austria	2.28	0.31	0.03[f]	0.07	0.72
Belgium	2.08	0.44	0.36	0.75	0.75
Canada	3.28	0.51	0.51	1.68	1.43
Denmark	2.30	0.18	0.25	0.57	−0.13
Finland	2.83	0.28	0.23	0.65	0.39
France	2.15	0.35	0.32	0.69	0.72
Germany	1.71	0.42	0.24[f]	0.41	0.02
Greece	2.75	0.37	0.40	1.10	1.36
Iceland	3.29	0.45	0.50	1.64	1.31
Ireland	7.66	0.55	0.49	3.75	2.92
Italy	1.60	0.19[f]	0.10[f]	0.16	0.12
Japan	1.13	0.07[f]	−0.15[f]	−0.17	0.20
Luxembourg	4.95	0.29	0.24	1.19	1.42
Netherlands	2.74	0.72	0.60	1.64	1.64
New Zealand	3.24	0.62	0.59	1.91	1.64
Norway	3.48	0.37	0.39	1.36	1.08
Portugal	2.59	0.45	0.43	1.11	1.13
Spain	2.95	0.80	0.75	2.21	1.42
Sweden	2.35	0.06[f]	0.08[f]	0.19	0.03
Switzerland	1.30	0.45	0.36	0.47	0.69
United Kingdom	2.73	0.22	0.18	0.49	0.22
United States	3.31	0.43	0.45	1.49	1.27

[a] The rate of growth of GDP (in constant local currency units) and employment elasticity are estimated by using regression equations.

[b] Estimate A, employment is measured by the number of persons actually in employment, irrespective of its type.

[c] Estimate B, employment is measured as [the number of persons in full-time employment + (1/2) the number of persons in part-time employment].

[d] Average annual growth of labour demand is derived by using the average annual growth of GDP and Estimate B of employment elasticity.

[e] Average annual growth of labour supply is the average annual growth of labour force estimated by using the average values for 1991–93 and 2001–03.

[f] Not significantly different from zero.

Sources: Derived from World Bank, World Development Indicators database (CD-ROM, 2005) and OECD OLISNET database (http://stats.oecd.org/WBOS/default.aspx).

Table 6.12 Growth of output and employment by sector, 1991–2003 (percentages)

Country	Average annual rate of growth							
	Agriculture		Manufacturing		Other industries		Services	
	Output	Employment	Output	Employment	Output	Employment	Output	Employment
Australia	3.50	0.12	2.41	0.13	3.51	1.65	4.26	2.41
Austria	−2.46	−1.59	2.24	−2.09	1.71	0.90	2.45	2.04
Belgium	−2.12	−3.28	1.59	−0.15	−0.78	0.10	2.70	1.51
Canada	0.01	−2.42	4.11	1.81	2.64	2.32	3.03	1.98
Denmark	−1.63	−4.48	1.48	−1.01	4.29	1.24	2.51	1.04
Finland	−1.13	−4.40	4.29	0.53	1.75	−0.10	3.31	1.31
France	0.24	−2.75	1.63	0.54	−8.04	−2.70	2.84	1.43
Germany	0.81	−4.16	0.18	−2.55	−1.58	−1.29	2.53	1.28
Greece	−1.28	−2.15	1.09	−1.52	2.70	1.39	3.84	2.71
Iceland	0.03	−1.37	1.97	−0.23	1.11	1.56	3.89	2.13
Ireland	−3.39	−2.61	9.66	2.44	9.75	7.89	7.68	5.22
Italy	−0.99	−4.11	0.34	0.36	0.28	−0.65	2.38	0.93
Japan	−3.84	−2.97	−1.04	−2.29	−1.09	−0.07	2.30	0.87
Luxembourg	−1.84	−6.21	0.37	−2.86	3.43	0.00	5.92	2.62
Netherlands	−1.65	−1.30	0.94	−0.37	2.23	1.84	3.41	2.56
New Zealand	2.14	0.09	1.89	1.17	2.68	3.60	3.94	2.61
Norway	−2.99	−2.50	1.88	−0.15	7.54	2.23	2.85	1.70
Portugal	−3.28	0.36	1.16	−0.25	3.22	4.12	3.24	1.18
Spain	−1.28	−2.71	1.74	0.97	2.64	3.68	3.83	3.26
Sweden	−1.58	−4.34	3.24	−1.11	−2.15	−2.15	2.87	0.78
Switzerland	−3.03	0.00	0.97	−1.24	−0.63	−0.54	1.77	1.20
United Kingdom	−3.32	−4.07	−0.32	−2.24	3.17	0.06	3.85	1.77
United States	−1.87	0.15	1.22	−0.73	3.26	2.28	3.91	1.82

Notes: The estimates of growth rates are based on average values in 1991–93 and in 2001–03. Employment is measured by the number of workers engaged irrespective of whether the engagement is full time or part time. "Other industries" includes "mining and quarrying", "electricity, gas and water" and "construction".

Sources: Derived from World Bank, World Development Indicators database (CD-ROM, 2005) and OECD OLISNET database (http://stats.oecd.org/WBOS/default.aspx).

happened, however, is that agriculture and manufacturing released low-skilled labour while services created jobs that went largely to new entrants into the labour force (mostly women). This is explained in large part by the rising skill intensity of employment, which is suggested by the fact that labour productivity growth was remarkably rapid in all sectors. In the case of agriculture and manufacturing, this involved shedding of low-skilled labour, while in the case of services it occurred through incremental employment of relatively high-skilled labour.

The most plausible explanations for the persistence of the employment problem in the post-1990 period therefore lie in skill-biased technological change and globalization. The arguments and evidence relating to skill-biased technological change and its adverse effects on employment of low-skilled labour are well known (Acemoglu, 2002; Ghose, 2003). It is also known that the growth of trade, associated with globalization, had the expected effect of inducing specialization in skill-intensive activities in developed countries. In the early phase of globalization, when trade with emerging developing countries was mainly in final manufactured goods, the effect on the employment of low-skilled labour was widely judged to have been small (Ghose, 2003). In the later part of the 1990s, however, growth of trade with developing countries was increasingly driven by growth of offshoring of labour-intensive activities to developing countries. In other words, there was rapid growth of what is now called "trade in tasks" in both manufacturing and services. Offshoring and the associated growth of trade has not prevented employment in developed countries from growing, as the evidence cited above shows (see also box 6.5). Its effect on employment has been quite similar to that of skill-biased technological change (Feenstra and Hanson, 2003; Grossman and Rossi-Hansberg, 2006; Feenstra, 2007): it has increased the skill intensity of employment in developed countries.[62]

Thus both technological change and globalization have had the effect of reducing demand for low-skilled labour and of increasing demand for high-skilled labour. In this context, the persistence of the employment problem has a rather simple explanation: labour market policies have not focused on transferring the low-skilled job losers in agriculture and manufacturing into new jobs in services.

---

[62] A currently favoured explanation for the labour market disadvantage of low-skilled labour in developed countries is the allegedly huge growth in supply of low-skilled labour in the global economy as a result of growing integration of China, India and other low-income economies. Freeman (2005b) estimates that the integration of China, India and the countries of Eastern Europe doubled the supply of labour force in the global economy. IMF (2007) suggests that "the effective global labour supply quadrupled between 1980 and 2005, with most of the increase taking place after 1990" (p.162). These estimates, in our view, are not just wildly exaggerated but also misleading. As shown in Chapter 4, in countries such as China and India only a small proportion of the labour force is in the formal segment, which produces tradable goods and services. Moreover, workers in the formal segment are not low skilled, nor are they employed with little capital and primitive technology.

The global employment challenge

> **Box 6.5   Offshoring and employment**
>
> The growth of offshoring activities in both manufacturing and services by firms in the developed world has aroused much concern about job losses. There is little doubt that trade with developing countries generally, and offshoring in particular, have led to job losses in certain sectors in developed countries. Rowthorn and Coutts (2004) estimate that, between 1992 and 2002, about 5 million manufacturing jobs were lost in developed countries as a result of trade with developing countries. Goldman Sachs estimates that, through 2003, some 300,000–500,000 service sector jobs were lost in the United States as a result of offshoring (Tilton, 2003). Projections by Forrester Research suggest that up to 3.4 million services sector jobs are likely to be lost in the United States between 2002 and 2015 for the same reason (McCarthy, 2004). Forrester Research also estimates that, between 2003 and 2015, the number of service sector jobs likely to be lost because of offshoring is 750,000 for the United Kingdom and 400,000 for the rest of EU-15 (Parker, 2004). Blinder (2007) estimates that between 30 and 40 million jobs in the United States are potentially "offshorable".
>
> None of this suggests that aggregate employment will decline in developed countries. During 1991–93 and 2001–03, in the United States 1.4 million jobs were lost in manufacturing while 17.1 million jobs were created in services. In the United Kingdom, net job loss in manufacturing was 1.1 million while net job gain in services was 3.3 million. Aggregate employment declined only in Germany and Japan, the two countries that suffered prolonged economic stagnation.
>
> Theoretically, as Samuelson (2004) has shown, it is possible to imagine situations where a developed country loses out from trade or offshoring in the long run. Whether or not such situations may arise in future is a matter for speculation, but no economist believes such situations to have already arisen (see Bhagwati et al., 2004; Rowthorn, 2005; Grossman and Rossi-Hansberg, 2006). At present there is no evidence to suggest that offshoring leads to declining aggregate employment in developed countries. The problem created by offshoring is the same as that created by skill-biased technological change: displaced workers tend to lack the skills required to occupy the new jobs being created in other parts of the economy. This is a problem that governments can and should address.

6.4 The labour market reforms of the 1990s and their effects

The reforms of labour market institutions[63] brought about changes in employment protection legislations, unemployment benefit systems, tax wedge and

---

[63] Detailed accounts of the reforms are available in OECD (2006).

Persistent employment problems in developed countries

Figure 6.16 Employment protection index (EPI) for regular employment, late 1980s and 2003

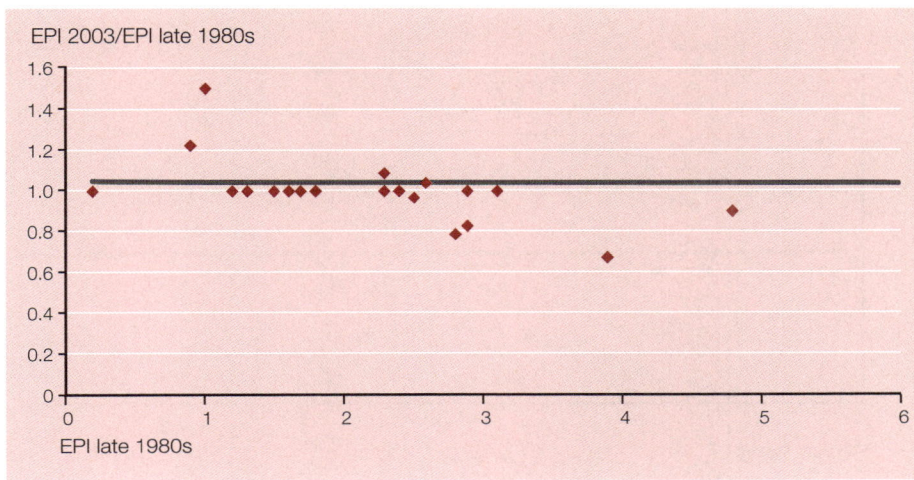

Note: Data for Iceland, Luxembourg and New Zealand are not available.

Source: Derived from OECD(2004).

working-time arrangements. What have these reforms achieved? Several studies claim to have found that changes in labour market institutions explain a large part of the movements in unemployment rates across countries (IMF, 2003; Nickell et al., 2005; Bassanini and Duval, 2006; OECD, 2006). Several others, however, refute the claim and make a counter-claim that changes in labour market institutions have not had much of an effect on unemployment (Baker et al., 2004; Baccaro and Rei, 2005; Howell et al., 2006). In short, empirical investigations have so far failed to produce a widely accepted set of results about the effects of the reforms on the employment problem (Freeman, 2005a and 2007). The view suggested by the analysis in this chapter is that labour market reforms have reduced long-term unemployment of low-skilled labour to a limited extent by expanding part-time and temporary jobs but have not addressed the core problem of transferring low-skilled job losers in manufacturing to new jobs in services.

Changes in employment protection legislation (the set of rules governing termination of employment relationships) relating to regular employment have not been substantive (figure 6.16).[64] The level of protection has declined

---

[64] The OECD has constructed employment protection indices separately for regular and temporary employees. These take account of requirements of fair dismissal of individual workers, requirements of collective dismissals, notice periods, rules for severance payments, rules allowing recourse to fixed-term contracts, maximum number of successive fixed-term contracts allowed, etc. These are the indices used in figures 6.16 and 6.17. Higher values of the indices indicate higher levels of protection. See OECD (2004) for details.

Figure 6.17 Employment protection index (EPI) for temporary workers, late 1980s and 2003

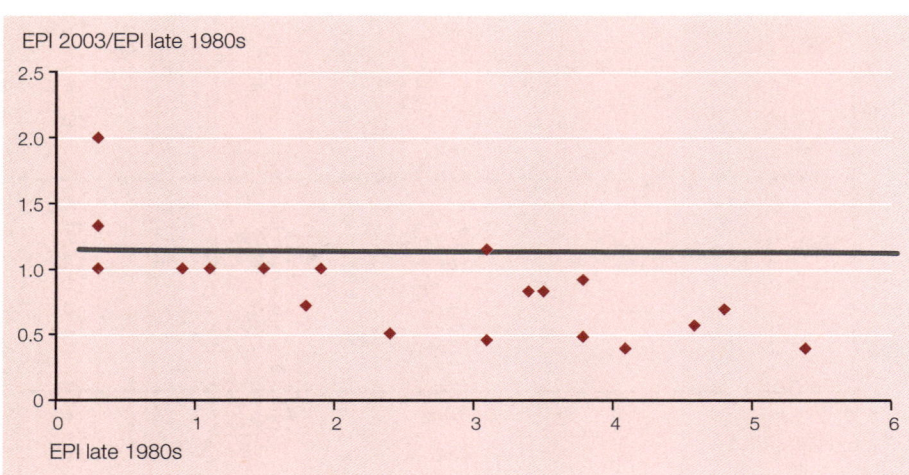

Note: Data for Iceland, Luxembourg and New Zealand are not available.

Source: Derived from OECD (2004).

in a few countries with an initially high level of protection and increased in a few others with an initially low level of protection, but in a majority of the countries it has basically remained unchanged. Much more substantive changes occurred in the level of protection for temporary employment, which has been lowered in a majority of the countries (figure 6.17). In effect, the reforms have "eased recourse to temporary employment, while leaving existing provisions for regular or permanent contracts practically unaltered" (OECD, 2006, p. 95).

Many of the countries implemented substantive reforms of the unemployment benefit system, which effectively reduced the level of benefits available to the unemployed (figure 6.18). Although there is heterogeneity across countries, a general pattern of change can be discerned (table 6.13 on page 194). Significant changes in the "generosity" of unemployment benefits (see note to table 6.13) have been rare. In most cases, the reforms have been designed to reduce coverage (the percentage of the unemployed receiving benefits), partly by forcing benefit recipients to find a job quickly and partly by excluding certain categories of the unemployed from the group of benefit recipients. Thus the scope for the unemployed to reject job offers has been circumscribed, eligibility conditions for receipt of benefits have been tightened (generally, the minimum period of insured employment required to qualify for benefits has been increased) and provisions for offering top-up

Figure 6.18 Unemployment benefit index (UBI), 1994 and 2001

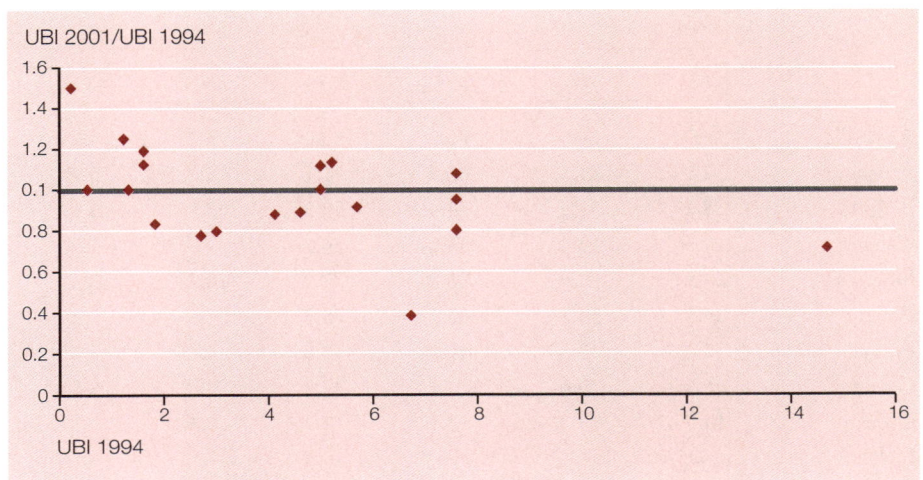

Note: Data for Iceland and New Zealand are not available.

Source: Derived from table 6.13.

benefits to those accepting part-time or low-wage jobs (i.e., wage subsidy schemes) have been introduced or expanded.

Tax wedge refers both to taxes on labour incomes and to non-wage labour costs (payroll taxes and social security contributions) to employers that drive a wedge between marginal productivity of labour and reward for work. In theory, a high tax wedge depresses both the demand for and the supply of labour; it thus leads to a sub-optimal level of employment but has no clear effect on the unemployment rate. This means that reduction in tax wedge could increase employment elasticity but has uncertain effects on unemployment. Yet it is widely believed that lowering the tax wedge reduces unemployment and, in the 1990s, governments in most of the developed countries made serious efforts to do this (OECD, 2006). However, empirical studies have so far failed to produce a consensus view on the effect of this reduction on unemployment. Some studies (IMF, 2003; Nickell et al., 2005; Bassanini and Duval, 2006) find that reduction in the tax wedge has helped reduce unemployment, while others (Baker et al., 2004; DiTella and MacCulloch, 2005) find that changes in the tax wedge have had no effect on unemployment. At any rate, given the perspective developed here (in which unemployment in general is not what needs to be explained), the issue is not of much relevance.

Reforms designed to introduce flexibility in working-time arrangements have been widespread (OECD, 2006). A major purpose of these reforms has

The global employment challenge

Table 6.13 Changes in the unemployment benefit system, 1994–2001

Country	Unemployment benefit generosity index		Percentage of unemployed receiving benefits		Unemployment benefit index	
	1994	2001	1994	2001	1994	2001
Australia	27.0	24.5	80.0	80.0	5.7	5.2
Austria	32.5	31.5	60.8	71.1	5.2	5.9
Belgium	38.7	38.5	74.4	59.9	7.6	6.1
Canada	19.3	15.3	36.0	36.0	1.8	1.5
Denmark	64.9	50.9	86.0	77.9	14.7	10.5
Finland	35.8	34.8	80.7	78.7	7.6	7.2
France	37.4	43.5	46.2	35.6	4.6	4.1
Germany	26.3	29.6	72.4	72.2	5.0	5.6
Greece	14.7	13.0	12.1	13.9	0.5	0.5
Iceland	–	–	–	–	–	–
Ireland	26.3	35.8	72.4	52.4	5.0	5.0
Italy	19.3	34.1	3.4	3.0	0.2	0.3
Japan	10.2	9.1	59.0	77.0	1.6	1.9
Luxembourg	–	–	–	–	–	–
Netherlands	52.3	52.9	48.3	18.3	6.7	2.6
New Zealand	–	–	–	–	–	–
Norway	38.8	42.0	74.0	74.0	7.6	8.2
Portugal	35.4	41.2	32.6	22.0	3.0	2.4
Spain	39.0	36.5	26.1	22.4	2.7	2.1
Sweden	26.9	23.6	58.0	58.0	4.1	3.6
Switzerland	30.0	37.5	15.0	15.0	1.2	1.5
United Kingdom	17.8	16.6	27.6	30.8	1.3	1.3
United States	11.9	13.5	50.0	50.0	1.6	1.8

Notes: The OECD **generosity index** is based on net **replacement rates** offered in the first four years of unemployment. The **unemployment benefit index** is calculated by using the formula: (OECD generosity index) * (percentage of the unemployed receiving benefits / 100) / (mean OECD generosity index + 2 standard deviation of OECD generosity index). The mean and the standard deviation are estimated across the sample of developed countries.
– = data not available.

Source: Derived from Boeri and Garibaldi (2006).

been to promote part-time work, including work outside the conventional work week (night work, weekend work and shift work). On the one hand, employers have been allowed flexible recourse to part-time employment and, on the other, some efforts have been made (though rather unsuccessfully in most cases, it appears) to make wages, as well as unemployment and social security benefits for part-time workers, equivalent (on a pro rata basis) to those applicable to comparable full-time employees.

When viewed together, it is not difficult to see what these reforms sought to achieve. On the one hand, they sought to increase labour market flexibility, not by reducing employment protection for permanent workers but by expanding the scope for temporary and part-time employment. On the other hand, reforms of unemployment benefit systems were designed to create pressures on the long-term unemployed to seek and accept the jobs that are available irrespective of their quality. The result has been a movement of some low-skilled workers from long-term unemployment to part-time and temporary jobs. At the same time, the expansion in the scope of part-time and temporary employment has brought new entrants, mainly women, into the labour force. This development has produced some positive benefits, as gender disparity in employment has declined and the average skill level of the labour force has increased, but it has done little to remove the labour market disadvantages of low-skilled workers.

6.5 Policies for the future

The persistence of the employment problem in the developed world is explained neither by lack of economic growth nor by jobless growth. Nor is it explained by labour market institutions (which, despite the reforms, remain quite heterogeneous across countries) since the nature of the employment problem is very similar across countries. The problem is explained by rapid decline in demand for low-skilled labour and lack of requisite adjustment on the supply side. Skill-biased technological change and globalization have set in motion a process of structural change leading to job losses for low-skilled labour in agriculture and manufacturing. While there are simultaneous job gains in services, it is not the job losers but the new labour force entrants who have been moving into the new jobs. The reason must be that the job losers' skills are less suited to the requirements of the new jobs in services than the skills of the new entrants.

In such a context, the reforms of labour market institutions have not, and could not have, solved the employment problem. They have reduced unemployment only to a very limited extent and have mainly altered its forms. In the process, they have brought two-tier labour markets into existence. Many countries now have one labour market for the low skilled, where temporary and part-time jobs with low wages and non-wage benefits predominate, and another labour market for the high skilled, where jobs are mostly regular and full time with high wages, non-wage benefits and legal protection.

The global employment challenge

A change in focus for labour market policy is both possible and desirable. If economic growth is not derailed by external shocks, aggregate employment growth in relation to labour force growth should remain healthy. The process of structural change, however, is most likely to continue in the foreseeable future. This means that demand for low-skilled labour will continue to decline in agriculture and manufacturing, and new jobs will continue to be created in services. The only effective way to improve the employment situation in this context will be to re-skill and re-orient job losers so as to enable them to move to new jobs in services.

One possibility is for governments to directly participate in the process of job creation by expanding public services. The advantage of this strategy is that governments can have direct control over skill development, employment and wages, and can therefore seek to influence not just the level of unemployment but also earnings inequality. The disadvantage is that such a strategy will require increasing taxes in many cases.

The other possibility would be to collaborate with private sector employers in the services sector to set up new kinds of apprenticeship schemes[65] combined with wage subsidy. Apprenticeship schemes can help in re-skilling and re-orientation of low-skilled job losers, thereby preparing them for new jobs in services. Wage subsidy schemes can help in guaranteeing a minimum level of living without undermining incentives to adapt to new conditions of work.

The two possibilities need not be regarded as mutually exclusive and the particular combination of the two measures can be expected to vary from country to country. The important point is that the focus of labour market policies has to be on facilitating movement of low-skilled labour from agriculture and manufacturing into services, made necessary by skill-biased technological change and globalization.

---

[65] Traditionally, apprenticeship schemes have been used to facilitate school-to-work transition for young persons. But, in principle, they can also be designed to facilitate job-to-job transition for older persons.

Appendix table A6.1 Average annual rate of unemployment[a] in developed countries, 1960–2004 (percentages)

Country	1960–64	1965–69	1970–74	1975–79	1980–84	1985–89	1990–94	1995–99	2000–04
Australia	1.37	1.72	2.21	5.53	7.52	7.29	9.28	7.90	6.21
Austria	–	1.62	1.01	1.48	2.57	3.99	4.83	5.48	5.20
Belgium	1.47	1.56	1.49	5.26	9.33	9.24	7.71	9.27	7.34
Canada	5.97	4.00	5.79	7.60	9.98	8.87	10.34	8.85	7.31
Denmark	–	–	1.20	4.76	7.36	5.80	8.17	5.54	4.79
Finland	1.41	2.52	2.15	5.01	5.16	4.65	10.82	12.87	9.20
France	1.37	2.07	2.76	5.12	8.20	10.19	10.52	11.59	9.37
Germany	0.49	0.66	0.71	2.15	4.47	5.89	6.21	7.79	7.86
Greece	6.08	4.60	2.92	1.90	5.80	7.54	8.54	10.51	11.04
Iceland	0.92	1.67	1.41	1.20	1.52	1.63	4.01	3.39	2.85
Ireland	5.41	5.31	6.43	9.23	12.60	16.71	14.96	9.59	4.33
Italy	3.46	4.12	4.26	5.10	7.00	9.89	9.56	11.75	9.24
Japan	1.34	1.22	1.29	2.04	2.40	2.60	2.35	3.74	5.02
Luxembourg	–	–	0.03	0.50	1.29	1.56	1.83	3.16	3.21
Netherlands	0.53	1.06	1.80	3.76	7.75	7.66	5.92	5.23	3.49
New Zealand	0.08	0.28	0.24	0.99	3.96	4.92	9.21	6.65	4.97
Norway	1.71	1.55	1.49	1.84	2.59	2.96	5.60	4.00	3.97
Portugal	2.47	4.40	2.84	6.94	8.20	7.17	5.12	6.10	5.22
Spain	–	–	2.57	4.90	12.93	15.67	14.83	15.81	10.72
Sweden	1.62	1.83	2.28	1.89	2.87	2.17	5.15	7.18	4.61
Switzerland	0.03	0.01	0.00	0.39	0.53	0.64	2.59	3.48	3.29
United Kingdom	1.37	1.62	2.27	4.35	9.29	9.17	8.63	7.17	5.09
United States	5.72	3.83	5.41	6.98	8.31	6.21	6.60	4.93	5.21

[a] Unemployment is defined as the state of a person who did not work even for one hour in the reference week but was seeking or available for work.

– = data not available.

Sources: Derived from Blanchard (2005) and OECD OLISNET database (http://stats.oecd.org/WBOS/default.aspx).

Appendix table A6.2 Part-time and temporary employment, 1960–2004 (percentages)

Country	Part-time employment[a] as share of total employment										Temporary employment[b] as share of total employment									
	1960–64	1965–69	1970–74	1975–79	1980–84	1985–89	1990–94	1995–99	2000–04		1960–64	1965–69	1970–74	1975–79	1980–84	1985–89	1990–94	1995–99	2000–04
Australia	–	10.44	11.15	14.86	16.87	19.50	23.14	25.44	28.19		–	–	–	–	–	–	–	–	–
Austria	–	–	5.28	5.87	6.46	6.13	8.18	11.40	21.29		–	–	–	–	–	–	–	6.50	6.81
Belgium	–	–	–	–	7.59	9.18	11.93	15.02	19.51		–	–	–	–	4.54	4.90	4.20	5.86	7.34
Canada	–	–	–	13.25	15.60	16.71	18.26	18.77	18.41		–	–	–	–	–	–	–	–	–
Denmark	–	–	–	–	22.17	23.68	22.52	21.62	21.17		–	–	–	–	11.24	10.04	10.13	9.84	8.49
Finland	–	–	–	6.29	7.44	8.17	10.42	11.40	12.64		–	–	–	–	–	–	–	14.46	14.18
France	–	–	5.71	8.09	9.08	11.57	12.77	16.12	16.22		–	–	–	–	2.77	5.84	8.94	11.41	12.44
Germany	–	–	–	–	12.14	12.79	14.73	17.29	20.82		–	–	–	–	8.72	9.7	9.18	10.43	10.98
Greece	–	–	–	–	5.78	5.27	4.38	5.35	4.51		–	–	–	–	8.76	9.39	6.74	6.51	7.58
Iceland	–	–	–	–	–	–	27.83	27.61	24.87		–	–	–	–	–	–	–	4.85	4.67
Ireland	–	–	–	–	6.15	6.90	9.41	13.98	16.83		–	–	–	–	4.88	6.44	6.91	7.06	4.26
Italy	–	–	5.95	5.54	4.96	5.32	5.40	6.90	9.32		–	–	–	–	4.14	3.79	4.27	5.90	7.53
Japan	16.15	14.60	13.52	14.56	15.61	16.54	20.05	22.16	24.28		–	–	–	–	–	–	–	–	–
Luxembourg	–	–	–	–	5.75	5.97	5.94	6.42	8.62		–	–	–	–	3.14	3.6	2.73	2.39	3.57
Netherlands	–	–	–	15.31	19.48	28.8	33.80	37.26	35.91		–	–	–	–	5.09	7.56	8.10	10.34	12.51
New Zealand	6.28	8.61	12.09	14.71	16.98	17.29	20.27	22.13	23.26		–	–	–	–	–	–	–	–	–
Norway	–	–	21.16	23.45	25.98	25.43	26.50	26.35	26.17		–	–	–	–	–	–	–	10.54	9.01
Portugal	–	–	–	14.74	13.33	6.40	7.10	9.84	11.22		–	–	–	–	–	12.14	9.69	10.52	15.74
Spain	–	–	–	–	–	5.05	5.47	7.40	7.98		–	–	–	–	–	15.55	24.03	25.85	26.12
Sweden	–	–	–	21.72	24.26	24.11	24.09	23.07	21.66		–	–	–	–	–	–	–	11.10	13.38
Switzerland	–	–	–	–	–	–	25.13	26.85	29.16		–	–	–	–	–	–	–	9.51	9.98
United Kingdom	–	–	–	–	19.26	21.35	22.52	24.49	25.18		–	–	–	–	5.10	5.43	4.75	6.01	5.51
United States	–	14.12	15.11	16.20	17.25	16.92	17.42	17.75	17.18		–	–	–	–	–	–	–	–	–

Notes: [a] Part-time employment is defined as employment that involves usual working hours of less than 30 hours per week. [b] Temporary employment is defined as workers on fixed-term contracts, temporary agency workers, workers on contracts for a specific task, workers on replacement contracts, seasonal workers, on-call workers, daily workers, trainees or apprentices without guarantee of permanent contract and workers employed under job creation schemes.
– = data not available.

Source: Derived from OECD OLISNET database (http://stats.oecd.org/WBOS/default.aspx).

Appendix table A6.3 Unemployment rate, 2003–05 (percentages)

Country	Unemployment rate			Long-term unemployment rate		
	2003	2004	2005	2003	2004	2005
Australia	6.05	5.53	5.10	1.29	1.14	0.90
Austria	4.21	4.93	5.16	1.13	1.36	1.30
Belgium	7.68	7.36	8.08	3.55	3.65	4.16
Canada	7.58	7.19	6.76	0.72	0.65	0.62
Denmark	5.40	5.20	4.80	1.06	1.18	1.24
Finland	9.05	8.87	8.43	2.12	1.97	1.96
France	9.80	9.93	9.83	3.83	3.97	4.03
Germany	9.27	10.29	11.15	4.86	5.45	6.01
Greece	9.34	10.21	9.62	5.26	5.60	5.17
Iceland	3.35	3.06	2.59	0.24	0.30	–
Ireland	4.38	4.38	4.25	1.58	1.52	1.45
Italy	8.65	8.04	7.73	5.12	3.80	3.78
Japan	5.22	4.68	4.41	1.74	1.55	1.46
Luxembourg	3.68	5.14	4.50	0.91	1.07	1.18
Netherlands	4.32	5.07	5.19	1.04	1.52	1.94
New Zealand	4.64	3.90	3.69	0.54	0.39	0.29
Norway	4.42	4.37	4.61	0.28	0.40	0.43
Portugal	6.37	6.65	7.62	2.02	2.73	3.48
Spain	11.30	10.97	9.16	4.19	3.82	2.65
Sweden	5.77	6.54	7.68	0.99	1.22	–
Switzerland	4.13	4.30	4.45	1.06	1.42	1.70
United Kingdom	4.84	4.63	4.58	1.08	0.98	1.00
United States	5.99	5.53	5.08	0.71	0.70	0.60

– = data not available.

Source: OECD (2006).

Appendix table A6.4 Modified Composite Employment Indicator (MCEI), 2003[a]

Country	MCEI
Australia	0.799
Austria	0.823
Belgium	0.783
Canada	0.817
Denmark	0.832
Finland	–
France	0.796
Germany	0.784
Greece (1999)	0.780
Iceland (2002)	0.852
Ireland	0.812
Italy	0.781
Japan (2001)	0.806
Luxembourg	0.808
Netherlands	0.789
New Zealand	0.821
Norway	0.824
Portugal	0.830
Spain	0.789
Sweden	0.826
Switzerland	0.826
United Kingdom	0.803
United States	–

[a] Unless otherwise indicated in parentheses.
– = data not available.

Sources: Authors' estimates based on data in text table 6.1 and appendix table A6.5.

Appendix figure A6.1 Unemployment rate and overall employment situation, 2003

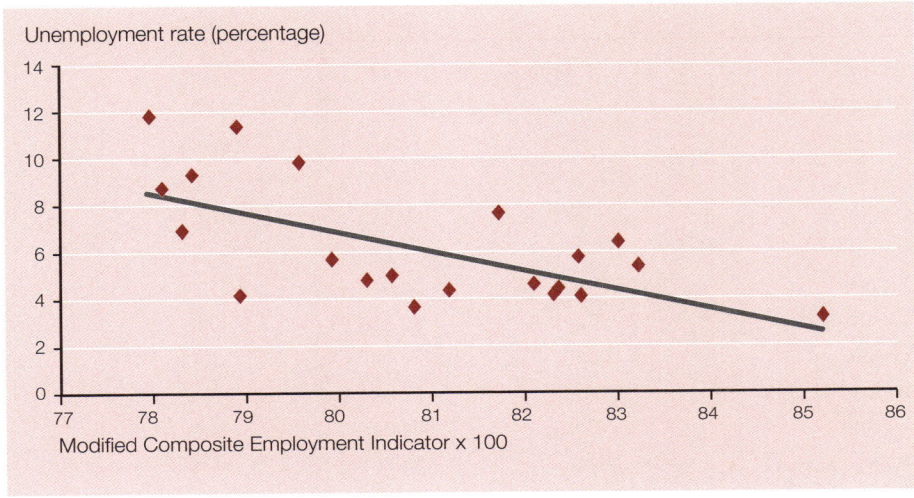

Note: The regression equation is: $Y = 73.166 - 0.827\,X$, $R^2 = 0.430$. The coefficient is significant at less than 1 per cent. Data for Finland and the United States are not available.

Sources: Derived from text table 6.1 and appendix table A6.4.

Appendix table A6.5 Voluntary part-time employment as percentage of total part-time employment, 2003

Country	All	Male	Female
Australia	71.08	67.44	72.86
Austria	92.31	92.63	92.26
Belgium	84.77	82.82	85.23
Canada	72.43	70.19	73.45
Denmark	87.26	89.47	86.03
Finland	–	–	–
France	74.65	78.57	73.67
Germany	87.46	80.35	88.89
Greece	74.75	79.06	72.75
Iceland (2002)	94.28	96.47	93.47
Ireland	90.82	84.23	92.82
Italy	84.55	84.86	84.44
Japan (2001)	92.45	93.70	91.84
Luxembourg	93.57	88.89	93.97
Netherlands	96.53	94.32	97.23
New Zealand	75.77	70.73	77.57
Norway	92.18	89.91	92.93
Portugal	82.42	90.45	78.68
Spain	81.16	81.25	81.14
Sweden	77.82	77.64	77.92
Switzerland	95.19	93.18	95.62
United Kingdom	93.08	86.64	94.97
United States	–	–	–

– = data not available.

Source: Derived from OECD OLISNET database (http://stats.oecd.org/WBOS/default.aspx).

Appendix figure A6.2   Gender disparity and overall employment situation, 2003

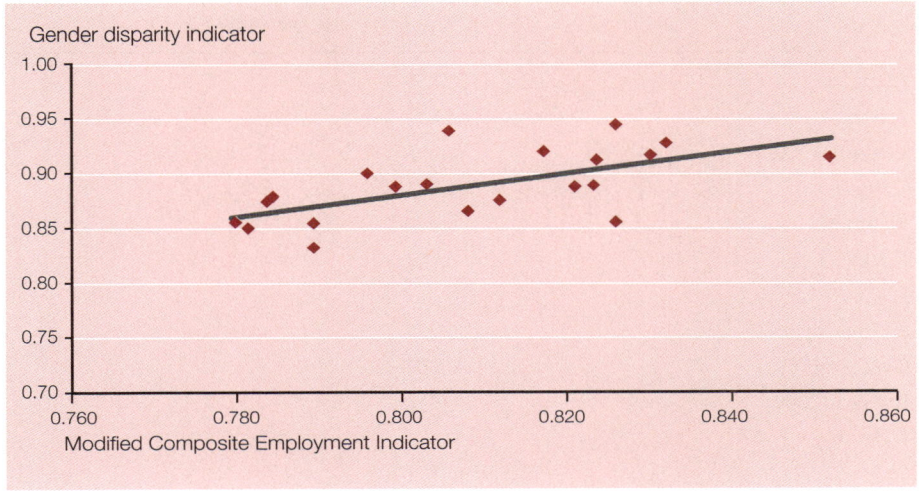

Note: The regression equation is: $Y = 0.115 + 0.959 X$, $R^2 = 0.382$. The coefficient is significant at less than 1 per cent. Data for Finland and the United States are not available.

Sources: Derived from appendix tables A6.4 and A6.6.

Appendix table A6.6   Modified Composite Employment Indicator, female to male ratio, 2003[a]

Country	Ratio of female to male MCEI
Australia	0.889
Austria	0.891
Belgium (2002)	0.876
Canada	0.921
Denmark	0.929
France	0.901
Finland	–
Germany	0.879
Greece (1999)	0.857
Iceland (2002)	0.916
Ireland	0.877
Italy	0.851
Japan (2001)	0.940
Luxembourg	0.866
Netherlands	0.834
New Zealand	0.889
Norway	0.913
Portugal	0.918
Spain	0.855
Sweden	0.946
Switzerland	0.857
United Kingdom	0.891
United States	–

[a] Unless otherwise indicated in parentheses.
– = data not available.

Sources: Authors' estimates based on data in text table 6.1 and appendix table A6.5.

Appendix table A6.7 Growth of employment and labour force, 1991–93 and 2001–03 (thousands)

Country	Employment					Labour force
	Agriculture	Manufacturing	Other industries	Services	Total	
Australia	4.8	14.1	127.9	1 459.3	1 606.0	1 345.0
Austria	−37.3	−174.6	32.9	446.0	267.0	272.9
Belgium	−27.3	−11.6	2.7	409.3	373.2	312.6
Canada	−120.4	375.9	242.2	2 033.0	2 530.7	2 184.9
Denmark	−50.6	−50.3	23.6	191.8	114.5	−38.4
Finland	−71.8	23.9	−1.6	194.2	144.7	98.7
France	−313.7	225.9	−565.1	2 214.2	1 561.3	1 831.9
Germany	−485.3	−2 512.0	−451.5	2 799.5	−649.2	69.3
Greece	−156.5	−93.3	45.4	583.7	379.3	579.6
Iceland	−1.8	−0.5	1.9	20.7	20.3	19.8
Ireland	−35.8	61.9	108.8	450.0	584.9	456.0
Italy	−581.7	177.5	−134.7	1 217.6	678.8	289.3
Japan	−1 057.7	−3 209.7	−48.5	3 409.9	−906.1	1 343.3
Luxembourg	−2.3	−7.3	0.0	32.7	23.1	25.3
Netherlands	−32.8	−41.5	91.1	1 313.0	1 329.7	1 237.3
New Zealand	1.6	32.0	41.7	296.3	371.5	301.1
Norway	−25.6	−4.4	42.0	259.9	272.0	241.3
Portugal	22.5	−27.2	217.0	302.3	514.6	570.2
Spain	−309.6	275.7	631.4	2 806.3	3 403.9	2 417.8
Sweden	−51.5	−85.7	−64.8	240.2	38.3	15.0
Switzerland	0.0	−88.9	−17.1	316.6	210.6	263.2
United Kingdom	−189.5	−1 100.8	14.0	3 288.6	2 011.4	641.0
United States	52.0	−1 425.7	2 306.2	17 061.3	17 993.9	17 151.0
Europe total	−2 350.3	−3 433.2	−24.9	17 086.8	11 278.4	9 302.9
Total	−3 470.1	−7 646.6	2 644.7	41 346.4	32 874.4	31 628.2

Source: Derived from OECD OLISNET database (http://stats.oecd.org/WBOS/default.aspx).

Appendix table A6.8 Composite Employment Indicator, 1991–2003

Country	Category	1991	1992	1993	1994	1995	1996	1997	1998	1999	2000	2001	2002	2003
Australia	All	0.77	0.76	0.76	0.76	0.77	0.77	0.76	0.77	0.77	0.77	0.77	0.77	0.77
	Male	0.84	0.83	0.83	0.84	0.84	0.84	0.83	0.83	0.84	0.84	0.83	0.83	0.83
	Female	0.68	0.68	0.68	0.68	0.69	0.69	0.69	0.69	0.69	0.70	0.70	0.70	0.70
Austria	All	–	–	–	–	0.81	0.81	0.81	0.81	0.81	0.81	0.81	0.80	0.80
	Male	–	–	–	–	0.88	0.88	0.88	0.87	0.87	0.88	0.87	0.87	0.87
	Female	–	–	–	–	0.74	0.74	0.74	0.74	0.73	0.73	0.74	0.73	0.74
Belgium	All	0.76	0.76	0.76	0.75	0.75	0.75	0.75	0.75	0.75	0.76	0.76	0.76	0.75
	Male	0.84	0.84	0.83	0.83	0.83	0.83	0.83	0.83	0.82	0.83	0.83	0.83	–
	Female	0.66	0.66	0.66	0.66	0.66	0.66	0.66	0.66	0.66	0.68	0.68	0.67	–
Canada	All	0.79	0.78	0.78	0.78	0.78	0.78	0.78	0.79	0.79	0.80	0.80	0.79	0.80
	Male	0.84	0.83	0.83	0.83	0.83	0.83	0.83	0.84	0.84	0.84	0.84	0.84	0.84
	Female	0.73	0.73	0.72	0.72	0.73	0.72	0.73	0.73	0.74	0.75	0.75	0.75	0.75
Denmark	All	0.80	0.80	0.79	0.80	0.80	0.81	0.81	0.81	0.82	0.82	0.82	0.82	0.81
	Male	0.85	0.85	0.84	0.84	0.86	0.85	0.85	0.86	0.86	0.86	0.86	0.86	0.85
	Female	0.74	0.74	0.74	0.74	0.74	0.75	0.76	0.76	0.77	0.77	0.78	0.78	0.77
Finland	All	0.83	0.81	0.78	0.78	0.79	0.79	0.79	0.80	0.80	0.80	0.81	0.80	0.80
	Male	0.85	0.83	0.81	0.80	0.81	0.82	0.82	0.82	0.83	0.83	0.83	0.83	0.83
	Female	0.81	0.79	0.77	0.76	0.76	0.76	0.76	0.77	0.77	0.77	0.78	0.78	0.78
France	All	0.78	0.77	0.77	0.76	0.76	0.76	0.76	0.76	0.76	0.77	0.77	0.77	0.78
	Male	0.84	0.83	0.83	0.82	0.82	0.82	0.82	0.82	0.82	0.82	0.83	0.83	0.83
	Female	0.71	0.70	0.70	0.69	0.69	0.69	0.69	0.69	0.69	0.70	0.71	0.71	0.72
Germany	All	0.81	0.80	0.79	0.79	0.78	0.78	0.77	0.77	0.77	0.77	0.77	0.76	0.76
	Male	0.88	0.88	0.87	0.86	0.86	0.85	0.85	0.85	0.85	0.85	0.84	0.84	0.83
	Female	0.72	0.71	0.70	0.70	0.70	0.69	0.69	0.69	0.69	0.69	0.69	0.68	0.68

Persistent employment problems in developed countries

Greece	All	0.78	0.77	0.77	0.77	0.77	0.77	0.77	0.77	0.77	0.78	0.78	0.79	0.79
	Male	0.84	0.84	0.84	0.84	0.83	0.84	0.83	0.83	0.83	—	—	—	—
	Female	0.69	0.70	0.69	0.69	0.70	0.69	0.69	0.69	0.69	0.77	—	—	—
Iceland	All	0.83	0.82	0.82	0.82	0.82	0.83	0.82	0.82	0.83	0.84	0.84	0.83	—
	Male	0.90	0.89	0.88	0.88	0.88	0.89	0.88	0.89	0.89	0.90	0.89	0.88	—
	Female	0.74	0.74	0.74	0.75	0.75	0.76	0.75	0.75	0.77	0.77	0.78	0.78	—
Ireland	All	0.76	0.75	0.75	0.75	0.76	0.76	0.76	0.77	0.78	0.79	0.79	0.79	0.79
	Male	0.83	0.82	0.82	0.82	0.83	0.83	0.83	0.84	0.86	0.86	0.87	0.86	0.86
	Female	0.67	0.67	0.66	0.66	0.67	0.68	0.68	0.68	0.69	0.70	0.70	0.70	0.70
Italy	All	0.77	0.76	0.76	0.76	0.75	0.75	0.75	0.75	0.75	0.75	0.76	0.76	0.76
	Male	0.85	0.84	0.84	0.84	0.83	0.83	0.83	0.83	0.83	0.83	0.83	0.83	0.84
	Female	0.67	0.67	0.66	0.66	0.65	0.66	0.65	0.65	0.66	0.66	0.67	0.67	0.67
Japan	All	0.81	0.81	0.80	0.80	0.80	0.79	0.79	0.79	0.78	0.79	0.78	0.77	0.77
	Male	0.89	0.88	0.88	0.88	0.88	0.88	0.87	0.87	0.86	0.87	0.86	0.85	0.85
	Female	0.72	0.71	0.71	0.71	0.71	0.70	0.70	0.69	0.69	0.69	0.68	0.68	0.67
Luxembourg	All	0.80	0.80	0.80	0.79	0.78	0.79	0.79	0.79	0.78	0.79	0.79	0.79	0.79
	Male	0.89	0.88	0.88	0.87	0.87	0.87	0.87	0.87	0.87	0.87	0.87	0.87	0.86
	Female	0.70	0.71	0.70	0.69	0.67	0.69	0.69	0.68	0.69	0.70	0.70	0.70	0.69
Netherlands	All	0.74	0.74	0.74	0.74	0.74	0.75	0.75	0.76	0.76	0.76	0.75	0.75	0.75
	Male	0.84	0.84	0.84	0.84	0.84	0.85	0.85	0.85	0.86	0.85	0.85	0.85	0.84
	Female	0.61	0.62	0.62	0.61	0.62	0.62	0.63	0.64	0.64	0.64	0.64	0.63	0.63
New Zealand	All	0.77	0.77	0.77	0.78	0.79	0.79	0.79	0.78	0.78	0.79	0.79	0.79	0.80
	Male	0.84	0.84	0.84	0.85	0.86	0.86	0.86	0.85	0.85	0.85	0.86	0.86	0.86
	Female	0.70	0.70	0.70	0.70	0.71	0.71	0.71	0.71	0.71	0.72	0.72	0.72	0.73
Norway	All	0.78	0.78	0.78	0.78	0.79	0.79	0.80	0.80	0.80	0.81	0.81	0.80	0.80
	Male	0.85	0.85	0.85	0.85	0.85	0.86	0.87	0.87	0.87	0.86	0.86	0.86	0.85
	Female	0.70	0.70	0.70	0.71	0.71	0.72	0.73	0.73	0.74	0.74	0.75	0.75	0.74

Appendix table A6.8 Composite Employment Indicator, 1991–2003 (continued)

Country	Category	1991	1992	1993	1994	1995	1996	1997	1998	1999	2000	2001	2002	2003
Portugal	All	0.83	0.82	0.82	0.81	0.81	0.81	0.81	0.82	0.82	0.83	0.83	0.82	0.82
	Male	0.88	0.88	0.87	0.86	0.86	0.86	0.86	0.87	0.87	0.87	0.87	0.87	0.86
	Female	0.77	0.76	0.76	0.75	0.76	0.76	0.76	0.77	0.78	0.78	0.78	0.78	0.77
Spain	All	0.77	0.75	0.74	0.73	0.73	0.74	0.74	0.75	0.76	0.77	0.78	0.78	0.78
	Male	0.85	0.84	0.82	0.81	0.81	0.81	0.82	0.83	0.84	0.84	0.85	0.85	0.84
	Female	0.66	0.65	0.64	0.63	0.63	0.64	0.64	0.65	0.66	0.68	0.69	0.69	0.70
Sweden	All	0.83	0.81	0.79	0.79	0.79	0.79	0.79	0.80	0.80	0.81	0.81	0.81	0.81
	Male	0.87	0.85	0.83	0.83	0.83	0.83	0.83	0.84	0.84	0.84	0.85	0.85	0.84
	Female	0.78	0.77	0.76	0.75	0.75	0.75	0.75	0.76	0.76	0.77	0.77	0.78	0.78
Switzerland	All	0.82	0.81	0.80	0.80	0.80	0.80	0.80	0.80	0.80	0.80	0.80	0.80	0.80
	Male	0.91	0.90	0.90	0.89	0.90	0.89	0.89	0.89	0.89	0.89	0.89	0.89	0.88
	Female	0.71	0.70	0.69	0.69	0.69	0.69	0.69	0.70	0.70	0.70	0.70	0.70	0.70
United Kingdom	All	0.78	0.77	0.76	0.76	0.76	0.76	0.77	0.77	0.77	0.77	0.77	0.77	0.77
	Male	0.86	0.85	0.84	0.84	0.84	0.84	0.84	0.84	0.84	0.84	0.85	0.84	0.84
	Female	0.68	0.68	0.68	0.68	0.68	0.68	0.69	0.69	0.69	0.69	0.70	0.70	0.70
United States	All	0.81	0.81	0.82	0.82	0.82	0.82	0.83	0.83	0.83	0.84	0.83	0.82	0.82
	Male	0.86	0.86	0.86	0.86	0.86	0.86	0.87	0.87	0.87	0.87	0.86	0.86	0.86
	Female	0.77	0.77	0.77	0.78	0.78	0.78	0.78	0.79	0.79	0.80	0.79	0.78	0.78

– = data not available.

Source: Authors' estimates based on data derived from OECD OLISNET database (http://stats.oecd.org/WBOS/default.aspx).

Appendix table A6.9   Adjusted Composite Employment Indicator, 1991–2003

Country	Category	1991	1992	1993	1994	1995	1996	1997	1998	1999	2000	2001	2002	2003
Australia	All	0.84	0.83	0.83	0.84	0.84	0.84	0.83	0.84	0.84	0.85	0.84	0.84	0.84
	Male	0.89	0.88	0.88	0.89	0.89	0.89	0.89	0.89	0.90	0.90	0.89	0.89	0.89
	Female	0.77	0.76	0.76	0.76	0.77	0.77	0.76	0.77	0.77	0.78	0.77	0.77	0.77
Austria	All	–	–	–	–	0.93	0.93	0.93	0.92	0.92	0.92	0.92	0.91	0.91
	Male	–	–	–	–	0.97	0.97	0.97	0.97	0.97	0.97	0.97	0.96	0.96
	Female	–	–	–	–	0.87	0.87	0.87	0.86	0.86	0.86	0.86	0.85	0.85
Belgium	All	0.89	0.89	0.89	0.88	0.88	0.88	0.88	0.88	0.87	0.88	0.88	0.88	0.87
	Male	0.95	0.96	0.95	0.94	0.94	0.94	0.94	0.94	0.93	0.94	0.94	0.94	0.93
	Female	0.79	0.80	0.79	0.79	0.79	0.79	0.79	0.79	0.78	0.80	0.80	0.80	0.79
Canada	All	0.86	0.85	0.85	0.85	0.86	0.86	0.86	0.86	0.87	0.88	0.87	0.87	0.87
	Male	0.90	0.89	0.88	0.89	0.90	0.90	0.90	0.90	0.91	0.91	0.91	0.90	0.90
	Female	0.81	0.81	0.80	0.81	0.81	0.81	0.81	0.82	0.82	0.83	0.83	0.83	0.82
Denmark	All	0.86	0.86	0.85	0.87	0.88	0.88	0.89	0.89	0.90	0.90	0.91	0.90	0.89
	Male	0.91	0.91	0.90	0.92	0.92	0.92	0.92	0.93	0.93	0.93	0.94	0.93	0.92
	Female	0.81	0.81	0.80	0.82	0.83	0.84	0.85	0.84	0.86	0.86	0.87	0.86	0.86
Finland	All	0.93	0.90	0.88	0.87	0.88	0.89	0.89	0.89	0.90	0.90	0.90	0.90	0.90
	Male	0.93	0.90	0.88	0.88	0.89	0.90	0.91	0.91	0.92	0.92	0.92	0.92	0.92
	Female	0.92	0.90	0.87	0.87	0.87	0.87	0.87	0.87	0.88	0.88	0.88	0.88	0.88
France	All	0.90	0.89	0.88	0.87	0.87	0.87	0.87	0.87	0.87	0.88	0.89	0.89	0.89
	Male	0.94	0.94	0.93	0.92	0.92	0.92	0.92	0.92	0.92	0.93	0.94	0.93	0.93
	Female	0.84	0.82	0.82	0.81	0.81	0.81	0.80	0.80	0.81	0.82	0.82	0.83	0.84
Germany	All	0.91	0.91	0.90	0.89	0.89	0.88	0.87	0.87	0.87	0.87	0.87	0.86	0.86
	Male	0.97	0.96	0.95	0.95	0.95	0.94	0.93	0.93	0.94	0.94	0.94	0.93	0.92
	Female	0.84	0.83	0.82	0.81	0.81	0.80	0.79	0.79	0.79	0.79	0.79	0.78	0.77

Appendix table A6.9   Adjusted Composite Employment Indicator, 1991–2003 (continued)

Country	Category	1991	1992	1993	1994	1995	1996	1997	1998	1999	2000	2001	2002	2003
Greece	All	0.93	0.92	0.92	0.92	0.92	0.91	0.91	0.90	0.90	0.92	0.92	0.92	0.93
	Male	0.96	0.95	0.95	0.95	0.95	0.95	0.94	0.94	0.94	0.95	0.95	0.95	0.96
	Female	0.88	0.87	0.87	0.87	0.86	0.85	0.86	0.84	0.84	0.87	0.88	0.87	0.88
Iceland	All	0.88	0.87	0.86	0.86	0.86	0.88	0.87	0.87	0.88	0.89	0.89	0.88	–
	Male	0.95	0.94	0.93	0.93	0.93	0.94	0.93	0.94	0.95	0.95	0.94	0.93	–
	Female	0.79	0.78	0.78	0.78	0.79	0.80	0.79	0.79	0.81	0.82	0.82	0.83	–
Ireland	All	0.87	0.87	0.86	0.86	0.87	0.87	0.87	0.87	0.88	0.89	0.89	0.89	0.88
	Male	0.90	0.90	0.89	0.90	0.91	0.91	0.91	0.92	0.93	0.94	0.95	0.94	0.94
	Female	0.82	0.81	0.80	0.80	0.81	0.81	0.81	0.80	0.81	0.81	0.82	0.81	0.81
Italy	All	0.90	0.89	0.90	0.90	0.89	0.89	0.89	0.89	0.88	0.89	0.89	0.90	0.90
	Male	0.94	0.94	0.94	0.94	0.93	0.93	0.93	0.93	0.93	0.93	0.94	0.94	0.94
	Female	0.82	0.82	0.82	0.82	0.81	0.81	0.81	0.81	0.81	0.81	0.82	0.82	0.82
Japan	All	0.89	0.89	0.88	0.88	0.89	0.88	0.87	0.86	0.86	0.87	0.85	0.85	0.85
	Male	0.94	0.94	0.93	0.93	0.94	0.93	0.92	0.92	0.91	0.92	0.91	0.90	0.90
	Female	0.82	0.82	0.81	0.81	0.81	0.80	0.80	0.79	0.78	0.79	0.78	0.77	0.77
Luxembourg	All	0.95	0.94	0.94	0.93	0.93	0.93	0.93	0.92	0.93	0.93	0.92	0.92	0.92
	Male	0.99	0.98	0.98	0.98	0.98	0.98	0.98	0.98	0.98	0.98	0.98	0.98	0.98
	Female	0.88	0.88	0.87	0.85	0.84	0.85	0.85	0.83	0.84	0.84	0.84	0.84	0.83
Netherlands	All	0.82	0.84	0.83	0.82	0.82	0.82	0.83	0.83	0.83	0.82	0.82	0.81	0.80
	Male	0.91	0.92	0.92	0.91	0.91	0.92	0.92	0.92	0.93	0.92	0.92	0.91	0.90
	Female	0.70	0.70	0.70	0.69	0.68	0.69	0.70	0.70	0.70	0.69	0.69	0.68	0.68
New Zealand	All	0.85	0.84	0.85	0.86	0.86	0.86	0.86	0.85	0.85	0.86	0.86	0.86	0.87
	Male	0.90	0.90	0.90	0.91	0.92	0.92	0.92	0.91	0.91	0.92	0.92	0.92	0.92
	Female	0.78	0.78	0.78	0.78	0.79	0.79	0.78	0.78	0.78	0.79	0.80	0.79	0.80

Country															
Norway	All	0.86	0.86	0.86	0.87	0.87	0.87	0.88	0.88	0.88	0.88	0.88	0.88	0.88	0.87
	Male	0.94	0.93	0.93	0.93	0.94	0.94	0.94	0.94	0.94	0.94	0.94	0.94	0.93	0.93
	Female	0.78	0.78	0.78	0.79	0.79	0.79	0.80	0.81	0.81	0.82	0.82	0.82	0.82	0.81
Portugal	All	0.93	0.94	0.93	0.92	0.92	0.92	0.92	0.93	0.93	0.93	0.93	0.93	0.93	0.92
	Male	0.96	0.96	0.96	0.95	0.95	0.95	0.94	0.95	0.96	0.96	0.96	0.96	0.95	0.94
	Female	0.89	0.90	0.89	0.88	0.89	0.88	0.88	0.89	0.90	0.90	0.90	0.90	0.90	0.89
Spain	All	0.90	0.88	0.86	0.85	0.85	0.85	0.86	0.87	0.88	0.89	0.91	0.91	0.91	0.90
	Male	0.93	0.92	0.90	0.89	0.90	0.90	0.91	0.92	0.93	0.94	0.95	0.95	0.95	0.95
	Female	0.83	0.81	0.78	0.77	0.77	0.77	0.77	0.78	0.80	0.82	0.84	0.84	0.84	0.84
Sweden	All	0.91	0.90	0.88	0.87	0.88	0.88	0.88	0.89	0.89	0.90	0.91	0.91	0.91	0.90
	Male	0.96	0.94	0.91	0.91	0.92	0.92	0.92	0.93	0.93	0.93	0.94	0.94	0.94	0.93
	Female	0.87	0.86	0.84	0.84	0.84	0.84	0.84	0.85	0.85	0.87	0.87	0.87	0.87	0.87
Switzerland	All	0.90	0.89	0.88	0.88	0.88	0.88	0.87	0.87	0.87	0.88	0.88	0.88	0.87	0.87
	Male	0.98	0.97	0.97	0.97	0.97	0.96	0.96	0.96	0.96	0.96	0.96	0.96	0.96	0.96
	Female	0.79	0.78	0.77	0.77	0.77	0.77	0.76	0.76	0.76	0.77	0.77	0.77	0.77	0.76
United Kingdom	All	0.86	0.84	0.84	0.84	0.84	0.84	0.85	0.85	0.85	0.86	0.86	0.86	0.86	0.86
	Male	0.93	0.91	0.90	0.91	0.91	0.91	0.92	0.92	0.92	0.93	0.93	0.93	0.93	0.92
	Female	0.76	0.76	0.76	0.76	0.76	0.76	0.77	0.77	0.77	0.77	0.78	0.78	0.78	0.78
United States	All	0.90	0.90	0.90	0.91	0.91	0.91	0.92	0.92	0.92	0.92	0.92	0.91	0.91	0.91
	Male	0.93	0.92	0.93	0.93	0.94	0.94	0.94	0.94	0.94	0.95	0.94	0.94	0.94	0.93
	Female	0.87	0.87	0.87	0.88	0.88	0.88	0.89	0.89	0.89	0.90	0.89	0.89	0.89	0.89

– = data not available.

Source: Authors' estimates based on data derived from OECD OLISNET database (http://stats.oecd.org/WBOS/default.aspx).

SYSTEMIC TRANSITION AND JOB CRISIS IN CENTRAL AND EASTERN EUROPEAN COUNTRIES

7

The Central and Eastern European (CEE) countries fall into two natural sub-groups. One sub-group comprises countries that are already members of the European Union and is referred to as New Member States (NMS).[66] The remaining six CEE countries are referred to as South-Eastern Europe (SEE).[67] The database for most SEE countries is extremely weak and the analysis below perforce relies mainly on statistical data for the NMS sub-group.[68]

7.1 The current state of employment

Overall employment situation

The main features of the employment problem in CEE countries today, as indicated by the data presented in table 7.1, can be summarized as follows:

- In both NMS and SEE countries, the labour force participation rate is very low, ranging from 49 per cent in Hungary to 60 per cent in Slovakia.[69]

- The rate of unemployment is very high in SEE countries, ranging from 14 per cent in Croatia to 37 per cent in the former Yugoslav Republic of

---

[66] The countries are: Bulgaria, Czech Republic, Estonia, Hungary, Latvia, Lithuania, Poland, Romania, Slovakia and Slovenia.

[67] The countries are: Albania, Bosnia-Herzegovina, Croatia, the former Yugoslav Republic of Macedonia, Montenegro and Serbia.

[68] The data on employment and unemployment used in this chapter are derived from labour force surveys. These surveys were launched in different countries at different points of time in the 1990s. In some SEE countries, full-fledged labour force surveys are yet to be conducted.

[69] By comparison, in nine of the 18 developed countries of Europe the participation rate exceeds 60 per cent (see Chapter 6, table 6.2).

The global employment challenge

Table 7.1 Employment and unemployment in Central and Eastern European countries, 2004 (percentages)

Country	Participation rate	Unemployment rate	Long-term unemployment rate	Part-time employment as share of total employment	Temporary employment as share of total wage employment	Self-employment as share of total employment
Bulgaria	49.6	12.0	7.2	2.4	7.4	15.2
Czech Republic	59.2	8.3	4.2	4.9	9.1	17.2
Estonia	58.4	9.6	5.0	8.0	2.6	9.7
Hungary	48.8	6.1	2.7	4.7	6.8	14.2
Latvia	57.9	10.4	4.6	10.4	9.5	13.1
Lithuania	57.0	11.4	5.8	8.4	6.3	18.6
Poland	53.7	19.0	10.3	10.8	22.7	26.7
Romania	54.7	8.0	4.5	10.6	2.5	34.7
Slovakia	59.5	18.1	11.8	2.7	5.5	12.4
Slovenia	58.9	6.3	3.2	9.3	17.8	15.4
Albania	58.8	–	–	–	–	–
Bosnia-Herzegovina	–	23.8	–	–	–	–
Croatia	50.5	13.8	7.3	8.5	12.2	23.5
Macedonia, former Yugoslav Rep.	52.2	37.2	–	5.3	–	–
Montenegro	51.7	27.7	–	–	–	–
Serbia	55.5	18.5	–	–	–	–

^a Unemployment of duration of one year or more as percentage of labour force.
– = data not available.

Sources: Derived from Landesmann and Vidovic (2006) and EUROSTAT database (http://epp.eurostat.ec.europa.eu/portal/page?_pageid=1090,30070682,1090_33076576&_dad=portal&_schema=PORTAL).

Macedonia. In NMS countries it is lower but is still quite high, ranging from 6 per cent in Hungary to 19 per cent in Poland; the unemployment rate exceeds 5 per cent in all ten NMS countries and exceeds 10 per cent in five of them.

- Much of the unemployment is long term in character (lasting one year or more). In most of the countries, over 50 per cent of the unemployed are found to have been in unemployment for one year or more. This stands in sharp contrast to the situation in the developed countries of Europe, where much of the unemployment is short term in character.

Systemic transition and job crisis in Central and Eastern European countries

- The incidence of non-standard employment is generally low. Part-time employment as a share of total employment ranges from 2.4 per cent in Bulgaria to 10.8 per cent in Poland. In only three (Latvia, Poland and Romania) of the ten NMS countries does the incidence reach 10 per cent.[70] Temporary employment as percentage of total wage employment is also low, except in Poland and Slovenia.

- Self-employment is significant in only three countries (Poland, Romania and Croatia). In general, the incidence of self-employment is no higher in CEE countries than in European developed countries.[71]

It is quite clear that the employment problem in CEE countries has two defining characteristics: low labour force participation (which reflects a large "discouraged worker effect") and high unemployment. Long-term unemployment is the dominant type of unemployment, and this is linked to low incidence of non-standard wage employment.

The seriousness of the problem is shown by the estimated values of the CEI,[72] presented in table 7.2. These values are low (ranging from 0.699 in the

Table 7.2 Overall employment situation, 2004

Country	Composite Employment Indicator (CEI)
Bulgaria	0.784
Czech Republic	0.820
Estonia	0.802
Hungary	0.793
Latvia	0.790
Lithuania	0.791
Poland	0.746
Romania	0.787
Slovakia	0.796
Slovenia	0.811
Croatia	0.761
Macedonia, former Yugoslav Rep.	0.699

Source: Derived from appendix table A7.7.

---

[70] In the case of the developed countries of Europe, the incidence falls short of 10 per cent in only two countries – Greece and Spain – and exceeds 20 per cent in seven countries (Chapter 6, table 6.1).

[71] Self-employment is significant in Greece, Italy and Portugal, too.

[72] As noted in Chapter 6, the CEI incorporates both the extent of employment and the extent of non-standard employment. The MCEI, which takes into account voluntary part-time employment (see Chapter 6), cannot be estimated here as data on voluntary/involuntary part-time employment are not available.

The global employment challenge

Figure 7.1 Unemployment and overall employment situation, 2004

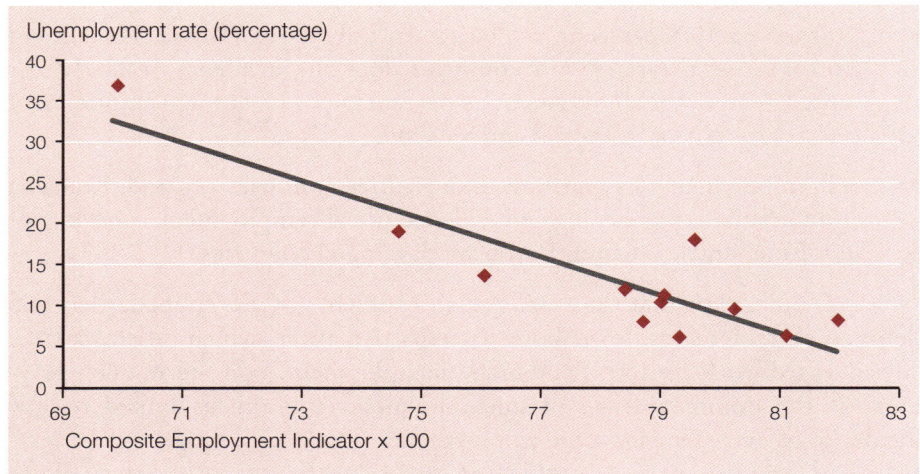

Note: The regression equation is: Y = 195.465 − 2.329 X, R^2 = 0.793. The coefficient is significant at less than 1 per cent.

Source: Derived from tables 7.1 and 7.2.

former Yugoslav Republic of Macedonia to 0.820 in the Czech Republic), suggesting a generally poor employment situation.[73] Across countries, a fairly strong inverse relation between the unemployment rate and the CEI is observed (figure 7.1). This shows that the unemployment rate remains a reasonably good indicator of the overall employment situation. Given that the incidence of non-standard employment is generally low, this is what we should expect.

Gender disparity in employment

Available data on employment and unemployment for men and women are set out in table 7.3. Four facts emerge: (1) the labour force participation rate is systematically and significantly lower for women than for men; (2) the unemployment rate for women is not systematically different from that for men; (3) the incidence of part-time employment is systematically higher for women than for men; and (4) the incidence of temporary employment for women is not systematically different from that for men.

It is clear that gender disparity in employment arises basically from differential participation rates and incidences of part-time employment for

---

[73] For the developed countries of Europe, CEI values range from 0.791 in the Netherlands to 0.887 in Iceland (Chapter 6, table 6.3).

Table 7.3 Employment profile by gender, 2004 (percentages)

Country	Male					Female				
	Participation rate	Unemployment rate	Long-term unemployment rate	Part-time employment as share of total employment	Temporary employment as share of total wage employment	Participation rate	Unemployment rate	Long-term unemployment rate	Part-time employment as share of total employment	Temporary employment as share of total wage employment
Bulgaria	55.0	12.5	7.3	2.1	7.7	44.6	11.5	7.0	2.7	7.0
Czech Republic	68.0	7.1	3.4	2.3	7.8	50.9	9.9	5.3	8.3	10.7
Estonia	65.9	10.4	5.6	5.4	3.5	52.0	8.9	4.4	10.6	1.8
Hungary	56.6	6.1	2.8	3.2	7.5	41.9	6.1	2.6	6.3	6.1
Latvia	65.7	10.6	4.8	7.7	11.6	51.4	10.2	4.3	13.2	7.3
Lithuania	63.4	11.0	5.5	6.5	8.7	51.6	11.8	6.2	10.5	3.9
Poland	61.0	18.2	9.6	8.2	23.7	47.1	19.9	11.0	14.0	21.5
Romania	61.4	9.0	5.2	10.2	2.9	48.5	6.9	3.6	11.2	2.0
Slovakia	67.6	17.3	11.3	1.4	6.0	52.2	19.1	12.4	4.2	5.1
Slovenia	65.8	5.8	3.1	7.9	16.7	52.4	6.8	3.4	11.0	19.1
Croatia	48.9	12.2	6.0	6.3	12.1	52.0	15.7	8.9	11.2	12.4
Macedonia, former Yugoslav Rep.	–	36.7	–	4.6	–	–	37.8	–	6.4	–
Montenegro	–	23.6	–	–	–	–	33.0	–	–	–
Serbia	–	15.1	–	–	–	–	22.9	–	–	–

– = data not available.

Sources: Derived from Landesmann and Vidovic (2006) and EUROSTAT database (http://epp.eurostat.ec.europa.eu/portal/page?_pageid=1090,30070682,1090_33076576&_dad=portal&_schema=PORTAL).

Table 7.4 Gender disparity in employment, 2004

Country	Ratio of female to male CEI
Bulgaria	0.958
Czech Republic	0.900
Estonia	0.920
Hungary	0.928
Latvia	0.921
Lithuania	0.933
Poland	0.909
Romania	0.951
Slovakia	0.920
Slovenia	0.931
Croatia	0.977

Source: Derived from appendix table A7.7.

men and women. A composite measure of this disparity is given by the CEI ratio for women to that for men: a higher value of this ratio indicates lower disparity. The estimated values are given in table 7.4. These indicate rather low levels of gender disparity. In fact, it is quite striking that the disparity is almost universally lower in NMS countries than in European developed countries.[74]

These facts seem to suggest that the pre-transition achievements in the area of gender disparity have survived the sharp deterioration in the employment situation during the transition from a centrally planned to a market system. However, contrary to the situation in developed countries, in the case of CEE countries the cross-country relationship between level of gender disparity and overall employment situation turns out to be negative (a better overall employment situation is associated with a higher level of gender disparity) (figures 7.2a and 7.2b). This seems rather surprising and the finding is taken up for further comments at a later point (see section 7.2 on page 221).

Skills and employment

The overall employment picture hides an important fact: the employment situation is far worse for low-skilled than for high-skilled workers (table 7.5).

---

[74] Compare table 7.4 and table 6.5 in Chapter 6.

Figure 7.2a Gender disparity and employment situation, 2004

Note: The regression equation is: $Y = 1.249 - 0.402\,X$, $R^2 = 0.138$. The coefficient is significant only at 26 per cent.

Source: Derived from tables 7.2 and 7.4.

Figure 7.2b Gender disparity and employment situation (excluding Poland), 2004

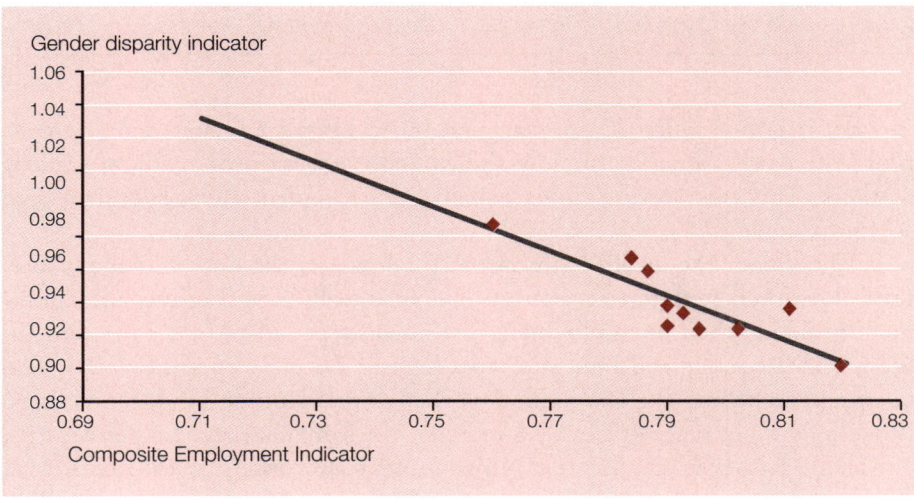

Note: The regression equation is: $Y = 1.900 - 1.218\,X$, $R^2 = 0.762$. The coefficient is significant at less than 1 per cent.

Source: Derived from tables 7.2 and 7.4.

Table 7.5 Unemployment and labour force[a] participation by level of education[b], 2004 (percentages)

Country	Unemployment rate (%)			Participation rate (%)		
	Level of education					
	Low	Medium	High	Low	Medium	High
Bulgaria	22.8	11.2	5.7	37.0	71.3	83.5
Czech Republic	26.5	7.6	2.3	31.0	77.0	87.3
Estonia	19.8	10.6	5.3	35.9	75.0	86.0
Hungary	12.5	5.8	2.3	31.6	69.5	84.1
Latvia	17.9	11.0	4.5	39.4	76.9	87.5
Lithuania	16.6	12.8	6.8	32.9	75.3	90.0
Poland	29.3	20.6	7.3	32.8	70.6	87.0
Romania	9.8	8.9	3.8	44.0	70.9	87.5
Slovakia	51.3	16.8	5.9	28.6	79.4	87.3
Slovenia	9.9	6.6	3.0	46.6	75.1	89.5
Croatia	15.3	15.5	7.8	41.6	70.3	86.2

[a] Labour force is defined as population in age group 15–64.
[b] Level of education: low – up to lower secondary; medium – above lower secondary and up to higher secondary; high – tertiary.

Sources: Derived from Landesmann and Vidovic (2006) and EUROSTAT database (http://epp.eurostat.ec.europa.eu/portal/page?_pageid=1090,30070682,1090_33076576&_dad=portal&_schema=PORTAL).

In fact, it is not much of an exaggeration to say that serious employment problems exist primarily for low-skilled (and a section of medium-skilled) workers. This observation holds equally well for men and for women (see appendix table A7.1).

The higher the level of education, the lower is the unemployment rate. Indeed, workers with tertiary education do not really face a serious unemployment problem: their unemployment rate ranges from a low of 2.3 per cent (in the Czech Republic and Hungary) to a high of 7.3 per cent (in Poland). The unemployment rate for low-skilled workers, on the other hand, tends to be shockingly high, ranging from 9.8 per cent (in Romania) to 51.3 per cent (in Slovakia). In seven of the ten NMS countries, workers with educational attainment of up to lower secondary level face unemployment rates exceeding 15 per cent.

Even these facts do not reveal the full extent of the gap in the employment situation between the high skilled and the low skilled. The labour force participation rate for low-skilled persons is very low (below 40 per cent) in eight of the 11 countries for which data are available and exceeds 50 per cent in only one (Slovakia). In general, the participation rate for high-skilled persons (i.e., those with tertiary education) tends to be higher than that for low-skilled persons by as much as 40–50 percentage points.

A summary view

Low labour force participation and a very high unemployment rate constitute the two main features of the employment problem in CEE countries. A closer look reveals, however, that they essentially characterize low-to-medium-skilled labour. For high-skilled labour, the participation rate tends to be high and the unemployment rate tends to be low. Observed at the level of the aggregate economy, the employment problem is in essence a problem for low-skilled labour.

7.2 Recent trends

Trends in employment

The process of transition from centrally planned to market economies in CEE countries began around 1990 with a deep economic recession that lasted between two and four years (table 7.6). The decline in output was astonishingly large: for example, real GDP in 1993 was only 56.4 per cent of that in 1990 in Latvia, 64.1 per cent in Croatia, 76.7 per cent in Slovakia and 84.9 per cent in Hungary. GDP declines of such magnitude could not but cause huge job losses. Employment recorded sharp drops, unemployment reached high levels and there were large-scale withdrawals by discouraged workers from the labour force.[75] By 1994, a very serious employment problem had emerged.

The focus of analysis here is the 1994–2004 period. It is clear from table 7.6 that this was a decade of post-contraction recovery in all countries except Bulgaria, where recovery really began only in 1998, and Poland, where recovery was complete by 1994. In most of the countries, real GDP regained 1990 levels sometime between 1999 and 2005. Thus 1994–2004 can reasonably be viewed as a period when CEE countries were on course to regain lost ground.

The main trends in employment and unemployment that can be discerned from the data in table 7.7 are as follows:

---

[75] Discussions of these developments are available in Nesporova (1999), Cazes and Nesporova (2003) and Boeri et al. (1998).

The global employment challenge

Table 7.6 Growth and recovery, 1990–2004

Country	GDP[a] in year preceding recovery as percentage of GDP in 1990	Year recovery begins	Year of full recovery[b]
Bulgaria	74.9 (1997)	1998	2004
Czech Republic	87.9 (1992)	1993	2000
Estonia	67.2 (1994)	1995	2002
Hungary	84.9 (1993)	1994	1999
Latvia	56.4 (1993)	1994	2004
Lithuania	56.1 (1994)	1995	2005
Poland	93.0 (1991)	1992	1994
Romania	79.4 (1992)	1993	2004
Slovakia	76.7 (1993)	1994	1999
Slovenia	86.1 (1992)	1993	1996
Croatia	64.1 (1993)	1994	2004

[a] In constant local currency unit.
[b] The year of full recovery is defined as the year in which GDP equalled or exceeded that in 1990.

Sources: Derived from data on GDP available from World Bank, World Development Indicators database (CD-ROM, 2006).

- The labour force participation rate continued to decline in the post-1994 period in most of the countries. In some countries (Lithuania, Poland, Romania and Croatia in particular) it witnessed a sharp decline.

- The unemployment rate declined in some countries and increased in others. In the former group, the participation rate was declining as well,[76] suggesting that the decline in unemployment resulted not so much from an increase in employment as from withdrawals by some of the unemployed from the labour force. Indeed, it is easy to see that declining labour force participation was the sole reason for the decline in unemployment in Lithuania and Romania. On the whole, it would be correct to say that the unemployment problem was generally worsening.

- Long-term unemployment became the increasingly dominant type of unemployment, its share in total unemployment increasing in seven of the 11 countries.

---

[76] The exception is Slovenia, where the unemployment rate declined while the participation rate rose.

Table 7.7 Change in employment profile, 1994–2004

Country	Change (in percentage points)					
	Participation rate	Unemployment rate	Ratio of long-term unemployment rate to overall unemployment rate	Part-time employment as share of total employment	Temporary employment as share of total wage employment	Self-employment as share of total employment
Bulgaria	−3.2	−8.2	4.4[b]	−0.8[c]	1.1[c]	0.1[b]
Czech Republic	−2.5	4.0	19.8[a]	−1.0[d]	2.1[d]	6.2
Estonia[a]	−1.2	0.5	5.7	−0.6	0.5	1.2
Hungary	−0.4	−4.8	−7.7[e]	1.0[d]	0.2[d]	−4.0[f]
Latvia	−1.2	−3.9	−11.1	−2.4	1.5	−4.4
Lithuania[a]	−4.1	−1.8	−5.9	−1.7	1.9	−1.9
Poland	−4.3	4.6	9.6[d]	0.2[d]	17.9[d]	−2.3[d]
Romania	−7.8	−0.2	14.6[d]	−4.3[d]	−0.5[d]	−2.9
Slovakia	0.1	4.5	13.2[a]	0.4[a]	1.3[a]	6.2
Slovenia	1.0	−2.8	4.2[e]	2.6[e]	6.2[d]	−2.7[f]
Albania	−4.6[e]	3.9[e]	−7.2[g]	0.2[g]	1.3[g]	−0.1[b]

Note: In Estonia, the participation rate declined by 4.9 percentage points during the period 1994–2004.
[a] Refers to 1998–2004.
[b] Refers to 2000–04.
[c] Refers to 2001–04.
[d] Refers to 1997–2004.
[e] Refers to 1996–2004.
[f] Refers to 1995–2004.
[g] Refers to 2002–04.

Sources: Derived from Landesmann and Vidovic (2006) and EUROSTAT database (http://epp.eurostat.ec.europa.eu/portal/page?_pageid=1090,30070682,1090_33076576&_dad=portal&_schema=PORTAL).

- No systematic trend in the incidence of non-standard employment is discernible. The incidence of part-time employment showed no significant trend in any of the countries and the incidence of temporary employment recorded significant increase in only one country (Poland).[77] The incidence of self-employment showed significant growth in three countries (Czech Republic, Estonia and Slovakia), where it was relatively low to start with, but declined or remained stable in others.

---

[77] What seems curious is that, despite the growth of temporary employment, in Poland both the unemployment rate and the share of long-term unemployment in total unemployment actually increased.

Table 7.8 Change in overall employment situation, ca. 1997–2004

Country	Period	Composite Employment Indicator	
		Initial year	Terminal year
Bulgaria	2001–2004	0.757	0.784
Czech Republic	1998–2004	0.830	0.820
Estonia	1998–2004	0.806	0.802
Hungary	1997–2004	0.781	0.793
Latvia	1998–2004	0.773	0.790
Lithuania	1998–2004	0.792	0.791
Poland	1997–2004	0.782	0.746
Romania	1997–2004	0.813	0.787
Slovakia	1998–2004	0.813	0.796
Slovenia	1999–2004	0.813	0.811
Croatia	2002–2004	0.759	0.761

Source: Derived from appendix table A7.7.

Thus the main changes during 1994–2004 were those in labour force participation and in unemployment. In four of the 11 countries considered (Czech Republic, Estonia, Poland and Croatia), the participation rate declined while the unemployment rate increased; in one country (Romania) the participation rate declined sharply while the unemployment rate remained virtually unchanged; and in one country (Slovakia) the unemployment rate increased sharply while the participation rate remained virtually unchanged. The overall employment situation unambiguously worsened in all these countries. Only in Slovenia did the employment situation unambiguously improve: the participation rate increased while the unemployment rate declined.

These conclusions more obviously emerge from the CEI estimates presented in table 7.8. Although these estimates generally cover shorter periods (because data on part-time employment are available for shorter periods), they confirm that the employment situation deteriorated in the Czech Republic, Estonia, Poland, Romania and Slovakia. They also suggest that the employment situation improved in Hungary and Latvia, and remained unchanged in Lithuania. In the case of Bulgaria and Croatia, the periods covered are simply too short, and all that can be said is that the employment situation in these countries may have begun improving after 2000, that is, after a long period of deterioration).

Trends in gender disparity

The estimated values of the gender disparity indicator (the ratio of the CEI for women to that for men), presented in table 7.9, show that gender disparity increased in a few of the countries, declined in a few others and remained unchanged in the remainder (see appendix table A7.2 for the detailed picture). Thus there is no general trend, positive or negative, observed across countries in the period of economic recovery. However, the observed change in gender disparity seems to be inversely related to the change in the overall employment situation across countries (figure 7.3). This means that improvement (deterioration) in the overall employment situation was associated with increased (reduced) gender disparity. The inverse relationship, it should be noted, is not really significant in statistical terms but is consistent with the fact (noted earlier, in section 7.1) that, across countries, the better the overall employment situation, the higher is the level of gender inequality.

Plausible explanations for these tendencies are not difficult to find, although empirical substantiation must await country-level investigations. It is known that childcare facilities were declining in CEE countries during both the transition and the recovery periods. This is likely to have increased gender disparity everywhere by forcing some women workers to withdraw from the labour force. It also seems, however, that the pattern of job destruction during

Table 7.9 Change in gender disparity in employment, ca. 1997–2004

Country	Period	Ratio of female to male CEI		Change in disparity
		Initial year	Terminal year	
Bulgaria	2001–2004	0.965	0.958	Increase
Czech Republic	1998–2004	0.896	0.900	Decrease
Estonia	1998–2004	0.921	0.920	Unchanged
Hungary	1997–2004	0.923	0.928	Decrease
Latvia	1998–2004	0.931	0.921	Increase
Lithuania	1998–2004	0.906	0.933	Decrease
Poland	1997–2004	0.901	0.909	Decrease
Romania	1997–2004	0.924	0.951	Decrease
Slovakia	1998–2004	0.921	0.920	Unchanged
Slovenia	1996–2004	0.959	0.931	Increase
Croatia	2002–2004	0.995	0.977	Increase

Source: Derived from appendix table A7.7.

The global employment challenge

Figure 7.3 Change in gender disparity and in overall employment situation, ca. 1997–2004

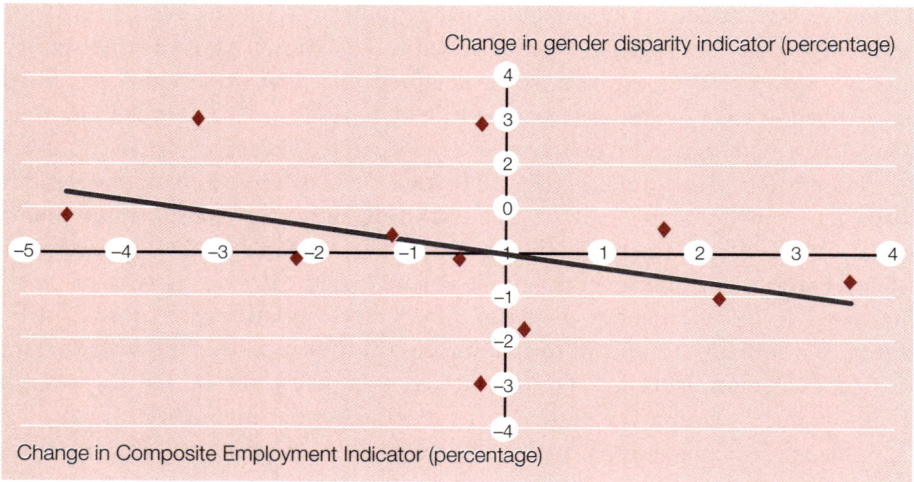

Note: The regression equation is: Y = − 0.050 − 0.305 X, R² = 0.162. The coefficient is significant only at 22 per cent.

Source: Derived from tables 7.8 and 7.9.

contraction was biased against men while the pattern of job creation during recovery was biased against women. As we shall see below, job losses have occurred in agriculture and in industry, sectors that traditionally employ more men than women (see appendix table A7.3). On the other hand, there were job gains in skill-intensive services (e.g., financial or management services), which usually employ mainly men. The combined effect of these developments was that gender disparity actually remained largely unchanged during economic contraction but increased during recovery.[78]

Trends in employment by skill category

It has been observed above that the employment problem in CEE countries as it exists today is essentially a problem for low-skilled (including a section of medium-skilled) labour. The data in table 7.10 suggest that this was already so

---

[78] If the process of job destruction had been indeed biased against men, the unemployment rate would have increased more and the "discouraged worker effect" would have been stronger for men than for women. On the other hand, the decline of childcare facilities would have reduced women's participation rate but not that of men. Overall, therefore, the employment situation would have worsened to similar extents for men and women during the period of contraction. If the process of job creation had been biased against women during recovery (while the decline of childcare facilities continued), men's employment situation would have improved while that of women would have continued to worsen.

Systemic transition and job crisis in Central and Eastern European countries

Table 7.10 Unemployment by level of education,[a] ca. 1997–2004 (percentages)

Country	Period	Unemployment rate (%)					
		Level of education					
		Low		Medium		High	
		Initial year	Terminal year	Initial year	Terminal year	Initial year	Terminal year
Bulgaria	2000–2004	28.1	22.8	16.1	11.2	7.3	5.7
Czech Republic	1998–2004	16.3	26.5	5.7	7.6	2.4	2.3
Estonia	1997–2004	17.1	19.8	11.8	10.6	7.2	5.3
Hungary	1997–2004	15.3	12.5	8.2	5.8	1.7	2.3
Latvia	1998–2004	19.9	17.9	15.1	11.0	6.5	4.5
Lithuania	1998–2004	19.5	16.6	16.5	12.8	8.9	6.8
Poland	1997–2004	15.5	29.3	11.7	20.6	3.4	7.3
Romania	1997–2004	5.0	9.8	7.6	8.9	2.3	3.8
Slovakia	1998–2004	28.9	51.3	11.4	16.8	3.7	5.9
Slovenia	1996–2004	9.9	9.9	6.7	6.6	2.8	3.0
Croatia	2002–2004	15.1	15.3	17.0	15.5	8.5	7.8

[a] Level of education: low – up to lower secondary; medium – above lower secondary and up to higher secondary; high – tertiary.

Note: The data refer to the age group 15–64.

Sources: Derived from Landesmann and Vidovic (2006) and EUROSTAT database (http://epp.eurostat.ec.europa.eu/portal/page?_pageid=1090,30070682,1090_33076576&_dad=portal&_schema=PORTAL).

at the beginning of the process of economic recovery. The economic contraction in the early phase of systemic transition had led to massive job losses for low-skilled labour but not for high-skilled labour. It is the low-to-medium-skilled labour that faced, and continues to face, an extraordinarily high level of unemployment. On the other hand, high unemployment has not been a major problem for high-skilled labour in a majority of the countries, either during contraction or during recovery.

Even these facts seriously understate the true scale of the labour market disadvantage of low-skilled labour, as the absolute number of low-skilled workers has been declining at a rapid rate in most CEE countries (table 7.11). It is evident that the demand for low-skilled labour declined at a rapid rate everywhere, and the observed change in the unemployment rate only reflects the extent to which the supply of low-skilled labour adjusted to this. In the

Table 7.11   Growth of labour force by level of education,[a] ca. 1997–2004 (percentages)

Country	Period	Average annual rate of growth of labour force (%)		
		Level of education		
		Low	Medium	High
Bulgaria	2001–2004	−1.9	−0.9	0.4
Czech Republic	1998–2004	−5.3	0.0	2.7
Estonia	1999–2004	−3.9	−0.1[b]	1.1
Hungary	1997–2004	−3.9	1.1	4.9
Latvia	1998–2004	1.0[b]	−0.8[b]	2.1
Lithuania	2001–2004	−2.7	−1.4	3.6
Poland	1997–2004	−5.8	0.6[b]	4.5
Romania	1997–2004	−5.8	−0.7[b]	−1.4[b]
Slovakia	1998–2004	−4.5	1.0	4.5
Slovenia	1996–2004	−4.1	0.8	4.4

[a] Level of education: low – up to lower secondary; medium – above lower secondary and up to higher secondary; high – tertiary.
[b] Statistically equivalent to zero.

Note: Growth rates estimated by using regression except for Bulgaria and Lithuania. In these two cases, the number of observations is too small and the compound interest formula has been used.

Sources: Derived from Landesmann and Vidovic (2006) and EUROSTAT database (http://epp.eurostat.ec.europa.eu/portal/page?_pageid=1090,30070682,1090_33076576&_dad=portal&_schema=PORTAL).

Czech Republic, Estonia, Poland, Romania and Slovakia, for example, the supply of low-skilled labour was declining at an average annual rate of 4–6 per cent, but even this proved insufficient to prevent a rise in unemployment as the demand for low-skilled labour was declining even faster.

In sharp contrast, the high-skilled labour force was growing in all the countries except Bulgaria and Romania (where this growth was negligible), and in a majority of them the increase was quite rapid. Yet the unemployment rate for high-skilled labour either fell or changed little in a majority of the countries. It is clear that, while the supply of high-skilled labour recorded rapid growth, demand for such labour tended to grow even faster.

The conclusion is clear: there was a rapid shift in the structure of labour demand in favour of high-skilled labour and this had a role to play in the worsening or persistence of the employment problem.

7.3 Explaining the trends

The labour market developments in CEE countries bear a distinct resemblance to those in European developed countries. In both groups, economic growth in recent years has been associated with a major shift in the relative demand for skill types, which has led to substantial redundancy of low-skilled labour (defined in broad terms to include the low-end part of medium-skilled labour). The problem of redundancy, of course, has been and remains much more extensive in CEE countries (and below we shall see why). The manifestations of the problem are also somewhat different in the two groups of countries. Unlike in the developed countries of Europe, in CEE countries non-standard wage employment has not increased. The explanation lies less in the nature of labour market institutions than in the depth of structural change (box 7.1). But the fact remains that while greater part-time and temporary

> **Box 7.1 Labour market institutions in CEE countries**
>
> At the inception of the process of transition to a market economy, labour market institutions similar to those existing in European developed countries were introduced in CEE countries (Boeri et al., 1998). Unemployment benefit systems, employment protection regulations and means-tested social assistance schemes were all put in place.
>
> A comparison of the labour market institutions in CEE countries with those in developed countries yields the following conclusions (Riboud et al., 2002; Vodopivec et al., 2003; Cazes and Nesporova, 2003). Where unemployment benefits are concerned, replacement rates, duration of benefits and coverage rates are quite similar to those found in Ireland, Italy and the United Kingdom but are much less generous than those in other developed countries of Europe. Employment protection regulations applicable to regular employees are stricter than those in Denmark, Ireland, Switzerland and the United Kingdom, and are about as strict as those in Austria, Germany and Sweden; regulations governing temporary employment are similar to those in Denmark, Netherlands and Switzerland (i.e., they are not really restrictive).
>
> This last fact has an important implication: the lack of growth in temporary employment seems to have had little to do with labour market policies and institutions. The likely explanation is the stagnant or declining demand for labour. Most enterprises are shedding labour and only a few are recruiting. And those few that are increasing employment are mainly recruiting skilled labour (Commander and Köllő, 2004). In these circumstances, the scope for growth of temporary employment is extremely limited. The same explanation is likely to hold for part-time employment.

Table 7.12 Economic growth and employment, ca. 1994–2004

Country	Period	GDP growth (%) (1)	Employment elasticity[a] (2)	Growth of labour demand[b] (%) (3)	Growth of labour supply (%) (4)	Growth of working-age population (%) (5)
Bulgaria	1994–2004	1.86	−0.24[c]	−0.4[c] (−0.8)	−1.1	−0.4
Czech Republic	1994–2004	2.01	−0.24	−0.5 (−0.6)	0.1[c]	0.3
Estonia	1998–2004	6.19	0.03[c]	0.2[c] (0.1[c])	−0.1[c]	0.2
Hungary	1994–2004	4.04	0.23	0.9 (0.9)	0.3	0.1
Latvia	1998–2004	6.90	0.11[c]	0.8[c] (0.7[c])	−0.1[c]	0.1
Lithuania	1998–2004	5.75	−0.05[c]	−0.3[c] (−0.6[c])	−1.0	0.2
Poland	1994–2004	4.17	−0.19	−0.8 (−1.0)	0.0	0.7
Romania	1994–2004	1.47	−0.68	−1.0 (−1.3)	−1.3	0.4
Slovakia	1994–2004	3.80	0.00	0.0 (−0.1[c])	0.8	0.8
Slovenia	1994–2004	3.83	0.17	0.7 (0.6)	0.4	0.6
Croatia	1996–2004	3.29	0.03[c]	0.1[c] (0.0)	0.7	1.9

[a] Estimated by using double-log regression equations.
[b] The figures outside parentheses are estimated by multiplying GDP growth rates by the corresponding values of employment elasticity, while the figures in parentheses are estimated directly from data on employment.
[c] Statistically insignificant.

Sources: Authors' estimates based on data on real GDP from World Bank (World Development Indicators database, CD-ROM, 2006) and data on employment, labour force and working-age population from Landesmann and Vidovic (2006) and EUROSTAT database(http://epp.eurostat.ec.europa.eu/portal/page?_pageid=1090,30070682,1090_33076576&_dad=portal&_schema=PORTAL).

employment have reduced long-term unemployment in European developed countries, long-term unemployment in CEE countries has remained high and its growth has only been restrained by large-scale withdrawals of discouraged workers from the labour force.

These differences can be traced to the remarkable fact that, unlike in European developed countries, economic growth in CEE countries was jobless. The pace of economic growth during 1994–2004 was rapid in most of the countries (table 7.12), but economic growth was associated with zero or negative growth of employment almost everywhere. In Poland, a rate of GDP growth in excess of 4 per cent per annum was associated with a decline of about 1 per cent per annum in the demand for labour. In five other countries (Estonia, Latvia, Lithuania, Slovakia and Croatia), high rates of GDP growth were associated with zero growth in the demand for labour. In two countries (Czech Republic and Romania), modest economic growth was associated with sharply declining demand for labour. Only in Hungary and Slovenia was GDP growth associated with job growth, although even in these countries employment elasticity was low.

What explains this jobless growth? The period under consideration, it is important to remember, was a period of post-contraction recovery. In any economy, severe output contraction destroys the least efficient producers. Subsequent recovery is then associated with the emergence of new producers who tend to use more modern (less labour-intensive) technologies. This means that the pre-contraction level of output is regained with a level of employment significantly lower than that prevailing in the pre-contraction period. Thus in any economy growth in a context of post-contraction recovery tends to be jobless for a certain period.

In CEE countries, rapid structural changes associated with systemic transition greatly strengthened the tendency.[79] These structural changes, moreover, were taking place in a period of rapid skill-biased technological change and intensified global competition. The result was a fairly radical rise in the skill intensity of employment.

Two types of structural change have been under way. The first involves restructuring of employment within production units, required to promote technological change and productivity growth, essential for viability in the new context of market orientation and openness of economies. The effect is a reduction in total employment together with an increase in the proportion of high-skilled labour in total employment in individual enterprises (Landesmann and Vidovic, 2006; Commander and Köllo, 2004; World Bank, 2006). The second type of restructuring has to do with reallocation of resources across sectors, required to correct the imbalances carried over from the past. The effects of this type of restructuring can be seen from the data in table 7.13. In general, employment in agriculture declined at a rapid rate, employment in industry either stagnated or declined and employment in services rose. Low-skilled workers have been losing jobs in large numbers in agriculture and industry; new jobs in services have been far fewer and in any case mostly unavailable to low-skilled workers.[80]

Absolute numbers for four countries (Czech Republic, Poland, Romania and Slovakia) provide a dramatic illustration of this point. During 1996–2004, employment declined by 2.3 million in agriculture and by 1.6 million in industry, while it increased by 0.6 million in services; thus total employment declined by 3.3 million (see appendix table A7.3). The changes in employment

---

[79] Landesmann and Vidovic (2006) argue that such structural changes give rise to a U-shaped trajectory of inter-temporal change in aggregate employment. Most CEE countries, it would appear, are still on the downward sloping segment of this trajectory.

[80] A detailed discussion of these trends and patterns is available in Landesmann and Vidovic (2006).

Table 7.13 Employment growth by sector, ca. 1994–2004 (percentages)

Country	Period	Average annual rate of growth of employment growth[a]		
		Agriculture	Industry	Services
Bulgaria	2000–2004	0.1[b]	1.4[b]	1.9
Czech Republic	1994–2004	−5.2	−0.6	0.5
Estonia	1998–2004	−5.8	0.1[b]	1.0
Hungary	1994–2004	−4.5	0.9	1.5
Latvia	1998–2004	−4.3	0.7[b]	1.9
Lithuania	1998–2004	−3.4	−0.6[b]	0.3[b]
Poland	1994–2004	−3.5	−1.0	0.9
Romania	1994–2004	−2.6	−1.3	1.0
Slovakia	1994–2004	−6.8	−0.1[b]	1.1
Slovenia	1994–2004	−1.6[b]	0.6	2.3
Croatia	1996–2004	−1.1[b]	0.1[b]	0.6[b]

[a] The growth rates are estimated by using regression.
[b] Statistically insignificant.

Source: Authors' estimates based on data from EUROSTAT database (http://epp.eurostat.ec.europa.eu/portal/page?_pageid=1090,30070682,1090_33076576&_dad=portal&_schema=PORTAL).

by skill type in the same countries during 1998–2004 were as follows (appendix table A7.4): low-skilled jobs declined by 2.2 million and medium-skilled jobs declined by 1.9 million while high-skilled jobs increased by 1.2 million; thus overall employment declined by 2.9 million and the share of high-skilled jobs in all jobs increased from 11.2 per cent to 16.5 per cent.[81]

It is clear that the process of change in CEE economies is similar to that observed in the developed economies of Europe. But while in CEE countries job losses in agriculture and industry were much larger than job gains in services, in European developed countries job gains in services were much larger than job losses in agriculture and industry. In short, growth was jobless in CEE countries essentially because employment growth in services was very low. This is an important fact and we shall come back to it.

This jobless growth increased unemployment but also forced a downward adjustment in labour supply. Of the nine countries where the growth in labour

---

[81] This number falls short of the number by which total employment declined (3.3 million). One reason is that the periods are different, and another is the fact that employment by sector refers to the age group 15 and older while employment by level of education refers to the age group 15–64.

demand was zero or negative, the growth of labour supply was positive in only two (Slovakia and Croatia). The adjustment in labour supply occurred partly through emigration and partly through a sharp decline in the participation rate, as large numbers of discouraged workers simply withdrew from the labour force. As we shall see below, emigration was substantial for all the countries and certainly restrained the growth of working-age population. Still, the working-age population was increasing in all the countries except Bulgaria, and the growth of labour supply was lower than that of working-age population in all the countries except Hungary and Slovakia (table 7.12). Evidently, had labour force participation remained stable, the growth of labour supply would have been significantly higher than it actually was. Also, without emigration and the sharp fall in participation rates, unemployment rates would have been much higher than those observed.

The decline in the overall participation rate essentially reflects a drastic fall in the participation rate of low-skilled persons; the participation rate of persons with tertiary education actually increased in a majority of the countries (appendix table A7.4). It also turns out that in a number of countries (particularly in Hungary, Poland and Slovenia), working-age population with low-level education was declining quite rapidly while that with medium and high-level education was rising almost across the board (table 7.14). General expansion of

Table 7.14 Growth of working-age population by level of education, ca. 1996–2004 (percentages)

Country	Period	Average annual rate of growth of working-age population[a]		
		Level of education[b]		
		Low	Medium	High
Czech Republic	1998–2004	−0.93[c]	0.53	3.11
Estonia	1999–2004	−1.01[c]	0.22[c]	1.08
Hungary	1997–2004	−3.33	1.25	4.64
Latvia	1998–2004	1.07[c]	−1.16	1.73
Poland	1997–2004	−2.99	1.66	4.70
Romania	1997–2004	−1.31	0.79[c]	−0.90[c]
Slovakia	1998–2004	−2.03	0.98	5.04
Slovenia	1996–2004	−4.24	1.48	3.98

[a] Working-age population refers to persons in age group 15–64.
[b] Level of education: low – up to lower secondary; medium – above lower secondary and up to higher secondary; high – tertiary.
[c] Statistically insignificant.

Sources: Derived from Landesmann and Vidovic (2006) and EUROSTAT database (http://epp.eurostat.ec.europa.eu/portal/page?_pageid=1090,30070682,1090_33076576&_dad=portal&_schema=PORTAL).

Table 7.15 Emigration to developed countries by level of education, period up to 2001

Country of origin	Extent of emigration[a]			Total
	Level of education[b]			
	Low	Medium	High	
Bulgaria	1.50	1.52	4.66	1.98
Czech Republic	1.58	1.10	5.07	1.63
Estonia	3.52	2.25	4.35	3.00
Hungary	2.40	3.02	9.19	3.41
Latvia	1.68	3.11	6.79	2.61
Lithuania	1.60	3.23	2.03	1.86
Poland	3.56	2.75	10.91	3.93
Romania	1.94	2.22	10.08	2.74
Slovakia	1.14	0.92	5.31	1.37
Slovenia	6.21	2.43	4.83	4.09

[a] Extent of emigration is defined as the number of emigrants as proportion of the total resident population plus the number of emigrants. Both emigrants and residents are taken to be persons belonging to the age group 15 years and older.

[b] Level of education: low – up to lower secondary; medium – above lower secondary and up to higher secondary; high – tertiary.

Sources: Authors' estimates based on data from Landesmann and Vidovic (2006), EUROSTAT database (http://epp.eurostat.ec.europa.eu/portal/page?_pageid=1090,30070682,1090_33076576&_dad=portal&_schema=PORTAL) and OECD database on immigrants and expatriates (http://www.oecd.org/document/51/0,2340,en_2649_33931_34063091_1_1_1_1.00.html).

education must be the main explanation for these trends. But was emigration also a contributory factor?

The answer appears to be no. Emigration of high-skilled labour was much more significant than that of low-skilled labour in all countries except Slovenia (table 7.15). Indeed, quite a few countries experienced serious brain drain (particularly Hungary, Poland and Romania). Emigration thus generally restrained the growth of high-skilled population much more than that of low-skilled population. The only exception was Slovenia, where emigration reduced the growth of the low skilled more than that of the high skilled.

7.4 Policy challenges

The analysis makes it abundantly clear that CEE countries face two main challenges.

The first concerns the need to substantially increase the employment intensity of economic growth. Most of the countries (with the exception of

Table 7.16 Growth of output and labour productivity by sector, ca. 1994–2004

Country	Period	Average annual rate of growth in output					
		Agriculture		Industry		Services	
		Total[a]	Per worker[b]	Total[a]	Per worker[b]	Total[a]	Per worker[b]
Bulgaria	2000–2004	–1.9	–1.9	4.6	4.6	6.1	4.2
Czech Republic	1994–2004	–3.1	2.1	7.0	7.6	3.4	2.9
Estonia	1998–2004	–1.4[c]	5.8	7.8	7.8	6.1	5.1
Hungary	1994–2004	–4.0	0.5	3.5	2.6	5.0	3.5
Latvia	1998–2004	7.2	11.5	4.0	4.0	7.9	7.9
Lithuania	1998–2004	–2.2[c]	3.4	6.3	6.3	6.5	6.5
Poland	1994–2004	–1.4[c]	3.5	1.9	0.9	6.0	5.1
Romania	1994–2004	–4.2	–1.6	–0.9[c]	1.3	6.0	5.0
Slovakia	1994–2004	–1.0	5.8	1.7	1.7	5.2	4.1
Slovenia	1994–2004	–2.1	–2.1	3.2	2.6	4.6	2.3
Croatia	1996–2004	0.2[c]	0.0	1.6	1.6	4.7	4.7

[a] The growth rates of output are estimated by using regression.
[b] The rate of growth of output per worker is estimated by subtracting the rate of employment growth (table 5.13) from the rate of output growth. In deriving this estimate, statistically insignificant values have been treated as zero.
[c] Statistically insignificant.

Sources: Authors' estimates based on data from Landesmann and Vidovic (2006), EUROSTAT database (http://epp.eurostat.ec.europa.eu/portal/page?_pageid=1090,30070682,1090_33076576&_dad=portal&_schema=PORTAL) and World Bank, World Development Indicators database (CD-ROM, 2006).

Bulgaria, the Czech Republic and Romania) achieved fairly rapid economic growth in the period since 1994, but in virtually all of them growth was associated with falling or stagnant demand for labour. Jobless growth is a main reason for the deterioration or persistence of the already very poor employment situations. And jobless growth, as already noted, is explained essentially by the extremely poor employment growth in services.

Economic growth in CEE countries during 1994–2004 was driven by growth in services[82] (table 7.16) but this growth is largely accounted for by growth in labour productivity. It is indeed quite remarkable that employment elasticity in services was much lower in CEE countries than in European developed countries (see appendix table A7.6). This is contrary to expectation. At the beginning of the 1990s, services were relatively undeveloped in CEE

---

[82] Industrial growth was high in only three of the 11 countries and agricultural growth was positive in only one country (Latvia).

economies and already well developed in the developed economies of Europe. Employment elasticity would thus normally be expected to be higher in the former than in the latter group.

Industrial growth, it might be noted, was also associated with growth of labour productivity and zero or negative growth of employment. But here plausible explanations exist. It is probable that even the severe economic contraction of the early 1990s did not eliminate the "hoarded" labour that had been carried over from the days of central planning. Quite apart from this, it is to be expected that industrial restructuring, involving extensive restructuring of old enterprises and establishment of new industries in a period of rapid technological change and globalization, would result in rising skill intensity of employment rather than in rising employment. In the case of agriculture, declining employment is not surprising since output itself was declining (although in some countries the decline in employment was sharper than the decline in output).

It is quite clear, therefore, that the extremely low employment elasticity in services provides the main explanation for jobless growth. And if growth is not to be jobless in future, it would be very important to consider policies that could help increase employment elasticity in services. Why was employment elasticity so low? The explanation cannot lie in the nature of labour market regulations and institutions, as these are very similar to those in the countries of Western Europe (see box 7.1). It might be thought that we are confronted with a statistical illusion: there may be much "informal" employment in services not captured by labour force surveys; but precisely why labour force surveys should fail to capture "informal" employment is far from clear. There remain two possible explanations. First, it is possible that employment in public services was declining even while employment in market services was growing. Second, it is possible that the growth has been confined to skill-intensive market services.

Landesmann and Vidovic (2006) investigate these issues in some detail and come up with the following findings. Employment in community, social and personal services declined in only three countries (Bulgaria, Poland and Slovakia) but generally showed slow growth mainly because education and health services, as well as social services such as childcare services, suffered a decline in many of the countries. On the other hand, in the case of market services, growth occurred basically in skill-intensive market services such as real estate, renting and business services. While some growth did occur in labour-intensive market services such as wholesale and retail trade and hotel and restaurant services, at the same time there was rapid decline in other employment-intensive market services such as transport, storage and communications; the net result was negligible growth of employment in labour-intensive market services.

So the reason why the employment intensity of services growth was low is that growth occurred mainly in skill-intensive market services. Future policies will clearly need to focus on the growth of both labour-intensive market services such as transport, storage and communication, and social services such as education, health and childcare.

The second major challenge faced by CEE countries involves increasing the employability of large sections of low- and medium-skilled workers made redundant (and who will, in all likelihood, continue to be made redundant) by the structural changes. This is a challenge also faced by developed countries. Just as in developed countries, this calls for active labour market policies focused on equipping the workers suffering job losses in agriculture and industry with new skills required for re-employment in the expanding service sector. Past experience with active labour market policies in Western European countries shows that skill development programmes improve the probability of re-employment of low-skilled job losers.[83] Some active labour market policies do exist in CEE countries, of course, but they are pitifully inadequate (Riboud et al., 2002). In addition, the policies are not particularly focused on imparting new skills to low-skilled job losers; they cover a vast array of programmes, including job search assistance and counselling, training for youth, wage subsidies to private employers, direct job creation in the public sector and special programmes for disadvantaged groups such as the disabled. What is required is not just greater expenditure but a much sharper focus on training programmes designed to enable low-skilled workers facing job losses in agriculture and industry to move to new jobs in the services sector.

---

[83] The main finding from macroeconomic evaluations is that while aggregate expenditure on active labour market policies per unemployed person does not have a significant effect on unemployment, expenditure on training programmes does have a significant effect. See Bassanini and Duval (2006) and Boone and van Ours (2004). Microeconomic evaluations show mixed results but on the whole suggest that training programmes and wage subsidies increase the probability of re-employment. See Kluve (2006).

Appendix table A7.1 Key employment indicators by gender and level of education, 2004 (percentages)

Country	Participation rate by level of education			Unemployment rate by level of education		
	Low	Medium	High	Low	Medium	High
Men						
Bulgaria	42.9	76.5	87.1	23.1	11.3	5.1
Czech Republic	30.8	84.7	93.3	29.2	6.4	2.3
Estonia (2003)	37.0	82.3	93.3	20.8	10.4	7.6
Hungary	36.2	76.2	88.8	14.5	5.5	1.7
Latvia	45.3	83.5	91.4	16.5	10.6	5.5
Lithuania	38.5	81.1	91.9	16.2	11.8	6.5
Poland	38.3	77.6	90.2	29.2	19.0	6.5
Romania	51.5	76.3	88.9	12.8	9.4	3.1
Slovakia	31.5	85.7	92.1	55.3	15.8	5.6
Slovenia	52.8	78.7	90.6	10.8	5.7	2.9
Croatia	51.3	75.0	86.5	14.3	13.0	7.4
Women						
Bulgaria	31.0	65.3	81.1	22.3	11.1	6.1
Czech Republic	31.3	69.0	80.0	24.6	9.2	2.3
Estonia (2003)	33.0	68.4	81.2	19.0	11.4	6.7
Hungary	27.9	62.2	80.3	10.3	6.2	2.8
Latvia	30.9	70.7	84.7	20.3	11.4	4.3
Lithuania	26.6	69.7	88.7	17.2	13.7	7.1
Poland	27.5	63.2	84.5	29.5	22.5	8.0
Romania	38.2	64.7	85.9	6.7	8.2	4.5
Slovakia	26.4	72.6	82.7	47.8	17.9	6.1
Slovenia	41.8	68.9	87.7	9.1	8.0	3.1
Croatia	34.7	65.0	85.0	16.3	19.0	8.1

Notes: Data refer to age group 15–64. Level of education: low – up to lower secondary; medium – above lower secondary and up to higher secondary; high – tertiary.

Sources: Derived from EUROSTAT database (http://epp.eurostat.ec.europa.eu/portal/page?_pageid=1090,30070682, 1090_33076576&_dad=portal&_schema=PORTAL).

Appendix table A7.2 Change in employment situation by gender, ca. 1996–2004

Country (year)[a]	Gender	Value (%) in initial year				Change to 2004 (percentage points)			
		PR	UR	PTE	TEMP	PR	UR	PTE	TEMP
Bulgaria (2001)	Male	54.6[b]	20.2[c]	2.9	6.6	0.5	−7.7	−0.8	1.1
	Female	44.7[b]	20.3[c]	3.6	5.9	−0.1	−8.8	−0.9	1.1
Czech Republic (1998)	Male	69.7	3.6[c]	2.6	5.7	−1.7	3.5	−0.3	2.1
	Female	53.1	5.2[c]	9.9	7.7	−2.2	4.7	−1.6	3.0
Estonia (1998)	Male	68.3	9.8	5.9	2.9	−2.4	0.6	−0.5	0.3
	Female	52.4	8.3	11.4	1.3	−0.4	0.6	−0.4	0.5
Hungary (1997)	Male	55.7[d]	11.8[c]	2.0	7.0	0.9	−5.7	1.2	0.5
	Female	39.9[d]	9.4[c]	5.6	6.1	2.1	−3.3	0.7	0.0
Latvia (1998)	Male	68.6	14.9	12.5	10.2	−2.8	−4.3	−4.8	1.4
	Female	51.3	13.6	13.1	5.7	0.1	−3.4	0.1	1.6
Lithuania (1998)	Male	69.5	14.6	9.0	5.9[b]	−6.1	−3.6	−2.5	2.8
	Female	53.9	11.7	11.2	3.1[b]	−2.4	0.1	−0.7	0.8
Poland (1997)	Male	64.2	13.1[c]	8.3	5.6	−3.2	5.1	−0.1	18.1
	Female	49.1	16.0[c]	13.6	4.0	−2.0	3.9	0.4	17.5
Romania (1997)	Male	71.9	6.3[d]	12.6	3.0	−10.5	2.7	−2.4	−0.1
	Female	58.1	7.4[d]	17.5	3.0	−9.6	−0.5	−6.3	−1.0
Slovakia (1998)	Male	67.2	13.3[c]	1.1	4.0	0.4	4.0	0.3	2.0
	Female	51.1	14.1[c]	3.8	4.4	1.1	5.0	0.4	0.7
Slovenia (1996)	Male	63.6	9.6[c]	5.2	9.9[e]	2.2	−3.8	2.7	6.8
	Female	52.7	8.5[c]	8.4	11.2[e]	−0.3	−1.7	2.6	7.9
Croatia (2002)	Male	47.9	9.5[d]	6.6	11.3	1.0	2.7	−0.3	0.8
	Female	53.8	10.5[d]	10.5	10.4	−1.7	5.2	0.7	2.0

[a] Figures refer to the year in parentheses unless otherwise indicated. [b] Refers to 2000. [c] Refers to 1994. [d] Refers to 1996. [e] Refers to 1999. PR – participation rate. UR – unemployment rate. PTE – part-time employment as share of total employment. TEMP – Temporary employment as share of total wage employment.
Sources: Derived from Landesmann and Vidovic (2006) and EUROSTAT database (http://epp.eurostat.ec.europa.eu/portal/page?_pageid=1090,30070682,1090_33076576&_dad=portal&_schema=PORTAL).

The global employment challenge

Appendix table A7.3 Change in employment by sector, selected countries, 1996–2004 (thousands)

Country	Total	Agriculture	Industry	Services
Czech Republic	−264.4	−103.1	−220.6	59.3
Poland	−1 174.3	−826.0	−762.5	414.2
Romania	−1 777.9	−1 254.6	−591.3	68.0
Slovakia	−58.7	−88.2	−33.1	62.6
Total	−3 275.3	−2 271.9	−1 607.5	604.1

Sources: Derived from Landesmann and Vidovic (2006) and EUROSTAT database (http://epp.eurostat.ec.europa.eu/portal/page?_pageid=1090,30070682,1090_33076576&_dad=portal&_schema=PORTAL)

Appendix table A7.4 Change in employment by level of education, selected countries, 1998–2004

Country	Change in employment[a] (thousands)	Level of education[b]		
		Low	Medium	High
Czech Republic	−115.1	−149.8	−71.3	106.0
Poland	−1 375.0	−974.8	−1 243.0	842.8
Romania	−1 379.3	−970.8	−593.3	184.8
Slovakia	−30.1	−101.4	4.3	67.0
Total	−2 899.5	−2 196.8	−1 911.9	1 200.6

[a] Refers to age group 15–64.

[b] Level of education: low – up to lower secondary; medium – above lower secondary and up to higher secondary; high – tertiary.

Sources: Derived from Landesmann and Vidovic (2006) and EUROSTAT database (http://epp.eurostat.ec.europa.eu/portal/page?_pageid=1090,30070682,1090_33076576&_dad=portal&_schema=PORTAL)

Appendix table A7.5 Participation rate by level of education, ca. 1998–2004 (percentages)

Country	Period	Level of education[a]					
		Low		Medium		High	
		Initial year	Terminal year	Initial year	Terminal year	Initial year	Terminal year
Bulgaria	2001–2004	39.3	37.0	71.1	71.2	82.4	83.5
Czech Republic	1998–2004	39.0	31.0	79.3	77.1	89.7	87.3
Estonia	1999–2004	39.6	35.9	76.6	75.0	85.5	86.0
Hungary	1997–2004	33.4	31.6	71.4	69.5	83.0	84.1
Latvia	1998–2004	41.6	39.4	76.2	76.9	85.6	87.5
Lithuania	2001–2004	32.8	32.9	78.3	75.3	89.3	90.0
Poland	1997–2004	40.1	32.8	75.6	70.6	87.3	87.0
Romania	1997–2004	59.1	44.0	77.5	70.9	87.8	87.5
Slovakia	1998–2004	33.4	28.6	79.6	79.4	91.7	87.3
Slovenia	1996–2004	43.9	46.6	76.5	74.3	86.3	88.9

[a] Data relate to persons belonging to age group 15–64. Level of education: low – up to lower secondary; medium – above lower secondary and up to higher secondary; high – tertiary.

Sources: Derived from Landesmann and Vidovic (2006) and EUROSTAT database (http://epp.eurostat.ec.europa.eu/portal/page?_pageid=1090,30070682,1090_33076576&_dad=portal&_schema=PORTAL).

Appendix table A7.6 Employment elasticity in services, selected CEE countries and European developed countries

Country	Period	Employment elasticity	Country	Employment elasticity
Selected CEE countries			**European developed countries**	
Bulgaria	2000–2004	0.311	Austria	0.833
Czech Republic	1994–2004	0.147	Belgium	0.559
Estonia	1998–2004	0.164	Denmark	0.414
Hungary	1994–2004	0.300	Finland	0.396
Latvia	1998–2004	0.241	France	0.504
Lithuania	1998–2004	0.000	Germany	0.506
Poland	1994–2004	0.150	Greece	0.706
Romania	1994–2004	0.167	Iceland	0.548
Slovakia	1994–2004	0.212	Ireland	0.680
Slovenia	1994–2004	0.500	Italy	0.391
			Luxembourg	0.443
Croatia	1996–2004	0.000	Netherlands	0.751
			Norway	0.596
			Portugal	0.364
			Spain	0.851
			Sweden	0.272
			Switzerland	0.678
			United Kingdom	0.453

Note: These are values of the arc elasticity derived by dividing the rate of growth of employment by the rate of growth of GDP. The rate of employment growth is taken to be zero when the estimated value is statistically insignificant.

Source: Estimated from data in tables 6.13 (Chapter 6), 7.13 and 7.16.

Appendix table A7.7 Composite Employment Indicator (CEI), 1997–2004

Country	Category	1997	1998	1999	2000	2001	2002	2003	2004
Bulgaria	All	–	–	–	–	0.757	0.765	0.777	0.784
	Male	–	–	–	–	0.772	0.781	0.794	0.801
	Female	–	–	–	–	0.745	0.750	0.762	0.768
Czech Republic	All	0.835	0.830	0.822	0.821	0.824	0.825	0.822	0.820
	Male	–	0.874	0.865	0.863	0.864	0.868	0.865	0.862
	Female	–	0.783	0.776	0.777	0.781	0.781	0.777	0.776
Estonia	All	–	0.806	0.797	0.792	0.793	0.799	0.799	0.802
	Male	–	0.842	0.828	0.826	0.829	0.833	0.835	–
	Female	–	0.776	0.771	0.763	0.762	0.770	0.768	–
Hungary	All	0.781	0.785	0.791	0.795	0.796	0.796	0.796	0.793
	Male	0.814	0.817	0.822	0.826	0.827	0.827	0.827	0.824
	Female	0.751	0.756	0.764	0.768	0.769	0.768	0.767	0.765
Latvia	All	–	0.773	0.772	0.770	0.777	0.785	0.789	0.790
	Male	–	0.804	0.806	0.800	0.805	0.816	0.823	0.825
	Female	–	0.749	0.745	0.745	0.755	0.758	0.759	0.760
Lithuania	All	–	0.792	0.823	0.778	0.771	0.777	0.786	0.791
	Male	–	0.850	–	0.795	0.789	0.800	0.813	0.820
	Female	–	0.770	–	0.765	0.757	0.757	0.762	0.764
Poland	All	0.782	0.783	0.770	0.764	0.758	0.748	0.745	0.746
	Male	0.822	0.821	0.810	0.801	0.793	0.782	0.779	0.782
	Female	0.741	0.746	0.729	0.726	0.722	0.713	0.712	0.711

Country									
Romania	All	0.813	0.805	0.802	0.798	0.796	0.786	0.787	0.787
	Male	0.845	0.838	0.833	0.828	0.826	0.815	0.811	0.807
	Female	0.781	0.773	0.772	0.770	0.769	0.758	0.766	0.768
Slovakia	All	–	0.813	0.802	0.796	0.796	0.797	0.798	0.796
	Male	–	0.847	0.833	0.825	0.825	0.826	0.828	0.830
	Female	–	0.780	0.773	0.769	0.769	0.769	0.769	0.763
Slovenia	All	0.814	0.813	0.814	0.815	0.819	0.817	0.812	0.811
	Male	0.859	0.838	0.839	0.841	0.847	0.844	0.840	0.840
	Female	0.824	0.818	0.789	0.790	0.792	0.790	0.785	0.782
Croatia	All	–	–	–	–	–	0.759	0.758	0.761
	Male	–	–	–	–	–	0.760	0.763	0.768
	Female	–	–	–	–	–	0.756	0.751	0.750

– = data not available.

Sources: Authors' estimates based on data derived from Landesmann and Vidovic (2006) and EUROSTAT database (http://epp.eurostat.ec.europa.eu/portal/page?_pageid=1090, 30070682,1090_33076576&_dad=portal&_schema=PORTAL).

EMPLOYMENT DRIFT IN COUNTRIES OF THE COMMONWEALTH OF INDEPENDENT STATES

8

Problems of data availability seriously limit the scope for analysis of the employment situation in countries of the Commonwealth of Independent States (CIS). Data required for studying gender disparity in employment and links between skills and employment, for example, are missing. Data on non-standard wage employment are available only for the Russian Federation. Even the basic data on employment and unemployment are not available for all countries and years.[84] The analysis that follows is thus, unavoidably, somewhat narrowly focused.

8.1 Overall employment situation and its evolution

The data presented in table 8.1 are derived from labour force surveys. For a number of countries, unfortunately, labour force surveys do not provide estimates of the unemployment rate. Data on registered unemployment rates are available, but these rates are known to be substantially lower than the actual unemployment rates in all the countries (see appendix table A8.1 for some evidence). In CIS countries unemployment benefits are generally small and eligibility conditions are stringent, so that there is little incentive for the unemployed to register. Underestimation of unemployment obviously leads to underestimation of labour force and hence of participation rate. Thus, in the case of five countries (Belarus, Azerbaijan, Tajikistan, Turkmenistan and Uzbekistan), the participation rates reported in table 8.1 are underestimates since the estimated labour force includes only the registered unemployed. In

---

[84] These observations refer to readily available data. It is possible, indeed likely, that more data actually exist, such that the database could be substantially improved through patient research at the country level over a period of time.

Table 8.1 Employment and unemployment in countries of the Commonwealth of Independent States (CIS), 2004 (percentages)

Country	Participation rate	Unemployment rate	Self-employment as share of total employment	Public (state) sector employment as share of total employment	Wage employment in private sector as share of total employment	Employment in agriculture as share of total employment	Employment in industry as share of total employment	Employment in services as share of total employment
Belarus	53.2	–	5.8	52.4	41.8	10.2	34.6	55.2
Russian Federation	59.9	8.3	6.9	36.0	57.1	10.3	29.0	60.7
Ukraine	54.9	8.6	10.9[a]	–	–	19.7	24.6	55.7
Armenia	47.7	9.6	50.7	20.7	28.6	46.5	15.3	38.2
Azerbaijan	64.1	–	34.4	31.7	37.0	39.5	11.9	48.6
Georgia	59.5	12.6	64.6[b]	–	–	–	–	–
Kazakhstan	68.4	8.4	37.8	24.7	37.5	33.5	17.4	49.1
Kyrgyzstan	59.7	9.0	59.9	19.1	21.0	49.9	11.5	38.5
Moldova	52.2	8.1	36.1	25.8	38.1	40.5	16.3	43.2
Tajikistan	53.8	–	48.7	26.5	24.8	60.4	8.9	30.7
Turkmenistan	53.0[a]	–	–	–	–	–	–	–
Uzbekistan	57.4[b]	–	26.1[c]	23.4[b]	–	33.1[c]	20.4[c]	46.5[c]

[a] Refers to 2003. [b] Refers to 2002. [c] Refers to 2001.
– = data not available.
Sources: Derived from data supplied by ILO Sub-Regional Office in Moscow and UNECE database (http://w3.unece.org/pxweb/Dialog/).

interpreting the data for these countries, we assume that the gap between actual and registered unemployment rates in Belarus is the same as that in the Russian Federation, and that the gap in Azerbaijan, Tajikistan, Turkmenistan and Uzbekistan is the same as that in Kyrgyzstan. It can then be said that the unemployment rate is high (in excess of 5 per cent) in all 12 countries. It can also be deduced that the actual participation rate in Azerbaijan is close to what is observed for Kazakhstan. In the other four countries (Belarus, Tajikistan, Turkmenistan and Uzbekistan), however, the actual participation rates, although higher than those reported in table 8.1, are still unlikely to exceed 60 per cent. It can thus be concluded that the labour force participation rate is low (less than 60 per cent) in ten out of the 12 countries.

One immediately noticeable and noteworthy fact is that in terms of employment structure, CIS countries fall into two distinct sub-groups. While in three of the countries – Belarus, Russian Federation and Ukraine (hereafter referred to as "European CIS countries") – the employment structure is similar to that in CEE countries, in the remaining CIS countries (hereafter referred to as "Other CIS countries") it is similar to what is typically found in developing countries. Self-employment, for example, is far more widespread in the Other CIS countries than in the European CIS countries,[85] while agricultural employment is insignificant in the latter but very significant in the former. These facts together suggest that it is only in the Other CIS countries that a large part of the labour force is self-employed in agriculture.

It emerges, then, that the employment problem in the European CIS countries is very similar to that in CEE countries: it is characterized by low labour force participation (indicating the existence of large numbers of "discouraged workers") on the one hand and high unemployment on the other. In these countries, neither self-employment nor non-standard wage employment is particularly widespread.[86] In addition to low labour force participation and high unemployment, in the Other CIS countries there is substantial low-productivity employment that conceals underemployment; at least this is what is suggested by the high incidence of self-employment in agriculture. Thus the seriousness of the employment problem is relatively obvious in the case of the European CIS countries but is partly hidden in the case of the Other CIS countries and can be properly appreciated only when time trends are examined.[87]

---

[85] On the other hand, the incidence of self-employment is noticeably lower in the European CIS countries than in CEE countries. This seems to be linked to the fact that restructuring of enterprises in the non-agricultural sectors has made much less progress in the former than in the latter.

[86] In the Russian Federation, in 2004 the share of part-time employment in total employment was 1.9 per cent and the share of temporary employment in total employment 11.1 per cent. It is fair to conclude from this evidence that, as in CEE countries, non-standard wage employment is generally insignificant in the European CIS countries.

[87] For one country, the Russian Federation, it is possible to derive CEI estimates. For 2004 the value is 0.832, which suggests that the employment situation there is better than in CEE countries.

Table 8.2   Employment levels (indexed to 1990 and/or 1992), 1990–2004

Country	1990	1992	1995	2000	2004
Belarus	100.0	95.0	85.6	86.2	83.8
		100.0	90.2	90.8	88.2
Russian Federation	–	100.0	90.3	90.7	94.6
Ukraine	–	100.0	96.7	82.5	82.9
Armenia	100.0	96.8	90.6	78.4	66.4
		100.0	93.5	81.0	68.6
Azerbaijan	100.0	100.5	97.6	100.1	102.9
		100.0	97.1	99.5	102.3
Georgia	100.0	71.9	62.6	64.1	62.1
		100.0	87.2	89.2	86.5
Kazakhstan	–	100.0	86.5	81.8	94.8
Kyrgyzstan	100.0	105.0	93.9	101.1	107.5
		100.0	89.4	96.3	102.4
Moldova	–	100.0	81.6	73.9	66.2
Tajikistan	100.0	98.5	97.5	90.0	107.7
		100.0	99.0	91.4	109.4
Turkmenistan[a]	100.0	106.9	118.5	129.3	(138.2)
		100.0	110.8	120.9	(129.3)
Uzbekistan	100.0	104.2	106.3	113.1	–
		100.0	102.0	120.9	–

[a] Figures in parentheses refer to 2003.
– = data not available.

Sources: Derived from data supplied by ILO Sub-Regional Office in Moscow and UNECE database (http://w3.unece.org/pxweb/Dialog/).

At first sight, time trends appear to have been quite diverse across countries (table 8.2). In five countries (Belarus, Ukraine, Armenia, Georgia and Moldova), employment declined more or less steadily throughout the period 1992–2004; in three (Russian Federation, Azerbaijan and Kyrgyzstan) it declined until the mid-1990s and started increasing thereafter; in two (Kazakhstan and Tajikistan) it declined through the end of the 1990s and then started growing; and in two (Turkmenistan and Uzbekistan) it actually showed steady growth throughout the period 1990–2004.

This apparent diversity notwithstanding, the employment situation was actually worsening everywhere. Two particular developments suggest this.

Employment drift in countries of the Commonwealth of Independent States

Table 8.3 Growth in employment by sector, 1992–2000 (percentages)

Country	Average annual rate of growth (%)				
	Self-employment	Employment by sector			
		Agriculture	Industry	Services	All sectors
Belarus	2.5	–5.6	–3.0	2.1	–1.2
Russian Federation	7.3	–3.1	–4.3	1.4	–1.2
Ukraine	4.7	–	–	–	–2.4
Armenia	3.1	1.7	–7.2	–4.0	–2.6
Azerbaijan	4.0	3.9	–9.1	–0.7	0.5
Georgia	11.9	–	–	–	0.5
Kazakhstan	28.3	0.9	–10.0	–0.3	–2.5
Kyrgyzstan	16.4	3.8	–9.4	–1.4	–0.5
Moldova	–0.7	–	–	–	–3.7
Tajikistan	7.7	2.9	–11.6	–3.0	–1.1
Turkmenistan	–	–	–	–	2.4
Uzbekistan	6.2	–2.2	0.6	4.5	1.0

– = data not available.

Sources: Derived from data supplied by ILO Sub-Regional Office in Moscow and UNECE database (http://w3.unece.org/pxweb/Dialog/).

First, both self-employment and employment in agriculture showed rapid growth in a number of the Other CIS countries even though total employment declined or stagnated (table 8.3). This indicates substantial growth of self-employment in agriculture, which helped restrain the decline in aggregate employment. Except in Uzbekistan, state and collective farms in these countries were dismantled early in the transition process, and land was distributed to farm employees and sometimes to some of the urban job losers.[88] The consequent growth of self-employment in agriculture, however, came at a price, for it was associated with declining labour productivity in agriculture (table 8.4).[89] Thus growth of low-productivity employment restrained the decline in aggregate employment.[90] The result was a radical reverse movement

---

[88] Land redistribution was carried out in Armenia around 1995, in Georgia between 1992 and 1996, in Kyrgyzstan between 1995 and 1998, in Moldova and Azerbaijan in the early 1990s, while Uzbekistan started dismantling state and collective farms only around 2000. See Verme (2006).

[89] The dismantling of state and collective farms severely disrupted the existing systems of maintenance of agricultural infrastructure and of extension services, but no new systems appropriate for small-scale household farming were put in place.

[90] Similar changes are likely to have occurred in Georgia and Turkmenistan as well, but no data for these countries are available.

Table 8.4   Growth in labour productivity by sector, 1992–2000 (percentages)

Country	Average annual rate of growth by sector (%)			
	Agriculture	Industry	Services	All sectors
Belarus	1.0	0.3	0.5	1.1
Russian Federation	−1.1	0.5	−2.3	−1.1
Ukraine	–	–	–	−5.3
Armenia	−0.4	9.4	11.0	6.1
Azerbaijan[a]	−6.3	22.3	7.2	6.6
Georgia[b]	–	–	–	0.4
Kazakhstan	−15.9	6.2	5.0	0.1
Kyrgyzstan	−1.0	4.8	3.4	1.7
Moldova	–	–	–	−2.5
Tajikistan	−9.5	3.0	−0.9	−5.5
Turkmenistan	–	–	–	−4.5
Uzbekistan	3.1	−4.8	1.9	−1.1

[a] Growth rates estimated by using the compound interest formula on initial and terminal values.
[b] Data available only from 1995.
– = data not available.

Sources: Derived from data supplied by ILO Sub-Regional Office in Moscow, UNECE database (http://w3.unece.org/pxweb/Dialog/) and World Bank, World Development Indicators database (CD-ROM, 2006).

of the employment structure and re-emergence of dualism that characterizes developing countries (see appendix table A8.3).

Second, in some countries, growth of low-productivity self-employment in non-agriculture and slow restructuring of state enterprises restrained the decline in aggregate employment. In Uzbekistan, employment in industry increased while labour productivity declined at almost 5 per cent per annum, indicating persistent labour hoarding. Labour productivity in services declined in the Russian Federation and virtually stagnated in Belarus, but employment was growing in both cases, indicating labour hoarding as well as growth in low-productivity self-employment. The stagnation of labour productivity in industry in Belarus and the Russian Federation also indicates persistent labour hoarding.

The general picture, therefore, is as follows. There was a sharp decline in demand for labour in all CIS countries. The decline in employment, however, was generally less sharp because growth of low-productivity employment was facilitated and overstaffing in state enterprises was allowed to persist. In a few

Employment drift in countries of the Commonwealth of Independent States

> **Box 8.1   Emigration from CIS countries**
>
> There was significant net emigration from many CIS countries during the period 1992–2002. Emigration from the Other CIS countries was particularly large. In some countries, this caused a decline of total and working-age population.
>
> In the early 1990s, emigration was driven mainly by non-economic factors. Following the transformation of the Soviet Republics into independent nation States, large settler populations – mainly Russians but also Ukrainians and Belarusians – returned to their homelands. Also, from certain countries, ethnic Germans left for Germany and many Jews left for Israel. The conflict between Armenia and Azerbaijan and the civil war in Tajikistan led to a swelling population of refugees.
>
> Alongside these movements, however, there was another kind of emigration – brain drain – from certain countries, particularly from Armenia, Georgia, the Russian Federation and Ukraine. Large numbers of qualified professionals from these countries emigrated in search of better jobs and a higher standard of living.
>
> From the mid-1990s onwards, migration flows slowed down but were increasingly driven by economic factors. Having suffered job losses in the course of the economic crisis, many people were forced to move, temporarily or permanently, to other countries in the region in search of livelihood. The resource-rich countries, in particular Azerbaijan, Kazakhstan and the Russian Federation, became major destinations for economic emigrants from other CIS countries.
>
> More detailed discussions are available in IOM (2000), World Bank (2006) and Verme (2006).

of the countries, such measures were significant enough to engender growth of aggregate employment.[91]

The decline in employment, however, did not lead to a commensurate rise in unemployment because there were downward adjustments in labour supply through declining labour force participation and, in some cases, substantial emigration (box 8.1). In the first half of the 1990s the labour force participation rate declined in all CIS countries except Ukraine (table 8.5). Although it

---

[91] The Russian Federation is the only country for which data on non-standard wage employment are available. Here the share of part-time employment in total employment showed no trend but the share of temporary employment in total employment increased from 2.5 per cent in 1992 to 11.1 per cent in 2004. For the Russian Federation, the value of the CEI declined from 0.859 in 1992 to 0.832 in 2004, suggesting a substantial deterioration in the overall employment situation.

Table 8.5 Key indicators of employment situation in CIS countries, selected years, 1992–2004 (percentages)

Country	Indicator	1992	1995	2000	2004
Belarus	Participation rate	61.8	55.6	55.4	53.2
	Unemployment rate	–	–	–	–
	Self-employment share	2.9	7.3	3.9	5.8
Russian Federation	Participation rate	64.8	60.7	60.6	59.9
	Unemployment rate	5.2	9.5	9.8	8.3
	Self-employment share	4.8	6.9	9.3	6.9
Ukraine	Participation rate	60.0	61.4	56.3	54.9
	Unemployment rate	–	6.0	11.4	8.6
	Self-employment share	5.1	14.9	8.9	10.9[a]
Armenia	Participation rate	63.1	61.1	60.8	47.7
	Unemployment rate	–	–	11.7	9.6
	Self-employment share	29.8	37.4	47.2	50.7
Azerbaijan	Participation rate	78.6	74.6	67.9	64.1
	Unemployment rate	–	–	–	–
	Self-employment share	–	56.5	67.1	65.6
Georgia	Participation rate	–	–	62.5[b]	59.5
	Unemployment rate	–	–	10.3	12.6
	Self-employment share	–	–	56.8	64.6[c]
Kazakhstan	Participation rate	65.1	63.7	65.5	68.4
	Unemployment rate	–	11.0	12.8	8.4
	Self-employment share	4.9	16.6	43.5	37.8
Kyrgyzstan	Participation rate	65.9	62.4	59.1	59.7
	Unemployment rate	–	5.7	7.6	9.0
	Self-employment share	17.2	44.0	60.1	59.9
Moldova	Participation rate	63.9	54.0	59.1	52.2
	Unemployment rate	–	–	8.5	8.1
	Self-employment share	29.1	14.2	37.2	36.1
Tajikistan	Participation rate	60.0	58.2	51.6	53.8
	Unemployment rate	–	–	–	–
	Self-employment share	21.1	32.3	41.8	48.7

Employment drift in countries of the Commonwealth of Independent States

Country	Indicator	1992	1995	2000	2004
Turkmenistan	Participation rate	–	–	64.7	53.0[a]
	Unemployment rate	–	–	–	–
	Self-employment share	–	–	–	–
Uzbekistan	Participation rate	65.6	63.3	59.4	57.4[c]
	Unemployment rate	–	–	–	–
	Self-employment share	17.5	20.2	26.1	–

Note: Self-employment is self-employment as share of total employment.
[a] Refers to 2003.
[b] Refers to 2001.
[c] Refers to 2002.
– = data not available.

Sources: Derived from data supplied by ILO Sub-Regional Office in Moscow and UNECE database (http://w3.unece.org/pxweb/Dialog).

stopped declining in the Russian Federation in the mid-1990s and increased in Kazakhstan from 1995 on, in the other countries it continued to decline steadily throughout the period 1995–2004. Emigration also appears to have played a role in reducing labour supply in some countries, particularly in Armenia, Georgia, Kazakhstan, Moldova and Ukraine. This is suggested by the fact that in these countries both the total population and the working-age population were declining (appendix table A8.2). It is clear, however, that the downward adjustment in labour supply throughout the region occurred mainly through flows from employment into inactivity.

However, even the growth of low-productivity employment, the persistence of labour hoarding in state enterprises and the downward adjustment in labour supply were not sufficient to prevent open unemployment from rising to high levels: by 2004, the rate of open unemployment was 8 per cent or more in all the countries.

8.2 Identifying the drivers

The sharp decline in labour demand was of course caused by a massive growth crisis, perhaps unprecedented in history, suffered by the countries in the aftermath of the break-up of the Soviet Union (table 8.6; box 8.2). Between 1990 and 1995, GDP had declined by between 20 and 70 per cent in all CIS countries. Economic growth resumed only in the late 1990s. Even in 2004, however, in as many as seven of the 12 countries GDP was substantially below

Table 8.6   Real Gross Domestic Product,[a] selected years, 1990–2004

Country	1990	1992	1995	2000	2004
Belarus	100.0	89.3	65.3	88.7	116.4
Russian Federation	100.0	81.2	62.1	67.3	85.2
Ukraine	100.0	82.7	48.0	43.5	61.2
Armenia	100.0	51.4	52.8	67.9	106.0
Azerbaijan	100.0	78.3	42.7	60.0	89.4
Georgia	100.0	43.5	28.3	37.5	48.8
Kazakhstan	100.0	84.3	61.4	69.4	103.6
Kyrgyzstan	100.0	79.4	50.7	66.6	80.4
Moldova	100.0	59.1	39.8	35.4	46.3
Tajikistan	100.0	66.0	38.0	38.1	55.8
Turkmenistan	100.0	90.3	62.3	76.3	–
Uzbekistan	100.0	88.4	81.1	98.0	119.2

[a] Indexed to 1990.
– = data not available.

Source: Derived from World Bank, World Bank Development Indicators database (CD-ROM, 2006).

Box 8.2   The output fall in CIS countries

The speed and extent of output decline in CIS countries have been quite staggering and have seemed puzzling to many. With hindsight, several reasons for the decline can be identified. First, the break-up of the Soviet Union led to the collapse of the hugely important trade relations among the ex-Republics, which meant loss of markets for producers in each of the newly formed States. Second, by the 1990s a large part of the industrial infrastructure built in the Soviet era was obsolete at world market prices so that new trade relations with the rest of the world could not be easily and speedily built. Third, there was massive disruption of well-established production and supply linkages among enterprises scattered across the ex-Republics. Fourth, many producers faced a credit crunch as a result of a sharp fall in state subsidies. Finally, political instability, civil conflicts and wars disrupted the functioning of the economy in many of the newly independent nation States.

Sources: Svejnar (2002); Campos and Coricelli (2002).

Table 8.7 Growth in GDP and employment by sector, 2000–04 (percentages)

Country	Average annual rate of growth[a] (%)							
	Agriculture		Industry		Services		Economy	
	GDP	EMP	GDP	EMP	GDP	EMP	GDP	EMP
Belarus	–1.6	–7.0	8.4 (10.7)	–0.8	8.2	0.9	7.0	–0.7
Russian Federation	1.4	–4.5	4.6 (–)	0.0	7.5	2.3	6.1	1.1
Ukraine	–0.1	–1.5	9.7 (14.0)	–5.5	11.2	3.9	9.0	0.1
Armenia	10.7	–2.7	14.1 (8.7)	–7.4	10.3	4.2	11.8	–4.1
Azerbaijan	1.3	–0.2	16.2 (9.1)	3.0	5.8	0.9	10.5	0.7
Georgia	1.6	–	11.3 (4.7)	–	6.8	–	6.8	–0.8
Kazakhstan	7.3	5.4	9.1 (9.5)	3.7	12.6	2.7	10.5	3.7
Kyrgyzstan	1.0	0.0	–1.7 (4.0)	3.1	12.8	3.2	4.8	1.6
Moldova	1.3	–8.8	9.3 (9.2)	0.4	10.1	1.6	7.0	–3.5
Tajikistan	4.5	2.9	7.1 (11.3)	4.3	16.7	8.5	10.0	4.6
Turkmenistan	–	–	–	–	–	–	–	2.4
Uzbekistan	2.6	–	8.3 (2.1)	–	5.0	–	5.0	–

[a] Growth rates are estimated by using the compound interest formula on initial and terminal values. Figures in parentheses show growth of manufacturing.
GDP – gross domestic product. EMP – employment.
– = data not available.

Sources: Authors' estimates based on data supplied by ILO Sub-Regional Office in Moscow, UNECE database (http://w3.unece.org/pxweb/Dialog/) and World Bank, World Development Indicators database (CD-ROM, 2006).

its 1990 levels; in Georgia and Moldova, it was less than 50 per cent of what it had been in 1990.

In recent years (2000–04), many CIS countries have achieved remarkably rapid economic growth (table 8.7), but for the most part this growth has not been employment intensive. In fact, rapid GDP growth has been associated with declining employment in a number of countries (Armenia, Belarus, Georgia and Moldova) and with negligible employment growth in some others (notably Azerbaijan and Ukraine); only in two countries (Kazakhstan and Tajikistan) has growth been employment intensive.

Unlike in CEE countries, recent economic growth in CIS countries has been led by both industry (except in Kyrgyzstan) and services. However, employment elasticity in industry in most CIS countries has been negative or insignificant (the only exceptions are Kazakhstan and Tajikistan). This is perhaps not particularly surprising. Given the slow restructuring and labour hoarding in the earlier period, there were large productivity gains to be made through rapid restructuring during 2000–04. Moreover, in some countries (e.g., Azerbaijan and Uzbekistan), industrial growth has been driven by the growth of extractive industries rather than that of manufacturing, and in extractive industries employment intensity tends to be low. More surprising is the fact that, as in CEE countries, employment elasticity in services in CIS countries has also been generally very low.

Developments in agriculture present a complex picture and there are substantial differences between the two sub-groups. In the European CIS countries, at the inception of the transition process agriculture was already relatively insignificant in terms of its share in national output and employment (appendix table A8.3). Throughout the 1990s its share declined (both output and employment were declining faster in agriculture than in other sectors) so that by 2000 it had become rather small. The same trends persisted during the 2000–04 period. In the Other CIS countries agriculture was an important sector in 1990. During the period 1990–2000, however, it experienced a much sharper output decline than the other sectors. And yet employment in the sector was actually growing, often quite rapidly, because of fast growth of low-productivity self-employment (table 8.3). Thus the share of agriculture in GDP was falling and its share in total employment rising. By 2000, agriculture had become the largest employer in four of the countries and the second largest employer in the other three for which we have data (appendix table A8.3). During 2000–04, growth in agricultural output resumed in most of the countries but was rapid in only three (Armenia, Kazakhstan and Tajikistan). In Armenia, however, rapid output growth was actually associated with a rapid decline in employment.[92] Only in Kazakhstan and Tajikistan was rapid growth in agriculture associated with rapid growth in both employment and productivity.

Overall, only two countries – Kazakhstan and Tajikistan – appear to have been on what might be called the right growth path during 2000–04: output growth was rapid in all sectors and growth was both employment intensive and productivity enhancing in all sectors.

8.3 Policy perspective

The above analysis suggests three basic objectives that future policies must seek to attain. First, increasing employment elasticity in services will be an important task in all CIS countries, particularly in the European CIS

---

[92] This is rather puzzling. Indeed, the entire growth experience of Armenia during 2000–04 is puzzling. Rapid output growth was combined with rapid decline in employment in all three sectors.

Employment drift in countries of the Commonwealth of Independent States

countries. As industry restructuring is still incomplete and will need to be carried forward, employment elasticity in industry will in all likelihood remain low for some time to come. Growth in non-agricultural employment will thus depend quite critically on the job-creating capacity of the services sector. As in the case of CEE countries, increasing employment elasticity in services will call for a focus on growth in labour-intensive services – education, health, transport, storage and communication, wholesale and retail trade, and hotel and restaurant services.

The second objective relates to employment in agriculture. In the European CIS countries, agriculture remains dominated by large-scale farms (state, collective and private), so there is scope for expanding employment through a transition to a household farming system. Given the magnitude of the employment problem, such a transition will need to be viewed as an important step. Redistribution of land, together with development of appropriate institutions for infrastructure maintenance and delivery of extension services, can generate substantial growth of productive self-employment in agriculture and it will be important for policies to focus on exploiting this potential. In the Other CIS countries, subsistence farming already engages a large section of the workforce; here the task is one of transforming subsistence farming into productive self-employment. This calls for establishment of new institutions for development and maintenance of infrastructure and delivery of extension services.

The third objective, particularly relevant for the Other CIS countries, relates to industrialization. In many of these countries, the level of industrial development has fallen considerably and there is much scope for employment-intensive industrialization. As many of these countries also happen to be rich in natural resources, exploiting and using these resources for employment-intensive industrialization must be high on the agenda. In this context, avoiding the "natural resource curse" will be a matter of critical importance.[93]

---

[93] Empirical research suggests that the pace of economic growth tends to be slower in countries with large natural resource wealth than in other countries (Sachs and Warner, 2001). The reasons are by now well understood. First, countries with large natural resource wealth are vulnerable to the so-called "Dutch disease": discovery and exploitation of natural resources often trigger a boom and cause appreciation of the real exchange rate, which discourages the production of tradable goods and can lead to de-industrialization. Second, countries with large natural resource wealth find it difficult to conduct sensible fiscal policies in the face of volatility of commodity prices in international markets. Finally, dominance of extractive industries in the economy encourages "rent-seeking" behaviour that can undermine the developmental orientation of the State.

Appendix table A8.1 Registered and actual unemployment rates in CIS countries, selected years, 1992–2004

Country	Unemployment rate	1992	1995	2000	2004
Belarus	Registered	0.5	2.9	2.1	1.9
	Actual	–	–	–	–
Russian Federation	Registered	0.8	3.5	1.6	2.8
	Actual	5.2	9.5	9.8	8.3
Ukraine	Registered	0.3	0.5	5.4	4.6
	Actual	–	6.0	11.4	8.6
Armenia	Registered	3.4	8.2	10.8	9.2
	Actual	–	–	11.7	9.6
Azerbaijan	Registered	0.2	0.8	1.2	1.5
	Actual	–	–	–	–
Georgia	Registered	–	–	6.0	2.6
	Actual	–	–	10.3	12.6
Kazakhstan	Registered	0.5	2.1	3.6	1.6
	Actual	–	11.0	12.8	8.4
Kyrgyzstan	Registered	0.1	3.0	3.2	3.0
	Actual	–	5.7	7.6	9.0
Moldova	Registered	0.7	1.5	1.9	1.6
	Actual	–	–	8.5	8.1
Tajikistan	Registered	0.4	2.0	2.4	1.8
	Actual	–	–	–	–
Turkmenistan	Registered	–	–	2.4	2.6[a]
	Actual	–	–	–	–
Uzbekistan	Registered	0.1	0.3	0.4	0.4
	Actual	–	–	–	–

Note: "Actual" refers to the rate derived from labour force surveys.
[a] Refers to 2003.
– = data not available.

Sources: Derived from data supplied by ILO Sub-Regional Office in Moscow and UNECE database (http://w3.unece.org/pxweb/Dialog/).

Appendix table A8.2   Population, working-age population and labour force, 1992–2004 (index numbers)

Country	Population category	1992	1995	2000	2004
Belarus	Population	100.0	100.0	97.0	95.2
	Working-age population	100.0	102.6	103.3	105.0
	Labour force	100.0	92.3	92.6	90.4
Russian Federation	Population	100.0	99.7	98.1	97.2
	Working-age population	100.0	100.9	101.9	106.0
	Labour force	100.0	94.6	95.4	97.9
Ukraine	Population	100.0	98.8	95.2	–
	Working-age population	100.0	100.1	98.8	–
	Labour force	100.0	102.4	92.7	–
Armenia	Population	100.0	100.0	86.9	86.9
	Working-age population	100.0	100.0	91.9	96.9
	Labour force	100.0	96.8	88.6	73.3
Azerbaijan	Population	100.0	101.4	109.6	113.2
	Working-age population	100.0	102.9	116.3	127.2
	Labour force	100.0	97.7	100.5	103.7
Georgia	Population	–	100.0	81.5[a]	79.9
	Working-age population	–	100.0	83.0[a]	83.9
	Labour force	–	100.0	103.1[a]	99.6
Kazakhstan	Population	100.0	97.6	88.0	89.2
	Working-age population	100.0	99.1	93.1	98.3
	Labour force	100.0	96.9	93.6	103.2
Kyrgyzstan	Population	100.0	100.0	109.1	113.2
	Working-age population	100.0	100.0	116.1	124.1
	Labour force	100.0	94.8	104.1	112.4
Moldova	Population	100.0	97.7	82.6	77.0
	Working-age population	100.0	97.7	87.1	85.4
	Labour force	100.0	82.7	80.7	69.8
Tajikistan	Population	100.0	103.6	108.9	117.9
	Working-age population	100.0	101.8	108.9	124.1
	Labour force	100.0	98.6	93.6	111.2
Turkmenistan	Population	–	100.0	126.3	165.8
	Working-age population	–	100.0	132.6	187.9
	Labour force	–	100.0	100.0	–
Uzbekistan	Population	100.0	106.1	114.5	–
	Working-age population	100.0	106.1	120.3	–
	Labour force	100.0	102.4	108.9	–

Note: Working-age population and labour force refer to persons aged 15 years or more.

[a] Refers to 2001.

– = data not available.

Sources: Derived from data supplied by ILO Sub-Regional Office in Moscow and UNECE database (http://w3.unece.org/pxweb/Dialog/).

Appendix table A8.3 Distribution of output and employment by sector, 1990, 2000 and 2004 (percentages)

Country	Year	Output			Employment		
		AG	IND	SER	AG	IND	SER
Belarus	1990	24	47	29	20	42	38
	2000	14	39	47	14	35	51
	2004	10	41	49	11	34	55
Russian Federation	1990	17	48	35	15[a]	39[a]	46[a]
	2000	6	38	56	13	30	57
	2004	5	36	59	10	29	61
Ukraine	1990	25	45	30	–	–	–
	2000	17	36	47	21	31	48
	2004	12	37	51	20	25	55
Armenia	1990	17	52	31	17	42	41
	2000	26	35	39	44	18	38
	2004	25	38	37	47	15	38
Azerbaijan	1990	29	33	38	31	19	50
	2000	17	45	38	41	11	48
	2004	12	55	32	40	12	48
Georgia	1990	32	33	35	–	–	–
	2000	22	22	56	–	–	–
	2004	18	26	56	–	–	–
Kazakhstan	1990	27	45	28	24	33	43
	2000	9	40	51	31	17	52
	2004	8	37	55	34	17	49
Kyrgyzstan	1990	34	36	30	38[a]	23[a]	39[a]
	2000	37	31	32	53	11	36
	2004	33	24	43	50	11	39
Moldova	1990	51[a]	31[a]	18[a]	–	–	–
	2000	29	22	49	51	14	35
	2004	21	24	55	41	16	43
Tajikistan	1990	33	38	29	47[a]	22[a]	31[a]
	2000	27	39	34	64	9	27
	2004	22	35	43	60	9	31

Employment drift in countries of the Commonwealth of Independent States

Country	Year	Output			Employment		
		AG	IND	SER	AG	IND	SER
Turkmenistan	1990	32	30	38	–	–	–
	2000	25	45	30	–	–	–
Uzbekistan	1990	33	33	34	44[a]	21[a]	35[a]
	2000	34	23	43	34	20	46

[a] Refers to 1992.
AG – agriculture. IND – industry. SER – services.
– = data not available.

Sources: Derived from data supplied by ILO Sub-Regional Office in Moscow, UNECE database (http://w3.unece.org/pxweb/Dialog/) and World Bank, World Development Indicators database (CD-ROM, 2006).

A SUMMING-UP

9

The world today is confronted with a substantial inadequacy of productive jobs in relation to the labour force. The nature and manifestation of this employment problem are different in different parts of the world, and the problem itself emerged earlier in some countries than in others, but there is no doubt that it is a serious concern in most parts of the world.

In developing countries, which have a dualistic economic structure, the main manifestation of the problem is not high unemployment but self-employment and casual wage employment, often in extremely low-productivity activities, of a large section of the workforce that has to find work outside the formal segment of the economy. Many other problems of global concern are intimately linked to this problem of employment. One of them is extreme poverty in the developing world. The poor work outside the formal segment, either as self-employed in intrinsically low-productivity activities or as casual wage labourers.[94]

In the developed world, the employment problem is of recent origin: it emerged in the mid-1970s, in the aftermath of the 1973 oil shock. Here the problem is one of lack of productive jobs for low-skilled labour. It manifests itself in low labour market participation, high unemployment and high incidence of non-standard (temporary and part-time) wage employment among this category of workers.

In CEE countries, the employment problem emerged in the early 1990s, as the process of their transition from centrally planned to market economies got under way. The problem in these countries is similar in nature to that in

---

[94] The problems of child labour and bonded labour, which we do not analyse in this book, are intimately linked to the problem of poverty and hence to the problem of employment.

the developed world but is larger in scale; its main manifestations are huge labour market disadvantages of low-skilled labour.

In CIS countries, the employment problem also dates back to the early 1990s and to the economically disruptive process of their emergence as independent States. The problem manifests itself in large flows of labour from employment into unemployment and inactivity, as well as from regular wage employment into low-productivity self-employment.

The trends in the post-1990 period have not been encouraging: they do not tell us that continuing the policies pursued during that period will improve the employment situation in most countries in the years to come. What they do indicate is that the global employment challenge will grow in seriousness if no corrective actions are taken at national and international levels.

In the developing world, the employment situation improved in a sizeable number of countries but deteriorated in many. The general reason for deterioration in the employment situation was poor economic growth. Remarkably, however, even the countries that achieved rapid economic growth did not always achieve significant improvement in their employment situation. In some of these countries, output and employment growth occurred almost exclusively in the formal segment of the economy so that employment conditions in the rest of the economy tended to deteriorate. In a larger number of countries, decent growth in the non-formal segment (i.e., the rest of the economy) reduced underemployment (and poverty) but growth in the formal segment was jobless. In very few countries do we find a combination of rapid employment growth in the formal segment and decent growth of output per worker in the non-formal segment.

In the developed world, during the period under review the overall employment situation was generally improving but the core problem persisted – high unemployment, high incidence of non-standard employment and low labour market participation of low-skilled workers (reflecting a large "discouraged worker effect"). The reason was neither lack of growth nor jobless growth; it was rather a persistent failure of the structure of labour supply to adjust to changes in the structure of labour demand brought about by rapid skill-biased technological change and globalization.

In CEE and CIS countries, economic growth was rapid but the employment problem was worsening. In CEE countries, the main reason was jobless growth, primarily attributable to a skill-intensive pattern of growth in services. In CIS countries, economic restructuring, necessitated by the twin transitions – from parts of a larger economic entity to independent economies and from centrally planned to market economies – was still in progress and had adverse consequences for employment.

A summing-up

A main lesson of the 1990s experience is that economic growth does not automatically improve the employment situation: many countries – developed, CEE, CIS and developing – achieved rapid economic growth in this period but still saw their employment situation stagnate or worsen. Economic growth improves the employment situation when it is designed to do so. This is why improving the employment situation must itself become a central concern, a core objective of policies worldwide.

Meeting the formidable employment challenge faced by developing countries will require policy responses at both international and national levels. At international level, two key asymmetries need to be recognized. First, there is the asymmetry in the distribution of productive resources: the developing world accounts for the bulk of the world's labour force but lacks capital and skills (which are concentrated in the developed world), the co-operant resources required to productively employ the labour force. Second, labour force growth is faster in poorer countries. These two asymmetries result in a third asymmetry: across countries, there is an inverse relation between the seriousness of the employment problem and the resources available to address it.

Despite its potential, globalization does not seem to have reduced these asymmetries to any significant extent. The growth of cross-border capital flows has not resulted in substantial flow of investment resources to capital-scarce developing countries. In addition, international migration has resulted in significant brain drain from some of the poorest countries of the world, restraining the growth of skill supply there.

This context calls for international policy to focus on two main objectives. The first consists in ensuring substantial "aid for investment" to the least developed countries. Here it needs to be recognized that humanitarian aid and debt relief, while extremely important, are complementary to and not substitutes for "aid for investment". The second objective concerns the development of a global framework for international migration that can transform brain drain into brain circulation. In this context, the possibility of establishing a transparent system of fixed-term migration, guaranteeing the same rights and working conditions for migrants and non-migrants, deserves serious consideration.

National policies in developing countries have to focus on achieving two basic objectives: (i) a rate of growth of employment in the formal segment that is higher than the rate of growth of labour force in the economy, and (ii) a substantially positive rate of growth of labour productivity in the rest of the economy. Such a focus has been lacking in the past. Indeed, growth strategies in most developing countries were concerned with maximizing output growth, mainly in the formal segment, and paid little attention (in practice, if not in theory) to the employment consequences. Future policies will need to be concerned with ensuring an adequate aggregate level of investment, an appropriate allocation of investment between formal and non-formal segments, labour market regulations and institutions that provide protection to those already employed in the formal segment without generating strong incentives for substitution of capital for labour, and public investment and institutions for support to household, micro- and small enterprises in the non-formal segment. Policy-makers will need to recognize, too, that greater openness to trade and capital flows can be helpful in achieving the employment objectives only if the aggregate investment in the economy can be increased at the same time. Greater openness alone does not increase the level of investment in an economy, as the experience of the 1990s shows. If unaccompanied by growing investment, it has adverse effects on employment in the non-formal segment and hence on poverty. In order to derive employment benefits from openness, therefore, national governments will need to find policies for stimulating investment.[95]

National policies in developed countries will need to focus on dealing with the problems encountered by low-skilled workers in the face of rapid skill-biased technological change and globalization. In concrete terms, this means adopting labour market policies specifically designed to enable low-skilled job losers in manufacturing to move to new jobs in services. Thus the focus of labour market policies has to be on imparting new skills to low-skilled job losers, on developing new forms of apprenticeship schemes and on guaranteeing a minimum level of welfare to low-skilled workers through wage subsidy schemes.

Such policies are needed in CEE countries, too, where labour market disadvantages of low-skilled workers also constitute the core of the employment problem. However, for these policies to work in these countries, another basic problem, that of jobless growth, will need to be addressed. Analysis shows that the root cause of the problem is the very low employment intensity of growth in services. The reason for this is that growth has been concentrated in skill-intensive services while at the same time employment-intensive non-market services have declined. Economic policies will need to focus on altering these trends, particularly by encouraging the growth of employment-intensive market services.

The problem of low employment intensity of growth in services is also observed in the European CIS countries (Belarus, Russian Federation and Ukraine) and needs to be addressed. However, in these three countries, where

---

[95] These will need to include policies for ensuring that foreign capital does not crowd out domestic capital. In the 1990s, such crowding out was a reason why investment failed to grow even in countries that received substantial inflow of foreign capital.

large-scale agricultural farms have not yet been dismantled, there is substantial scope for generating productive self-employment in agriculture. It would be both necessary and sensible to exploit this potential. But here it would be important to bear in mind that mere redistribution of land would create subsistence farming and not productive self-employment. Policies would need to focus on developing new institutions for managing infrastructure and providing credit, training and extension services to the self-employed in agriculture.

These policies are also very relevant for the Other CIS countries, where land distribution has already created subsistence farming. The task now is to transform subsistence farming into productive self-employment. Apart from this, given their current low level of industrial development, in these countries there is considerable scope for industrialization. Many of them are rich in natural resources (including petroleum and gas) and must find ways of exploiting and using these resources for employment-intensive industrialization. Avoiding the "natural resource curse" will thus be of critical importance.

REFERENCES

Acemoglu, D. 2002. "Technical change, inequality, and the labor market", in *Journal of Economic Literature*, Vol. 40, No. 1, pp. 7–72.

Aisbett, E. 2005. *Why are the critics so convinced that globalization is bad for the poor?*, Working Paper No. 11066 (Cambridge, MA, National Bureau of Economic Research).

Baccaro, L.; Rei, D. 2005. *Institutional determinants of unemployment in OECD countries: A time series cross-section analysis*, International Institute for Labour Studies Discussion Paper Series 160/2005 (Geneva, ILO).

Baker, D.; Glyn, A.; Howell, D.R.; Schmitt, J. 2004. "Labour market institutions and unemployment: A critical assessment of the cross-country evidence", in D.R. Howell (ed.): *Fighting unemployment: The limits of free market orthodoxy* (Oxford, Oxford University Press), pp. 72–118.

Banerjee, A.; Galiani, S.; Levinsohn, J.; Woolard, I. 2006. *Why unemployment is so high in South Africa*, Center for International Development Working Paper No. 134 (Cambridge, MA, Harvard University).

Barro, R.J.; Lee, J.-W. 2000. *International data on educational attainment*, Working Paper No. 42, Center for International Development (Cambridge, MA, Harvard University).

Bassanini, A.; Duval, R. 2006. *Employment patterns in OECD countries: Reassessing the role of policies and institutions*, Working Paper No. 486 (Paris, OECD).

Basu, K. 1984. *The less developed economy: A critique of contemporary theory* (Oxford, Basil Blackwell).

Berg, A.; Krueger, A. 2003. "Trade, growth and poverty: A selective survey", in B. Pleskovic and N. Stern (eds): *The Annual World Bank Conference on Development Economics: The new reform agenda* (Washington, DC, World Bank; New York, Oxford University Press), pp. 47–90.

Besley, T.; Burgess, R. 2003. "Halving global poverty", in *Journal of Economic Perspectives*, Vol. 17, No. 3, pp. 3–22.

Bhagwati, J.; Panagariya, A.; Srinivasan, T.N. 2004. "The muddles over outsourcing", in *Journal of Economic Perspectives*, Vol. 18, No. 4, pp. 93–114.

Blanchard, O. 2005. *European unemployment: The evolution of facts and ideas*, Working Paper No. 11750 (Cambridge, MA, National Bureau of Economic Research).

Blinder, A. 2007. *How many U.S. jobs might be offshorable?*, Center for Economic Policy Studies Working Paper No. 142 (Princeton, NJ, Princeton University).

Boeri, T.; Burda, M.C.; Köllö, J. 1998. *Mediating the transition: Labour markets in Central and Eastern Europe* (London, Centre for Economic Policy Research).

—; Terrell, K. 2002. "Institutional determinants of labour reallocation in transition", in *Journal of Economic Perspectives*, Vol. 16, No. 1, pp. 51–76.

—; Garibaldi, P. 2006. *Labour market protection in Europe and other OECD countries*, Background Paper (Geneva, ILO).

Boone, J.; van Ours, J.C. 2004. *Effective active labour market policies*, Discussion Paper Series 4707 (London, Centre for Economic Policy Research).

Booth, A.; Francesconi, M.; Frank, J. 2002. "Temporary jobs: Stepping stones or dead ends?", in *Economic Journal*, Vol. 112, No. 480, pp. F189–F213.

Bruno, M.; Sachs, J. 1985. *The economics of worldwide stagflation* (Oxford, Basil Blackwell).

—; Ravallion, M.; Squire, L. 1998. "Equity and growth in developing countries: Old and new perspectives on the policy issue", in V. Tanzi and K.-Y. Chu (eds): *Income distribution and high-quality growth* (Cambridge, MA, MIT Press), pp. 117–164.

Campos, N.F.; Coricelli, F. 2002. "Growth in transition: What we know, what we don't and what we should", in *Journal of Economic Literature*, Vol. 40, No. 3, pp. 793–836.

Cazes, S.; Nesporova, A. 2003. *Labour markets in transition: Balancing flexibility and security in Central and Eastern Europe* (Geneva, ILO).

Chen, S.; Ravallion, M. 2004a. "How have the world's poorest fared since the early 1980s?", in *World Bank Research Observer*, Vol. 19, No. 2, pp. 141–170.

—;—. 2004b. *China's (uneven) progress against poverty*, Policy Research Working Paper No. 3408 (Washington, DC, World Bank).

Clemens, M.; Radelet, S.; Bhavnani, R. 2004. *Counting chickens when they hatch: The short-term effect of aid on growth*, Working Paper No. 44 (Washington, DC, Center for Global Development).

Collier, P. 2006. *Globalization, employment and poverty in low-income Africa*, Background Paper (Geneva, ILO).

Commander, S.; Köllö, J. 2004. *The changing demand for skills: Evidence from the transition*, Discussion Paper Series 1073 (Bonn, Institute for the Study of Labour (IZA)).

—; Kangasniemi, M.; Winters, L.A. 2003. *The brain drain: Curse or boon?*, Discussion Paper Series 809 (Bonn, IZA).

DiTella, R.; MacCulloch, R. 2005. "The consequences of labour market flexibility: Panel evidence based on survey data", in *European Economic Review*, Vol. 49, pp. 1225–1259.

References

Docquier, F.; Marfouk, A. 2004. *Measuring the international mobility of skilled workers (1990–2000): Release 1.0*, Policy Research Working Paper No. 3381 (Washington, DC, World Bank).

Dolado, J.J.; Garcia-Serrano, C.; Jimeno, J.F. 2002. "Drawing lessons from the boom of temporary jobs in Spain", in *Economic Journal*, Vol. 112, No. 480, pp. F270–F295.

Dollar, D.; Kray, A. 2002. "Growth is good for the poor", in *Journal of Economic Growth*, Vol. 7, No. 3, pp. 195–225, reprinted in A. Shorrocks and R. van der Hoeven (eds): *Growth, inequality and poverty* (Oxford, Oxford University Press for UNU–WIDER, 2004), pp. 29–61.

—; —. 2004. "Trade, growth and poverty", in *Economic Journal*, Vol. 114, No. 493, pp. F22–F49.

Dumont, J.-C.; Lemaître, G. 2004. *Counting immigrants and expatriates in OECD countries: A new perspective*, Social, Employment and Migration Working Paper No. 25 (Paris, OECD).

European Commission (EC). 1997. *Employment in Europe 1997* (Luxembourg).

Feenstra, R.C. 2007. "Globalization and its impact on labor", paper presented at the Global Economy Lecture, Vienna, 8 Feb. (Vienna, Vienna Institute of International Economic Studies).

—; Hanson, G.H. 2003. "Global production sharing and rising inequality: A survey of trade and wages", in K. Choi and J. Harrigan (eds): *Handbook of international trade* (Oxford, Basil Blackwell), pp. 146–187.

Fields, G. 1989. "Changes in poverty and inequality in developing countries", in *World Bank Research Observer*, Vol. 4, No. 2, pp. 167–186.

Freeman, R.B. 2005a. *Labour market institutions without blinders: The debate over flexibility and labour market performance*, Working Paper No. 11246 (Cambridge, MA, National Bureau of Economic Research).

—. 2005b. "The great doubling: Labour in the new global economy", paper presented at the Usery Lecture in Labor Policy, Atlanta, 8 Apr. (Atlanta, Georgia State University).

—. 2007. "How well do the clothes fit?: Priors and evidence over flexibility and labour market performance", in B. Eichengreen, M. Landesmann and D. Stiefel (eds): *The European economy in an American mirror*, Vol. 1 (Abingdon and New York, Routledge), pp. 104–116.

Ghose, A.K. 2003. *Jobs and incomes in a globalizing world* (Geneva, ILO).

—. 2004a. "The employment challenge in India", in *Economic and Political Weekly*, Vol. 39, No. 48, pp. 5106–5116.

—. 2004b. *Capital inflows and investment in developing countries*, Employment Strategy Paper No. 11 (Geneva, ILO).

—. 2005a. *Employment in China: Recent trends and future challenges*, Employment Strategy Paper No. 14 (Geneva, ILO).

—. 2005b. "Foreign capital, investment and reserve accumulation in developing countries", Economic and Labour Market Analysis Background Paper, unpublished (Geneva, ILO).

—. 2005c. "High-wage-low-productivity organised manufacturing and the employment challenge in India", in *Indian Journal of Labour Economics*, Vol. 48, No. 2, pp. 231–242.

—. 2006. "Economic growth and employment in labour-surplus economies", in *Economic and Political Weekly*, Vol. 41, No. 31, pp. 3430–3434.

Grossman, G.M.; Rossi-Hansberg, E. 2006. "The rise of offshoring: It's not wine for cloth anymore", paper presented at the *New economic geography: Effects and policy implications* Symposium, Jackson Hole, Wyoming, 24–28 Aug. (Jackson Hole).

Harrison, A. 2006. *Globalization and poverty*, Working Paper No. 12347 (Cambridge, MA, National Bureau of Economic Research).

Holmlund, B.; Storrie, D. 2002. "Temporary work in turbulent times: The Swedish experience", in *Economic Journal*, Vol. 112, No. 480, pp. F245–F269.

Howell, D.; Baker, D.; Glyn, A.; Schmitt, J. 2006. *Are protective labour market institutions really at the root of unemployment? A critical perspective on the statistical evidence*, Policy Paper (Washington, DC, Center for Economic and Policy Research).

Hussmanns, R. 2005. *Measuring the informal economy: From employment in the informal sector to informal employment*, Policy Integration Working Paper No. 53 (Geneva, ILO).

Inter-American Development Bank (IADB). 2006. *Sending money home: Leveraging the development impact of remittances* (Washington, DC).

International Labour Organization (ILO). 2002. *Resolution concerning decent work and the informal economy*, International Labour Conference, 90th Session, Geneva, 2002 (Geneva).

—. 2004. *HIV/AIDS and work: Global estimates, impact and responses* (Geneva).

International Organization for Migration (IOM). 2000. *World Migration Report, 2000* (Geneva).

International Monetary Fund (IMF). 2003. "Unemployment and labour market institutions: Why reforms pay off", in *World Economic Outlook* (Apr.) (Washington, DC), pp. 129–150.

—. 2005. "Two current issues facing developing countries", in *World Economic Outlook* (Apr.) (Washington, DC), pp. 69–107.

—. 2006. *Labour market performance in transition* (Washington, DC).

—. 2007. "The globalization of labour", in *World Economic Outlook* (Apr.) (Washington, DC), pp. 161–192.

Jansen, M.; Lee, E. 2007. *Trade and employment: Challenges for policy research* (Geneva, ILO and WTO).

Kakwani, N.; Son, H.H. 2006. *New global poverty counts*, Working Paper No. 29 (Brasilia, UNDP International Poverty Centre).

Kingdon, G.G.; Knight, J. 2004. "Unemployment in South Africa: The nature of the beast", in *World Development*, Vol. 32, No. 3, pp. 391–408.

References

Kluve, J. 2006. *The effectiveness of European active labour market policy*, Discussion Paper Series 2018 (Bonn, IZA).

Kose, M.A.; Prasad, E; Rogoff, K.S.; Wei, S.-J. 2006. *Financial globalization: A reappraisal*, Working Paper No. 12484 (Washington, DC, National Bureau of Economic Research).

Landesmann, M.; Vidovic, H. 2006. *Employment developments in Eastern and Central Europe: Trends and explanations*, Economic and Labour Market Analysis Background Paper, unpublished (Geneva, ILO).

Lewis, W.A. 1954. "Economic development with unlimited supplies of labour", in *The Manchester School*, Vol. 22, pp. 139–191.

Lindbeck, A; Snower, D.J. 1989. *The insider–outsider theory of employment and unemployment* (Cambridge, MA, MIT Press).

Lundberg, M; Squire, L. 2003. "The simultaneous evolution of growth and inequality", in *Economic Journal*, Vol. 113, No. 487, pp. 326–344.

Maddison, A. 2003. *The world economy: Historical statistics* (Paris, OECD).

McCarthy, J.C. 2004. "Near-term growth of offshoring accelerating", in *Trends*, 14 May (Cambridge, MA, Forrester Research).

Nesporova, A. 1999. *Employment and labour market policies in transition economies* (Geneva, ILO).

Nickell, S.; Nunziata, L.; Ochel, W. 2005. "Unemployment in the OECD since the 1960s: What do we know?", in *Economic Journal*, Vol. 115, No. 500, pp. 1–27.

Nunziata, L. 2006. *Some notes on OECD labour markets*, Economic and Labour Market Analysis Background Paper, unpublished (Geneva, ILO).

Nurkse, R. 1953. *Problems of capital formation in underdeveloped countries* (Oxford, Basil Blackwell).

Organisation for Economic Co-operation and Development (OECD). 1994. *Jobs Study: Evidence and explanations*, Parts I and II (Paris).

—. 1999. *Employment Outlook: Giving youth a better start* (Paris).

—. 2001. *Employment Outlook: Reconciling social and employment goals* (Paris).

—. 2002. *Employment Outlook: Surveying the jobs horizon* (Paris).

—. 2004. *Employment Outlook: Reassessing the OECD jobs strategy* (Paris).

—. 2006. *Employment Outlook: Boosting jobs and incomes* (Paris).

Parker, A. 2004. "Two-speed Europe: Why one million jobs will move offshore", in *Trends*, 18 Aug. (Cambridge, MA, Forrester Research).

Pissarides, C. 1990. *Equilibrium unemployment theory* (Oxford, Basil Blackwell).

Rajan, R.G.; Subramanian, A. 2005a. *Aid and growth: What does cross-country evidence really show?*, Working Paper No. 05/127 (Washington, DC, IMF).

—. 2005b. *What undermines aid's impact on growth?*, Working Paper No. 05/126 (Washington, DC, IMF).

Ravallion, M. 1995. "Growth and poverty: Evidence for developing countries in the 1980s", in *Economic Letters*, Vol. 48, No. 3, pp. 411–417.

—. 2001. "Growth, inequality and poverty: Looking beyond averages", in *World Development*, Vol. 29, No. 11, pp. 1803–1815.

—. 2007. "Looking beyond averages in the trade and poverty debate", in M. Nissanke and E. Thorbecke (eds): *The impact of globalization on the world's poor* (Basingstoke, Palgrave Macmillan), pp. 118–144.

Riboud, M.; Sánchez-Páramo, C.; Silva-Jauregui, C. 2002. "Does Eurosclerosis matter? Institutional reform and labour market performance in Central and Eastern Europe", in B. Funck and L. Pizzati (eds): *Labour, employment, and social policies in the EU enlargement process* (Washington, DC, World Bank), pp. 243–311.

Rodrik, D. 2006. *Understanding South Africa's economic puzzles*, Center for International Development Working Paper No. 130 (Cambridge, MA, Harvard University).

Rosenstein-Rodin, P.N. 1943. "Problems of industrialisation of Eastern and South-Eastern Europe", in *Economic Journal*, Vol. 53, No. 210/211, pp. 202–211.

Rowthorn, R.; Coutts, K. 2004. "De-industrialisation and the balance of payments in advanced economies", in *Cambridge Journal of Economics*, Vol. 28, No. 5, pp. 767–790.

—. 2005. "The impact on advanced economies of north–south trade in manufacturing and services", in *Brazilian Journal of Political Economy*, Vol. 25, No. 2, pp. 60–73.

Samuelson, P.A. 2004. "Where Ricardo and Mill rebut and confirm arguments of mainstream economists supporting globalization", in *Journal of Economic Perspectives*, Vol. 18, No. 3, pp. 136–146.

Sachs, J.D.; Warner, A.M. 2001. "The curse of natural resources", in *European Economic Review*, Vol. 45, No. 4/6, pp. 827–838.

Schultz, T.W. 1964. *Transforming traditional agriculture* (New Haven, CT, Yale University Press).

Sen, A.K. 1966. "Peasants and dualism with or without surplus labour", in *Journal of Political Economy*, Vol. 74, No. 5, pp. 425–450.

—. 1993. "Capability and well-being", in M. Nassbaum and A. Sen (eds): *The Quality of Life* (Oxford, Clarendon Press), pp. 30–53.

Svejnar, J. 2002. "Transition economies: Performance and challenges", in *Journal of Economic Perspectives*, Vol. 16, No. 1, pp. 3–28.

Tilton, A. 2003. "Offshoring: where have all the jobs gone?", in *US Economic Analyst*, 19 Sep. (New York, Goldman Sachs Group).

United Nations (UN). 2002. *World Population Ageing, 1950–2050* (New York).

—. 2006. *Trends in Total Migration Stock: The 2005 revision* (New York).

References

United Nations Conference on Trade and Development (UNCTAD). 2002. *The Least Developed Countries Report 2002* (New York and Geneva).

United Nations Millennium Project (UNMP). 2005. *Investing in development: A practical plan to achieve the Millennium Development Goals* (London, Earthscan).

Viner, J. 1957. "Some reflections on the concept of disguised unemployment", in *Indian Journal of Economics*, Vol. 38, pp. 17–23.

Verme, P. 2006. *Constraints to growth and job creation in low-income Commonwealth of Independent States countries*, Policy Research Working Paper No. 3893 (Washington, DC, World Bank).

Vodopivec, M.; Wörgötter, A.; Raju, D. 2003. *Unemployment benefit systems in Central and Eastern Europe: A review of the 1990s*, Social Protection Discussion Paper Series 0310 (Washington, DC, World Bank).

Winters, L.A.; McCulloch, N.; McKay, A. 2004. "Trade liberalization and poverty: The evidence so far", in *Journal of Economic Literature*, Vol. 42, No. 1, pp. 72–115.

World Bank. 1990. *World Development Report 1990: Poverty* (New York, Oxford University Press).

—. 2000. *World Development Report 2000/2001: Attacking Poverty* (New York, Oxford University Press).

—. 2005. *Enhancing job opportunities: Eastern Europe and the former Soviet Union* (Washington, DC).

—. 2006. *Global economic prospects: Economic implications of remittances and migration* (Washington, DC).

INDEX

Note: Page numbers in **bold** refer to Tables, Boxes and Annexes; those in *italics* refer to Figures

Afghanistan **54**
age
    changes in structure 32–4, **32, 33**
    and structure of labour force 17, **18**, *19*, **19**
agriculture
    CIS countries 249, **251**, 251$_{88, 89}$, **252**, 258, 269
    and dualism **65**, 67–8
    and employment growth 93$_{30}$, 231, **232**
    exports 140
    growth and output **188**, 258
    self-employment in CIS countries 249, 251, 259, 269
    and skills 195, 196
Albania **214, 223**
Algeria **54, 66, 70, 74, 76, 86, 94, 117, 120**
Angola 49
apprenticeship schemes 196$_{and\ 65}$
Argentina **54, 66, 70, 74, 76, 84, 86, 92, 94, 97, 111, 117, 119, 120,** 146
    economic change 100, *101*, 153
Armenia **252, 254, 256, 257, 260, 261, 262**
    emigration 255
    employment growth **251**, 258$_{and\ 92}$
    employment and unemployment **248**, 250, **250**, 257
Australia **157, 158, 162, 164, 166, 171,** 172, **180, 187, 188, 194, 197, 198, 199, 200, 202, 204, 205, 206–11**
    education and employment **168,** 170, **182, 183**

Austria **157, 158, 162, 164, 166, 171, 180, 187, 188, 194, 198, 200, 202, 204, 206–11, 243**
    education and employment **168,** 170, **182, 183**
    labour force growth 186, **205**
    unemployment 155, **197, 199**
Azerbaijan 7, **16, 251, 252, 254, 256, 257, 260, 261, 262**
    employment and unemployment 247, **248,** 249, 250, **250**
    industrial growth 258

Bahrain **54**
Bangladesh **43, 54, 67, 71, 75, 80, 87, 95, 96, 118, 122, 147, 149, 151**
    FDI 42, **42**
    productive resources 39, 40, **40**
Belarus **254, 256, 257, 260, 261, 262**
    employment growth **251, 257,** 268
    employment and unemployment 247, **248,** 249, 250, **250,** 257
    labour productivity growth 252, **252**
Belgium **157, 158, 166, 168, 171, 180, 182, 183, 187, 188, 194, 197, 198, 199, 202, 204, 205, 243**
    CEI estimates (all) 162, **162, 200, 204, 206–11**
    employment indicators **164,** 165
Belize **67, 80, 95, 118, 153**
Benin **54, 147**
Bhutan **43**
Bolivia **54, 66, 70, 74, 76, 86, 117, 120,** 146, **149, 151**

279

Bosnia-Herzegovina **214**
Botswana 30, **54**, **66**, **70**, **74**, **76**, **84**, **86**, **92**, **94**, **111**, **117**, **119**, **120**, **146**
　economic change *101*, **153**
brain drain 49, **50**, 51, 110, 267
　from CEE countries 234
Brazil 43, 49, **54**, **65**, **66**, **70**, **74**, **76**, **82**, **84**, **86**, 90, **92**, **94**, **117**, **119**, **120**, **146**, 149
　economic change 100, *101*, **151**, **153**
　FDI 42, **42**
　formal segment 95, **97**, **111**
Bulgaria 215, 217, 218, 220, 223, 224, 225, 227, 230, 234, 238, 239, 242, 243, 244
　economic output 221, **222**, 235, **235**
　employment and unemployment **214**, **224**, **232**
　part-time employment 215
Burkina Faso **147**, **149**, **151**
Burundi 49, **147**, **149**, **151**

Cambodia 71, 75, 80, 87, 122, **147**
Cameroon **54**, **70**, **76**, **86**, **96**, **120**, **146**, **149**, **151**
Canada **157**, **158**, **162**, **164**, **166**, **168**, **171**, **180**, **182**, **183**, **187**, **188**, **194**, **198**, **200**, **202**, **204**, **205**, 206–11
　unemployment rates 155, **197**, **199**
capital flows
　in developing countries 41–4, **42**
　employment effects 102–7
capital investment
　allocation between formal and non-formal segments 108–9, 268
　and economic growth 108, 267–8
　per worker 38, **39**, 40–1, **40**
　and trade growth 140, 143, 267
　see also foreign direct investment (FDI)
Caribbean, poverty **127**, 128
casual wage employment **60**, **65**, 265
　and unemployment rates 75, 79
Central African Republic 30, **54**, **147**
Central and Eastern European (CEE) countries 2, **5**, 6, 213–37
　CEI estimates 215
　change in employment profile **223**
　current employment situation 213–21, **214**, **216**, **224**
　economic growth and labour market 229–30, **230**, 234–5
　economic recession 221

employment trends 221–8, 236, 265–7
explanation for trends 229–34
gender disparity 216, 217, 218, **218**, *219*
labour force 10
　age structure **18**, *19*, **19**, **32**
　gender composition *13–14*, **13**, **31**
　growth **25**
　participation rates *11*, *12*, **28**, 213, 222
　skill structure 20–4, **21**, **22**, **23**, **24**, **34**, **35**
labour market institutions 229
migrants 46, 233–4
policy challenges 234–7
population growth *28*, 36
productive resources 39
skills and employment 218, 220–1
structural changes 229, 231, 265–6
see also EU New Member States (NMS); South-Eastern Europe (SEE)
Chile **54**, **66**, **70**, **74**, **76**, **86**, **94**, **96**, **97**, **112**, **117**, **120**, **146**
　economic change 100–1, *101*, **153**
　employment situation **84**, **91**, **92**, **119**
China 3, 16, 43, 49, **54**, **66**, **74**, **76**, **84**, **92**, **117**, **119**, **146**, 149
　economic growth rate 101, *101*, **151**, **153**
　effect of trade growth on employment 103, 105, **105**
　employment indicators **70**, **72**₃, **94**
　FDI 42, **42**
　formal segment 95, **97**, **98**, **98**, **112**
　and global labour force 189₆₂
　labour force 10
　poverty reduction **127**, **143**
　trade growth 103, 105, **105**, **143**
Colombia **54**, **70**, **76**, **86**, **120**, **146**, **149**, **151**
Commonwealth of Independent States (CIS) countries 2, **5**, 6, 247–59
　agriculture 249, 251, **251**, 251₈₈, ₈₉, **252**, 258, 259, 269
　economic disruption 266
　economic output 255–8, **262**
　employment growth 251–2, **251**
　factors in employment trends 255–8, 266
　key employment indicators **254–5**
　labour force **10**, **261**
　　age structure **18**, *19*, **19**, **32**
　　gender composition *13–14*, **13**, **31**
　　growth **25**

Index

participation rates *11*, *12*, **28**
skill structure 20–4, **21**, *22*, *23*, **24**
labour productivity growth **252**
land redistribution 251$_{88}$, 259, 269
migration 45, 46, **253**, 255
output and employment (by sector) **262**
output fall **256**
overall employment situation 247–55, **248**, **250**
policies for 258–9
population *28*, 36, **261**
productive resources **39**, 259$_{and\ 93}$, 269
real GDP **256**
unemployment 247, 253, 255, **260**
Composite Employment Indicator (CEI) 160–3, **162**, 176, *177*, 206–8, 244–5
Adjusted *177*, **179**, 209–11
and gender disparity 178, *178*, **179**, 225
Modified CEI 163, 165, 176$_{60}$, 200, 204
Congo 54
Congo, Democratic Republic 54
consumption/income (per capita), and change in poverty 130–1
Costa Rica 54, 66, 70, 74, 76, 84, 86, 92, 94, 96, 97, 112, 117, 119, 120, 146, 149
economic change *101*, 151, **153**
trade growth 103, 105, **105**
Côte d'Ivoire 146, 149, 151
Croatia 215, 217, 218, 220, 224, 225, 227, 238, 239, 243, 245
economic growth and employment 230, **230**
economic output 221, **222**, **235**
employment and unemployment 213, **214**, 224, **232**
labour supply growth 233
self-employment 215
Cuba 54, 66, 76, 94, 117, 153
cultural norms, and female labour force participation 16
Cyprus 54
Czech Republic 215, 217, 218, 223, 224, 225, 227, 234, 238, 239, 240, 243, 244
economic growth and employment 230, **230**
economic output **222**, 235, **235**
education and employment 220, **220**, 238, 241, 242
employment and unemployment **214**, 224, 231–2, **232**
low-skilled labour 228

self-employment 223
working age population growth 233, **233**

Denmark 157, 158, 166, 171, 180, 187, 188, 194, 197, 198, 199, 202, 204, 205, 243
CEI estimates (all) 162, **162**, 200, 204, 206–11
education and employment 168, 170, **182**, **183**
employment indicators **164**, 165
developed countries 2, **5**, 6–7, 155–96, 265
current employment situation 156–73
employment trends 173–84
explanations for persisting unemployment 184–90, **184–5**
labour force 10
age structure *18*, *19*, **19**, 32
gender composition *13–14*, **13**, 31
growing concentration in 24–5, *27*, 28–30, *28*, **28**, **29**
participation rates *11*, *12*, **28**
skill structure 20–4, **21**, *22*, **23**, **24**, **34**, **35**
migrants 46
off-shoring of manufacturing 189, **190**
population growth *28*
productive resources **39**
skills and employment 167–73, 179–81, 184
unemployment rates **197**
developing countries 123–45
assessment of employment situation 61–82
capital flows 41–4, **42**
labour market growth 189$_{62}$
migration from 47, 49, 50, 51, 54–6
overall employment situation 83, **84**, **85**, 266
public employment policies 145
social security 58
trade orientation 139–40
unskilled labour 37
see also Central and Eastern European (CEE) countries; Commonwealth of Independent States (CIS) countries; least developed countries; medium-income developing countries; other high income countries; petroleum exporter developing countries
development, primary education and primary health care 145
distributional inequality, and reduction of poverty 124
domestic savings, least developed countries 43, 109$_{and\ 43}$, 110

281

Dominica 70
Dominican Republic **54, 66,** 70, 74, 76, **86, 94, 96,**
   117, 120, 146, 153
dualism
   in developing economies 57, 265
   empirical view of 64–8
   indicators **66–7**
   and labour market 60
   and poverty reduction 134

earnings inequality, in developed countries **172,** 173
economic growth
   annual change rates **153**
   and employment 99–101, *100, 101,* 125, 186,
      256, 257–8, 266–7
   and labour productivity (CEE countries)
      235–6, **235**
   obstacles to 124–5
   and poverty reduction 124, 130–4, **132–3,**
      151–2
   and unemployment (CEE countries) 229–31
economies
   CIS countries 255, **256,** 257–8
   formal and non-formal segments 57–61, **58**
   macroeconomic shocks 184, **184**
   restructuring 99
   see also formal segment; non-formal segment
Ecuador **54, 66,** 70, 74, 76, **84, 86,** 92, **94,** 97, **112,**
   117, 119, 120, 146, 149
   economic change *101,* **151**
education
   as anti-poverty programme 145
   attainment levels **34**
   average years, and economic development **22**
   and chronic unemployment **81–2**
   employment indicators (CEE countries) **238**
   gender disparity *23,* **35**
   and labour force growth **183, 233**
   and labour force participation 20–4, **21,** 168,
      170, **220, 242**
   and non-standard wage employment **169–70**
   and skills gap **69**
   and unemployment 167, **182, 220, 227**
Egypt 16, **54, 66,** 70, 74, 76, **84, 86,** 92, **94,** 97, **112,**
   117, 119, 121, 146, 149
   economic change *101,* **151, 153**
El Salvador **54, 66,** 70, 74, 76, **84, 86,** 92, **94, 96,**
   97, **113, 117, 119, 121, 146,** 149

economic change *101,* **151, 153**
trade growth 103, 105, **105**
employment
   and economic growth 99–101, *100, 101,* 125,
      186, 257–8, **257**
   formal segment 57–61, **58, 64,** 68, 71–2,
      111–16
   future policies 195–6, 267–9
   global factors in 1, 266
   indicators 61–3, **70–1, 94–5, 164, 254–5**
   measurement 2–3
   output in non-formal segment 63, 67, 72–3,
      74–5, 117–18
   and poverty reduction 125–6, 136
   public works programmes 144–5
   ranking **84**
   and skills in developed countries 167–73,
      179–81
   see also Composite Employment Indicator
      (CEI); employment situation; productive
      employment; unemployment
employment elasticity 61$_{19}$, **187,** 236
   in CIS countries 257–9
   and output growth 109, 134
   in services **243**
   and tax wedge 193
employment growth
   and labour force growth 109$_{41}$, 186, **187,** 189,
      205
   by sector (CEE countries) 231, **232**
employment protection index (EPI)
   regular employment *191*
   temporary workers *192*
employment protection legislation 190, 191–2
   OECD indices 191$_{64}$
employment situation
   CEE countries 213–21
   CIS countries 247–55
   current overall state 83–9, **84,** 85, 266–7
   developed countries 156–73, **157,** *201, 203*
   developing countries 61–82
   gender disparity 85, **86–7,** 87–9, **88,** 89, **120–2,**
      181
   output growth 95, 97–8, **97**
   recent trends 89–99, **92, 94–5**
Employment Situation Index (ESI) 89, 91, **119**
entrepreneurs 65
Equatorial Guinea 49

Index

Estonia **215**, **217**, **218**, **220**, **222**, **223**, **224**, **225**, **227**, **233**, **234**, **235**, **238**, **239**, **242**, **243**, **244**
   economic growth and employment 230, *230*
   employment and unemployment 214, **224**, **232**
   low-skilled labour 228
   self-employment 223
Ethiopia 67, 71, 148, 149, 151
EU New Member States (NMS)
   gender employment disparity 218
   labour force participation rates 213
   unemployment 214
Europe
   employment elasticity in services 243
   labour force and employment growth 205
   see also individual countries
European CIS countries, employment situation 249

Fiji 54, 153
Finland 157, 158, 164, 166, 168, 171, 172, 180, 182, 183, 187, 188, 194, 197, 198, 199, 202, 204, 205, 243
   CEI estimates (all) **162**, *163*
foreign aid **44**, 110, 267
   and poverty reduction 123–4
foreign direct investment (FDI) 41–2, **41**, **44**, 268
   effect on employment 102–7
formal segment
   effect of trade growth *104*
   employment 57–61, **58**, **64**, 68, 71–2, **111–16**, 266
   employment growth 97–8, 99, 108, 134–5$_{52}$, 266
   employment share 63, 91–2
   output growth 95, 97–8, *97*
   and reduction of poverty 134–5$_{\text{and }52}$
   restructuring 99
   see also non-formal segment
France 157, 158, **162**, 164, 166, 171, 172, 180, 187, 188, 194, 197, 198, 199, 200, 202, 204, 205, 206–11, 243
   education and employment 168, 170, **182**, 183

Gambia 54, 148, 150, 151
GDP *see* per capita GDP
gender
   composition of labour force 11–12, *13–14*, **13**, 15–17, **16**, 30–2, **31**

employment indicators
   CEE countries 238
   in developed countries 164
   and job queuing 88–9, **90**
   labour force participation 180
gender disparity
   education *23*, **35**
   employment 85, **86–7**, **87–9**, **120–2**, *181*
      in CEE countries 216, **217**, 218, **218**, *219*, 225–6, **225**, *226*
      in developed countries 165–7, **166**, *167*, 203
   Modified Composite Employment Indicator 204
   self-employment 88, *89*
   trends in 93, **96**, 178–9, *178*, *179*
   unemployment 87–9, **88**, *89*, 120–2
   see also women
Georgia 251, 252, 254, 260, 261, 262
   emigration 255
   employment and unemployment **248**, 250, **250**
   GDP **256**, 257, *257*
Germany 3, 157, 158, 164, 166, 171, 172, 180, 188, 194, 198, 202, 204, 243
   CEI estimates (all) **162**, *162*, 200, 204, 206–11
   economic growth 186, **187**
   education and employment 168, 180–1, **182**, 183
   labour force growth 186, 205
   unemployment rates 155, 179, **197**, 199
Ghana 49, 54, 66, 70, 74, 76, 94, 117, 146, 149, 151, 153
globalization
   employment 1, 266
   labour force 9–10, **9**, 24–35, 189$_{62}$
   and productive employment 38
Greece 157, 158, **162**, 166, 171, 180, 182, 183, 187, 188, 194, 198, 200, 202, 204, 205, 206–11, 243
   employment indicators 164, 165
   unemployment rates 155, **197**, 199
Guatemala 54, 66, 70, 74, 76, 86, 94, 117, 121, 146, 149, 151, 153
Guinea-Bissau 49, 54
Guyana 54

Haiti 54, 80, 148
health care, primary, as anti-poverty programme 145
HIV/AIDS, and labour force participation 29–30, **30**

Honduras 54, 66, 70, 74, 76, 84, 86, 92, 94, 96, 97, 113, 117, 119, 121, 146, 149
   economic change 100, *101*, 151, 153
Hong Kong, China 54
household enterprises, economic policies for 109$_{\text{and 40}}$
Hungary 215, 217, 218, 223, 224, 225, 227, 238, 239, 243, 244
   economic growth and employment 230–1, **230**
   economic output 221, **222**, **235**
   education and employment 220, **220**, **238**, **242**
   employment and unemployment 213, 214, **214**, **224**, **232**
   migration from **234**, 234
   working age population growth **233**, 233

Iceland 157, 158, 162, 166, 171, 180, 187, 188, 194, 198, 200, 202, 204, 205, 206–11, 243
   education and employment **168**, **180**, **182**, **183**
   employment indicators **164**, 165
   unemployment rates 155, **197**, **199**
India 3, 15, 16, 20, 49, 54, 65, 66, 70, 74, 76, 81, 84, 86, 90, 92, 94, 96, 97, 113, 117, 119, 121, 146, 149
   economic growth rate 100–1, *101*, 151, 153
   and global labour force 189$_{62}$
   labour force 10, **20**
   trade growth 103, 105, **105**
Indonesia 16, 54, 66, 70, 74, 76, 84, 86, 94, 113, 117, 121, 146
industry
   CIS countries 251, 252, **252**, 256, 257–8, 259, 269
   as formal segment 95
   growth and output **188**, 231, **232**, **236**
   off-shoring of manufacturing 189, **190**
inequality
   distributional 124
   earnings **172**, 173
Iran, Islamic Republic of 16, 54, 86, 117, 120
Iraq 54
Ireland 155, 157, 158, 162, 164, 166, 171, 180, 187, 188, 194, 197, 198, 199, 200, 202, 204, 205, 206–11, 243
   education and employment **168**, 170, **182**, **183**
Israel 54
Italy 157, 158, 162, 166, 168, 171, 180, 182, 183, 188, 194, 197, 198, 199, 200, 202, 204, 206–11, 243

economic growth 186, **187**
employment indicators **164**, 165
labour force growth 186, **187**, 205

Jamaica 54, 66, 70, 74, 76, 84, 86, 92, 94, 96, 97, 113, 117, 119, 121, 146
   economic change 100, *101*, 153
Japan 157, 158, 162, 164, 166, 168, 171, 172, 180, 182, 183, 188, 194, 198, 200, 202, 204, 206–11
   economic growth 186, **187**
   labour force growth 186, **205**
   unemployment rates 155, 179, **197**, **199**
job destruction, in CEE countries 225–6
job insecurity, in developed countries 155
job queuing 80, 87, 88–9
   and gender 88–9, **90**
Jordan 54, 76, 146

Kazakhstan 252, 254, 256, 257, 260, 261, 262
   emigration 255
   employment growth 251, 257, 258
   employment and unemployment 248, 249, **250**, 250
   labour participation rate 255
Kenya 54, 66, 114, 147, 149, 151
Korea, Republic of 54
Kuwait 54
Kyrgyzstan 251, 252, 254, 256, 257, 260, 261, 262
   economic growth 257
   employment and unemployment 248, 250, **250**

labour flows 45–53, **54**–6
labour force
   defined 9$_1$
   future trends 35–6
   global estimates 9–10, **9**
   global trends 24–35
   structure and characteristics 10–24, 266
      age structure 17, **18**, *19*, 19, 32–4, **33**
      concentration in low-income countries 10–11
      gender composition 11–12, *13–14*, 13, 15–17, 30–2, **31**, 178
      skill and education 20–4, **21**, **22**, **23**, **24**, 180–1
labour force growth 25, 61–3, 107, **183**, 189$_{62}$
   and employment growth 109$_{41}$, **187**, 189, **205**, 267

Index

and skills level 227–8
and unemployment 186
labour force participation
    CEE countries 222, 224, **233**
    CIS countries 249, 253
    developed countries **158**, 174, 176, *176*, 265
    and education level 168, 170, **171**, 220–1, **220**, 266
    and incidence of HIV/AIDS 30
    and part-time employment 159–60, *161*
    rates *11*, *12*, **28**
    and unemployment 224
    women 166, **171**, 178–9
labour force surveys 1, 2–3
    CIS countries 247, **248**, 249, 250, **250**
labour market
    in CEE countries 233–4, 236, 268
    CIS countries 252–3
    in dual economies 60
    and economic policies 109, 237
    flexibility 160
    formal and non-formal segments 57–61, **58**
    OECD reforms 185
    surplus labour 57–8, **58**
    two-tier 195
labour market institutions
    CEE countries **229**, 236
    reforms 190–1, 195, 269
    and unemployment 184, **185**
labour market reforms 190–5
labour productivity, and output growth (CEE countries) 235
Lao People's Democratic Republic 148, 150, 151
Latin America
    poverty 127, 128
    remittances from USA 53
    trade growth 103, 105–6, 105$_{and\ 38}$
    see also individual countries
Latvia 215, 217, 218, 220, 222, 223, 224, 225, 227, 233, 234, 235, 238, 239, 242, 243, 244
    economic growth and employment 230, **230**
    employment and unemployment 214, 224, **232**
    part-time employment 215
least developed countries 2, **6**
    brain drain 50
    domestic savings **43**, 109$_{and\ 43}$, 110
    dual economy indicators 68
    employment situation trends 92, 95

    FDI 42
    gender disparity in employment 87, 96
    investment per worker 40
    labour force 10
        age structure 18, *19*, 19, 32
        employment status 71
        gender composition *13–14*, **13**, 31
        growth 25
        participation rates *11*, *12*, **28**
        skill structure 20–4, **21**, **22**, **23**, **24**, 34, 35
    migration 46, 47, 48
    population growth *28*
    poverty statistics 147–8, 149–50
    productive resources 39
    value added per non-formal worker 75
Lesotho 30, 54, 148
Lewis, Arthur 59
Liberia 49, 54
Lithuania 214, 215, 217, 218, 220, 222, 223, 224, 225, 227, 232, 234, 235, 238, 239, 242, 243, 244
    economic growth and employment 230, **230**
Luxembourg 155, **157**, **158**, 162, 164, 166, 168, 171, 180, 182, 183, 187, 188, 194, 197, 198, 199, 200, 202, 204, 205, 206–11, 243

Macedonia, former Yugoslav Republic of 215, 217
    employment and unemployment 214, **214**
Madagascar 70, 75, 80, 87, 116, 122, 148, 150, 151
Malawi 30, 54, 71, 87, 116, 122, 148, 150, 151
Malaysia 54, 66, 70, 74, 76, 86, 94, 96, 117, 121, 147, 153
Maldives 71, 80, 87, 96, 122
Mali 54, 116, 148, 150, 151
manufacturing *see* industry
Mauritania 49, 148, 150, 151
Mauritius 54, 66, 70, 86, 121
medium-income developing countries 2, 6, **6**
    brain drain 50
    domestic savings 43
    dual economy indicators 66–7
    employment situation trends 92, 94–5
    FDI 106$_{39}$
    gender disparity in employment 86–7, 96
    investment per worker 40
    labour force 10
        age structure 18, *19*, 19, 32
        employment status 70–1
        gender composition *13–14*, **13**, 31

growth 25
participation rates *11*, *12*, 28
skill structure 20–4, **21**, **22**, **23**, **24**, **34**, **35**
migration 46, **47**, **48**
population growth *28*
poverty statistics 146–7, **149**
productive resources 39
ranking by employment situation **84**
value added per non-formal worker **74–5**
Mexico 43, 49, 54, 66, 70, 74, 76, 84, 86, 92, 94, 96, 97, 114, 117, 119, 121, 147, 149
economic change 100, *101*, **151**, **153**
FDI 42, **42**
trade growth 103, 105, **105**
migration 45–53, **47**, **48**, 54–6
brain drain 49, **50**, 51, 110, 267
from CEE countries 233–4, **234**
from CIS countries **253**, 255
fixed-term 267
remittances 51, **52**–3, 53
as share of total population **46**
statistics **45**
Millennium Development Goals, on poverty 123
Moldova 251, 252, 254, 260, 261, 262
emigration 255
employment and unemployment 248, 250, **250**
GDP 256, 257, **257**
Mongolia 66, 70, 75, 76, 94, 117, 147, 153
Montenegro 214, 217
Morocco 70, 75, 76, 86, 121, 147
Mozambique 54, 148
Myanmar 54, 67, 71, 80, 92, 95, 116, 118, 119
economic change *101*, **153**

Namibia 30, 66, 71, 75, 76, 86, 94, 118, 121, 147, 153
Nepal 54, 67, 80, 148, 150, 151
Netherlands 157, 158, 164, 166, 171, 172, 180, 187, 188, 194, 197, 198, 199, 202, 204, 205, 243
CEI estimates (all) 162, **162**, 200, 204, **206–11**
education and employment 168, 180–1, **182**, **183**
New Zealand 157, 158, 162, 164, 166, 171, 172, 180, 188, 194, 197, 198, 199, 200, 202, 204, 205, 206–11
education and employment 168, 170, **182**, **183**
Nicaragua 54, 66, 71, 75, 77, 84, 86, 92, 94, 96, 97, 114, 118, 119, 121, 147, 149

economic change *101*, **151**, **153**
Niger 54, 148
non-formal segment
and economic growth 108
effect of trade growth 106–7, *107*, **142**
employment 57–61, **58**, **64**, 68, 71–2, 144
and employment growth 93_{30}, 266
output 63, 67, 72–3, **74–5**, **117–18**
and reduction of poverty 134–5, 136–7, **138**, 144
skills gap **69**
value added per worker **74–5**, **117–18**
wages 60
see also formal segment; output growth
non-standard wage employment 186
in CEE countries 215, 223
in developed countries 158–9, 265
and level of education **169–70**
Russian Federation 253_{91}
and skills 170, 173
and unemployment rate 160–1
Norway 157, 158, 162, 164, 166, 168, 171, 180, 182, 183, 187, 188, 194, 198, 200, 202, 204, 205, 206–11, 243
unemployment rates 155, **197**, **199**

Organization for Economic Co-operation and Development
employment protection indices 191_{64}
on labour market institutions 184
migration database 45
recommendations for labour market reforms 185
other high income countries 2, 5, 6
brain drain **50**
labour force 10
age structure **18**, *19*, 19, 32
gender composition *13–14*, **13**, 31
growth 25
participation rates *11*, *12*, 28
skill structure 20–4, **21**, **22**, **23**, **24**, **34**, **35**
migration 46, **48**
population growth *28*
productive resources 39
output
decline in market transition 221, 258
in non-formal segment 63, 67, 72–3, **74–5**, **117–18**

Index

output growth 95, 97–8, **97**
   agriculture **188**, 258
   and employment elasticity 109, 134
   and employment growth 98, 108–9
   industry **188**, 231, **232**, 236
   and labour productivity **235**
   and per capita GDP *136*
   and poverty reduction 134–5, *135*, 136–7, **138**, 144, **151–2**
   service sector **188**, 231–2, **232**, 235–7, **235**
   and trade growth 140, *141*, 142

Pakistan 54, 66, 71, 75, 77, 86, 94, 96, 118, 121, 147, 149, 151, 153
Panama 54, 67, 71, 75, 77, 84, 86, 92, 94, 96, 97, 114, 118, 119, 121, 147, 149
   economic change *101*, **151, 153**
Papua New Guinea 54, 67, 77
Paraguay 54, 67, 71, 75, 77, 84, 86, 92, 94, 96, 97, 114, 118, 119, 121, 147, 149
   economic change 100, *101*, **151, 153**
part-time employment 155$_{56}$, 156
   in CEE countries 215
   in developed countries 174, *175*, **198**
   involuntary 165
   and labour force participation 159–60, *161*
   and long-term unemployment *160*
   voluntary 159–60, 176$_{60}$, **202**
   women 165
   and working-time flexibility 191, 193–5
per capita GDP
   and output per worker 135–6, *136*
   and poverty (annual change) *137*, **151–2**
   and poverty reduction 131, *132*, 134
   and trade growth 141
Peru 54, 67, 147, 149, 152
petroleum exporter developing countries 2, 5, 6
   brain drain 50
   dual economy indicators 66
   employment situation trends 92, 94
   gender disparity in employment 86, 96
   labour force 10
      age structure 18, *19*, **19**, 32
      employment status 70
      gender composition *13–14*, **13**, 31
      growth 25
      participation rates *11*, *12*, 28
      skill structure 20–4, **21**, **22**, **23**, **24**, 34, 35
   migration 46, 48
   population growth *28*
   productive resources 39
   ranking by employment situation 84
   value added per non-formal worker 74
Philippines 16, 54, 67, 71, 75, 77, 86, 94, 118, 121, 147, 149, 152, 153
Poland 215, 217, 218, 223, 224, 225, 227, 238, 239, 240, 243, 244
   economic growth and employment 230, **230**
   economic output 221, **222**, 235
   education and employment 220, **220**, 238, 241, 242
   employment and unemployment 214, **214**, 224, 231–2, **232**
   low-skilled labour 228
   migration from 234, **234**
   part-time employment 215
   self-employment 215
   temporary employment 215
   working age population growth 233, **233**
population
   and HIV/AIDS in Africa 30
   and labour force ageing **33**, 233
population growth
   average rates *28*
   demographic transition 26
   and economic development 29
   and labour force 25, 233, 261
   regional shares 27
Portugal 157, **158**, 166, 168, 171, 180, 182, 183, 187, 188, 194, 197, 198, 199, 202, 204, 205, 243
   CEI estimates (all) 162, **162**, **200**, **204**, 206–11
   employment indicators 164, 165
poverty
   in developing world 127
   and employment 134–7, 265
   and GDP *137*
   measurement and statistics on 128–9, **128**, 146–8
   World Bank definition 123$_{44}$, 126
poverty reduction
   in 1990s 127–30, *130*
   and economic growth 124, 130–4, **132–3**
   and employment 125–6
   global 123–6
   and mean expenditure/income growth *133*, *154*

287

and output growth in non-formal segment 134–5, *135*, 136–7, **138**
and per capita GDP 131, *132*, 134
policies for 144–5
strategies for **125**
productive employment 37–8
asymmetric distribution 38, **39**, 40–1
globalization and 38
need for skills 37–8, 265
policy challenges 107–10, 267–9
productive resources **39**, 267
public services, job creation in 196
public works programmes 144–5

refugees, CIS countries 252
religion, and female labour force participation **16**
remittances 51, **52–3**, 53
resources
natural 259$_{and\ 93}$, 269
productive **39**, 267
Romania 215, 217, 218, 223, 224, 225, 227, 230, 233, 238, 239, 240, 243, 245
economic output **222**, 235, **235**
education and employment 220, **220**, 238, 241, **242**
employment and unemployment **214**, 224, 231–2, **232**
low-skilled labour 228
migration from 234, **234**
part-time employment 215
self-employment 215
Russian Federation **254**, **256**, 257, 260, 261, 262
CEI estimates 249$_{87}$
employment growth **251**, 257, 268
employment and unemployment **248**, 249, **250**, 250
labour productivity growth 252, **252**
non-standard wage employment 253^{91}
Rwanda 49, **54**, 71, 87, 122, 148

Samoa **80**
Sao Tome and Principe 49
Saudi Arabia **117**
savings, domestic 42–4, **43**, 109$_{and\ 43}$, 110
self-employment **60**, **65**, 68, **70–1**, 72
in agriculture (CIS countries) 249, 251, 259, 269
CEE countries 215, 223

CIS countries 249$_{and\ 85}$, 252
in developing countries 265
gender disparity 88, *89*
part-time 156
policies for productivity growth 109$_{40}$
and unemployment 79
Sen, Amartya **59**
Senegal **54**, **148**, **150**, **152**
Serbia **214**, 217
service sector 196, 268
CIS countries **251**, **252**, 257–8, 259
community and social 236
and female labour force participation 15
growth and output **188**, 231–2, **232**, 235–7, **235**
market 236–7
short-term employment *159*
Sierra Leone 49, **54**
Singapore 6–7, **54**
skills 20–4
distribution *24*
and earnings inequality **172**, *173*
and emigration 49$_{and\ 14}$, 51, 53
and employment in CEE countries 218, 220–1, 226–8, 231–2, 237
and employment in developed countries 167–73, 179–81, 184
gap between formal and non-formal segments 69
and labour market 195–6, 268
and technological change 189, 231
see also education
Slovakia 215, 217, 218, 223, 224, 225, 227, 234, 238, 239, 240, 243, 245
economic growth and employment 230, **230**
economic output 221, **222**
education and employment 220, 221, 238, 241, **242**
employment and unemployment 213, **214**, 224, 231–2, **232**
low-skilled labour 228
self-employment 223
working age population growth 233, **233**
Slovenia 215, 217, 218, 220, 222, 223, 224, 225, 227, 238, 239, 242, 243, 245
economic growth and employment 230–1, **230**
employment and unemployment **214**, 224, **232**
migration from 234, **234**

Index

temporary employment 215
working age population growth 233, **233**
social security, absent in developing countries 58–61
Somalia 49
South Africa 30, **54**, 67, 71, 75, 77, 80, 84, 87, 94, 115, 118, 121, 147, 149, 152
South-Eastern Europe (SEE)
   labour force participation rates 213
   unemployment 213–14
Spain 157, 158, 162, 164, 166, 168, 171, 180, 182, 183, 187, 188, 194, 197, 198, 199, 200, 202, 204, 205, 206–11, 243
Sri Lanka 54, 67, 71, 75, 80, 84, 87, 92, 95, 96, 97, 115, 118, 119, 121, 147, 149
   economic change *101*, 152, 153
sub-Saharan Africa 49
   employment situation 99$_{\text{and 33}}$
   poverty 127, 128
Sudan 54
surplus labour 57–8, **59**
Swaziland 30, **54**, 115, 147
Sweden 157, 158, 162, 164, 166, 171, 172, 180, 187, 188, 194, 197, 198, 199, 200, 202, 204, 206–11, 243
   education and employment 168, 170, 182, 183
   labour force growth 186, **205**
Switzerland 157, 158, 162, 164, 166, 168, 171, 180, 182, 183, 188, 194, 198, 200, 202, 204, 205, 206–11, 243
   economic growth 186, **187**
   unemployment rates 155, 179, **197**, 199
Syrian Arab Republic **16**, 54

Tajikistan 252, 254, 256, 257, 260, 261, 262
   employment growth **251**, 257, 258
   employment and unemployment 247, **248**, 249, 250, **250**
Tanzania, United Republic of 3, **54**, 67, 71, 75, 80, 95, 118, 148, 150, 152, 153
tax wedge 190, 193
technological change 103$_{36}$, 189, 231
temporary employment 155$_{57}$, 156, 158, 159, *159*, 161
   developed countries 174, *175*, **198**
   women 165
Thailand 54, 67, 71, 75, 80, 87, 95, 96, 118, 122, 147, 149, 152, 153

Togo **54**
trade growth
   and capital investment 140, 143, 267
   and economic growth **139**
   employment effects 102–7, *107*
   and employment policies 108
   and formal segment *104*
   and per capita GDP 141, **142**
   and poverty 139–43
   and poverty reduction **143**
trade relations, CIS countries **256**
training, effectiveness of 237$_{83}$
transfer payments, for poverty relief 144–5
Trinidad and Tobago 54, 66, 70, 74, 76, 87, 94, 96, 117, 120
Tunisia 54, 71, 80, 147
Turkey 16, 54, 67, 71, 75, 80, 87, 95, 96, 118, 122
Turkmenistan 16, 251, 252, 255, 256, 257, 260, 261, 263
   employment and unemployment 247, **248**, 249, 250, **250**

Uganda 54, 67, 71, 75, 80, 95, 118, 148, 150, 152, 153
Ukraine 252, 254, 256, 257, 260, 261, 262
   emigration 255
   employment growth **251**, 257, 268
   employment and unemployment **248**, 249, 250, **250**
UN (Population Division of the Department of Economic and Social Affairs), migration database 45
underemployment 61, 62, 63, 64, 93
   CIS countries 249
   in developed countries 155
   in non-formal segment 107–8, 266
unemployment
   in CIS countries 247, 253, 255
   in developed countries 156, **157**, 167, *173*, 176, 184–90, **184–5**, 265
   and education (skills) 167, **168**, 170, 179, **182**, 220
   explanations 184, **184–5**, 186, 189
   gender disparity 87–9, *88*, *89*, **120–2**, 165
   and job queuing 80, 87, 88–9
   long-term 156, 158, *160*, 165, 214, 222, 230–1
   and overall employment situation *163*, **214**, 268

short-term 159, 165, 174
in South Africa 80
transient 80, 87
see also underemployment
unemployment benefit
   changes 190, 192–3, 199
   CIS countries 247
   Index (UBI) *193*
unemployment rate 63, 73–5, **76–7**, 79–80, *201*
   CEE countries 222, 224
   chronic **81–2**
   and level of economic development *81*
   nature of data 78
   and self-employment 79
United Kingdom 157, 158, 162, 164, 166, 171, 172, 180, 187, 188, 194, 197, 198, 199, 200, 202, 204, 205, **206–11**, 243
   education and employment 168, 170, **182**, 183
United Nations, Millennium Summit (2000) 123
United States 157, 158, 164, 166, 171, 172, 180, 187, 188, 194, 198, 202, 204, 205
   CEI estimates (all) 162, **162**, 163, 200, 204, **206–11**
   education and employment 168, 170, **182**, 183
   unemployment rates 155, **197**, 199
unskilled labour
   concentration in developing countries 37
   decline in demand 184, 186, 189, 227
   see also education; skills
Uruguay 54, 67, 71, 75, 80, 84, 115, 118, 147
   gender in employment 85, 87, **122**
Uzbekistan 251, 255, 256, 257, 260, 261, 263
   agriculture 251
   employment and unemployment 247, 248, 250, **250**

industrial growth 258
labour productivity growth 252, **252**

Venezuela, Bolivarian Republic of 54, 66, 70, 74, 76, 84, 86, 92, 94, 96, 97, 111, 117, 119, 120
   negative economic growth 100, *101*
Viet Nam 16, 67, 71, 75, 80, 87, 95, 96, 118, 122, 147, 149, 152, 153

wages
   in non-formal segment 60
   subsidy schemes 196
   see also casual wage employment; non-standard wage employment
women
   education 23, *23*
   and job queuing 87, 88–9
   in labour force 11–12, *13–14*, 13, 15–17, 85$_{28}$, 178–9, 216
   religious and cultural norms 16
   temporary employment 165
   see also gender disparity
working-time flexibility 191, 193–5
World Bank
   data on domestic savings 109$_{43}$
   data on FDI 106$_{39}$
   and decline in poverty 127
   definition of poverty 123$_{\text{and } 44}$
   poverty reduction strategy 125

Yemen 71, 80, 87, 122, 148, 150, 152

Zambia 30, 54, 148, 150, 152
Zimbabwe 30, 54, 71, 87, 115, 122, 147, 149, 152